New England Writers and Writing

MALCOLM COWLEY

New England Writers
and Writing

Edited and with an Introduction

by Donald W. Faulkner

UNIVERSITY PRESS OF NEW ENGLAND

Hanover and London

ACKNOWLEDGMENTS

The editor thanks Robert Cowley, executor of his father's estate, Tulin D. Faulkner, the staff of the University Press of New England, Bennett Graff, and Sarah Bray for assistance in bringing this book before the public eye.

University Press of New England, Hanover, NH 03755

© 1996 by University Press of New England and the Estate of Malcolm Cowley; introduction © 1996 by Donald W. Faulkner

All rights reserved

Printed in the United States of America   5   4   3   2   1

CIP data appear at the end of the book

New England is quite as large a lump of earth
as my heart can really take in.

—NATHANIEL HAWTHORNE

Contents

NEW ENGLAND LIFE: ESSAYS
AND REFLECTIONS

Editor's Introduction

❧ Although Malcolm Cowley was born in western Pennsylvania, he lived the majority of his life, fifty-five of his ninety years, in Sherman, Connecticut, where he died in 1989. An adoptive but stalwart Yankee, he made a reverse migration typical of his generation to the New England sources of American literature. Drawn first to Harvard, where he was educated and met many of the figures he would later write about (such New England denizens as Edward Arlington Robinson, Amy Lowell, E. E. Cummings, Conrad Aiken, and S. Foster Damon, among many others), Cowley later noted in his book, *Exile's Return,* a systematic inattention to New England, or even American, culture at Harvard in his college years:

"Of the [American literature] texts we studied," Cowley wrote, "I can remember only one, 'The Legend of Sleepy Hollow,' that gave us any idea that an American valley could be as effectively clothed in romance as Ivanhoe's castle or the London of Henry Esmond. It seemed to us that America was beneath the level of great fiction. . . . Here was a university that had grown immediately out of a local situation, out of the colonists' need for trained ministers of the Gospel. It had transformed itself from generation to generation with the transformations of New England culture. Farming money, fishing money, trading money, privateering money, wool, cotton, shoe and banking money, had all contributed to its vast endowment. It had grown with Boston, a city whose records were written on the face of its buildings. Sometimes on Sundays I used to wander through the old sections of Beacon Hill and the North End and admire the magnificent doorways, built in the chastest Puritan style with profits from the trade in China tea. Behind some of them Armenians now lived, or Jews; the Old North Church was in an Italian quarter, near the house of Paul Revere, a silversmith. Back Bay had been reclaimed from marshland and covered with mansions during the prosperous years after the Civil War (shoes, uniforms, railroads, speculation in government bonds). On Brattle Street, in Cambridge, Longfellow's house was open to the public, and I might have visited Brook Farm. All these things, Emerson, doorways, factory hands and fortune, the Elective System, the Porcellian Club, were bound together into one civilization, but of this I received no hint. I was studying Goethe's *Dichtung und Warheit* and the Elizabethan drama, and perhaps, on my way to classes in the morning, passing a Catholic church outside of which two Irish boys stood and looked at me with unfriendly eyes."

In the early 1930s, after a postwar "exile" in France, a sojourn in New York City, and frequent weekend trips to upstate New York or Connecticut's upper Fairfield and Litchfield counties (all written about in his *Exile's Return*), Cowley returned to New England to stay. He settled into a slowly renovated tobacco drying barn in the hamlet of Sherman, Connecticut, which was to be his home for the rest of his life. There, using his books and long country walks as mapping tools, he surveyed both the New England landscape and the American literary tradition it had generated. He examined the makers of an emerging American literary tradition and shaped our understanding of them, often by reading old works with a fresh eye in order to "get under," as he said, what other critics and historians had written. He pointed public understanding of those nineteenth-century works toward continuity with writers of his own generation. In so doing he deepened our sense of a national literature, a literature with an ongoing, ever-unfolding and ever-enhanced sense of tradition "bound together in one civilization." The cradle of that tradition, Cowley said, is the region of America east of the Hudson River.

All of the work presented here reflects that insight. Its shape is diverse. It ranges from extensive work on Hawthorne and Whitman, the objects of much of Cowley's research through the 1940s, to writers as disparate as Horatio Alger, the Boston prophet of the gospel of success; the ever-enigmatic Henry James, who wished upon himself glories of the stage as his own novelistic dramas transcended easy acclaim; the sometimes reclusive, sometimes cantankerous poets Edward Arlington Robinson, Robert Frost, E. E. Cummings, and Hart Crane; and the Quincy-born scop of suburbia, John Cheever. Along the way, we find telling estimations of the haunted playwright Eugene O'Neill, examens of teachers of an emerging American perspective such as George Santayana and Van Wyck Brooks, and a generation of new New Englanders inspired by its landscape, mores, and people. These authors alternately looked deeper into the region's past, measured its present, or used it as a touchstone for reflections on life's future. It was a generation ranging from J. P. Marquand to Thornton Wilder, and from Conrad Aiken to John Cheever.

Much of the material gathered in this book hasn't been collected previously. Some pieces are brief reviews of works by New England authors written for publications such as the *New Republic* and New York's *Herald Tribune* or *Times*. Others are equally brief reviews of biographies and critical works on major figures of New England writing. (It nonetheless remains perplexing that, given the extent of his writing on Hawthorne and Whitman, Cowley wrote relatively little on those confounding characters, Thoreau, Melville, and Dickinson. And of Emerson, the figure in American letters who came to dominate Cowley's perspective on New England literary culture, Cowley wrote only in broad comparison to writers of his own generation.)

But the bulk of the collection is the extended work for which Cowley is broadly praised and best known, work that led Wallace Stegner to note, "Malcolm Cowley is certainly our best and wisest student of American writing. . . . No student of our literature can afford not to know everything he writes." Given that Cowley is known primarily as an expositor of twentieth-century American writing, particularly as an apologist for and explorer of such coevals as Ernest Hemingway, F. Scott Fitzgerald, and William Faulkner, it may be surprising to some of his newer readers that he devoted so much of his writing life to New England as a scene of writing, and that both his devotion to major New England writers and his heralding of its minor ones are amplified by Cowley's rich sense of the importance of New England in literary life and culture.

When Robert M. Adams wrote in the *New York Times Book Review,* "The remarkable thing about Mr. Cowley is not that he wrote so frequently for so long, but that so much of his work is worth preserving," he was confirming Cowley's clarity of insight and his straightforward writing style. "I like a *thingy* style, not an abstract style," Cowley remarked in the conversation with his son, Robert, that ends this volume. "Sometimes when I read writing full of abstractions I stop and say, 'Now what the hell does he mean?' When you read something I write you know damn well what I mean. The language is simple, and the figures of speech have to do with actual objects, persons, and animals." For example, when Cowley sized up the emerging form of critical biography and said, "Most of them turn out to be half-length and unoriginal biographies combined with half-length critical studies; the biographies and studies are each sliced into chapter lengths and the chapters are heaped up alternately, like the ham and dry chicken in a club sandwich," he demonstrated his aversion to abstraction: the assertion is as accessible as the sandwich. Or take his evaluation of Frost, when another critic called him "the only living New Englander in the great tradition, fit to be placed beside Emerson, Hawthorne and Thoreau." Cowley reacted by saying "when [Frost] is so placed and measured against them, his stature seems diminished; it is almost as if a Morgan horse from Vermont, best of its breed, had been judged by the standards that apply to Clydesdales and Percherons. Height and breadth and strength: he falls short in all these qualities of the great New Englanders." The point is taken: in a backhanded compliment Frost is at least a standardbred, versatile, a natural charger, good for riding, cutting, and light farm labor. The others are heavy breeds, bred to haul weight. Descendents of ancient war horses like Bucyrus, Clydesdales and Percherons stand three to four hands above Morgans, work unflaggingly, and were replaced in New England farming of the twentieth century only by tractors. Unpacked, Cowley's "thingy" style is sharp, concise, and undiminished.

Beyond the imagery of his shorter efforts, in Cowley's longer work the reader has the feeling of being told a story. Cowley's senses of narrative and theme are basic components of his writing style. So a long essay on Hawthorne becomes a story of how one man used the dimensions of his own solitude to create a singular voice. The beginning of the piece reads like the beginning of a short story his subject might have written: "After four moderately happy, moderately social years at Bowdoin College, Hawthorne came back to Salem in 1825 and disappeared like a stone dropped into a well." The tale could end there, but another hangs upon that line. There's an element of narrative urgency informed by the reader's knowledge of Hawthorne's success; a story begs to be told. How did Hawthorne get from that frightening anonymity to *The Scarlet Letter*? Whether enhancing a reader's awareness of an old tale now told fresh, or building for the reader dramatic information about an unheralded subject, most of Cowley's longer critical essays conform to the conventions of short stories: there is a clear beginning, middle, and end, and a "something happened" which sets forth an irreversible movement such that a "something changed" is a clear result of what occurred. Thus Hawthorne finds in his own silence access to what Melville later put bluntly: "the past is usable!" In a new country, lacking a discernible past, Hawthorne found in New England tales and folklore a way to fashion his writerly vision. From such efforts Cowley learned how to embrace New England.

Although Cowley was an adoptive, and finally an adopted, New Englander, through his readings he laid claim to a well-worn New England mantle. He would reweave it in his writings. Still, he didn't feel accepted in his own hamlet until the people of Sherman provided him with an inscribed silver plate in honor of thirty years of service upon his retirement from the local zoning board. He helped keep the land nearby from being "condominiumized," and worked to keep farmers free from the encroachment of suburbia. Regardless of his adoptive status as a Connecticut Yankee, he acted like a native one, and he enjoyed the role. His laconic manner is remembered by earnest interviewers who after a paragraph-length question would receive a sometimes terrifying "uhh yup"-like answer. His typifying frugality is remembered by scholars working through his papers at the Newberry Library in Chicago who treasure his reuse of carbon copy backing paper. A foolscap carbon sheet of a letter to his Fairfield County neighbor Robert Penn Warren, another adoptive, if less embracing, New

Englander, might have on its verso a deleted page from Cowley's assessment of a writer's worthiness for an American Academy prize. Cowley took his role as a New Englander seriously. He took it upon himself to reforest acreage of his own land with the famous New England white pine that was originally there. ("This is the southernmost stand of white pine in New England," Cowley once proudly said to me as I drove him, just below his home acreage, along the backroads above Lake Zoar from a reading at Yale.) He was intending to make his plantings rejoin a larger ridgeline. Cowley attended religiously to the plights of local dairyfarmers, shopkeepers, and countrymen, and remembered fondly and self-deprecatingly the obituary of a lifelong Cape Cod resident who died at age eighty-six. "Although not a native," the local paper's obituary grudgingly stated, "Mr. Jones came to Orleans at the age of two." The nuance of that, of a man slighted because two of his long-lived years were spent elsewhere, won't be lost on a New England reader.

Despite Cowley's service as twice president of the National Institute of Arts and Letters and chancellor of the American Academy, despite his huge accomplishments on behalf of American literature worldwide, and despite the fact that he had so many literary neighbors, he once quipped, "It's gotten so you can't fire a load of buckshot around here without hitting some Pulitzer prize-winning author," he often stood by an autobiographical "tag line" that embraced his sense of home. "Mr. Cowley," the line would often read in the "contributor's acknowledgment" section of a journal or book in which his work appeared, "lives on seven acres in Sherman, Connecticut. He says of his country place that it is 'just enough for a hayfield and a lawn (you can't tell them apart), a vegetable garden, half an acre of pine trees and a trout stream called the Naromiyocknowhusnkatankshunk. The signboard on the state highway that gives its name is wider than the stream itself. When I'm not reading or writing I chop wood in the winter, fish in the spring months and raise vegetables in the summer. Next to writing a perfect poem, what I'd most like to do is grow a perfect melon."
Some of Cowley's most accessible writing comes of his regard for the good stewardship of New England (here assembled in the third section of this volume), but it is clear as one reads these efforts that he redoubles the stewardship of those writers a century before him, writers like Thoreau and members of the Brook Farm and Fruitlands communities. Cowley exhibits in his critical writing an awareness of the New England landscape attended by Emerson and his literary progeny. It is all too often ignored by campus-bound scholars and students. In his critical writings, Cowley was profoundly aware of landscape as a character force within the story provided. Imagine, for example, Frost's narrative poems without a brook, or *The Scar-*

let Letter without the forest meeting of Dimmesdale and Hester. Moreover, as Cowley attends to writers of New England cityscapes, among them Alger, James, Marquand, Wilder, and Cheever, he makes clear that for them an urban horizon is as valuable as a nonurban landscape is for Hawthorne, Emerson, Frost, or Whitman.

It is Whitman who is the odd man out in this anthology, and I should attend to his seemingly ill-matched presence immediately. He's technically not a New Englander, but Cowley's seminal work on Whitman (written across two major essays, the first an examination of the 1855 edition of *Leaves of Grass,* and the second a path-breaking examination of Whitman's philosophy) is included because Whitman is *of* New England, because his beloved starting point, Paumanok, Long Island, was, and still is, closer to New England's shore than it is to New York City and the rest of the country; because he sought sanction from New England writers such as Emerson; because his emotional and writing center came of a New England context (Cowley refers to Whitman's "drawling Yankee self-ridicule"); and because, frankly, Cowley believed in him, earnestly and sincerely, as an extension of the New England pantheon.

But equally, one could say that Cheever is an odd inclusion. Though born and buried in Quincy, Massachusetts, Cheever wrote most often of the suburbs of New York City. Of his later work Cowley said, "He rebecame a New Englander. One can be more specific: he became a Bay Stater, a native son of the Massachusetts seaboard, which has a different voice and different traditions from those of the Connecticut Valley. If Bay Staters are of Puritan descent, they trace their ancestral histories back to the founder of the family. In John's case the founder was Ezekiel Cheever, a minister highly respected by Cotton Mather, who preached his funeral sermon. John quotes Mather as saying, 'The welfare of the Commonwealth was always upon the conscience of Ezekiel Cheever . . . and he abominated periwigs.' The commonwealth of letters was always on John's conscience and he abominated all sorts of pretension, almost as much as he abominated pollution and superhighways."

And Wilder. Though he lived the majority of his life in Hamden, Connecticut (where part of the town library was renamed after him before his death), he was born in Wisconsin and raised in China. And there are others, like Santayana, who, though he was born in Madrid and lived long in Rome, nonetheless had a shaping effect on New England life and letters through its erstwhile center, Harvard.

In his writing Cowley continually wove his New England theme, grounded by Emerson, into otherwise diverse personalities and subjects. Collected thematically for the first time, his essays on New England writers demonstrate the value of what F. O. Matthiessen called "The Problem of the Artist as New Englander," but which Cowley (who called his own generation "lucky" rather than "lost") might as easily have called "The *Asset* of the Artist as New Englander." For example, of Wilder, just mentioned, Cowley noted "the brilliant series of lectures that he gave at Harvard in 1950–1951 [which] started with Emerson, Thoreau, and other classical American writers, notably Melville and Whitman. What he tried to deduce from their works was the character of the representative American, but what he actually presented was, I suspect, partly a reflection of his own character. . . . Wilder is neo-classical . . . he goes back to Pope and Addison in his attitude toward the art of letters, but in other habits of thought he clearly goes back to the Transcendentalists. His work has more than a little of the moral distinction they tried to achieve, and like their work it deals with the relation of one to one, or of anyone to the All, the Everywhere, and the Always." Cowley similarly called Cummings "the latest—though I suspect not the last—of the New England Transcendentalists," and spoke broadly of Aiken's Emersonianism while noting that he wrote his verse and prose with a "candid, scrupulous, self-deprecatory, yet reckless and fanciful New England voice."

There are, too, homeless and haunted writers reflected in this collection, among them Eugene O'Neill and Hart Crane, neither of whom ever found a home, though each searched for it in New England. O'Neill lived in the 1920s in Ridgefield, Connecticut, in a grand house dubbed by its former owners "Brook Farm," a dim echo of the community established by nineteenth-century writers, and a dim echo too of the only steady abode O'Neill knew as a child, the "Monte Cristo Cottage" in New London, farther along the Connecticut coast, bought, and named, with his actor-father's earnings from playing the role of the Count of Monte Cristo for many years on the stage. That house, which provided the setting for both O'Neill's comedy *Ah! Wilderness* and his tragedy *Long Day's Journey Into Night,* proved to be a greater match for O'Neill than the "Brook Farm" in which, during Prohibition, O'Neill laid out applejack for each Cowley and Crane.

And Crane. "There is so much I forget about him, as if part of my own life had been erased," Cowley wrote, "and so much I remember too. Hart, Hart . . . ," he intoned, like Horatio remembering his ill-fated friend, Hamlet. Although Hart Cane's sojourn in New England was matched by others in Cuba, New York, and Mexico, he dwelled, if such a term could be used in Crane's case, with Cowley's friends, Sue Jenkins and William Slater Brown, and Carolyn Gordon and Allen Tate, in their New England redoubts. "Hart was at home in the country without belonging to the country," Cowley wrote. "He did not go trouting in the spring, or plant a garden, or have a dog to follow him, or gather apples for his own cider, or saw and split a winter's supply of wood. . . . He read classical authors, slowly and intently; his favorites were Dante, Rabelais, Marlowe, Shakespeare, Melville, Whitman, and Rimbaud. I think he approached them," Cowley added, "as if they had written the standard textbooks of advanced engineering; he was looking for models that would help in designing his Bridge."

Cowley's writers of the twentieth century dig back, interconnect, and interrelate with each their New England heritage and prospect. Just as E. E. Cummings, for example, can look back to his father's long friendship with William James and even deeper into New England culture, it is S. Foster Damon with whom Cummings connects, and whom he credits with his insight into literary and cultural modernism: "Practically everything I know about painting or poetry came to me through Damon," Cowley quotes Cummings saying to his biographer. And of Damon's poetry, iambic pentameters giving rise to unexpected trochees and spondees, Cowley says, "reading such lines makes me think of New Hampshire fields that are strewn with boulders." Anyone who knows the interruptive presence of such unexpected rhythms in an iambic poetic line could appreciate Cowley's allusion. It's like mowing a clean field and hitting a rock in August. Of Marquand's compositional method Cowley writes, "Imagine that a highly trained anthropologist had led an expedition into New England to study its native folkways. Imagine that he had become friendly with the headmen and headwomen of the aborigines and had been allowed to participate in all their particular rites, including the Friday Afternoon Sewing Circle. Imagine too that he had received expert advice from a former Brahmin who had become partly westernized by living in New York [and then turned that] material into a novel that will be easy to read, but without sacrificing any of its value as scientific observation."

Beyond Emerson, whom Cowley most often echoed as a theorist and historian, it is Hawthorne to whom he most frequently returned in his New England writing. As with all of the writers he examined, Cowley was as intrigued by personality as by the products of the work. His research often led him to valuable biographical insights. Cowley, rather than explaining away the fiction at hand (as some critics do, proclaiming a one-to-one correspondence between author's biography and work), provided his readers an insight into the context of the work's development and production. Discussing Hawthorne's activities and the writing that came with them in a review of Van Doren's Hawthorne biography, Cowley stated: "No sharp division has to be made; life and books can be treated in the same passage and sometimes in the same paragraph." The reader shouldn't mistake the simple sentence for the context in which it is provided. Cowley maintained that although life and art can be treated in the same passage, the reduction of books to thinly veiled autobiography isn't to be condoned. Writers work with the material available to them, but they transform rather than record.

The five pieces on Hawthorne gathered here reflect a concern with the writer that lasted more than half of Cowley's long life. There is of course the introduction to the *Portable Hawthorne* ("Hawthorne in Solitude"), which is a gem. But precious too is its natural companion, the unabashed love story Cowley writes about the courtship and marriage of Nathaniel Hawthorne and Sophia Peabody ("The Hawthornes in Paradise"). Cowley wrote the piece in the late 1950s for *American Heritage*, where his son had recently begun working as an editor. Norman Holmes Pearson, a professor of English and American Studies at Yale, had equally recently acquired an unexpurgated set of the correspondence of the Hawthornes and, blocked about what to do with it, passed it along to Cowley. Cowley, obviously moved by the material, turned it into an homage to both marriage and literature.

The opening paragraph of "The Hawthornes in Paradise" deserves to be quoted in full:

There are only a few great love stories in American fiction, and there are fewer still in the lives of famous American writers. Nathaniel Hawthorne wrote one of the greatest, *The Scarlet Letter.* He also lived a story that deserves to be retold with all the new knowledge we can bring to bear on it—as long as there are lovers in New England; it was his courtship and conquest of Sophia Peabody. Unlike his first novel, the lived story was neither sinful nor tragic. Everything in the foreground was as softly glowing as a June morning in Salem, but there were shadows in the background and obstacles to be surmounted; among them were poverty, seemingly hopeless invalidism, conniving sisters, political intrigues, a silken temptress, a duel that might have been fought to the death, and inner problems more threatening than any of these. It was as if Hawthorne had needed to cut his way through a forest of thorns—some planted by himself—in order to reach the castle of Sleeping Beauty and waken her with a kiss, while, in the same moment, he wakened himself from a daylong nightmare.

Delightfully, Cowley delivers on his promises as a storyteller, and the tale is told through to its happy ending. The other pieces on Hawthorne are more like semiprecious gems. Among them is Cowley's demonstration of the Racinian and Aristotelian nature of *The Scarlet Letter,* more an argument for Hawthorne's naive dramatic insight than a brief for Hawthorne's dramatic mastery. Then too comes Cowley's case for Hawthorne's *The Blithedale Romance,* which "contains one scene—Zenobia's trial in front of a rock in the woods called Eliot's Pulpit—that is almost as powerful as anything Hawthorne wrote. Perhaps American realism began with *The Blithedale Romance*; at any rate Howells got his start from it and always named it as his favorite among Hawthorne's novels. . . . In many ways Hawthorne's work foreshadowed the literary trends of a whole century," Cowley says in that piece on *Blithedale,* and goes on to maintain that Hawthorne's unfinished *Dolliver Romance* is as oddly experimental as Kafka's work. Finally, Cowley, age 85, responds to a Hawthorne family skeleton brought to light in a short book by Philip Young. Cowley acknowledges the younger critic's discoveries yet states, "but Young simplifies, too, by making Hawthorne a less complicated person than he was in the flesh." I think it both bizarre and wonderful that Cowley, in old age and still sharper than critics a generation younger than he, had acquired so intuitive a sense of his subject. Reading Cowley one—at times stubbornly—begins to acknowledge that not only did he understand his fellows, he understood their forebears as though he had met them.

Finally, one comes in the last section of this book to "the supporting evidence" of Cowley's regard for New England life. It is a series of informal pieces (with a handful of some of his best nature poetry) written across more than forty years and variously regarding inhabitants of his region and their environs. All of them confirm a sense of living in New England. There is a 1931 piece on Zebulon Trumbull, a local roustabout, whose family came to New England in 1652. Trumbull worked alternately as a tobacco farmer, sawmiller, horsetrader, and furniture restorer. "He can lift the rear axle of a Buick unaided," Cowley wrote. "He can lift a fifty-gallon barrel of cider, but he won't take a drink of it afterwards, not even to slake his thirst. Years ago his only brother died of drinking cider." There is a portrait of Cowley's town during wartime rationing in 1942 ("One effect of this war has been to broaden our political interests while narrowing our social horizons. Friends who live thirty miles from us used to be regarded as neighbors; now we can see them only by saving gasoline for weeks to have a little surplus. Our cousins in Pennsylvania might as well be living in Omaha, or on the moon"). And another profile of it during the election night of 1944 ("'Hello, Minnie,' they said, and 'How many times did you vote?' and there was a great deal of laughter. A table was spread in the back of the hall, with pies and a big homemade layer cake; the ladies of the Opportunity Club were serving lunch to the twelve election officials. The kitchen door was open and you could smell a big pot of chowder simmering on the stove. Going down to vote was almost like paying a Sunday afternoon visit to a French village cafe"). These are balanced by late-life estimates of the future of rural New England and its farming life, written at peak form.

When Cowley noted, "What I'd most like to do is grow a perfect melon," he wasn't joking. He wrote an epistle on the subject and called attention to the long-standing appreciation of that art: "On the last day in August

1839, when Henry and John Thoreau set out for a famous week on the Concord and Merrimack rivers, their homemade rowboat carried melons from their home patch as part of its cargo. At Hooksett, not ten miles south of Concord, New Hampshire, they found a commercial grower so proud of his melons that he guarded them at night with a loaded musket." On another occasion Cowley reflected upon his first encounter with New England rural living:

When I first came to Sherman more than forty years ago [Cowley was writing in 1974], it was reported by the census as having 330 people and something like 100 farms. . . . Most of the farms didn't deserve the name; they were simply fields and a house where an old couple subsisted with the help of a cow, a flock of chickens, and usually a team of superannuated horses. In the valley north of the Center, though, were rich tobacco and dairy farms. The hills were grassy there and dotted with cattle to their rounded tops. On the valley floor were big white houses, red barns, and silos like baronial donjons standing guard over luxuriant fields of corn, alfalfa and tobacco. Driving past them on a winding dirt road was like exploring Arcadia.

It was in this Arcadia, this seven acres of personal Eden, that Cowley lived and wrote, where he entertained artist neighbors (like his dear friend, the painter Peter Blume, who lived only two hundred yards across a country road, and comrades across the hills like Alexander Calder, James Thurber, and Robert Penn Warren, among many others). It was here too during the dark days of McCarthyism and its "witch hunts" that he wrote of the haunting witches that moved Hawthorne and another Cowley neighbor, Arthur Miller, to explore their history. More important, it was here where Cowley found his writerly voice, here where, to use lines from one of his poems, he planted his "urn of native soil," and found "the smell of home."

Cowley wrote well and lived long in New England. He wrote of its landscape, its people, its literature, and its legacy for both a nation and a world. Though Cowley wrote of *all* American literature, and wrote with particular delight in its regionalism, be it western, midwestern, or southern, enhanced by mountains or coasts, by plains or cities, he loved New England, its majesty, and its simplicity. At his interment in 1989 his granddaughter Miranda read his unintended valediction, the closing stanza of his poem, "Here With the Long Grass Rippling":

I pray simply for this:
to walk as humbly on the earth as my mother and father did;
to greatly love a few;
to love the earth, to be sparing of what it yields,
and not leave it poorer for my long presence;
to speak some words in patterns that will be remembered,
and again the voice be heard to exalt or to mourn—

all this, and in some corner where nettles grew in black soil,
to plant and hoe a dozen hills of corn.

Cowley's deep pleasure in the land may well have died with him, but his remembered words of exaltation and mourning serve to keep it fertile ground.

THE NINETEENTH CENTURY

Hawthorne

Hawthorne in Solitude

After four moderately happy, moderately social years at Bowdoin College, Hawthorne came back to Salem in 1825 and disappeared like a stone dropped into a well. He used to say that he doubted whether twenty persons in the community so much as knew of his existence. He had thought that while writing his first books he might support himself by working for his uncles, who were prosperous stagecoach proprietors; then later he might travel into distant countries. But the books didn't come out—except for a poor little romance called *Fanshawe* that was printed at his own expense—and meanwhile the place in his uncles' counting house was deferred from month to month, the travels from year to year. Day after day he spent in his room; it was an owl's nest, he said, from which he emerged only at dusk.

If he had lived in Boston he might have found others who shared his ambitions or at least understood them. Boston in 1825 had the beginnings of a literary society, but Salem was a little desert where it seemed impossible for any writer to flourish. Salem was shipping and politics; it was the waterfront, the new Irish slums, and the big houses on Chestnut Street where people asked, "Who are the Hawthornes?" Any young man of Salem who tried to enter literature as others entered business or the law was condemned to solitude; and Hawthorne was doubly condemned, by his character as well as by his interests. He was intensely shy and proud—shy *because* he was proud, with a high sense of personal merit, a respect for his ancestors, and a fear of being rebuffed if he went into society. The fear grew stronger as his clothes grew shabbier and his manners more reserved. "I sat down by the wayside of life," he said, "like a man under enchantment, and a shrubbery sprung up around me, and the bushes grew to be saplings, and the saplings became trees, until no exit appeared possible, through the tangling depths of my obscurity."

As the years passed he fell into a daily routine that seldom varied during autumn and winter. Each morning he wrote or read until it was time for the midday dinner; each afternoon he read or wrote or dreamed or merely stared at a sunbeam boring in through a hole in the blind and very slowly moving across the opposite wall. At sunset he went for a long walk, from which he returned late in the evening to eat a bowl of chocolate crumbed thick with bread and then talk about books or politics with his two adoring sisters, Elizabeth and Louisa, both of whom were already marked for spinsterhood; these were almost the only household meetings. The younger Hawthornes were orphans; their father was a sea captain who had died of yellow fever at Surinam when Nathaniel was four years old. Madame Hawthorne, as his mother was called, had fallen into the widow's habit of eating in her room, and Elizabeth often missed dinner because of her daylong solitary rambles. There was an old aunt dressed in black who wandered through the house or, in summer, worked among the flowers like the ghost of a gardener.

In summer Hawthorne's routine was more varied; he went for an early-morning swim among the rocks and often spent the day wandering alone by the shore, so idly that he amused himself by standing on a cliff and throwing stones at his shadow. Once, apparently, he stationed himself on the long toll bridge north of Salem and watched the procession of travelers from morning to night. He never went to church, but on Sunday mornings he liked to stand behind the curtain of his open window and watch the congregation assemble. At times he thought that the most desirable mode of existence "might be that of a spiritualized Paul Pry, hovering invisible round man and woman, witnessing their deeds, searching into their hearts, borrowing brightness from their felicity and shade from their sorrow, and retaining no emotion peculiar to himself." At other times—and oftener with the passing years—he was seized by an impulse to throw himself into the midst of life. He came to feel there was no fate so horrible as that of the mere spectator, condemned to live in the world without any share in its joys or sorrows.

No man is a mere spectator, and even Hawthorne had a somewhat larger share in worldly events than he was afterwards willing to remember. Each summer he took a fairly long trip through New England, riding in his uncles' coaches, and once he traveled westward to Niagara and Detroit. During the trips he talked—or rather, listened—to everyone he met in coach or tavern, and "enjoyed as much of life," he said, "as other people do in the whole year's round." Even at home he was less of a hermit than he later portrayed himself as being; sometimes there was company in the evening and sometimes he paid visits to his three Salem friends. One of these, William B. Pike, was a carpenter and a small Democratic politician, in that Whig stronghold. Hawthorne shared his political opinions and must have discussed with him the questions of party patronage that would play an important part in both their lives. He could sometimes be seen at a bookstore that stocked the latest novels and, as time went on, he began writing for the Salem *Gazette*. But there were not enough of these contacts with the world to destroy his picture of himself as a man completely alone. He began to be obsessed by the notion of solitude, both as an emotional necessity for a person like himself and also as a ghostly punishment to which he was self-condemned. "By some witchcraft or other," he said in 1837 when he was trying to escape from his owl's nest and had started to correspond with his Bowdoin classmate, Longfellow, ". . . I have been carried apart from the main current of life, and find it impossible to get back again. Since we last met, which you remember was in Sawtell's room, where you read a farewell poem to the relics of the class,—ever since that time I have secluded myself from society; and yet I never meant any such thing, nor dreamed what sort of life I was going to lead. I have made a captive of myself, and put me into a dungeon, and now I cannot find the key to let myself out,—and if the door were open, I should be almost afraid to come out."

Those years of self-imprisonment in Salem were the central fact in Hawthorne's training as a writer. They served as his apprenticeship and his early travels, corresponding to the years that other American writers of his time spent wandering in Europe or making an overland expedition to Oregon or sailing round Cape Horn on a whaler. In recent terms they were his postgraduate work, his year in Paris or Rome, his military service, everything that prepared him for his career. He worked or idled under his own supervision, traveled into himself, and studied the inner landscape. It was the Salem years that deepened and individualized his talent.

Talent cannot be acquired, cannot be explained, and in Hawthorne's case we have to start with the fact that he possessed it from boyhood. Moreover, it was a sturdier sort of talent than has usually been attributed to him, at least by critics with the habit of regarding him as a delicate plant that was incapable of bearing much fruit and would have withered in the sun. His Concord neighbors had a different picture of him. Emerson, for example, was convinced that he had greater resources than he ever displayed in his works, and Margaret Fuller said of him in the Brook Farm days, "We have had but a drop or two from that ocean." We never had more than a trickle and perhaps the inner ocean was not so vast as she believed; yet Hawthorne's hundred-odd stories were only a few of those foreshadowed in his notebooks. Besides his four published novels he once had five others fully outlined in his head. The wonder is not that he never wrote them, but rather that some of his projects were finished with careful workmanship at a time when circumstances were unfavorable to Hawthorne's type of richly meditated fiction. His talent had to be robust in order to survive and had to be exceptionally fertile in order to produce, against obstacles, the few books he succeeded in writing.

We can merely wonder at the talent in itself, but we can try to understand some of the factors that contributed to its development. When Hawthorne was nine years old he injured one foot in a game of bat-and-ball and the doctors judged that he might be permanently lame. The lameness disappeared after two years, but meanwhile it had kept him home from school and left him to follow his own bent. It was at this time that he formed the habit of reading for hour after hour as he lay stretched out on the parlor carpet. *Pilgrim's Progress* was his favorite book—later it was to be the only one that he often mentioned in his stories—but he also liked Shakespeare and *The Faery Queen* and the crimes described in *The Newgate Calendar*; in fact the boy would read anything, no matter how difficult, so long as it told a story. He raced through the Waverley novels one after another, almost as fast as they reached Salem.

When he wasn't reading or building castles with blocks for a series of kitten-princesses, he listened to the stories that could be heard in a New England household. There were family traditions; many of them dealt with Colonel John Hathorne, as the name used to be spelled, who had been a judge in the Salem witchcraft trials and who had been cursed, with all his descendants, by one of the women he condemned to death. Other traditions dealt with a vast tract of land in Cumberland County, Maine, which rightfully belonged to the family although the title-deeds had been lost; and still others clustered round Daniel Hathorne, the Revolutionary privateer, known as the sternest man who ever walked a quarterdeck. The voyage of his brig, the *Fair American,* had been the subject of a ballad:

> Bold Hathorne was commander, a man of real worth,
> Old England's cruel tyranny induced him to go forth.

The little boy liked stories of the Revolution and he also liked to hear about the superstitions that survived in the New England countryside. Much later Hawthorne was to speak of an old woman who "made it her serious business and sole amusement," he said, "to tell me stories at any time from morning till night, in a mumbling, toothless voice, as I sat on a log of wood, grasping her check-apron in both my hands. . . . There are a thousand of her traditions lurking in the corners and by-places of my mind."

Besides listening to stories, the boy invented long and fanciful stories of his own, which he told to his two admiring sisters. Usually they were about the wonderful adventures he would have when he was grown up, and they always ended with the words, ". . . and I'm never coming back again." He had picked a career for himself long before he went away to college: he was going to write books, a whole shelf of them, with "Hawthorne's Works" printed on the back. The books were going to deal with his native land; that requirement was clear in his mind from the beginning. Later his purpose became a little more specific. He was going to write romances in which he would retell the history and preserve the vanishing myths of New

England; and he would thus make its soil "fertile with poetry," in the same way that Scotland—"cold, cloudy, barren, insignificant little bit of earth," as he later called it—had been transformed by Sir Walter Scott into a motherland of legends known everywhere in the world.

When Nathaniel was fourteen years old he spent a year in Maine, on the shore of Sebago Lake. He used to go skating alone till midnight, before the great snows fell; and in summer he fished for trout or wandered through the woods with his gun. Those nights and days became his image of remembered happiness. "I lived in Maine like a bird of the air," he said not long before his death, "so perfect was the freedom I enjoyed. But it was there I first got my cursed habits of solitude." One such habit was that of talking silently to himself. In his boyhood he started an inner monologue that lasted for most of his waking hours and went on, apparently, from youth to age. It was his principal solace in Salem, during the lonely years that followed his graduation from college. Even after he had emerged from his "owl's nest," it continued to be his substitute for spoken conversation; and he once observed in his notebook that he doubted whether he had ever really talked with half a dozen persons in his life, either men or women.

But the inner monologue also served another purpose, as time went on; it was the workshop where he forged his plots and tempered his style. Before writing his stories he told them to himself, while walking by the sea or under the pines; he liked a solitary place where there was nothing to distract his attention. In Rome, much later, he preferred the Pope's garden on the Quirinal: "It would suit me to have my daily walk along such straight paths," he said in his notebook, "for I think them favorable to thought, which is apt to be disturbed by variety and unexpectedness." When he was living at The Wayside, in Concord, he tramped through the sweetfern and huckleberry bushes on the hilltop until his feet had made a path that was visible for thirty years after his death. He said in a letter to his friend and publisher, James T. Fields, "In compliance with your exhortations, I have begun to think seriously of that story, not, as yet, with a pen in my hand, but trudging to and fro on my hilltop." He trudged out and, in his silent fashion, talked out all his stories before he tried to set them down.

There is more to be said about this inner monologue which played an essential part in his life and work. In one sense it was a dialogue, since Hawthorne seems to have divided himself into two personalities while working on his stories: one was the storyteller and the other his audience. The storyteller uttered his stream of silent words; the audience listened and applauded by a sort of inner glow, or criticized by means of an invisible frown that seemed to say, "But I don't understand."—"Let me go over it again," the storyteller would answer, still soundlessly; and then he would repeat his tale in clearer language, with more details; perhaps he would go over the doubtful passages again and again, until he was sure that the listener would understand. This doubleness in Hawthorne, this division of himself into two persons conversing in solitude, explains one of the paradoxes in his literary character: that he was one of the loneliest authors who ever wrote, even in this country of lost souls, while at the same time his style was that of a social man eager to make himself clear and intensely conscious of his audience. For him the audience was always present, because it was part of his own mind.

Another paradox is also connected with his solitude and self-absorption. Hawthorne was reserved to the point of being secretive about his private life, and yet he spoke more about himself, with greater honesty, than any other American of his generation. Not only did he write prefaces to all his books, in which he explained his intentions and described his faults more accurately than any of his critics; not only did he keep journals in which he recorded his daily activities; but also most of his stories and even, in great part, his four novels are full of anguished confessions. One can set side by side two quotations from his work. In the preface to his *Mosses* he said, "So far as I am a man of really individual attributes I veil my face; nor am I, nor have I ever been, one of those supremely hospitable people who serve up their own hearts, delicately fried, with brain sauce, as a tidbit for their beloved public." But he also said at the end of *The Scarlet Letter,* when drawing a moral from Mr. Dimmesdale's tragic life, "Be true! Be true! Show freely to the world, if not your worst, yet some trait whereby the worst may be inferred." Divided between his two impulses, toward secrecy and toward complete self-revelation, he achieved a sort of compromise: he revealed himself, but usually under a veil of allegory and symbol.

No other writer in this country or abroad ever filled his stories with such a shimmering wealth of mirrors. Poe detested mirrors; when he wrote an essay on interior decoration he admitted one of them—only one—to his ideally furnished apartment, but on condition that it be very small and "hung so," he said, "that a reflection of the person can be obtained from it in none of the ordinary sitting places of the room." Hawthorne went to the other extreme by adorning his imagined rooms and landscapes with mirrors of every description—not only looking-glasses but burnished shields and breastplates, copper pots, fountains, lakes, pools, anything that could reflect the human form. And the mirrors in his stories have supernatural functions as well: sometimes they are tombs from which can be summoned the shapes of the past (as in "Old Esther Dudley"); sometimes they prophesy the future (like Maule's Well, in *The House of the Seven Gables*); often they reveal the truth behind a delusion (as in "Feathertop," where the scarecrow impresses people as a fine gentleman until they look at his image in a mirror); and always they serve as "a kind of window or doorway into the spiritual world."—"I am half convinced that the reflection is indeed the reality—the real thing which Nature imperfectly images to our grosser sense," Hawthorne said in his notebook after describing a scene mirrored in the little Assabet River. He even wrote a story, "Monsieur du Miroir," in which the hero is simply his own reflected image.

"From my childhood I have loved to gaze into a spring," says the narrator of another Hawthorne story, "The Vision of the Fountain." One day the young man sees his own eyes staring back at him, as usual; but then he looks again—"And lo!" he says, "another face deeper in the fountain than my own image, more distinct in all the features, yet faint as thought. The vision had the aspect of a fair young girl with locks of paly gold." This substitution of a girl's face for that of the youth bending over the spring makes one think of Narcissus in love with his twin sister—according to one version of the Greek myth—and gazing into a pool because he fancies that his own mirrored features are hers.

In Hawthorne's life as well as in his stories there are curious suggestions of the Narcissus legend. He had been a beautiful boy, petted by his relatives and admired by strangers; I think it was one of his aunts who said of him that he had "eyelashes a mile long and curled up at the end." Always he loved to wander by the edge of little streams. One characteristic he showed from the beginning was an abhorrence for ugliness in women. "Take her away!" the little boy said to one woman who tried to be kind to him. "She is ugly and fat and has a loud voice." Forty years later he would be roused to homicidal anger by looking at English dowagers. "The grim, red-faced monsters!" he said in his usually even-tempered notebook. "Surely a man would be justified in murdering them—in taking a sharp knife and cutting away their mountainous flesh, until he had brought them into reasonable shape." At times he was like Thomas Bullfrog in one of his own stories. "So painfully acute was my sense of female imperfection," Mr. Bullfrog says, "and such varied excellence did I require in the woman whom I could love, that there was an awful risk of my getting no wife at all, or of being driven to perpetrate matrimony with my own image in the looking-glass."

Mr. Bullfrog's predicament was like the one in which Hawthorne involved himself during the Salem years when he had no other companions: in a sense he did marry his own image. Many of his tales read like confessions of a self-love that was physical as well as moral. It is true that he continued to elaborate the New England legend, but after 1834 another note appeared in his stories: more and more of them were allegories that dealt with self-absorption, self-delusion, self-condemnation, a whole series of reflexive emotions. They also expressed feelings of guilt, as one can see from the development of Hawthorne's mirror images. Thus, Roderick Elliston, the hero of "The Bosom Serpent," is tormented by a snake that lives in his own breast. The snake has come from an innocent-looking fountain (another mirror), where it had lurked since the time of the first settlers. Elliston spends "whole miserable days before a looking-glass with his mouth wide open, watching, in hope and horror, to catch a glimpse of the snake's head far down within his throat." "The Bosom Serpent" was published in 1843, when Hawthorne was happily married and living in Concord, at the Old Manse. By that time he was able to look back almost tranquilly on his old dilemma and even to give the story a happy ending—for Elliston is freed from the snake by his wife's love. But some of the stories that Hawthorne wrote in his Salem days—I am thinking especially of "Young Goodman Brown" and "The Minister's Black Veil"—so testify to his sense of being judged and condemned that they might have been cries from the pit.

There are of course other secret sins than the one to which Hawthorne may have yielded. What we know, as distinguished from mere probabilities, is that he came to regard his separation from normal society as something sinful in itself, a crime that was also a punishment. He began to think of himself as a man not only self-judged and condemned, but self-confined in a prison that had no visible bars. The key was in the lock; at any moment he might have stepped over the threshold and lived among his neighbors. What kept him in his solitary chamber was the feeling that year by year the world was becoming more unreal for him and, even worse, that he was becoming less real than the world; he was a shadow effectively walled in by shadows. As time went on he came to resemble one of his own characters, Gervayse Hastings of "The Christmas Banquet," who considered himself the unhappiest of men. "You will not understand it," Hastings tells his rivals in misery. "None have understood it—not even those who experience the like. It is a chilliness—a want of earnestness—a feeling as if what should be my heart were a thing of vapor—a haunting perception of unreality! . . . Mine—mine is the wretchedness! This cold heart. . . ."

Sometimes Hawthorne pictured himself as caught in a whirlpool or drifting helplessly towards a cataract; one of his despondent letters to his classmate Horatio Bridge closed with the words, "I'm a doomed man and over I must go." The fact was that he had already been carried down into a sort of private hell, exactly the size of the room in which he brooded out his days. Ice, not fire, was the torment he suffered there. The images that recur in his work are those of coldness and torpor from coldness; among his favorite adjectives are "cold," "icy," "chill," "benumbed," "torpid," "sluggish," "feeble," "languid," "dull," "depressed." He spoke of having "ice in the blood" and sometimes thought of the heart as being congealed or turned to stone. He also expressed a longing, not for mere warmth, but for an all-consuming fire to melt the ice and calcify the stone. It is curious to note how he fell into the habit of burning his letters to the family as soon as he returned home, how he burned all the available copies of his first novel, and how he burned a whole group of his early stories, which, from the reports of those who read them, were somber and fanciful works that the world would be glad to possess; it was as if he were trying to immolate himself. One of his few amusements in Salem was going to fires—but only after sending his sister Elizabeth to the top of the house to report whether they were big enough to be worth watching. "Come, deadly element of Fire,—henceforth my familiar friend!" is a last prayer uttered by one of his solitary heroes, Ethan Brand. With a burst of laughter Brand leaps into the lime kiln, as into hell. When the fire in the kiln burns down, there is the outline of a skeleton on top of the lime; and within the ribs is the shape of a human heart, like calcified marble.

But these metaphors of ice and fire were not all that Hawthorne learned from his years of self-absorption. He also learned—or at least he learned to suspect—that he was not alone in his nether world; others might be as bad as himself. Some of his stories began to express the notion of companionship in evil doing; for example, the good Mr. Hooper explains on his deathbed why he had insisted for years on hiding his face. "When the friend," he says, "shows his inmost heart to his friend; the lover to his best beloved; when man does not vainly shrink from the eye of his Creator, loathsomely treasuring up the secret of his sin; then deem me a monster, for the symbol beneath which I have lived, and die! I look around me, and lo! on every visage a Black Veil!" The same idea is expressed in "Young Goodman Brown." When the young man goes at nightfall into a forest that might be his own subconscious mind, he finds himself, not alone, but in the midst of a multitude assembled for a witch's sabbath. Among those pledged to Satan he recognizes everyone he had most admired in Salem village: the pious minister, the senior deacon, and even old Goody Cloyse, who had taught him his catechism. At last he stands before an unholy altar with Faith, his wife, while Satan addresses them both. "Evil is the nature of mankind. Evil must be your only happiness," Satan says. "Welcome again, my children, to the communion of your race."

For Hawthorne, too, evil was a sort of communion. He loathed it and struggled against it, most of all when he found it in his own heart; but nevertheless he recognized that it humbled his pride and bound him to other sinners. He might have said of himself what he later said of Mr. Dimmesdale, in *The Scarlet Letter*: "His intellectual gifts, his moral perceptions, his power of experiencing and communicating emotion, were kept in a state of preternatural activity by the prick and anguish of his daily life. . . . This very burden it was that give him sympathies so intimate with the sinful brotherhood of mankind, so that his heart vibrated in unison with theirs, and received their pain into itself, and sent its own throb of pain through a thousand other hearts, in gushes of sad, persuasive eloquence."

It is characteristic of Hawthorne that he should have drawn a social lesson from a solitary experience. He was more of an individualist than Emerson, to judge by his life as a whole, and yet he did not preach the virtue of self-reliance; instead his moral in story after story was that every person must submit to the common fate. "The truly wise," he said in one of his early sketches—and often said again in different words—"after all their speculations, will be led into the common path, and, in homage to the human nature that pervades them, will gather gold, and till the earth, and set out trees, and build a house." Hawthorne, too, wished to gather gold and build a house; on one side of his nature he was a sturdy and harshly practical New Englander like the magistrates and sea captains from whom he was descended. "Let them scorn me as they will," he said of his ancestors, "strong traits of their nature have intertwined themselves with mine"; but he also had strong traits of the Byronic rebel. Everywhere in his character one finds a sort of doubleness: thus, he was proud and humble, cold and sensuous, sluggish and active, conservative and radical, realistic and romantic; he was a recluse who became involved in party politics and a visionary with a touch of cynicism and a hard sense of money values. These contradictions, these inner tensions, lend force to his stories and make their author an endless study.

Out of his struggles with his conscience and his sense of guilt, Hawthorne evolved a sort of theology that was peculiar to himself, but was also profoundly Christian and on most points orthodox. He believed in original sin, which consisted—so I think he would have said—in the pride and self-centeredness of every individual. He believed that evil existed in all hearts, including his own, and he therefore had no patience with the modernists of his time who explained that evil was merely accident or illusion. He believed in the brotherhood of men, based on their common sinfulness and their weakness before God. He believed in predestination, as his Calvinist ancestors had done; but at the same time he had an instinctive faith in the value of confession and absolution that sometimes brought him close to Roman Catholicism. He never went to church after leaving college and apparently he seldom prayed. One might say that he was both too proud and too humble for prayer: too proud to ask for help and too humble to plead his own desires against the divine wisdom: "Men's accidents are God's purposes" was the motto he scratched with a diamond ring on a window of the Old Manse. He trustingly submitted himself to Providence, and he believed in a future life where each guilty person would be punished, if only as he himself had been, by self-knowledge of his sins. On the whole his faith was close to that of the Puritan fathers, but it was not derived from their teaching; it was a practical Puritanism based on his own experience. It was expressed in story after story, not philosophically—for he did not think in abstractions—but in terms of symbols as powerfully simple as those in *Pilgrim's Progress,* and so much closer to the modern mind that in some respects he seems nearer to Kafka than to John Bunyan.

In his plots he laid more emphasis on sin and retribution than on redemption through divine grace; yet one can hardly say that he regarded all sinners as hopelessly damned. Some, it is true, might be led by gradual steps into what he regarded as the Unpardonable Sin; it was an intellectual pride and selfishness that permitted them to manipulate human souls in order to satisfy their cold curiosity and lust for power; such men deserved the fate of Ethan Brand. Others, however, might be taught human brotherhood by their very crimes and, if they publicly confessed, might be taken back into the community. Still others might be redeemed simply by their love for one human being, and that was Hawthorne's salvation. When he fell in love with Sophia Peabody, it seemed to him that he had been drawn from the shadows and made real, together with the world about him, by the intensity of his passion. "Indeed, we are but shadows," he said in one of those letters to Sophia in which he poured out his feelings for the first time; "we are not endowed with real life, all that seems most real about us is but the thinnest substance of a dream,—till the heart be touched. That touch creates us,—then we begin to be."

It was Sophia's older sister, Elizabeth, who first brought the lovers together. Miss E. P. Peabody, as she called herself, was the friend of all the Boston cranks and reformers, a transcendental spirit who fluttered from enthusiasm to enthusiasm like an iron-willed butterfly. She had been excited by "The Gentle Boy" and other stories that appeared anonymously in the giftbooks and magazines; she suspected that they were all the work of the same author and hoped to discover a genius. When *Twice-Told Tales* appeared in 1837, she learned that the genius was a neighbor in Salem—indeed, one of her childhood playmates—and at once she laid siege to the Hawthorne household. It was a matter of patient months before she had charmed Louisa, the lively sister, who she said disappointedly was "just like other people," and Elizabeth, the intellectual sister, whom she admired as "the hermitess." Nathaniel was harder to entice from his solitude; but at last her evening of triumph came when the whole family paid her a visit. Miss Peabody excused herself and rushed upstairs to the room where Sophia was recovering from one of her daily headaches. "Oh, Sophia," she said, "you must get up and dress and come down! The Hawthornes are here, and you never saw anything so splendid as he is,—he is handsomer than Lord Byron!"

Sophia didn't feel strong enough to meet him. "If he has called once, he'll call again," she said.

Hawthorne did call again, in the afternoon, and this time Sophia came down in her simple white wrapper and sat on the sofa. When Miss Peabody said, "My sister Sophia," he rose and looked at her so intently that both women were frightened. Many years later Sophia told her children that she felt a magnetic power in his eyes and instinctively drew back. Then, as the weeks passed by and Hawthorne became a daily visitor, she began to realize that they had loved each other at first sight.

"Poor children," one thinks while reading the story of their courtship; for they both were children in their knowledge of the world. But again one thinks, "Lucky children," after picturing the fates that both of them escaped, in a provincial society full of old maids and cranky bachelors. Sophia was twenty-seven years old when they met; she suffered from violent headaches that had defied treatment by all the doctors and half the quacks in Boston. Often she had told her older sister that nothing would tempt her to marry and inflict on a husband the care of an invalid. Hawthorne was thirty-four and was trying to venture out from his solitary life, which had led him to fears of suicide or madness; but he seemed too shy and aloof ever to risk a proposal of marriage, and his sisters, moreover, were determined to keep him a bachelor. Somehow he groped his way to Sophia and she to him, both surmounting their inner obstacles, both cutting through a little maze of family intrigues; and they clung together as if they furnished, each to each, the only present refuge or hope of future salvation. Soon they were secretly engaged and were even addressing each other in their letters as husband and wife; but the marriage ceremony couldn't take place until Hawthorne was able to support a family.

In 1839 he obtained the first of his political appointments, as weigher and gauger in the Boston Custom House. He had a salary now, even if it was only $1,500 a year, but other obstacles delayed the wedding. Sophia decided that it would have to wait until she had recovered from her twenty-years' illness. "If God intends us to marry, He will let me be cured," she said; "if not, it will be a sign that it is not best." Hawthorne's sisters warned him against marrying an invalid; they said that his mother would die of the shock. Miss E. P. Peabody seems to have hoped that Hawthorne would recognize her own superior merits—that is one inference to be drawn from the family correspondence—but nevertheless she provided a meeting place for the lovers and helped them to exchange letters. She also encouraged Hawthorne's next step, which was to join the utopian community at Brook Farm in the hope that it would provide a home for himself and Sophia. For a time he shared the ideals of the other Brook Farmers and outdid them in physical labor; indeed, he worked so hard in the fields and the cow stable that he had no energy left for dreaming. "A man's soul," he said in a letter to Sophia, "may be buried and perish under a dung-heap or in the furrow of a field, just as well as under a pile of money." He left Brook Farm in the autumn and later resigned his post as chairman of the finance committee. His literary prospects looked brighter and at last he determined to tell his mother about the approaching marriage. "I already knew about it," Madame Hawthorne said, ". . . almost as long as you knew it yourself, and Sophia Peabody is the wife of all others I would have chosen for you." The sisters now declared that they were delighted with his choice. Sophia's headaches miraculously disappeared. After an engagement that had lasted for nearly four years, the wedding took place on July 9, 1842, and the lovers went to live in Concord, where they had rented the Old Manse. "I have married the Spring!" Hawthorne exclaimed in a letter. "I am husband to the month of May!"

Springlike as she was, Sophia had her faults, some of which were regarded as virtues by the Bostonians. She was painfully high-minded, even priggish; and when Hawthorne admiringly painted her portrait (as Hilda, in *The Marble Faun*), he presented a character that seems to us heartless and almost monstrous in its ideality. She tried to see nothing but the beautiful, the good, and the true. Unconsciously she acted as a censor of her husband's work, by admiring it for the wrong qualities; and she also played the conscious censor when she edited the notebooks for publication after his death. The fact remains that her love for him was earthly as well as ethereal. She made him an admirable wife, devoted, uncomplaining in their early hardships, respectful of his need for solitude, and always regarding him as the sun around which her life revolved. In practical ways she also helped: she protected him from intrusions on his time and demanded little for herself; after he lost his second political post, in the Salem Custom House, it was her savings from her household allowance that enabled him to start writing *The Scarlet Letter*. Hawthorne made her an admirable husband, too; besides playing the father to her, and the dutiful son, he was also her passionate lover—at least until their younger daughter, Rose, was born in 1851; afterwards they decided to have no more children and their passion seems to have subsided into a steady and lifelong affection. Without this domestic security, his public career as a writer would have been impossible. All his novels and many of his stories were written for and because of Sophia.

After the popular success of the first three novels, there was a further change in Hawthorne: he became more conservative and directed more of his attention towards the external world. Brook Farm had been his farthest venture into radicalism and it had frightened him, especially when his associates began talking about sexual liberty. Now, forsaking the reformers who had been his first friends when he emerged from solitude, he began to see more of "the merchants, the politicians, the Cambridge men, and all those respectable old blockheads, who still, in this intangibility and mistiness of affairs, kept a death-grip on one or two ideas which had not come into vogue since yesterday morning." He tried to forget his earlier dilemmas and even came to dislike the stories in which he had expressed his sense of guilt. The change is implicit in one of his letters to James T. Fields, the junior partner of the publishing house that had taken over his work and, in 1854, was bringing out a revised edition of *Mosses from an Old Manse*. "When I wrote these dreamy sketches," Hawthorne said, "I little thought that I should ever preface an edition for the press amidst the bustling life of a Liverpool consulate. Upon my honor, I am not quite sure that I entirely comprehend my own meaning, in some of these blasted allegories; but I remember that I always had a meaning, or at least thought I had. I am a good deal changed since those times; and, to tell you the truth, my past self is not very much to my taste, as I see myself in this book."

Thanks chiefly to his marriage he had become a success by public standards; not only a famous romancer but a highly respected citizen like his Salem ancestors, a government official and the head of a family. He had even lived out his fable of the Great Stone Face: orphaned and seeking year after year for a father image, he had at last discovered in himself the benignant parent. Only one side of his double character was now revealed to the world and his own children. His son Julian, who didn't read the romances until after Hawthorne's death, found himself continually bewildered by them and "unable to comprehend," he said, "how a man such as I knew my father to be could have written such books. He did not talk in that way; his moods had not seemed to be of that color." The fact was that the books continued to mirror his earlier self; even the last unfinished novels, for all their details copied from life, were still based on his discoveries in that inner world where he had lived in desperate isolation. Now he had roofed over the entrance to the abyss and had built another life above it. He was honored, he was financially secure, and, after 1860, he found it impossible to write the novels that he started one after another—partly because he was tired and in ill health, partly because he kept setting higher standards for himself, but chiefly because he had blocked off the source of his inspiration.

"The best things come, as a general thing, from talents that are members of a group," says Henry James in his little book on Hawthorne; "every man works best when he has companions working in the same line, and yielding the stimulus of suggestion, comparison, emulation." Hawthorne never had such a stimulus, and for a long time after his work began to be printed he even lacked the feeling that it was being read; he wrote like a prisoner talking aloud in his cell. When he did find admirers, after 1837, they usually agreed with Sophia in praising him for the wrong reasons: most of them were Emersonian and idealistic, whereas Hawthorne's bent was towards psychological realism even when he was writing allegories. Fortunately he resisted their efforts to change him, and justified his own description of himself as "a most unmalleable man." Working alone, he had to look in himself for the answer to each of his literary problems. He often made elaborate mistakes, as might have been expected; the wonder is that so many of the answers he found were usable. Not in his life, but in his work, he foreshadowed the ideals that later American writers would try to realize and fixed the patterns that many of them would instinctively follow.

During his years of solitude Hawthorne learned more than others did in the marketplace. He learned, for example, that he had to respect his own limitations. "Four precepts," he wrote in his notebook for 1835: "To break off customs; to shake off spirits ill-disposed; to meditate on youth; to do nothing against one's genius." He learned—and this was a lesson he never forgot—that the best things he wrote were uttered by a voice deep within himself, whose speech he was unable to control. He surrendered himself to a power that was, so he said, "higher and wiser than himself, making him its instrument." The crowning effect that he hoped to achieve was "a happiness which God, out of His pure grace, mixes up with only the simplehearted best efforts of men." Yet this inner voice, which he sometimes regarded as divine, more often seemed to him infernal; thus, he spoke of *The Scarlet Letter* as being "baked in hell-fire."—"When I get home, I will try to write a more genial book," he said when he was working on *The Marble Faun*; "but the Devil himself always seems to get into my inkstand, and I can only exorcise him by pensful at a time." There were months and years, however, when the Devil stayed out of his inkstand, and that was worse; at such periods Hawthorne felt that his work was contrived and inconsequential. "I have an instinct that I had better keep quiet," he said in one of his last letters to James T. Fields. "Perhaps I shall have a new spirit of vigor if I wait quietly for it; perhaps not."

He learned a wise patience that he sometimes explained as indolence. It was really watchfulness; he was crouching in wait for his own thoughts like a duck-shooter hidden in the reeds. There was, however, another side of the picture and he also learned to be active in pursuit of his thoughts. He collected impressions and stored them away in his notebook, so that a background would be ready for the inspiration when it came at last; and he learned to wrestle with it and force it from its obscurity. "This forenoon," he said in a diary for 1843, "I began to write, and caught an idea by the tail, which I intend to hold fast, though it struggles to get free. As it was not ready to be put on paper, however, I took up the *Dial,* and finished the article on Mr. Alcott." The *Dial,* organ of the Concord intellectuals, was one of his trusted tools, but it served a different purpose from that intended by its editors; Hawthorne read it when he was tired and it usually put him to sleep.

Catnaps over the *Dial* were part of his routine, for he had learned a system of working, resting, exercising, and returning to work with a fresh mind. In the summer—I am speaking of the first years after his marriage— he made entries in his notebook and hoed the garden, trying, as he said, to be "happy as a squash, and in much the same mode."—"I am never good for anything in the literary way," he wrote to Fields, "till after the first autumnal frost, which has somewhat the same effect on my imagination that it does on the foliage here about me,—multiplying and brightening its hues." All his four novels were finished during the winter, when he made a practice of writing from two to four hours each day—seldom longer than that, except when he was working excitedly on *The Scarlet Letter,* for he had found that the mood on which he depended was likely to vanish when he became weary. One respects him for insisting on leisure when he hadn't money to pay for it. He was willing to live on the cheapest foodstuffs available in Concord—his Christmas dinner in 1843 consisted of "preserved quince and apple, dates, and bread and cheese, and milk"; but, poor as he was, he refused to hurry along a story that needed time to ripen.

He wrote much more than one would infer from his easy schedule or from merely looking at the little shelf of books with "Hawthorne's Works" on the back. Besides the early stories he burned in his fireplace—there were many of them and once, he said, they set the chimney on fire—he did a quantity of hackwork when trying to break away from Salem and later when he was earning a living for himself and Sophia. In 1836, for a promised salary of five hundred dollars a year (of which he received twenty dollars in all), he not only edited but wrote almost the entire contents of the *American Magazine of Useful and Entertaining Knowledge.* After the magazine went bankrupt, through no fault of the editor's, he wrote for a fee of one hundred dollars (this time actually paid) a history of the world that went through scores of editions and eventually had a sale of more than a million copies. In England, during the four years when he was consul at Liverpool, he wrote nothing for publication except a preface to Delia Bacon's crazy book on Shakespeare; but he kept a journal that ran to 300,000 words, and it was more carefully expressed than most published novels. One might say that he taught himself to write by writing a great deal.

He also learned to write by constant reading. Having acquired the habit at the age of nine, he never relinquished it; in his last years he went through the Waverly novels a second time, reading them aloud to his family. We have a record of the books he borrowed from the Salem Athenaeum during most of his solitary period. His average was a hundred titles each year: biography, travel, New England history, encyclopedias (which he seems to have read from beginning to end), and bound volumes of English magazines; the record shows that he had a thirst for general information. He also read the latest novels, which he rented from a circulating library. In some respects his choice of books seems curious and impractical for a Romantic writer trying to keep abreast of the movement to which he belonged. Thus, he studied the French classics, especially Racine and Voltaire, but nowhere in his notebooks does he mention Balzac, Stendhal, Hugo, or any other French rebel of his own time. He was closer in spirit to the German Romantics, but not because he read them; once, with a German phrase book open beside him, he puzzled through a story by Johann Ludwig Tieck, but he never repeated the experiment. Some of his favorite English authors, besides Scott and Bunyan, were Pope, Swift, Addison, and Dr. Johnson—all of whom represented the classical standards against which his fellow Romantics had risen in revolt.

It was from these and other Augustan writers that he seems to have learned the style of his early work. The style was old-fashioned, balanced, formal, one might almost say white-silk-stockinged and periwigged; it was a curious manner of writing for an author bent on penetrating the shadowy places of the heart. It was full of personified abstractions. "Sometimes," he said in describing one of his early heroines, "she stole forth by moonlight and visited the graves of venerable Integrity, and wedded Love, and virgin Innocence, and every spot where the ashes of a kind and faithful heart were mouldering." The sentiment is Romantic, while the language is that of an eighteenth-century drawing-room poet. But Hawthorne's style changed gradually as he grew older, until he was writing better and easier prose than any other American of his time. One reason for the change was his habit of walking out his stories, repeating them to himself as he wandered along the seashore or under the pines. The result was that his rather provincial drawing-room English developed into a natural, a *walked* style, with a phrase for every step and a comma after every phrase like a footprint in the sand. Sometimes the phrases hurry, sometimes they loiter, sometimes they march to drums. Although Hawthorne had no ear for music and couldn't tell one melody from another, his sense of rhythm was extraordinary.

Since he could never express himself in company—except sometimes in his later years over a bottle of wine—writing became his principal means of communication with the world; and he therefore tried to make each statement clear. He learned to use what he called "the humblest medium of familiar words and images."—"Every sentence," he said in the introduction to *Twice-Told Tales,* "so far as it embodies thought or sensibility, may be understood and felt by anybody who will give himself the trouble to read it, and will take up the book in the proper mood." He liked children and was proud of his ability to write for them without condescension: "I never did anything else so well as these old baby stories," he said when working on *Tanglewood Tales*.

Apparently he agreed with Poe in thinking that the writer's principal problem was how to produce "effects," which might be defined as states of feeling induced in his readers. Writing to his classmate Horatio Bridge, who had become a naval officer and was planning to keep a journal of his cruise to Africa, Hawthorne mentioned some of the methods by which effects might be achieved. "Begin to write always before the impression of novelty has worn off from your mind," he said, "else you will be apt to think that the peculiarities which at first attracted you are not worth recording; yet those slight peculiarities are the very things that make the most vivid impression upon the reader. Think nothing too trifling to write down, so it be in the smallest degree characteristic. You will be surprised to find on re-perusing your journal what an importance and graphic power these little particulars assume." In the course of time Hawthorne had trained himself to observe "little particulars"; he insisted on being a good reporter as well as an artist. He was a good journalist or magazinist, too; and one reads his articles on occasional subjects with wonder at the many original methods he found for presenting his rather tame material. Everything he published had the charm of solid craftsmanship. He was perhaps the first American writer with a professional attitude towards all his work.

One problem that obsessed him all his life was the relation between the inner and the outer world. Hawthorne tried different means of solving it, one after the other, but none of them proved satisfactory.

The inner world of dreams and moral compulsions had been the real subject of almost all his stories. Of course they had an outward setting, too, but it often lacked substance, being a mere projection or symbol of the landscapes inside his mind. Most of his plots were based on an inner event; it was usually some transgression, vaguely stated, that led to its own punishment without the intervention of policemen or magistrates; and there was always a moral implicit in the story.

As the plots were jotted down in his early notebooks, they were quite brief; often they consisted of a few phrases. "To trace out the influence of a frightful and disgraceful crime," he would say, "in debasing and destroying a character naturally high and noble—the guilty person alone being conscious of the crime." Again he would say: "A person to be in the possession of something as perfect as mortal man has a right to demand; he tries to make it better, and ruins it entirely." The first of these plots was never used, while the second, after lying in Hawthorne's mind for six years, developed into one of his better stories, "The Birthmark." When they were first noted down, however, one seemed as promising or unpromising as the other; both were inner dramas and both carried an implicit moral: the first, that crime is self-punished; the second, that striving for perfection in this imperfect world is an act of sinful pride.

Before any of his plots became a narrative, Hawthorne had to find characters, invent actions for them that would reveal the inner conflict, and describe an outward setting that would symbolize the inner truth. The characters, the actions, and the setting would all have to be woven out of his mind, like a spider extruding its web. In the beginning, at least, Hawthorne couldn't copy from other lives than his own, because his experience, though deep, was too narrow. "I have another great difficulty in the lack of materials," he said in an early letter to Longfellow; "for I have seen so little of the world that I have nothing but thin air to concoct my stories of, and it is not easy to give a lifelike semblance to such shadowy stuff."

Having diagnosed his weakness, Hawthorne tried to cure it. The best remedy, he thought, would be more observation of the world; and so he began taking notes on every new scene or person he encountered in his summer wanderings. He practiced writing descriptions like a painter doing watercolor sketches; once, for example, he sat alone in the woods near Concord with his notebook in his lap and made a record of everything that came under his eyes. He filled eight pages with his small handwriting, then made a final comment: "How narrow, scanty, and meagre is this record of observation, compared with the immensity that was to be observed, within the bounds which I prescribed to myself. . . . When we see how little we can express, it is a wonder that any man ever takes up a pen a second time." Yet Hawthorne kept trying to express more and more of what he saw and more of what he heard and thought (his ears were always less keen than his eyes). Without being a naturalist like Thoreau, he learned to catch the changing moods of nature; and he developed his naturally keen sense of character. Said Lawyer Haynes, the one-armed drunken soapmaker he met in North Adams, "My study is man." Then, looking straight at Hawthorne, he added, "I do not know your name, but there is something of the hawk-eye about you too."

His notebooks came to play a curious part in his creative process: they were a hoard of objects and persons; they were the outer world reduced to words and made usable in his fiction. Instead of concocting his backgrounds out of thin air, he began to take them from his notebooks, as if he had requisitioned them from a warehouse, where they might have been stored for a decade or more. "Ethan Brand," published in 1851, is an example of this new method; it combines an inner drama over which he had brooded for several years with a collection of notes he had made during his visit to

North Adams in 1838. One of the most effective chapters in *The Blithedale Romance* (1852) is the one describing the search for Zenobia's drowned body. Hawthorne had fished for the body of a suicide in 1845, when he was living at the Old Manse, and now he merely revised the notes he had taken on that occasion. More than two-thirds of *The Marble Faun* (1860) consists of descriptive passages transcribed from the Italian notebooks. The novel combines his two worlds, but without fusing them; inner drama and outer setting tend to separate like oil and water. Hawthorne kept looking for another answer to his problem.

He often thought of completely shifting his approach. Instead of starting with a drama from his inner world and surrounding it with objects copied from nature, might it not be better to start with the external world and brood over its meaning until he forced it to reveal its inner drama? That had been the "wiser effort" suggested in his introduction to *The Scarlet Letter,* where, as usual, he insisted on disparaging the work he had actually performed. "It was a folly," he said, "with the materiality of this daily life pressing so intrusively upon me"—he had been describing his three years in the custom house—"to attempt to fling myself back into another age; or to insist on creating the semblance of a world out of airy matter, when, at every moment, the impalpable beauty of my soap-bubble was broken by the rude contact of some actual circumstance. The wiser effort would have been to diffuse thought and imagination through the opaque substance of to-day, and thus to make it a bright transparency." Hawthorne greatly admired the seventeenth-century Dutch painters, especially Gerhard Douw, for their treatment of natural objects. "These painters," he said in his notebook, "accomplish all they aim at—a praise, methinks, which can be given to no other men since the world began. They must have laid down their brushes with perfect satisfaction, knowing that each one of their million touches had been necessary to the effect, and that there was not one too little or too much. And it is strange how spiritual, and suggestive the commonest household article—an earthen pitcher, for example—becomes when represented with entire accuracy. These Dutchmen get at the soul of common things, and so make them types and interpreters of the spiritual world." At times Hawthorne tried to copy their method. "Many passages of this book," he said when writing *The House of the Seven Gables,* "ought to be finished with the minuteness of a Dutch picture, in order to give them their proper effect."

There was no violent change in Hawthorne's theories when he tried to work inward from the surface of things instead of outward from the heart. All his life he believed that a sort of correspondence existed between the two worlds of nature and spirit; one might start with either and, with sufficient effort, one might end by expressing the same truths. In some respects his notion of correspondences brought him close to the Puritan divines like Cotton Mather, who also found a double meaning in everything. Mather was ready to explain even the humblest events—like a cow's going dry or finding her way home from the forest—as tokens of God's providence or Satan's wiles. Hawthorne had a similar faith in tokens that often made him sound old-fashioned; but he was an explorer, too, and some of his work looked forward to the still undiscovered fields of psychiatry and psychosomatic medicine. Here are a few entries from his notebooks that have a prophetic ring:

(1836). An article on fire, on smoke. Diseases of the mind and soul,—even more common than bodily diseases.
(1841). To symbolize moral or spiritual disease by disease of the body;—thus, when a person committed any sin, it might cause a sore to appear on the body;— this to be wrought out.
(1842). Imaginary diseases to be cured by impossible remedies—as, a dose of the Grand Elixir, in the yolk of a Phoenix's egg. The diseases may be either moral or physical.
(1842). A physician for the cure of moral diseases.

In working with these notions about moral diseases—which we have learned to call psychoses—and about the operation of the spirit on the body, Hawthorne was far in advance of his time and he was a little frightened by his boldness. Often his speculations played a part in his stories; a famous example of psychophysical parallelism is the scarlet A that appears on Mr. Dimmesdale's flesh after he has brooded for years over his guilt. In describing such incidents, however, Hawthorne always protects himself from the skeptics by saying "perhaps," or "it was the general belief," or "if all the stories were true." This ambiguity is carried to great length in his account of Mr. Dimmesdale's confession. Most of the spectators testify to having seen a scarlet letter imprinted on the minister's flesh, but they give three different explanations of its presence, and there are some who flatly deny that it could be seen, or indeed that Mr. Dimmesdale had confessed to anything improper. Hawthorne reports the controversy without taking sides, and yet he makes his attitude fairly clear in spite of all the conflicting statements: he believed that there was really a scarlet A on Mr. Dimmesdale's breast, and he believed that it was "the effect of the ever-active tooth of remorse, gnawing from the inmost heart outwardly." What happened in the heart became manifest in the flesh; and, conversely, one could arrive at inner truths by scrutinizing appearances.

Towards the end of his life, Hawthorne became more and more impatient with the books in which he embodied his misty theories. "My own individual taste," he complained in a letter to Fields, "is for quite another class of works than those which I myself am able to write. If I were to meet with such books as mine, by another writer, I don't believe I should be able to get through them. Have you ever read the novels of Anthony Trollope? They precisely suit my taste; solid and substantial, written on the strength of beef and through the inspiration of ale, and just as real as if some giant had hewn a great lump out of the earth and put it under a glass case, with all its inhabitants going about their daily business, and not suspecting that they were made a show of." That was the sort of novel he admired, and it was even a sort of novel he had prepared himself to write—or so one judges after reading his English notebooks, with their solid grasp of character and their substantial pictures of persons and places. It was not, however, a sort of novel that he judged to lie within the limits of his genius. "I wish God had given me the faculty of writing a sunshiny book," he said; but he bowed to fate or Providence in this respect as in others; he wrote or tried to write the books that he had within him.

He was working towards a conception of the novel—or of the romance, as he preferred to call it—that was completely different from the notions prevailing at his time. "In writing a romance," he had said in a letter to Fields, "a man is always, or always ought to be, careering on the utmost verge of a precipitous absurdity, and the skill lies in coming as close as possible, without actually tumbling over." The last books he planned would have been a mixture of fantasy and realism; they would have been realistic in their method, with all the details copied from life, and realistic in their reading of human nature; but they would have been based on plots that were flatly impossible. Thus, in *The Dolliver Romance,* the book with which he struggled during the last year of his life, he would have told us how Grandsir Dolliver grew younger year by year and finally became a child again. Each step towards that impossible goal would have been as carefully visualized as any of the real scenes described in Hawthorne's notebooks. The book as a whole would have had the circumstantiality of a dream, while at the same time it would have been a vehicle for Hawthorne's broodings over mortality. If he had been able to finish *The Dolliver Romance,* it might have served as the bridge for which he had always been seeking, between the inner and the outer world.

Hawthorne was always dissatisfied with his own work and at the end he became obsessed with a sense of failure. One day when Emerson found him on the path that his feet had made among the sweetfern and the huckleberry bushes, Hawthorne said to him, "This path is the only remembrance of me that will remain." Yet he was a failure only when his achievements are measured against the inordinately high standards he set for himself. Measured by the easier standards of his time, the same achievements seem almost Himalayan. He advanced the art of fiction. Even before Poe, he was the first American—and possibly the first in any country—to write short stories in the modern sense of the term: not sketches or episodes, but stories built around a single effect and having the unity of a lyric poem. Moreover, he carried his prose experiments farther than Poe, for he was also the first American to write novels that were as tightly constructed as short stories.

There is more to be said about his conception of the novel. One can see by internal evidence that he was faced with difficulties in the longer form; his training as a story writer made it hard for him to keep the action continually moving forward; but he solved this problem by dividing his novels into scenes or tableaus, each strikingly visualized and balanced one against another; it was the dramatic method that Henry James would rediscover in his final period. Within the limitations of his technique and personality, each of his novels was different from all the others, not only in subject but in mood and treatment. One principle he followed instinctively was that every work of art must be right by its own laws, which are never quite the same as those governing any other work of art. Another principle was that each novel should be a painting complete within its frame. Besides being a series of balanced tableaus, the action of his novels consists of *interactions* among a few characters—usually four—with voices from the crowd as a sort of dramatic chorus; and the result is that each book becomes a system of relationships, a field of force as clearly defined and symmetrical as a magnetic field. He was the first American writer to develop this architectural conception of the novel; and even in France *Madame Bovary* wasn't published until seven years after *The Scarlet Letter* had appeared in Boston.

Flaubert and Hawthorne had not a little in common; their work revealed the same search for perfection (though Flaubert carried it farther), the same mixture of realism and romanticism, the same feeling that each new novel was a totally new problem in mood and organization. Hawthorne's work has a New England sparseness and accuracy of detail that is almost like Flaubert's Norman economy. Frederic Moreau, of *Sentimental Education,* was said to be a self-portrait of Flaubert; and one cannot fail to note his resemblance to Miles Coverdale, of *The Blithedale Romance,* who was said to be a self-portrait of Hawthorne. The striking difference between the two authors was that Flaubert regarded himself as living and working at the center of the civilized world, on an eminence from which life could be judged without moral preconceptions, whereas Hawthorne remained the complete provincial even when living in Europe. He was provincial in both the good and the bad sense of the word: in the good sense because he knew his province, accepted his part in it, and tested everything else in the world by New England standards (so that he carried the Puritan conscience to Rome, in *The Marble Faun,* and transferred the Greek legends to the Berkshires, in *The Wonder-Book,* after purifying them, as he said, of all moral stains); and provincial in the bad sense because his localism made him blind to other values than those accepted in Boston.

Sometimes his work had a sort of New England stuffiness, as if it were meant to be read in an unaired parlor. At his worst he wrote and acted less like Flaubert than like the late George Apley—as when he quailed at the notion of meeting George Eliot, who was living with a man she couldn't marry, and when he refused to admit that any sculptor was a genius unless he was able to portray heroism in frock coat and breeches. "I do not altogether see the necessity of ever sculpturing another nakedness," he said in his notebook for 1858. "Man is no longer a naked animal; his clothes are as natural to him as his skin, and sculptors have no more right to undress him than to flay him." Hawthorne had always been interested in clothes as symbols that revealed a man's nature while concealing it, and now his interest had become an obsession. Having dressed his thoughts in trousers, he no longer moved with the freedom of the naked mind.

Yet he was, for all his decorum, a man of strong passions who liked to write about women of strong passions. Two of his four novels deal with adultery and a third, *The Blithedale Romance,* is about a woman trying to escape from an undesirable husband who has reduced her sister to moral slavery. The heroine of *The Scarlet Letter* justifies her life in terms that shocked some of Hawthorne's early critics: "What we did," she says to her lover, "had a consecration of its own." In the background of *The Marble Faun,* adultery is compounded with incest and fratricide. Miriam is married to a near relative—one would guess her half-brother—who is a mixture of saint and devil. When the devilish side comes uppermost and he tries to resume their relationship, she encourages Donatello to kill him; and one assumes that she and Donatello became lovers that same night. I cannot imagine that Howells, for example, would have dared to tell such a story even discreetly and by implication, as Hawthorne told it; in most of the New England writers passion was not only censored in its expression but expunged from the heart. It is only the surface that is censored in Hawthorne and it is chiefly the surface that has aged; his underlying problems are as real to us today as when he first presented them.

Although he doubted that his work would be remembered, Hawthorne fixed a pattern for writers who came after him; and it was by no means the pattern that critics expected to find. It had been taken for granted that American literature would somehow correspond to the physical and social features of a new country: that it would be as broad as the continent, as hardy and uncouth as the pioneers, and as noisy as an election campaign. But the correspondence that really exists between literature and society can seldom be reduced to such parallels, because books are written by men of special training, from their special type of experience. Not many American writers have been frontiersmen or politicians or even businessmen; most of them have had the feeling of being more or less isolated from their neighbors. Whitman, a lonely man, tried to create a literature of democratic comradeship. After those first great poems in which he poured out his feelings, he made the mistake of conforming to a preconception of what he should write, and that is why much of his later work seems forced. Hawthorne in his solitude wrote what he had to write. Because he obeyed his instinct, which he personified as his genius or demon, he proved to be a better prophet than Whitman of the books that would be written after his death.

So far as there has been a continuous literary tradition in this country, it is the one that Hawthorne had a share in founding. So far as there has been a prevailing tone in our literature, it is not the one that critics tried to deduce from American geography or American politics. In one respect the critics proved to be right. Most of our writers have been democratic, for the simple reason that they were reared in a democratic society and that, in spite of their isolation, they shared its feelings. Hawthorne, who started in life as a Jacksonian Democrat, became more conservative as he grew older; but he retained an interest in ordinary persons—as persons, not as specimens—that set him apart from most of his European contemporaries. That faith runs through American literature; one finds it even in Henry James.

In other respects the best of our writing has taken a course that contradicts most of the prophecies made a century ago. To speak in general terms it has been, not broad and sweeping, but narrow and deep; not epical, but lyrical; not optimistic, but somber and self-questioning in its mood; not young, but middle-aged—one might almost say from the beginning; not realistic as a whole, but marvelously realistic in its grasp of details; not careless and uncouth, but often formalized and troubled by the search for perfection; not prevailingly social, but psychological, and interested from the first in what afterwards came to be known as depth psychology. On the whole it has been a literature of loneliness and one in which persons, however real in themselves, tend to dissolve into symbols and myths. Hawthorne's work continues to stand as one of its archetypes, at the beginning of a double line that runs through James to Eliot, with all his imitators, and through Stephen Crane to Faulkner and Hemingway.

1948

The Hawthornes in Paradise

I

There are only a few great love stories in American fiction, and there are fewer still in the lives of famous American writers. Nathaniel Hawthorne wrote one of the greatest, *The Scarlet Letter*. He also lived a story that deserves to be retold with all the new knowledge we can bring to bear on it—as long as there are lovers in New England; it was his courtship and conquest of Sophia Peabody. Unlike his first novel, the lived story was neither sinful nor tragic. Everything in the foreground was as softly glowing as a June morning in Salem, but there were shadows in the background and obstacles to be surmounted; among them were poverty, seemingly hopeless invalidism, conniving sisters, political intrigues, a silken temptress, a duel that might have been fought to the death, and inner problems more threatening than any of these. It was as if Hawthorne had needed to cut his way through a forest of thorns—some planted by himself—in order to reach the castle of Sleeping Beauty and waken her with a kiss, while, in the same moment, he wakened himself from a daylong nightmare.

When he first met Sophia, Hawthorne was thirty-three years old, and he had spent twelve of those years in a dreamlike seclusion. Day after day he sat alone in his room, writing or reading or merely watching a sunbeam as it bored through the blind and slowly traveled across the opposite wall. "For months together," he said long afterward, in a letter to the poet R. H. Stoddard, "I scarcely held human intercourse outside of my own family; seldom going out except at twilight, or only to take the nearest way to the most convenient solitude." He doubted whether twenty people in Salem even knew of his existence.

In remembering those years, Hawthorne sometimes pictured his solitude as being more nearly absolute than it had been. There were social moments even then. Every summer he took a long trip on his Manning uncles' stagecoach lines and "enjoyed as much of life," he said, "as other people do in the whole year's round." In Salem he made some whist-playing acquaintances and learned a little about the intricacies of Democratic party politics. He had a college friend, Horatio Bridge, of Augusta, Maine, to whom he wrote intimate letters, and Bridge was closely connected with two rising political figures, also Democrats and college friends of Hawthorne's, Congressman Jonathan Cilley of Maine, and Franklin Pierce, the junior senator from New Hampshire. All three were trying to advance Hawthorne's career, and Bridge had rescued him from complete obscurity by guaranteeing a publisher against loss and thereby inducing him to issue the first book with Hawthorne's name on it, *Twice-Told Tales.*

After the book appeared in the early spring of 1837, its author made some mild efforts to emerge into Salem society, where the young ladies admired him for his courtesy, his deep-set eyes—so blue they were almost black—and his air of having a secret life. He thought of marriage and even fancied himself in love that spring, as Romeo did before meeting Juliet, but his courtship of a still-unidentified woman was soon broken off. Hawthorne was beginning to fear that he would never be able to rejoin the world of living creatures. His true solitude was inward, not outward, and he had formed the habit of holding long conversations with himself, like a lonely child. His daylong nightmare was of falling into a morbid state of self-absorption that would make everything unreal in his eyes, even himself. 'None have understood it," says one of his heroes, Gervayse Hastings of "The Christmas Banquet," who might be speaking for the author, "—not even those who experience the like. It is a chilliness—a want of earnestness—a feeling as if what should be my heart were a thing of vapor—a haunting perception of unreality! . . . All things, all persons . . . have been like shadows flickering on the wall." Then putting his hand on his heart, he says, "Mine—mine is the wretchedness! this cold heart . . ."

Sophia Amelia Peabody, five years younger than Hawthorne, never suffered from self-absorption or an icy heart, but she had a serious trouble of her own. A pretty rather than a beautiful woman, with innocent gray eyes set wide apart, a tiptilted nose, and a mischievous smile, she had beaux attending her whenever she appeared in society: the trouble was that she could seldom appear. When Sophia was fifteen, she had begun to suffer from violent headaches. Her possessive mother explained to her that suffering was woman's peculiar lot, having something to do with the sin of Eve. Her ineffectual father had her treated by half the doctors in Boston, who prescribed, among other remedies, laudanum, mercury, arsenic, hyoscyamus, homeopathy, and hypnotism, but still the headaches continued. Once as a desperate expedient she was sent to Cuba, where she spent two happy years on a plantation while her quiet sister Mary tutored the planter's children. Now, back in Salem with the family—where her headaches were always worse—she was spending half of each day in bed. Like all the Peabody women, she had a New England conscience and a firm belief in the True, the Beautiful, and the Transcendental. She also had a limited but genuine talent for painting. When she was strong enough, she worked hard at copying pictures—and the copies sold—or at painting romantic landscapes of her own.

Sophia had been cast by her family in a role from which it seemed unlikely that she would ever escape. Just as Elizabeth Peabody was the intellectual sister, already famous as an educational reformer, and Mary was the quiet sister who did most of the household chores, Sophia was the invalid sister, petted like a child and kept in an upstairs room. There were also three brothers, one of them married, but the Peabodys were a matriarchy and a sorority; nobody paid much attention to the Peabody men. It was written that when the mother died, Sophia would become the invalid aunt of her brother's children; she would support herself by painting lampshades and firescreens, while enduring her headaches with a brave smile. As for Hawthorne, his fate was written too; he would become the cranky New England bachelor, living in solitude and writing more and more nebulous stories about other lonely souls. But they saved each other, those two unhappy children. Each was the other's refuge, and they groped their way into each other's arms, where both found strength to face the world.

2

It was Elizabeth, the intellectual sister, who first brought them together, unthinkingly, in a moment of triumph for herself. She had long admired a group of stories, obviously by one author, that had been appearing anonymously in the annual editions of a gift book, *The Token,* and in the *New England Magazine.* Now she learned that the author was a Salem neighbor. Always eager to inspire a new genius, she made patient efforts to inveigle him into the Peabody house on Charter Street, with its square windows looking over an old burying ground where Peabodys and Hathornes—as the name used to be spelled—were sleeping almost side by side. She even took the bold step of paying several visits to the Hawthorne house on Herbert Street, known as "Castle Dismal," where nobody outside the family had dared to come for years.

Usually she was received by Hawthorne's younger sister, Louisa, who, Miss Peabody said disappointedly, was "quite like everybody else." The older sister, Elizabeth—usually called Ebe—was known with good reason as "the hermitess," but she finally consented to take a walk with her enterprising neighbor. Madam Hawthorne, the mother, stayed in her room as always, and Nathaniel was nowhere to be seen. He did, however, send Miss Peabody a presentation copy of his book, and she replied by suggesting some journalistic work that he had no intention of doing. Then, on the evening of November 11, 1837, came her moment of triumph. Elizabeth was sitting in the parlor, looking at a five-volume set of Flaxman's classical engravings that she had just been given by Professor Felton of Harvard, when she heard a great ring at the front door.

"There stood your father," she said half a century later in a letter to her nephew Julian Hawthorne, "in all the splendor of his young beauty and a hooded figure hanging on each arm." The figures were Louisa and Ebe. Miss Peabody bustled them into the parlor and set them to looking at Flaxman's illustrations for *The Iliad*. Then she ran upstairs to the invalid's room and said, "Oh, Sophia, Mr. Hawthorne and his sisters have come, and you never saw anything so splendid—he is handsomer than Lord Byron! You must get up and dress and come down. We have Flaxman too."

Sophia laughed and said, "I think it would be rather ridiculous to get up. If he has come once he will come again."

A few days later he came again, this time in the afternoon. "I summoned your mother," Miss Peabody said in the same letter,

and she came down in her simple white wrapper, and glided in at the back door and sat down on the sofa. As I said, "My sister, Sophia—Mr. Hawthorne," he rose and looked at her—he did not realize how intently, and afterwards, as we went on talking, she would interpose frequently a remark in her low sweet voice. Every time she did so, he looked at her with the same intentness of interest. I was struck with it, and painfully. I thought, what if he should fall in love with her. . . .

Miss Peabody explained why that was a painful thought: it was because "I had heard her so often say, nothing would ever tempt her to marry, and inflict upon a husband the care of such a sufferer." But there was an unspoken reason too, for it is clear from other letters that Elizabeth Peabody wanted Nathaniel Hawthorne for herself. Whether she hoped to marry him we cannot be sure, but there is no question that she planned to come his spiritual guide, his literary counselor, his muse and Egeria.

Sophia had no such clear intentions. She told her children long afterward that Hawthorne's presence exerted a magnetic attraction on her from the beginning, and that she instinctively drew back in self-defense. The power she felt in him alarmed her; she did not understand what it meant. By degrees her resistance was overcome. . . . That was Sophia's story, and Hawthorne did not contradict her. There is some doubt, however, whether he told her about everything that happened during the early months of their acquaintance.

3

What followed their first meeting was a comedy of misunderstandings with undertones of tragedy. Hawthorne was supposed to be courting Elizabeth—Miss Peabody, as she was called outside the household: *the* Miss Peabody, as if she had no sisters. There was a correspondence between them. In one of her missives—and that is the proper word for them—she warned Hawthorne that her invalid sister would never marry. His answer has been lost, but Miss Peabody quoted him as saying, "Sophia is a rose to be worn in no man's bosom." Satisfied on this point, she advised him to study German, write books for children, and have no truck with Democratic politicians. She liked to think of him as an otherworldly genius who might save the soul of America, if only he would read the German philosophers in the original. Hawthorne obediently studied German, but he did not take kindly to advice about his personal affairs, and Miss Peabody went off to West Newton to live with her married brother. While she was there, Sophia wrote her a series of letters. Most of them mentioned Mr. Hawthorne, more and more warmly, but Sophia maintained the pretense that her interest in him was intellectual, or at most sisterly, and that he was still Elizabeth's suitor. Meanwhile Hawthorne himself was secretly involved with a Salem heiress.

The story of his involvement, and of the duel to which it nearly led, was told in some detail by Julian Hawthorne in his biography of his parents. Unfortunately Julian did not give names (except "Mary" and "Louis") or offer supporting evidence. Poor Julian, who was sometimes irresponsible, has never been trusted by scholars, and the result is that later biographers of Hawthorne either questioned the story or flatly rejected it. Norman Homes Pearson of Yale, who was preparing a definitive edition of Hawthorne's letters, discovered an interesting document in the Morgan Library. He wrote an article about it for the *Essex Institute*'s quarterly, one for which other scholars stand in his debt. The article was a memorandum by Julian on a conversation with Miss Peabody, one in which she described the whole affair, giving names and circumstances and supporting Julian's story at almost every point. She even explained by implication why the principal figures in the story had to be anonymous. Two of them were still living in 1884, when Julian's book was published, and one of them was the widow of a president of Harvard.

Her name when Hawthorne knew her was Mary Crowninshield Silsbee, and she was the daughter of former United States Senator Nathaniel Silsbee, a great man in New England banking and shipping. Julian says that she was completely unscrupulous, but admits that she had "a certain kind of glancing beauty, slender, piquant, ophidian, Armida-like." Armida—in Tasso's *Jerusalem Delivered*—was a heathen sorceress, daughter of the king of Damascus, who lured the boldest of the Crusaders into her enchanted garden. Mary Silsbee exercised her lures on the brilliant young men she met in her travels between Salem and Washington. One of them was John Louis O'Sullivan of Washington, who was laying ambitious plans for a new magazine to be called the *Democratic Review.*

The young editor was a friend of Hawthorne's classmate Jonathan Cilley, the rising congressman from Maine. Cilley had given him a copy of *Twice-*

Told Tales as soon as the book appeared. O'Sullivan was impressed by it and wrote to the author soliciting articles at the generous rate, for the time, of five dollars a page. He also told Miss Silsbee about Hawthorne. Fascinated by O'Sullivan's picture of a mysterious Salem genius, Armida at once determined, Julian says, "to add him to her museum of victims."

Her method of operation was to cast herself on Hawthorne's mercy by revealing what she told him were the secrets of her inmost soul. She read him long and extremely private passages from her diary—"all of which," Julian says, "were either entirely fictitious, or such bounteous embroideries on the bare basis of reality, as to give what was mean and sordid an appearance of beauty and a winning charm." Hawthorne, who had never considered the possibility that a Salem young lady might be a gratuitous liar, began to regard himself as Miss Silsbee's protector and champion. But he disappointed her by offering none of his own confidences in return.

She tried a new stratagem. Early in February 1838, she summoned Hawthorne to a private and mysterious interview. With a great deal of calculated reluctance she told him that his friend O'Sullivan, "presuming upon her innocence and guilelessness"—as Julian tells the story—"had been guilty of an attempt to practise the basest treachery upon her; and she passionately adjured Hawthorne, as her only confidential and trusted friend and protector, to champion her cause." Hawthorne promptly wrote a letter to O'Sullivan, then in Washington, and challenged him to a duel. The letter has disappeared, but there is another to Horatio Bridge written on February 8—possibly the same day—in which he speaks darkly of a rash step he has just taken.

O'Sullivan must have discussed the challenge with their friend Jonathan Cilley; then he wrote a candid and friendly letter to Hawthorne refusing the challenge. But he did more than that; he made a hurried trip to Salem and completely established his innocence of the charge against him. Although Hawthorne could scarcely bring himself to believe that Miss Silsbee had made an utter fool of him, he had to accept the evidence. In Miss Peabody's words, he called on Armida and "crushed her."

To this point the story had been a comedy, or even a farce, but it soon had a tragic sequel on the national scene. In 1838 the House of Representatives was equally divided between conservatives and radicals, not to mention the other division between southerners and northern antislavery men. Jonathan Cilley was a rising leader among the radical free-soil Democrats, and there are some indications that his political enemies had decided to get rid of him. On a flimsy pretext, he was challenged to a duel by a fire-eating southern congressman, William J. Graves of Kentucky. He was still hesitating whether to accept the challenge when somebody said to him—according to Julian's story—"If Hawthorne was so ready to fight a duel without stopping to ask questions, you certainly need not hesitate." Horatio Bridge denied this part of the story, but there is no doubt that Hawthorne considered himself partly responsible for what followed. The duel, fought with rifles at ninety yards, took place on the afternoon of February 24. After the first exchange of shots, and again after the second, Cilley's second tried to effect a reconciliation, but Graves and his second both declined. Cilley said, "They thirst for my blood." On the third exchange, he was hit in the body and fell dying.

Hawthorne brooded over the duel for a long time. His memorial of Cilley, which was among the first of his many contributions to the *Democratic Review*, reads as if he were making atonement to the shade of his friend. In a somewhat later story, "The Christmas Banquet," from which I have quoted already, he describes a collection of the world's most miserable persons. One of them is

a man of nice conscience, who bore a blood stain in his heart—the death of a fellow creature—which, for his more exquisite torture, had chanced with such a peculiarity of circumstances, that he could not absolutely determine whether his will had entered into the deed or not. Therefore, his whole life was spent in the agony of an inward trial for murder.

Julian's story would lead us to believe that Hawthorne, once again, was thinking of himself.

4

There were other causes for worry in those early months of 1838, when Hawthorne was still supposed to be courting Sophia's intellectual sister. One of the chief causes was Mary Silsbee, who refused to let him go. Miss Peabody's memorandum says that Mary somehow "managed to renew relations with him," and that she then offered to marry him as soon as he was earning $3,000 a year, a large income for the time. Hawthorne answered that he never expected to have so much. When his sister Ebe heard the story, she remarked—according to Miss Peabody—"that he would never marry at all, and that he would never *do* anything; that he was an ideal person." But Hawthorne did something to end the affair; he disappeared from Salem.

Before leaving town on July 23, he paid what was known as a take-leave call on Sophia. "He said he was not going to tell any one where he should be for the next three months," she told Elizabeth in a letter: "that he thought he should change his name, so that if he died no one would be able to find his gravestone. . . . I feel as if he were a born brother. I never, hardly, knew a person for whom I had such a full and at the same time perfectly quiet admiration." Then, suspecting that she had gone too far, she added, "I do not care about seeing him often: but I delight to remember that *he is*." It was as near as she could come to telling Elizabeth that she was already in love.

At the end of September when Hawthorne came back to Salem—from North Adams, his mysterious hiding place—Miss Silsbee had disappeared from his life. She had renewed her acquaintance with another suitor, now a widower of forty-nine with an income well beyond her minimum requirement; he was Jared Sparks, the editor of George Washington's papers, who would become president of Harvard. Hawthorne now had more time to spend at the house on Charter Street. He was entertained by whichever sister happened to be present, or by all three together, but it began to be noticed that his visits were longer if he found Sophia alone. One day she showed him an illustration she had drawn, in the Flaxman manner, for his story, "The Gentle Boy." It showed the boy asleep under the tree on which his Quaker father had been hanged.

"I want to know if this looks like your Ilbrahim," she said.

Hawthorne said, meaning every word, "He will never look otherwise to me."

Under the Peabody influence, he was becoming almost a social creature. There was a sort of literary club that met every week in one of the finest houses on Chestnut Street, where the Salem merchants lived. The house belonged to Miss Susan Burley, a wealthy spinster who liked to patronize the arts. Hawthorne was persuaded to attend some of Miss Burley's Saturday evenings—usually as an escort for Mary or Elizabeth, since the invalid sister was seldom allowed to venture into the night air. There was one particularly cold evening when Sophia insisted that she was going to Miss Burley's whether or not she was wanted. Hawthorne laughed and said she was not wanted: the cold would make her ill. "Meanwhile," Sophia reported in a letter, "I put on an incalculable quantity of clothes. Father kept remonstrating, but not violently, and I gently imploring. When I was ready, Mr. Hawthorne said he was glad I was going. . . . We walked quite fast, for I seemed stepping on air."

The evening at Miss Burley's marked a change in their relations. From that time Sophia began taking long walks with Mr. Hawthorne in spite of the winter gales. Elizabeth was busy with her affairs in Boston, and Mary, the quiet sister, looked on benevolently. Sophia never felt tired so long as she could hold Mr. Hawthorne's arm. It was during one of their walks, on a snowy day just before or after New Year's 1839, that they confessed their love for each other. Clinging together like children frightened of being so happy, they exchanged promises that neither of them would break. They were married now "in the sight of God," as old-fashioned people used to say, and as Hawthorne soon told Sophia in slightly different words, but that was a secret they would keep to themselves for a long time to come.

5

In the middle of January Hawthorne went to work as a weigher and gauger for the Boston Custom House. It was a political appointment made by the collector of the port, who was George Bancroft, the historian. Hawthorne had been recommended to him by several influential persons, including Miss Peabody, who may have hoped to get him out of Salem. Bancroft justified the appointment to Washington by writing that Hawthorne was "the biographer of Cilley," and thus a deserving Democrat. Cilley again. . . . It was as if the college friend for whose death Hawthorne felt responsible had reached out of the grave to help him. Many other deserving Democrats had sought for the post, but it was not a sinecure, and he worked as hard as Jacob did for Rachel, while saving half his salary of $1,500 a year. Every other Saturday he took the cars to Salem and spent an evening with Sophia. On the Saturdays in Boston he sent her a long letter, sometimes written in daily installments.

"What a year the last has been!" he wrote on January 1, 1840. " . . . It has been the year of years—the year in which the flower of our life has bloomed out—the flower of our life and of our love, which we are to wear in our bosoms forever." Three days later he added,

Dearest, I hope you have not found it impracticable to walk, though the atmosphere be so wintry. Did we walk together in any such weather, last winter? I believe we did. How strange, that such a flower as our affection should have blossomed amid snow and wintry winds—accompaniments which no poet or novelist, that I know of, has ever introduced into a love-tale. Nothing like our story was ever written— or ever will be—for we shall not feel inclined to make the public our confidant; but if it could be told, me-thinks it would be such as the angels might delight to hear.

As a matter of fact, Hawthorne wrote the story from day to day, in that series of heartfelt letters to Sophia, and the New England angels would delight to read them. It is true that the tone of them is sometimes too reverent for the worldly taste of our century. "I always feel," Hawthorne says in July 1839, "as if your letters were too sacred to be read in the midst of people, and (you will smile) I never read them without first washing my hands." We also smile, but in a different spirit from Sophia's. We feel a little uncomfortable on hearing the pet names with which he addresses her, almost all superlatives: "Dearissima," "mine ownest love," "Blessedest," "ownest Dove," "best, beautifullest, belovedest, blessingest of wives." It is confusing to find that he calls her "mine own wife," and himself "your husband" or "thy husband," for three years before the actual marriage. His use of "thee" and "thou" in all the letters written after March 1840, though it reveals his need for deeper intimacy of expression, still gives an archaic look to the writing. But the feelings expressed are not in the least archaic; they are those of a restrained but passionate man, truly in love for the first and last time, and gifted with an extraordinary talent for self-awareness.

Long afterward Sophia, then a widow, tried to delete the passion before she permitted the letters to be read by others. She scissored out some of the dangerous passages, and these are gone forever. Others she inked out carefully, and most of these have been restored by the efforts of Randall Stewart—the most trustworthy biographer of Hawthorne—and the staff of the Huntington Library. They show that Hawthorne was less of an other-worldly creature than Miss Peabody pictured him as being. "Mine own wife," he says in one of the inked-out passages (November 1839), "what a cold night this is going to be! How I am to keep warm, unless you nestle close, close into my bosom, I do not by any means understand—not but what I have clothes enough on my mattress—but a husband cannot be comfortably warm without his wife." There is so much talk of beds and bosoms that some have inferred, after reading the restored text, that Hawthorne and Sophia were lovers for a long time before their marriage—and most of these readers thought no worse of them. But the records show that this romantic notion has to be dismissed. Much as Hawthorne wanted Sophia, he also wanted to observe the scriptural laws of love. "Mr. Hawthorne's passions were under his feet," Miss Peabody quoted Sophia as saying. If he had made Sophia his mistress, he would have revered her less, and he would have despised himself.

"I have an awe of you," he wrote her, "that I never felt for anybody else. Awe is not the word, either, because it might imply something stern in you; whereas—but you must make it out for yourself. . . . I suppose I should have pretty much the same feeling if an angel were to come from Heaven and be my dearest friend. . . . And then it is singular, too," he added with his Salem obduracy, "that this awe (or whatever it is) does not prevent me from feeling that it is I who have charge of you, and that my Dove is to follow my guidance and do my bidding." He had no intention of submitting to the Peabody matriarchs. "And will not you rebel?" he asked. "Oh, no; because I possess the power to guide you only so far as I love you. My love gives me the right, and your love consents to it."

Sophia did not rebel, but the Peabodys were confirmed idealists where Hawthorne was a realist, and sometimes she tried gently to bring him round to their higher way of feeling. Once she refused to kiss him good night because she had smelled a cigar on his breath. Another time she made the mistake of urging him to hear the famous Father Taylor, who preached to the sailors. "Dearest," he said,

I feel somewhat afraid to hear this divine Father Taylor, lest my sympathy with thy admiration of him should be colder and feebler than thou lookest for. Belovedest wife, our souls are in happiest unison; but we must not disquiet ourselves if every tone be not re-echoed from one to the other—if every slightest shade be not reflected in the alternate mirror. . . . I forewarn thee, sweetest Dove, that thy husband is a most unmalleable man; thou art not to suppose, because his spirit answers to every touch of thine, that therefore every breeze, or even every whirlwind, can upturn him from his depths.

But this conflict of wills is a minor note of comedy in the letters. In time Sophia learned to yield almost joyfully, not so much to Hawthorne's unmalleable nature as to his love. It is love that is the central theme of the letters—unquestioning love, and beneath it the sense of almost delirious gratitude that both of them felt for having been rescued from death-in-life. Sophia refused to worry about her health. "If God intends us to marry," she said to Hawthorne, "He will let me be cured; if not, it will be a sign that it is not best." She depended on love as her physician, and imperceptibly, year by year, the headaches faded away. As for Hawthorne, he felt an even deeper gratitude for having been rescued from the unreal world of self-absorption in which he had feared to be imprisoned forever. "Indeed, we are but shadows," he wrote to Sophia, "—we are not endowed with real life, and all that seems most real about us is but the thinnest substance of a dream—till the heart is touched. That touch creates us—then we begin to be. . . ." In the same letter he said:

Thou only hast taught me that I have a heart—thou only hast thrown a deep light downward, and upward, into my soul. Thou only hast revealed me to myself; for without thy aid, my best knowledge of myself would have been merely to know my own shadow—to watch it flickering on the wall, and mistake its fantasies for my own real actions. . . . Now, dearest, dost though comprehend what thou hast done for me?

His four novels, beginning with *The Scarlet Letter,* were written after his marriage and written because Sophia was there to read them. Not only Nathaniel Hawthorne but the world at large owes the gentle Sophia more than can be expressed.

6

When Miss Peabody was told of the engagement, after more than a year, she took the news bravely. Her consolation was that having Hawthorne as a brother-in-law might be almost as rewarding as having him for a husband; she could still be his Egeria. Not yet knowing how unmalleable he was, she still thought of forging him into the shape of her dream. Meanwhile she offered to serve as a secret courier and forward his letters to Salem. With Sophia's health improving, it was Hawthorne's inability to support a wife—especially a delicate wife who needed a servant in the household—that now seemed to be the chief remaining obstacle to the marriage.

The post in the Boston Custom House did not solve the problem. It left him with little time alone or energy for writing, and he could not be sure of keeping it after the next election. Hawthorne resigned at the end of 1840, a few months before he would have been dismissed—as were almost all his colleagues—by the victorious Whigs. After some hesitation he took a rash step, partly at the urging of Miss Peabody. He invested his Custom House savings in George Ripley's new community for intellectual farmers: Brook Farm. It was the last time he would accept her high-minded advice.

The dream was that Hawthorne would support himself by working in the fields only a few hours each day, and only in the summer; then he could spend the winter writing stories. He and Sophia would live in a cottage to be built on some secluded spot. Having bought two shares of stock in the community at $500 each—later he would lend Ripley $400 more—he arrived at Brook Farm in an April snowstorm. Sophia paid him a visit at the end of May. "My life—how beautiful is Brook Farm!" she wrote him on her return. " . . . I do not desire to conceive of a greater felicity than living in a cottage, built on one of those lovely sites, with thee." But Hawthorne, after working for six weeks on the manure pile—or gold mine, as the Brook Farmers called it—was already disillusioned. "It is my opinion, dearest," he wrote on almost the same day, "that a man's soul may be buried and perish under a dung-heap or in a furrow of the field, just as well as under a pile of money." By the middle of August he had decided to leave Brook Farm. "Thou and I must form other plans for ourselves," he told Sophia; "for I can see few or no signs that Providence purposes to give us a home here. I am weary, weary, thrice weary of waiting so many ages. Yet what can be done? Whatever may be thy husband's gifts, he has not hitherto shown a single one that may avail to gather gold."

"Thy husband" and "mine own wife" were drawing closer to marriage, simply because they had exhausted their vast New England patience. "Words cannot tell," Sophia had written, "how immensely my spirit demands thee. Sometimes I almost lose my breath in a vast heaving toward thy heart." Hawthorne, now vegetating in Salem—while the Peabodys were in Boston, where Elizabeth had opened a bookshop—was looking desperately for any sort of literary work. In March 1842, he went to Albany to see John Louis O'Sullivan, who was again editing the *Democratic Review*. On the strength of the promises that O'Sullivan was always ready to make, Hawthorne decided to wait no longer; he would try to support a wife on what he could earn as a writer. It was a bold decision for an age when American writers were miserably paid and when Poe, his principal rival, had never earned as much as $1,000 in one year.

The wedding was set for the last day of June. During a visit to the Emersons, Miss Peabody found a home for the young couple; it was the Ripley house in Concord, where the parson used to live. Hawthorne could no longer defer telling his family about the engagement, after keeping it secret for three years. Now at last it became evident that there was and had always been another obstacle to his marriage.

The final obstacle was his older sister, Ebe the hermitess. She adored her handsome brother and clung to him as her only link with the world. The stratagem she found for keeping him was to insist that their mother would die of shock if she learned that he was marrying an invalid. Hawthorne loved his mother, though he had never been able to confide in her. This time he finally took the risk. "What you tell me is not a surprise to me," Madam Hawthorne said, ". . . and Sophia Peabody is the wife of all others whom I would have chosen for you." When Ebe had recovered from her fury at hearing the news, she wrote Sophia a frigid letter of congratulation.

Your approaching union with my brother [she said] makes it incumbent upon me to offer you the assurance of my sincere desire for your mutual happiness. With regard to my sister and myself, I hope nothing will ever occur to render your future intercourse with us other than agreeable, particularly as it need not be so frequent or so close as to require more than reciprocal good will.

There would be, in fact, no intercourse with Ebe. She retired to a farmhouse in Beverly, where she spent the rest of her long life reading in her room and walking on the shore.

Three weeks before the date set for the wedding, Sophia terrified everyone by taking to her bed. There was talk of an indefinite postponement. Fortunately a new doctor explained that it was nothing unusual for a bride to run a fever, and so another date was chosen: Saturday morning, July 9. It was a few days after Hawthorne's thirty-eighth birthday, while Sophia was almost thirty-three. At the wedding in the parlor behind Miss Peabody's bookshop, there were only two guests outside the immediate family. It started to rain as the bride came down the stairs, but then the sun broke through the clouds and shone directly into the parlor. Hawthorne and Sophia stepped into a carriage and were driven across the Charles River, along the old road through Cambridge and Lexington, into the Land of Eden.

7

And so they lived happily ever after? They lived happily for a time, but as always it came to an end, and the lovers too. For Hawthorne after twenty years of marriage, the end was near when he went feebly pacing up and down the path his feet had worn along the hillside behind his Concord house, while he tried to plan a novel that refused to be written. For Sophia the end was a desolate widowhood without the man who, she never ceased to feel, "is my world and all the business of it." But the marriage was happy to the end, and at the beginning of it, during their stay at the Old Manse, they enjoyed something far beyond the capacity of most lovers to experience: three years of almost unalloyed delight.

On the morning after their first night in the Old Manse, Hawthorne wrote to his younger sister, Louisa, the one who was quite like everybody else. "Dear Louse," he said affectionately, "The execution took place yesterday. We made a christian end, and came straight to Paradise, where we abide at the present writing." Sophia had the same message for her mother, although she expressed it more ecstatically. "It is a perfect Eden round us," she said. "Everything is as fresh as in first June. We are Adam and Eve and see no persons round! The birds saluted us this morning with such gushes of rapture, that I thought they must know us and our happiness." The Hawthornes at thirty-eight and thirty-three were like children again—like children exploring a desert island that every day revealed new marvels. Their only fear was that a ship might come to rescue them. Once the great Margaret Fuller wrote them and suggested that another newly married couple, her sister Ellen and Ellery Channing, might board with them at the Manse. Hawthorne sent her a tactful letter of refusal. "Had it been proposed to Adam and Eve," he said, "to receive two angels into their Paradise, *as boarders,* I doubt whether they would have been altogether pleased to consent." The Hawthornes were left happily alone with Sarah the maid and Pigwiggin the kitten.

They were exercising a talent that most New Englanders never acquire, that of living not in the past or in dreams of the future, but in the moment itself, as if they were already in heaven. Sophia wrote letters each morning or painted in her studio, while Hawthorne worked meditatively in the garden that Henry Thoreau had planted for them. In the afternoon they explored the countryside together or rowed on the quiet river, picking waterlilies. Hawthorne wrote in his journal,

My life, at this time, is more like that of a boy, externally, than it has been since I was really a boy. It is usually supposed that the cares of life come with matrimony; but I seem to have cast off all care, and live with as much easy trust in Providence, as Adam could possibly have felt, before he had learned that there was a world beyond his Paradise.

Sometimes they ran footraces down the lane, which Sophia grandly called "the avenue." Sometimes in the evening she wound the music box and, forgetting her Puritan training, danced wildly for her lover. "You deserve John the Baptist's head," he teased her. In the records of that time—there are many of them, and all a delight to read—there is only one hint of anything like a quarrel. It arose when one of their walks led them to an unmown hayfield. Hawthorne, who had learned about haying at Brook Farm, told Sophia not to cross it, and trample the grass. "This I did not like very well and I climbed the hill alone," Sophia wrote in the journal they were keeping together.

We penetrated the pleasant gloom and sat down upon a carpet of dried pine leaves. Then I clasped him in my arms in the lovely shade, and we laid down a few moments on the bosom of dear Mother Earth. Oh, how sweet it was! And I told him I would not be so naughty again, and there was a very slight diamond shower without any thunder or lightning and we were happiest.

There was some thunder and lightning even during those three sunny years at the Old Manse. Sophia's mother and her sister Elizabeth had insisted that she must never bear children, but she longed for them ardently. One day in the first February she fell on the ice—where she had been sliding while Hawthorne skated round her in flashing circles—and suffered a miscarriage. When her first baby was born in March 1844, it lingered, as Hawthorne said, "ten dreadful hours on the threshold of life." It lived and the parents rejoiced, but now they had financial worries: O'Sullivan took years to pay for the stories he printed, and Ripley hadn't returned the money advanced to Brook Farm. There were weeks when Hawthorne was afraid to walk into Concord for the mail, lest he meet too many of his creditors. Sophia's love did not waver, then or for the rest of her life, nor did her trust in the wisdom and mercy of Providence. It had snatched her from invalidism and spinsterhood and transported her to Paradise. It had made her "as strong as a lion," she wrote to her sister Mary, "as elastic as India rubber, light as a bird, as happy as a queen might be," and it had given her a husband whose ardent love was as unwavering as her own. She was expressing in five words all her faith in Providence, and indeed all her experience in life, when she stood at the window in Hawthorne's study one April evening at sunset and wrote with her diamond ring on one of the tiny panes—for him to see, for the world to remember:

Man's accidents are God's purposes.

Sophia A. Hawthorne 1843

1958

The Five Acts of The Scarlet Letter

When he finished *The Scarlet Letter* in 1850, at the age of forty-five, Nathaniel Hawthorne had accomplished something new in his own career and something new in the craft of fiction. By accident or design he had invented a form that was closer to stage drama than it was to ordinary novels. That was perhaps the greatest of his technical achievements, and I plan to discuss it at some length, but it was not the last of them. In the first of his four romances, as he called them, he had also applied to a longer work the exacting standards that he and Edgar Poe, working separately, had developed in writing their tales or short stories.

Poe had defined the standards eight years before, when he reviewed and praised the second edition of *Twice-Told Tales*. The skillful writer of tales, he said, does not fashion his thoughts to accommodate his incidents. No, "having conceived, with deliberate care, a certain unique or single *effect* to be wrought out, he then invents such incidents—he then combines such events as may best aid him in establishing this preconceived effect. If his very initial sentence tend not to the outbringing of this effect, then he has failed in his first step. In the whole composition there should be no word written of which the tendency, direct or indirect, is not to the one pre-established design." Thus, unity of effect and economy of means were two of the principal standards by which Poe judged the short story. He did not think that the two could be enforced in a novel or in any other work too long to be finished at a single reading. In his one book-length story, *The Narrative of Arthur Gordon Pym*, he did not even try to enforce them; after starting with a realistic story of boys on the waterfront, he launched into a grotesque recital of horrors at sea and ended with a Freudian nightmare of returning to the womb. It remained for Hawthorne to make the attempt in *The Scarlet Letter*—that is, to conceive "a certain unique or single effect" and then to invent such incidents, but only such, as would help him to re-establish the effect in a reader's mind.

He was thereby disregarding another standard, one that was accepted by the leading critics of the time and even by Hawthorne himself when he thought in critical terms. The critics were imbued with what they called the Shakespearian principle that the tragic should be mingled with the comic in any longer work; their ideal was the drunken porter grumbling while fate knocked at the gate. Although most of them praised Hawthorne's novel, they complained about the lack of comic relief. "In his next work," said E. P. Whipple, who was Hawthorne's favorite among them, "we hope to have a romance equal to *The Scarlet Letter* in pathos and power, but more relieved by touches of that beautiful and peculiar humor, so serene and searching, in which he excels almost all living writers." Hawthorne agreed with the criticism, as he showed when writing his next novel, *The House of the Seven Gables,* which presented a mixture of moods, somber and hu-morous, romantic and realistic; it was "a work," he said a little less self-perceptively than was his custom, "more characteristic of my mind." But he also reported, in a letter to his publisher, that the writing of it went more slowly and seemed more laborious than that of *The Scarlet Letter.*

His first romance was written by a sort of inner compulsion that would be reawakened at moments in his later career, but never with quite the same driving power. The theme of secret guilt and public confession was one that had haunted him all his life. The controlling symbol of the scarlet A was one over which he had been brooding for many years. When he finally started writing the book, after a series of personal disasters—the loss of his position in the custom house, the death of his mother, illness in the family, and the threat of destitution—he worked on it like a man possessed by Satan. "*The Scarlet Letter,*" he told his friend Horatio Bridge, "is positively a hell-fired story into which I found it almost impossible to throw any cheering light." But writing it seemed easy, so long as he followed the bent and inclination of his mind. "I had only to get my pitch," he told his pub-lisher, "and then could go on interminably." Written all in one pitch, *The Scarlet Letter* was the first novel in English—perhaps in any language, con-sidering that the book appeared six years before *Madame Bovary*—that had the unity of effect and the strict economy of means of a perfect tale.

The symbol of the scarlet A had first appeared as a detail in one of Haw-thorne's New England legends, "Endicott and the Red Cross," published in 1838. There, in describing the colonists who watched a muster of Endi-cott's trainband, he had mentioned "likewise a young woman, with no mean share of beauty, whose doom it was to wear the letter A on the breast of her gown, in the eyes of all the world and her own children." Six years later the detail reappeared in one of his notebooks, this time as the plot of a new story he planned to write. Here are a few of the other notebook entries that, as he brooded over the symbol, eventually grouped themselves around the central theme of Hester's public atonement:

1838. A perception, for a moment, of one's eventual and moral self, as if it were another person,—the observant faculty being separated, and looking intently at the qualities of the character. There is a surprise when this happens,—this getting out of one's self,—and then the observer sees how queer a fellow he is.

In Chapter XIV of *The Scarlet Letter* we read that poor Chillingworth "lifted his hands with a look of horror, as if he had beheld some frightful shape, which he could not recognize, usurping the place of his own image in the glass. It was one of those moments—which sometimes occur only at the interval of years—when a man's moral aspect is faithfully revealed to his mind's eye."

1838. Character of a man who, in himself and his external circumstances, shall be equally and totally false: his fortune resting on baseless credit,—his patriotism assumed—his domestic affections, his honor and honesty, all a sham. His own misery in the midst of it,—making the whole universe, heaven and earth alike, an unsubstantial mockery to him.

Hawthorne would say of the Reverend Mr. Dimmesdale, at the end of Chapter XI, "It is the unspeakable misery of a life so false as his, that it steals the pith and substance out of whatever realities there are around us, and which were meant by Heaven to be the spirit's joy and nutriment. To the untrue man, the whole universe is false,—it is impalpable,—it shrinks to nothing within his grasp. And he himself, in so far as he shows himself in a false light, becomes a shadow, or, indeed, ceases to exist."

1838. Dr. Johnson's penance in Uttoxeter Market. A man who does penance in what might appear to lookers-on the most glorious and triumphal circumstance of his life. Each circumstance of the career of an apparently successful man to be a penance and torture to him on account of some fundamental error in early life.

Arthur Dimmesdale's career is a torture and a penance, merely intensified by his outward success; and at the moment when he rises to "the very proudest eminence of superiority, to which the gifts of intellect, rich lore, prevailing eloquence, and a reputation of whitest sanctity, could exalt a clergyman in New England's earliest days," he leaves the triumphal procession to stand with his former mistress on the scaffold of the pillory.

1841. To symbolize moral or spiritual disease by a disease of the body;—thus, when a person committed any sin, it might cause a sore to appear on the body; this to be wrought out.

There is a scarlet A imprinted on Dimmesdale's flesh; "and those best able to appreciate the minister's peculiar sensibility, and the wonderful operation of his spirit upon the body . . . whispered their belief, that the awful symbol was the effect of the ever-active tooth of remorse, gnawing from the inmost heart outwardly, and at last manifesting Heaven's dreadful judgment by the visible presence of the letter."

1842. A physician for the cure of moral diseases.

This is one of several notebook entries in which Hawthorne seems to be thinking in terms of what would afterward be called psychoanalysis and psychosomatic therapy. In Chapter X, "The Leech and His Patient," Chillingworth assumes the role of analyst. "You, Sir," he says to Dimmesdale, "of all the men whom I have known, are he whose body is the closest conjoined, and imbued, and identified, so to speak, with the spirit whereof it is the instrument. . . . Thus, a sickness . . . a sore place, if we may so call it, in your spirit, hath immediately its appropriate manifestation in your bodily frame. Would you, therefore, that your physician heal the bodily evil? How may this be, unless you first lay open to him the wound or trouble in your soul?"

1842. Pearl—the English of Margaret—a pretty name for a girl in a story.
1842. In moods of heavy despondency, one feels as if it would be delightful to sink down in some quiet spot, and lie there forever, letting the soil gradually accumulate and form a little hillock over us, and the grass and perhaps flowers gather over it. At such times, death is too much of an event to be wished for;—we have not spirits to encounter it; but choose to pass out of existence in this sluggish way.

At the end of Chapter XVI, before his meeting with Hester and little Pearl, Dimmesdale walks through the forest with a listlessness in his gait, "as if he saw no reason for taking one step farther, nor felt any desire to do so, but would have been glad, could he be glad of anything, to fling himself down at the root of the nearest tree, and lie there passive, for evermore. The leaves might bestrew him, and the soil gradually accumulate and form a little hillock over his frame, no matter whether there were life in it or no. Death was too definite an object to be wished for or avoided." This is a passage that Hawthorne seems to have written with the notebook open in front of him. He had started that practice in "Ethan Brand," which was written, probably, a year before *The Scarlet Letter*. In his last years the practice would become an obsessive habit, with the result that more than two-thirds of *The Marble Faun* would be copied directly from his Roman notebooks.

1844. The Unpardonable Sin might consist in a want of love and reverence for the Human Soul; in consequence of which the investigator pried into its dark depths, not with a hope or purpose of making it better, but from a cold philosophical curiosity,—content that it should be wicked in whatever kind or degree, and only desiring to study it out. Would not this, in other words, be the separation of the intellect from the heart?

1844. The life of a woman, who, by the old colony law, was condemned always to wear the letter A, sewed on her garment, in token of her having committed adultery.

There is no indication in the notebooks that Hawthorne was immediately conscious of having found a theme for the novel he had long been planning to write. But he had the habit of patient meditation, and many of his ideas gradually rearranged themselves around this new center. The idea of the Unpardonable Sin was of course to be used in "Ethan Brand," but it would reappear in the novel—with other ideas from some of his earlier stories, notably "Young Goodman Brown" and "The Minister's Black Veil." Chillingworth commits the Unpardonable Sin as a means of wreaking his revenge on Dimmesdale. The minister says of him in Chapter XVII, "We are not, Hester, the worst sinners in the world. There is one worse than even the polluted priest! That old man's revenge has been blacker than my sin. He has violated, in cold blood, the sanctity of a human heart."

1845. In the eyes of a young child, or other innocent person, the image of a cherub or an angel to be seen peeping out;—in those of a vicious person, a devil.

Sometimes an angel can be seen peeping from the eyes of little Pearl; but once, in Chapter VI, when Hester looks into them she sees "a face, fiend-like, full of smiling malice . . . as if an evil spirit possessed the child, and had just then peeped forth in mockery." A diabolical light often glimmers out of Chillingworth's eyes; in Chapter X it is "burning blue and ominous, like the reflection of a furnace, or, let us say, like one of those gleams of ghastly fire that darted from Bunyan's awful doorway in the hillside."

1845. It was believed by the Catholics that children might be begotten by intercourse between demons and witches. Luther was said to be a bastard of this hellish breed.

At the end of Chapter VI, some of the townspeople assert "that poor little Pearl was a demon offspring; such as, ever since old Catholic times, had occasionally been seen on earth, through the agency of their mother's sin, and to promote some foul and wicked purpose. Luther, according to the scandal of his monkish enemies, was a brat of that hellish breed."

1847. A story of the effect of revenge, in diaboling him who indulges in it.

In Chapter XIV Chillingworth is offered as "a striking evidence of man's faculty of transforming himself into a devil, if he will only, for a reasonable space of time, undertake a devil's office." The old physician says of Dimmesdale that he fancied himself given over to a fiend. "But it was the constant shadow of my presence!" he continues, "—the closest propinquity of the man whom he had most vilely wronged!—and who had grown to exist only by this perpetual poison of the direst revenge! Yea, indeed!—he did not err!—there was a field at his elbow! A mortal man, with once a human heart, has become a fiend for his especial torment!"

During the spring and summer of 1849, Hawthorne was occupied with family and business worries—his mother's illness and the political intrigues against him that did not end when he lost his post in the custom house— with the result that he scarcely tried to do any serious work. He had time, however, for some unusually long entries in his notebooks, most of them concerned with the behavior of his children: Julian, aged three, and Una, aged five. He looked at them with a father's eye, but also with the capacity for absolutely detached observation that he retained even at his mother's deathbed, in "the darkest hour I ever lived." Part of one entry, written on July 30, the day before his mother died, shows clearly how Una was serving as the model for Hester's only half-angelic brat:

. . . there is something that almost frightens me about the child—I know not whether elfin or angelic, but, at all events, supernatural. She steps so boldly into the midst of everything, shrinks from nothing, has such a comprehension of everything, seems at times to have but little delicacy, and anon shows that she possesses the finest essence of it; now so hard, now so tender; now so perfectly unreasonable, soon again so wise. In short, I now and then catch an aspect of her, in which I cannot believe her to be my own human child, but a spirit strangely mingled with good and evil, haunting the house where I dwell.

At this point, after brooding over the subject for eleven years or more, Hawthorne had fixed the time and place of his novel and had chosen the strands that would be woven into the plot. He had found his four essential characters: the woman condemned to public penance, the man who suffered even more from concealing his guilt, their unearthly child, and the wronged husband diabolized by his revenge. There were important technical problems still to be solved, and they happen to be the ones that particularly interest us today, but Hawthorne does not mention them in his working notebooks. Although we know that he solved them brilliantly, we cannot be certain whether it was by conscious reasoning or simply by his instinct for what, in the special circumstances, was right.

Perhaps the first of the technical problems was one of social background. The persons of Hawthorne's story existed in relation to a particular society, whose standards—which they fully accepted—intensified their guilt and lent drama to their atonement. How could the society be brought directly into the story—not merely talked about and explained by the author, but presented in life? Hawthorne's solution was to invent a few additional characters, not to be studied in depth, but merely to be put forward as representatives of the society in its essential aspects. Three of these characters are Governor Bellingham (representing the secular authorities), the Reverend John Wilson (representing sanctity), and Mistress Hibbins the witch-lady (representing evil and rebellion inside the community). Except for the four principals—and except for Master Brackett the jailer, mentioned in passing—these are the only named persons in the story; but there are also two unnamed characters of some importance. One is a Bristol shipmaster, representing the moral freedom or indifference of the world outside, and the other is the Boston crowd, which, at the beginning and the end of the story, speaks in the voices of complacent ignorance.

The author has some comments of his own to offer, and they sometimes seem obtrusive to readers trained in the impersonal technique of more recent fiction, but they are not essential to our understanding of the story. Except in the last chapter—which is an epilogue conceived in the expository manner of other early nineteenth-century writers—Hawthorne lets his characters act out their fates. No information is needed by the reader beyond that suggested by the behavior of the characters or imparted in their dialogues. The action of the novel is completely an *interaction* among four persons in a particular environment that is also presented in its own terms. Hawthorne had solved the problem of social background in a fashion that enabled him to write, for the first time in American literature, a novel that was a completely framed and self-subsistent work of art.

There was, however, another technical problem that required a more radical solution, arising as it did from the author's special experience and cast of mind. Until that time the novel in all its forms had been essentially a chronicle of events, and Hawthorne had no great talent or practice as a chronicler. When a very young man he had written a short and artlessly romantic novel called *Fanshawe*, which demonstrated not very much except that its author admired Sir Walter Scott and, in pure storytelling, could never hope to equal him. Feeling ashamed of the little book, Hawthorne had withdrawn it from circulation and had destroyed every copy on which he could lay his hands. In the twenty years since *Fanshawe* he had written nothing else of equal length, but he had published nearly a hundred tales or sketches, and these had given a special direction to his thinking. What he had learned from writing them was, among other lessons, how to work intensively in smaller forms and how to present his subjects as moral essays or allegorical pictures rather than as continually moving narratives.

His final problem, then, was to devise some method by which a larger theme could be adjusted to his training and personality as a writer. It was the solution he found, whether by reason or instinct, that became the truly important technical innovation in *The Scarlet Letter.* Instead of conceiving the novel as a single or double narrative moving ahead in a straight or zigzag line and revealing the social landscape as if to the eyes of a traveler on horseback, Hawthorne approached it dramatically, almost as if his characters were appearing on a stage. Instead of dividing his book into narrative episodes—now the hero falls in love, now he fights a duel, now he escapes from prison—Hawthorne divided it into scenes, each of which is a posed tableau or a dramatic confrontation. The advantage of the method for this particular author was that it enabled him to work on each scene intensively, almost as if it were a separate tale. Although there was little movement within the separate scenes, he could create a general sense of movement by passing rapidly from one scene to another, for example, from the marketplace at night to the seashore and thence to the forest. Unity of mood was not one of his problems—that had already been achieved by his years of brooding over the central symbol—but the method enabled him to give the book architectural unity as well, by balancing one scene against another and by ending the story where it really began, on the scaffold of the pillory.

This dramatistic method followed by Hawthorne was also, in effect, the "divine principle" that Henry James would rediscover in 1895, when he went back to writing fiction after the failure of his career as a playwright. "Has a *part* of all this wasted passion and squandered time (of the last 5 years)," James would ask in his notebook shortly after having been hissed from the stage at the first night of *Guy Domville*—has part of it "been simply the precious lesson, taught me in that roundabout and devious, that cruelly expensive, way, *of the singular value for a narrative plan too* of the (I don't know *what* adequately to call it) divine principle of the Scenario?" It was the principle that enabled him to achieve what he called his *big* effects— "scenic, constructive, 'architectural'"—and he would follow it in all the novels of his later years. "Yes, I *see* thus, I think, my little *act* of my little drama here," he said in his notebook when he was working on *What Maisie Knew.* "Ah, this *divine* conception of one's little masses and periods in the scenic light, as rounded ACTS: this patient, pious, nobly 'vindicative' application of the scenic philosophy and method—I feel as if it *still* (above *all*, YET) had a great deal to give me and might carry me as far as I dream!"

It carried him nobly through *The Wings of the Dove* and *The Golden Bowl,* as it has carried later novelists through hundreds of more or less distinguished works. But Hawthorne in his solitude had discovered the "divine principle" almost fifty years before the first night of *Guy Domville,* and the fact seems all the more amazing when we reflect that, unlike James, he had never tried to write for the stage. As a matter of fact, he had never even engaged in amateur theatricals, having shown little talent or taste for mimicry. Although he liked going to the Boston theatres, he seems to have had no consuming interest in acted plays; at most they may have confirmed him in his taste for conveying moods by visual effects. Hawthorne's knowledge of the drama came mostly from his reading, which—according to the records of the Salem Athenaeum—included all of Racine, besides other classical French dramatists; he had been familiar with Shakespeare's works since boyhood. It might well be argued that his cast of mind was not Shakespearian, as Melville thought, but Racinian. The fact is that *The Scarlet Letter* can be read, and gains a new dimension from being read, as a Racinian drama of dark necessity.

It is a novel in twenty-four chapters, but, considered as a tragic drama, it is divided into the usual five acts and subdivided into eight scenes. (My principle would be that any act may include two scenes if the second follows without any great lapse of time.) There are of course some chapters that fall outside the dramatic framework, since each of them deals with a single character (Chapter V with Hester, VI with Pearl, IX with Chillingworth, XI with Dimmesdale, XIII with Hester again, XX with Dimmesdale, and XXIV, the epilogue, chiefly with Hester) and since the method they follow is narrative or expository. These seven chapters serve as interludes in the dramatic action—or in one case as a postlude—and they provide some additional information about the characters that would have been difficult to incorporate into the dialogue. The essential chapters, however, are the other seventeen, in which Hawthorne is applying the scenic philosophy and method. Here is how they arrange themselves into rounded acts and scenes:

Act I, Scene I (Chapter I to III) is laid in the marketplace of Boston, fifteen or twenty years after the founding of the city. On the right, rear, is the enormous nail-studded door of the prison, with a wild rosebush growing beside it. On the left is the meeting house, with a balcony projecting over the stage. Under the balcony is the scaffold of the pillory, which will be the effective center of the drama. Hester Prynne emerges from the blackness of the prison, with the child on her arm not hiding the letter A in scarlet cloth pinned to her breast; in the whole scene it is the one touch of brilliant color. She moves through the gray crowd and climbs the scaffold. From the balcony overhead the Reverend Mr. Dimmesdale adjures her to reveal the father of her child. "Believe me, Hester," he says, "though he were to step down from a high place and stand beside thee, on thy pedestal of shame, yet better were it so than to hide a guilty heart through life." Hester shakes her head. Looking down at the crowd she recognizes her wronged husband, who had been missing for two years, but he puts his finger on his lips to show that she must not reveal his identity. All the named characters of the drama—including Governor Bellingham, John Wilson, and Mistress Hibbins—appear in this first scene; and there is also the Boston crowd, which speaks in strophe and antistrophe, like a Greek chorus.

Scene 2 of the first act (Chapter IV) is a room in the prison that same June evening. Here, after the public tableau of the first scene, comes a private confrontation. Hester and the child have fallen ill, a leech is summoned to care for them, and the leech is Chillingworth, the betrayed husband. He tells her that the scarlet letter is a more effective punishment than any he might have imagined. "Live, therefore," he says, "and bear about thy doom with thee." After revealing his determination to find the lover and be revenged on him, Chillingworth extracts one promise from Hester: that just as she has kept the lover's identity a secret, so she must keep the husband's.

Act II, Scene 1 (Chapter VII and VIII) is laid in the governor's hall, three years after the events of the first act. Little Pearl is thought to be such a strange and willful child that there has been talk among the Puritan magistrates of taking her away from her sinful mother. When Hester, now a seamstress, comes to deliver a pair of embroidered gloves to Governor Bellingham, there is an informal trial of her case. Chilingworth plays an ambiguous part in it, but Dimmesdale—when Hester demands that he speak—makes such an eloquent plea that she is allowed to keep the child. All the named characters are again present—down to Mistress Hibbins, who, at the end of the scene, invites Hester to attend a witches' sabbath in the forest. Hester refuses with a triumphant smile:

"I must tarry at home," she says, "to keep watch over my little Pearl. Had they taken her from me, I would willingly have gone with thee into the forest, and signed my name in the Black Man's book, and that with mine own blood!"

This tableau and its brief epilogue are followed once more by a private confrontation. *Scene 2* of the second act (Chapter X) is set in Chillingworth's laboratory, among the retorts and crucibles. The old leech suspects Dimmesdale and has taken up residence in the same house, to continue all through the scene his relentless probing of Dimmesdale's heart. The minister will not confess, but, at the curtain, Chillingworth accidentally finds proof that he is indeed the guilty man.

Act III (Chapter XII) has only one scene, the scaffold of the pillory. Four years have passed since the second act. Subtly tortured by Chillingworth and finally driven half-insane, Dimmesdale has dressed in his ministerial robes and left his room at midnight, hoping to find relief in a private mimicry of public confession. Standing on the scaffold he shrieks aloud, but nobody recognizes his voice. Governor Bellingham and Mistress Hibbins both open their windows to peer into the night. On his way home from Governor Winthrop's deathbed, good John Wilson walks through the marketplace in a halo of lanternlight; he does not look up at the pillory. Then, coming from the same deathbed, Hester appears with little Pearl, and Dimmesdale invites them to join him on the scaffold. Holding one another's hands they form what Hawthorne calls "an electric chain," and Dimmesdale feels a new life, not his own, pouring like a torrent into his heart.

"Minister!" Pearl whispers. "Wilt thou stand here with mother and me, tomorrow noontide?"

When Dimmesdale refuses, she tries to pull her hand away. At this moment a meteor gleams through a cloud, forming a scarlet A in the heavens while it also reveals the little group on the scaffold. It is another of Hawthorne's many lighting effects, based partly on his Emersonian belief that the outer world is a visible manifestation of the inner world, but also based partly on his instinct for theatre; one might also speak of his staginess. While the meteor is still glowing, Chillingworth appears to lead the minister back to his torture chamber. This tableau, occurring at the exact center of the drama, is the turning point of *The Scarlet Letter*; from now the tempo will be quicker. The first half of the story has covered a space of seven years; the second half will cover no more than fifteen days.

Act IV is in two intimate scenes, the second of which is the longest in the drama. Scene 1 (Chapters XIV and XV) is laid on the seashore, where Chillingworth is gathering herbs to concoct his medicines. While Pearl goes wading in a tidal pool, Hester accosts the old leech and begs him to release her from her promise not to tell Dimmesdale that he is the wronged husband. Chillingworth answers in a speech that reveals not only his own heart but the other side of Hawthorne's philosophy. The Emersonian side contributed to his stage effects, but it was his surviving Calvinism (in some ways close to Racine's Jansenism) that enabled him to conceive a tragic drama.

"Peace, Hester, peace!" the old man says. "It is not granted me to pardon. . . . My old faith, long forgotten, comes back to me, and explains all that we do, and all we suffer. By thy first step awry thou didst plant the germ of evil; but since that moment, it has all been a dark necessity. Ye that have wronged me are not sinful, save in a kind of typical illusion; neither am I fiend-like, who have snatched a fiend's office from his hands. It is our fate. Let the black flower blossom as it may! Now go thy ways, and deal as thou wilt with yonder man."

He goes back to gathering herbs. Hester calls to Pearl, who, as they leave the stage, keeps asking her, "Mother!—Why does the minister keep his hand over his heart?"

Scene 2 of the fourth act (including four chapters, XVI to XIX) is set in the forest, which forms another contrast with the marketplace and helps to reveal the moral background of Hawthorne's drama. The forest, he tells us in what might almost be a stage direction, is an image of the moral wilderness in which Hester has long been wandering. But it was more than that for Hawthorne himself, and a close reading shows that the forest is also an image of the world men enter when they follow their passions and revolt against the community. In this sense little Pearl, the natural child, is a daughter of the forest, and we observe in this scene that she is perfectly at home there. Witches like Mistress Hibbins go into the forest to dance with Indian powwows and Lapland wizards, and Hester has been tempted to follow them. When she meets Dimmesdale in the forest, although she intends only to warn him against Chillingworth, it is natural in this setting that she should also urge him to defy the laws of the tribe and flee with her to a foreign country. The minister agrees; they will take passage on a Bristol cruiser then moored in the harbor. For a moment Hester unpins the scarlet A from her dress and lets down her long black glossy hair; but Pearl, who has been called back from playing at the brookside, sulks until she pins the letter on her breast again.

On his way back to Boston (in Chapter XX) Dimmesdale meets Mistress Hibbins. "So, reverend Sir, you have made a visit into the forest," says the witch-lady, nodding her high head-dress at him. "The next time, I pray you to allow me only a fair warning, and I shall be proud to bear you company."

Act V, in a single scene (Chapters XXI to XXIII), takes place three days after the meeting in the forest and is the culmination toward which the drama has been moving. Once again it is laid in the marketplace, with all the named characters present, as well as the Bristol shipmaster and the Boston crowd that speaks with the voices of the tribe. Dimmesdale preaches the Election Sermon, the climax of his ministerial career, while Hester listens outside the meeting house. The shipmaster tells her that Chillingworth has taken passage on the same vessel; there will be no escape. Then Dimmesdale appears in a great procession of Puritan worthies and, instead of marching with them to the official banquet, he totters up the steps of the scaffold after calling on Hester to support him. At last they are standing together, in public, on the pedestal of shame.

"Is not this better?" Dimmesdale murmurs, "than what we dreamed of in the forest?" Facing the crowd he tears open his ministerial band and shows that there is a scarlet A imprinted on his own flesh. He has made his public confession and now, at the point of death, he feels reconciled with the community. As he sinks to the scaffold, Chillingworth kneels over him repeating, "Thou hast escaped me." Pearl kisses her father on the lips, and the tears that she lets fall are the pledge that she will cease to be an outcast, an embodiment of the scarlet letter, a daughter of the forest, and instead will grow up among human joys and sorrows.

I spoke of Hawthorne's kinship with Racine, but at this point, if not before, one begins to feel that his drama might have another ancestry as well, even though the author was not conscious of it. He has presented us with distinguished, even noble, characters who are inevitably brought to grief for having violated the laws of heaven and the tribe. He has presented "an action that is serious and also, as having magnitude, complete in itself . . . with incidents arousing pity and fear, wherewith to accomplish its catharsis of such emotions." This familiar quotation from Aristotle seems appropriate in a discussion of *The Scarlet Letter.* In telling his story by a new method, Hawthorne had done more than to extend the unity and economy of the brief tale into the realm of the novel; and more than to discover a new architectural form that would be rediscovered by Henry James and copied by scores of respectably talented novelists after him. It is not too much to say that he had recaptured, for his New England, the essence of Greek tragedy.

1958

A Case for Blithedale

Mark Van Doren's *Hawthorne* is the third and by far the best of the volumes published in the American Men of Letters Series. It is the best not only because the author comes really close to his subject, as Joseph Wood Krutch somehow failed to do in his "Thoreau"; and not only because he is intelligently critical instead of being merely reverent, like Emery Neff in his "Robinson"; but also because he has found the right form for a critical biography.

That was no small achievement in itself. Critical biographies are easy to write, as hundreds of candidates for the doctorate in the humanities, or Ph. Doodlers, have proved during the last few years; but they are extremely difficult to write well. Most of them turn out to be half-length and unoriginal biographies combined with half-length critical studies. The biographies and studies are each sliced into chapter lengths and the chapters are heaped up alternately, like the ham and dry chicken in a club sandwich.

Mr. Van Doren has written a full-length and satisfying book about Hawthorne instead of two short books jumbled between the same covers. His method was to start with a unifying conception, that of Hawthorne as a tragic artist. The conception is discussed in reference to Hawthorne's tales and romances, while at the same time it is set against the background of his not too eventful life. No sharp division has to be made; life and books can be treated in the same passage and sometimes in the same paragraph.

Having made his critical statement in the course of the narrative, Mr. Van Doren is not compelled to write one of those concluding chapters, "In Retrospect," which are the occupational hazard and stale ham of most critical biographers. "In retrospect Hawthorne's work might be characterized briefly as . . ." the chapters usually begin by saying; and then they characterize it briefly in thirty or forty pages as illuminating as the blank wall of a fireproof warehouse. Instead of the chapter Mr. Van Doren writes a concluding paragraph, only one, but it contains a poet's discerning tribute to Hawthorne's genius:

His one deathless virtue is that rare thing in any literature, an utterly serious imagination. It was serious, and so it was loving; it was loving, and so it could laugh; it could laugh, and so it could endure the horror in every human heart. But it saw the honor there along with the horror, the dignity by which in some eternity our pain is measured.

The serious imagination—or perhaps we might call it the tragic sense of life—is the quality by which Mr. Van Doren judges and assigns a place to each of Hawthorne's tales and romances. He finds that the quality is most richly present in *The Scarlet Letter,* and therefore he praises it not only as Hawthorne's best novel but as "the high mark in American fiction." The quality is also present in "Young Goodman Brown," which he ranks a little below *The Scarlet Letter* but only because it is shorter; he says that it is one of the world's great tales. After "Rappaccini's Daughter," which seems to be third on his list, come six other stories—"The Gentle Boy," "Roger Malvin's Burial," "My Kinsman, Major Molineux," "The Birthmark," "Ethan Brand," and "The Wives of the Dead." There are, apparently, no other works that he would place on the first level of Hawthorne's talent.

The House of the Seven Gables and *The Marble Faun* stand high, Mr. Van Doren says, "among his works of the second level." There, too, would belong a few of the moral allegories, like "The Celestial Railroad," and some of the strictly historical stories. On the other hand, he seems to think that all the sketches of contemporary life, except "The Custom House," are merely graceful exercises. *The Blithedale Romance* he describes as an utter failure: "Few poorer novels have been produced by a first-rate talent."

I like Mr. Van Doren's selection among the tales: he has omitted almost all the schoolbook favorites, like "The Great Stone Face," while including some neglected stories that have more depth and meaning for our own time.

There are questions to be raised about his judgment of the four novels; and I should like to make a special plea for *The Blithedale Romance* as the one book in which Hawthorne wrestled with a problem in human relations that was both native and contemporary.

Blithedale is of course concerned with the Utopian colony at Brook Farm, of which Hawthorne himself had been a member. If the book seems a little thin-bodied in contrast with the rich material at his disposal, still it contains one scene—Zenobia's trial in front of a rock in the woods called Eliot's Pulpit—that is almost as powerful as anything Hawthorne wrote. Perhaps American realism began with *The Blithedale Romance*; at any rate Howells got his start from it and always named it as his favorite among Hawthorne's novels.

Yet Hawthorne himself was never strictly a realist. In his later work, including parts of *Blithedale,* he was often an accuratist, but that is not the same thing. Besides his tragic or Greek side, which Mr. Van Doren celebrates, he also had a "Dutch side" that Mr. Van Doren rejects as not being sufficiently imaginative and as leading to the mere depiction of surfaces; perhaps this feature of his work should be examined more closely. It was called Dutch because of his sympathy with the seventeenth-century Dutch painters; but what Hawthorne admired in them was something more than their faithfulness to nature.

"It is strange how spiritual and suggestive the commonest household article—an earthen pitcher, for example—becomes when represented with entire accuracy," he said in one of his later notebooks. "These Dutchmen get at the soul of common things, and so make them types and interpreters of the spiritual world." To interpret the spiritual, or, as we now call it, the inner world was Hawthorne's lifelong purpose as a writer. The real scene of all his stories, early or late, was the human heart.

It was only his method of depicting the scene that changed with the years. In his early stories he started with something in the inner world—an emotion or a moral principle—and then surrounded it with objects and events from the world outside, much as if he were furnishing a bare room. In some of his later work he tried to reverse the process by copying the method of the Dutch painters: that is, he started with the outer world and brooded over it in the effort to discern its inner meaning. He was trying, as he once said, "to diffuse thought and imagination through the opaque substance of today, and thus to make it a bright transparency." That was an imaginative effort, too, and I think that Mr. Van Doren is wrong not to acknowledge the value of the passages in which—not too often—the effort succeeded.

In many ways Hawthorne's work foreshadowed the literary trends of a whole century. The last books he planned, without completing them, would have resembled some of the experimental fiction that is being written today. They would have been accuratistic in their method, with the details copied from life, and realistic in their reading of human nature; but they would have been based on plots that were flatly impossible. In three fragments of *The Dolliver Romance,* the book on which he was working until his last illness, realism and fantasy are mixed in about the same proportions as in Kafka's *The Trial,* which is now being copied by scores of younger novelists—often without their knowing that they are following Hawthorne, too.

Slowly he has been coming back into favor, as readers discovered that he wrote as much or little for our time as for his own. Five books on the man or his work have appeared since last summer and others, I know, are being written or are making their rounds of the publishers. Mr. Van Doren's *Hawthorne* will survive the competition; it is well balanced, sensitive and—in spite of what seems to me some weaknesses in judgment and interpretation—generally the best of the critical books about Hawthorne since Henry James wrote the first of them, in 1879. For the rest, it revives one's early hopes for the American Men of Letters Series, by setting a pattern that other authors in the series might be encouraged to follow.

1949

Mystery at the Old Manse

🌸 Philip Young is a sleuth and scholar best known for his *Ernest Hemingway* (1952), which is still a landmark in Hemingway criticism. Now he has turned his attention to Hawthorne. His new book* reveals, and documents, a scandal among the romancer's Salem ancestors, not the Hathornes (as the name was then spelled), but his mother's wealthier family, the Mannings. The scandal—if Hawthorne learned about it early in his career—may have affected his picture of himself as a solitary dreamer.

It goes back to the years 1680 and 1681. Two sisters, Anstice and Margaret Manning, were convicted of "incestuous carriage with their brother Nicholas Manning who is fled or out of the way." They were sentenced "to be

Hawthorne's Secret: An Un-Told Tale.

whipt upon the Naked body at Ipswich, & that the next Lecture day at Salem then shall stand or sitt upon an high stoole during the whole time of the Exercise in the open middle ally of the meeting house with a papper upon each of their heads, written in Capital Letters This is for whorish carriage with my naturall Brother." A Massachusetts law passed a dozen years later would also have condemned them to wear "a capital I, two inches long of a proportionable bigness, cut in cloth of a contrary colour to their cloathes."

The trial is summarized, but with no names mentioned, in Joseph B. Felt's *Annals of Salem* written in 1827, a book that Hawthorne borrowed on two occasions; the second was for three months in 1849, when he was writing *The Scarlet Letter*. Felt, however, does not quote the damning testimony, which was that of a servant named Elizabeth Watters. This was copied by Philip Young after a friend directed him to page 69, Ledger 35, of the Records and Files of the Quarterly Courts of Essex County, preserved with other volumes acquired in 1980 by the Essex Institute. There he read that Elizabeth Watters

. . . saw the offor said Anstis Manning arise out of the bed without her clothes except only an under petticote which we conceived she had then sliped on & presently I saw my master . . . arise out of the same bed without his clothes . . . and put on his clothes siteing by the bed side. . . . She further testifieth that the morning above mentioned . . . An Kelegrew called her to Look in the bed when she made it & saw the bed much stained of a Red colour.

This is hard evidence, confirmed under oath by the other two serving maids, Ann Kelegrew and Grace Stiver. If Hawthorne indeed came across it during his researches into Salem history, it would have suggested a different version of the ancestral sin that weighed on his family. The sin was not Judge Hathorne's sentencing to death of innocent persons. It was Nicholas Manning's incest with two of his sisters. But did Hawthorne read the damning testimony? Young assumes that he did. Of course he might have found it in a ledger then stored on an open shelf of the Essex County courthouse; or again he might have learned about the scandal from his relatives, one of whom was an antiquarian. But he seldom talked to the relatives and there is no record of his having paid visits to the courthouse. Young's hard evidence, after being weighed, dissolves into suppositions.

Still, Young makes use of it—together with his reading of several *Twice-Told Tales*—to create a sort of mystery novel out of Hawthorne's life, as if he had solved a puzzling case. His plot? Hawthorne nourished incestuous fantasies about his slightly older sister Elizabeth, or Ebe. These may have been only fancies, but they would leave behind them, in a mind like Hawthorne's, a stain of guilt—as indeed he intimated in one of his slighter tales, "Fancy's Show-Box." There he asks,

... will guilty thoughts—of which guilty deeds are no more than shadows—will these draw down the full weight of a condemning sentence, in the supreme court of eternity? In the solitude of a midnight chamber ... the soul may pollute itself even with those crimes, which we are accustomed to deem altogether carnal.

Rather hesitantly and with apologies, Young conjectures that there may have been some carnal sin as well. In either case, Sister Ebe was Hawthorne's guilty secret.

This supposition lends salience to the Manning scandal. If or when Hawthorne learned about it, he might well have regarded the story as a brutal foreshadowing of his own situation. To pass from supposition to fact, we know that he sometimes pondered on ancestral crimes and how they tainted one generation after another. Some of his tales embodied more than a hint of incestuous relations. One detail of the scandal that might have colored his work is Watters's testimony that the bed was "much stained of a Red colour." Blood and guilt became synonymous in his imaginings. Satan in "Young Goodman Brown," one of Hawthorne's greatest tales, promises the Goodman and his wife that they shall "exult to behold the whole earth one stain of guilt, one enormous bloodspot." As for the scarlet letter that Hester Prynne was condemned to wear, Young conjectures that, in the mind's eye of the author, it was not an *A* for adultery but an *I* for incest.

All this is a simplified version of Philip Young's scenario, which he renders more plausible by offering scores of quotations. But Young simplifies, too, by making Hawthorne a less complicated person than he was in the flesh. Young's portrait makes him a pallid figure who deserves the other-worldly nickname "Oberon." Determined as he is to win fame by transcribing his fancies, he neglects his relations with living men and women. Hawthorne's persona in his fiction has something of that weakness, as witness Miles Coverdale of *The Blithedale Romance*; but Hawthorne in life had another aspect as well, especially after his marriage to Sophia Peabody. More and more he displayed the practical, the merchant-like, the Bay State side of his character. He became a householder who was obeyed and almost worshiped by his little family, as well as a widely respected civil servant.

Young neglects this other side of Hawthorne, besides disparaging the solid achievements to which it led. It is true that he lost contact with the dreams that had given a somber radiance to his early fiction, but I would not say with Young that his work "declined steadily in value" after *The Scarlet Letter*. Young is unfair to the published romances that followed, forgetting what Hawthorne said about *The House of the Seven Gables*—that, in its mixture of several moods, romantic and realistic, it was "a work more characteristic of my mind." He is even more unfair to *The Blithedale Romance,* which he could hardly bear to read, let alone to write about; he calls it "a feeble book, badly put together and to no particular point." But I go back to it with pleasure, while noting that it had a discernible effect on Henry James and Howells; and hence on the history of American fiction. As for *The Marble Faun,* largely a guidebook to Rome read by generations of tourists, it contains two superbly dramatic chapters.

And the *English Notebooks,* not published as he wrote them until nearly eighty years after his death and never widely read? They form a substantial work in themselves, full of shrewd observations. They make us feel that Hawthorne might have become a realistic novelist of stature if he had turned his mind in that direction. Instead, with his health ruined, he spent his declining years trying vainly to finish four romances after losing touch with the sources of his inspiration. The fact remains that Hawthorne, on his Yankee or practical side, was not the utter failure that Young presents him as being.

Whether he had a secret of any sort is a question that has been argued and obfuscated for more than a century. Herman Melville believed in its existence. When Julian Hawthorne was writing a biography of his father, Melville told him that he was "convinced Hawthorne had all his life concealed some great secret, which would, were it known, explain all the mysteries of his career." Julian disagreed; he wrote that his father "had no stain . . . upon his conscience." Others might conjecture that there was indeed something to conceal, but of a nature less shocking to modern sensibilities than incest.

One of the tales that Hawthorne wrote while living happily at the Old Manse might offer a clue; it is "Egotism; or, The Bosom Serpent." A wealthy and talented young man, Roderick Elliston, is afflicted with the notion that a serpent lives in his breast. "It gnaws me! It gnaws me!" he keeps muttering. Elliston wanders the streets accosting neighbors under the delusion that they, too, nourish bosom serpents. His mania has given him a sharp eye for the sins of others. After his release from an asylum, Elliston is visited by a young sculptor, the cousin of his deserted wife, Rosina. The sculptor has first consulted "an eminent medical gentleman," who assured him that Elliston's case was not unprecedented. His symptoms, including morbidity and a sickly green complexion, are in fact those assigned by nineteenth-century opinion to victims of self-abuse. Thus, for the word "egotism" in the title of the story, one is tempted to substitute "onanism." Elliston himself is finally redeemed by a reawakened affection for Rosina.

This clue to one of Hawthorne's meanings might also be applied to some of his other tales, as notably to "Young Goodman Brown," with its vision of universal human depravity, and even more to "The Minister's Black Veil."

There the saintly Mr. Hooper wears a black veil on his face in token of an unacknowledged sin. Nobody can persuade him to remove it, not even his beloved Elizabeth, who thereupon bids him farewell. Years later he rises from his deathbed to proclaim, "I look around me, and lo! on every visage a Black Veil!" What was the universal sin of which it was an emblem? In another tale, "The Birthmark," the blemish on Georgiana's lovely face was in the shape of a hand—and why a hand?

One is tempted to pursue such queries and speculations, but I have come to feel that the temptation should be resisted. Too many critics have been yielding to it, and not with fruitful results. In Hawthorne's case especially, though also in others, it may lead to the simplification of a rich and baffling personality, as well as to the neglect of the works themselves in the effort to reveal the usually sexual, usually familiar aberrations that they conceal. Philip Young tries to avoid those faults, and most often succeeds (though he has little of interest to say about Sister Ebe, an essential figure in his story). One feels grateful to him for unearthing an item of hard evidence about Hawthorne's ancestors, and also for offering persuasive readings of some tales that are often misinterpreted. I read his book with keen interest, then went back to read it again. Still, as for Hawthorne's secret, if a secret there was, that reserved and reclusive man has told us as much of it as he could bear to tell. His contribution to American letters had earned him the right to carry the rest of it with him into Sleepy Hollow cemetery.

1984

The External Emerson

❧ Ralph L. Rusk's life of Emerson contains 508 large pages of text, besides 43 pages in which he identifies his sources and 40 crowded pages of index and bibliography. It is the first book on Emerson since 1889 to be based on a fresh study of the family papers. Scholarly, exhaustive, accurate, it is destined to remain a standard work for a long time—and I wonder why Rusk devoted ten years of his own life to writing it.

Or twice ten years, if we go back to the beginning. For the first half of the longer period he was preparing a copiously annotated edition of Emerson's letters, which appeared in six volumes in 1939. Then, starting with the Emerson family in colonial times, he began collecting more facts and still more facts. Besides rereading the family papers preserved by the Ralph Waldo Emerson Memorial Association, to which he has been the only scholar outside the family circle to be granted free access, he worked for many months in the Houghton Library at Harvard, and that was only the beginning of his labors.

He read through the Emerson collections of the Columbia University Libraries, the New York Public Library, the Union Theological Seminary Library, the Massachusetts Historical Society, the Concord Free Public Library, the Concord Antiquarian Society, the Emerson House in Concord, the Harvard Historical Society (of Harvard, Mass.), the Andover-Harvard Theological Library, the Abernethy Library of Middlebury College—"and other libraries—" he adds in his preface, "more than can be named here." Town by town, almost step by step, he followed Emerson's travels in America and Europe. He became known in the academic world of two continents as "the Emerson man." Not deliberately, but simply by the rumor of his prodigious studies, he frightened away other scholars who might have worked in the same field. Then, taking advantage of a Guggenheim fellowship, a sabbatical leave from Columbia University and all his other academic vacations, he wrote this immense, authoritative book—and again I wonder why.

In his style, in his arrangement of facts, in his critical explanations he reveals no more than a tepid admiration for Emerson. Not once does he make us feel by comment or quotation that Emerson was a very great writer. Not once does he descend to those deeper levels—his own or Emerson's—where the author speaks for himself, risks himself and pronounces each word as if he were carving it in stone. Rusk works ahead like a bookkeeper copying rows of figures, proud of their accuracy and not much concerned with their ultimate meaning. Twenty years ago Emerson must have fired his imagination and given him a picture of the long course that he would follow; but now the fire has died away, leaving chiefly the determination to finish the task once grandly conceived.

"To write, not merely a book about Emerson, but one fit to be called his life": that was the project he has carried to completion. Here in this volume is Emerson's joyless childhood; here are his family tragedies, including the death of three brothers and his first wife by consumption; here are the posts he held, the lectures he gave, the fees he earned and the cities he visited. Seldom do we read a biography that follows its hero so closely from cradle to grave.

Rusk has many new facts to present, and they make us feel that Emerson was less of a serene sage than we had pictured him; more of a rebellious student, a faithful and grieving brother, a passionate lover of his first wife. We perceive what we may have missed before: that Emerson's optimistic sermons were being preached for himself as well as the public, in the midst of his sorrows.

Yet this light on the inner man is offered indirectly and almost inadvertently. What Rusk is really presenting in this book is the external Emerson, in terms of behavior—the author as seen by his family, his friends and his lecture audiences; not the lonely man who lived in his own mind and wrote by flashes of inspiration that were sometimes mystical experiences. There were moments when he felt that his personality was being merged in the universal life and when he redoubled his energy by drawing, as he said, on "a great public power . . . by unlocking, at all risks, his human doors, and suffering the ethereal tides to roll and circulate through him." These moments are mentioned at some length in the essays and the journals, but I cannot remember that Rusk ever refers to them. Instead he talks about Emerson's pear orchard and his investments in railroad bonds.

Rusk doesn't ask the questions that are suggested by Emerson's career; for example, he never seems to wonder about the reasons for the poet's slow growth and sudden flowering. At Harvard Emerson was not a distinguished or a popular student. His scholastic rank was thirtieth in a class of fifty-nine and he was named as class poet only after six others had declined the honor. He was not a success as a schoolmaster nor famous as a young preacher—at least until he resigned his pulpit at the age of twenty-nine— yet a few years later he had become the recognized leader of the younger generation in New England. "I think Mr. Emerson is the greatest man that ever lived. *As a whole* he is satisfactory," Sophia Peabody wrote in her diary for 1838, when she was being courted by Hawthorne.

Emerson had become a cult with the Peabody clan; but so had he also become with all the reformers and all the representatives of what was then called "the newness." It was a wave of individual rebellions that had swept over New England, carrying with it freaks of every nature; Emerson listed them once as "Madmen, madwomen, men with beards, Dunkers, Muggletonians, Come-outers, Groaners, Agrarians, Seventh-day Baptists, Quakers, Abolitionists, Calvinists, Unitarians and Philosophers"; but he might also have mentioned feminists, vegetarians, no-money enthusiasts, primitive communists and future railroad financiers then sowing their intellectual wild oats. Emerson stood aside from them, yet they all read his books and most of them regarded him as their patron and prophet. Another question that Rusk fails to ask is how much Emerson's work was a product of the same forces that produced the general movement, and how much "the newness" was the lengthened shadow of Emerson.

There is one period of his life that is admirably suited to Rusk's external method of biography. It is the period after 1866, when Emerson was losing his memory, when he had no new ideas, when he reread his own books and murmured in his daughter Ellen's hearing, "Why, these things are really very good." Since his life by then had lost most of its inner meaning, it can be fully described in terms of travels, encounters, lectures and financial records (on which Rusk is especially good). He is also good at collecting anecdotes, like the one about Emerson's conducted tour of a San Francisco opium den. "There is not much aspiration there—or inspiration," was his very mild comment. At home in Concord he entertained Bret Harte and invited him, Harte said, to spend a "wet evening" over a glass of sherry.

Emerson in his old age was serene, Buddha-like and sometimes ridiculous in a large, lovable fashion. Rusk tells that story well, but it is not a story of great moment to our age or any other. The Emerson whose memory should be revived—and his work reread, after years of neglect—is the young rebel against all forms of the mob spirit. "Let us affront and reprimand," he said, "the smooth mediocrity, the squalid contentment of the times."—"The timidity of our public opinion is our disease, or, shall I say, the publicness of opinion, the absence of private opinion." These are statements we need to hear again in these days when private citizens are being asked to support and expound intolerance as the only true Americanism. Emerson had good advice for scholars, too; he liked to repeat for them the Arabian proverb: "A fig tree, looking on a fig tree, becomes fruitful." He meant that each new labor of scholarship should become a creative work; but Rusk has failed to follow the master's advice. The figs on his branches have a dusty taste and the smell, not of new ideas, but of old letters in a Concord attic.

1949

Melville Among His Champions

We are still in the midst of the Melville boom-or-bust. During the past year it has produced two remarkable contributions to Melville scholarship and soon there will be a third—Jay Leyda's *A Melville Log* (Harcourt, Brace)—which may or may not be remarkable but which promises at the very least to cast new light on Melville's career; it will be discussed in due time. Meanwhile I should like to talk about the other two books, which are in danger of being confused with each other since both are critical studies and both have the title *Herman Melville*. These are, however, almost their only similarities.

Newton Arvin's *Herman Melville* is remarkable simply because it is *good*; that is, perceptive, reasonable, balanced, and persuasive in its judgments. Arvin has mastered an art that is essential to sound criticism: the art of making qualifications that seem to weaken his direct statements, but really strengthen them by bringing them closer to the complicated truth. Thus, in discussing the form of *Moby Dick,* he does not say, "It is an epic poem," a statement or challenge that would simplify the truth. He says, with all the restricting clauses, "If one must look for analogies that will do a little to express the effect *Moby Dick* has on us in form—and they can do no more than that at the very most—it is not to tragedy that one should turn but to heroic poetry, to the epic."

He does not stop at this point. Having limited his statement—much as if he was retiring to a fortified position—he brings up the evidence that will support and expand it. He explains how American life at the time, and Melville's life in particular, had about them an epic feeling like that of the Homeric age. He says that *Moby Dick* combines two epic themes, the voyage and the chase. He shows that the fourfold, wavelike movement of the novel (which he describes at length) suggests the sixfold design of the *Odyssey* or the fivefold design of the *Lusiads*. At the end one feels that, with his qualifications behind him, he has reached something close to a final statement.

Another critical art he has mastered is that of rising to the level of his subject without overleaping it. When he discusses Melville's earlier narratives from *Typee* to *White-Jacket,* he pays perhaps a little more than the right degree of attention to their half-disclosed psychological depths, but usually his tone is as factual and happily adventurous as Melville's was in those early days. When he discusses *Moby Dick,* his tone rises as Melville's did and his very long chapter, "The Whale," is not only the best he has written but stands high among the achievements of recent criticism.

He does not overestimate the later books. "Critically speaking," he says, "and from the point of view of poetic value, almost nothing Melville later did is comparable to his one very great book. Much that he later did has so real an interest, and has incited so much commentary, as to blur and becloud the fact that it is work not only on a lower level but on a level that is lower by several wide degrees." Arvin praises only one novel, *Billy Budd,* among the four that followed *Moby Dick* and he speaks of it in terms that reveal more affection than critical admiration. On the other hand, he is mildly enthusiastic about Melville's poems and persuades us to accept the value he sets on them by quoting exactly the right lines. His book is remarkable not only for its positive qualities but also for the absence of serious faults. For a long time it will serve as the best general introduction to Melville's work.

Richard Chase's *Herman Melville* is remarkable for quite a different reason: because there is no other book of our time, and perhaps no other in the long history of critical writing, that seizes on a method so eagerly and rides it so far into the clouds. The method sometimes called "mythological criticism," is becoming fashionable in the universities; it consists in looking for the myths embodied in or suggested by an author's work. Chase, however, carries or is carried by the method far beyond the point of merely looking for myths in Melville's writings. Seeming to regard them as Holy Scripture, he sets out on a search like Swedenborg's in the *Arcana Coelestia,* with the aim of fully revealing their inner or spiritual meaning.

There are suggestions of such a meaning in Melville's work. In the spirit of his age, which strengthened his personal inclinations, he was interested in what Swedenborg called "correspondences." He made conscious use of emblems, tokens or symbols; and sometimes, like his friend Hawthorne, he wove the symbols into connected allegories—although he distrusted the allegorical method after using it in *Mardi* and deciding that the book was a failure. Chase therefore has a real field for research, besides the ingenious type of mind that leads him to look for the implications hidden beneath hidden implications. There is at least a germ or possibility of truth in almost everything he says; but unlike Arvin he has never learned to qualify his statements.

One weakness of his method is revealed by his continual misuse of the copulative verb—the "is" that joins subject to predicate like a sign of identity. Thus, he says that Bulkington, a very minor character in *Moby Dick,* "is"—not "suggests" or "carries with him a hint of being," but flatly *is*— "the titanic body of America (as the word 'Bulkington' suggests) stirring out of the uncreated night and passing ponderously into motion and consciousness." Those are big phrases to use in connection with a character whom Melville introduces in one paragraph and soon afterwards dismisses in a "six-inch chapter," which he says will serve as Bulkington's "stoneless grave"—and a small one, too, in which to inter the titanic body of America. Chase devotes more than twice as many words to Bulkington as Melville does, but it is not until he begins writing about the characters in Melville's next novel, *Pierre,* that he reveals his full talent for discovering spiritual correspondences and for abusing the word "is." I quote:

"Like Ahab, Pierre is the vessel of the Promethean fire. He is 'stone,' charged 'with the fire of all divineness'; he is the human clay, transfigured into a Titan. . . . Isabel, or Bell, as she is also called, is Darkness. . . . Lucy is light in more than name. . . . Isabel . . . is the 'clog from Chaos' who drags the world back into the womb of Old Night." Turning a few pages, we find that Chase has finished with his fire-day-night identities and is now comparing *Pierre* with the Apocalypse of St. John. "Pierre is Christ," he says. ". . . Glen is Antichrist. Pierre's mother is History or Society, the old, established, conventional, unredeemed Jewish church. The Reverend Ms. Falsgrave is the Laodicean church. Lucy is the New Jerusalem. Isabel is Babylon." And so on for page after page until we reach the statement that "Perhaps at less conscious levels"—were all these identities consciously present in Melville's mind?—"there are other relationships. . . . Lucy may be the silver cord, Isabel the golden bowl, Mrs. Glendinning the pitcher, the cycles of history the wheel, Pierre the body which contains these symbolic organs"—namely, cords, bowls, pitchers and wheels, and in addition, let us hope, lungs, liver and heart.

It would seem to most critics that the whole attempt to reinterpret *Pierre* in terms of the Bible is an exercise of pedantic ingenuity and an attempt to read back into Melville all the wealth of literary allusions that Joyce put into his *Ulysses* after working over the manuscript for eight years (whereas *Pierre* was written in a few months, by an exhausted man on the edge of a nervous breakdown). Nor is this Chase's only mistake. Even if the correspondences were really suggested in *Pierre*—they could not be more than suggested, and in a shadowy fashion—Chase would still be wrong to use the copulative verb, since it gives a radically false impression of the symbolic method that Melville sometimes followed. Symbols are not equivalents or identities of the values symbolized; they are real persons or objects that suggest those values among others. To say that Isabel, for example, *is* Darkness or Babylon amounts to saying she *is no more than* Darkness or Babylon and that accordingly she *is not* a human being (as perhaps she isn't) or even truly a character in a novel.

There is, however, a still greater weakness in Chase's mythological or mystagogic criticism. It encourages him to misjudge the artistic quality of the works he is discussing, by tempting him to believe that the greatest novels are those which suggest the greatest wealth of allegorical meanings. In his book on Melville, for example, it leads him to magnify *Pierre* as a companion novel on the same level as *Moby Dick*; whereas Arvin, after making the necessary qualifications, gives us the final judgment on *Pierre* by saying that all its high qualities are not enough to keep it from being "four-fifths claptrap, and sickly claptrap to boot." *The Confidence Man* is as tired and dismal a novel as was ever published by a first-rate writer, but Chase finds it rich in allegorical values (including sermons to use against Henry Wallace, whom Chase obsessively doesn't like) and therefore he raises it to a very high place among Melville's works: "*The Confidence Man*," he says, "is a supreme achievement."

The sort of myths and puns and dreamlike symbols for which he is seeking depend more on an author's subconscious than they do on his conscious mind. Often the subconscious functions best when the author is close to a mental collapse and is writing at top speed to support his family. This seems to have been the case with Melville and it explains the qualities that Chase admires in *Pierre* and *The Confidence Man*; it also explains why both books failed as works of art. But the qualities, good and bad, were not confined to Melville. I am speaking seriously when I say that the works of Horatio Alger Jr. are rich in symbolic meanings and that they embody in striking images not only the American myth of the poor boy making good but the greater and older myth of the orphan seeking his spiritual father. The works of Frederick Van Rensselaer Dey, who wrote most of the Nick Carter stories, are much admired by the French Surrealists—and with good reason, for they too are myths and fantasies and they depict a struggle between gods and titans. Here is a rich field neglected by the mythological critics. Chase would earn the gratitude of every scholar if he would devote his talents to revealing the mantic, oneiric, parabolic and anagogic values embodied in the works of Horatio Alger and Freddie Dey.

*　*　*

It is impossible for the life of a truly great man to remain forever concealed. No matter if he lost his faith in the public and hid himself for thirty years; no matter if his heirs had such a fear of notoriety that they burned his letters and memoranda; no matter if the products of his genius were forgotten for half a century and only rediscovered when all who knew him intimately had vanished—still the great works will be resurrected and the life of the author will be deciphered little by little from the traces it could not fail to leave on other lives. The difficulty of the search will be a challenge to hundreds of learned detectives till at last the great recluse is better known than any of his famous contemporaries.

That has been the fate of Herman Melville. Thirty years after his death in 1891 he suddenly became a popular author. Fifty years after his death he became the great subject of American literary scholarship, so that "When are you publishing your book on Melville?" was a stock question at faculty teas. For more than a decade he has been the victim of interpretations and misinterpretations that have been weaving themselves into a Melville legend. Now, in 1951, we are at last given the sort of book about him that only national heroes receive, a collection, in two volumes, of passages from the actual documents that record his early years, his success and failure with the American public and his long life in retirement.

The documents quoted in *The Melville Log* were gathered by many scholars from many sources. They include letters from Melville that somehow escaped the flames, letters from his friends and relatives preserved in various collections, extracts from publishers' files, books from Melville's library with passages that he underlined, newspaper gossip about him—in all, a comprehensive collection of items few of which are important when taken by themselves, but all of which, taken together, give us a factual record of his life from day to day. It is refreshing to find that the editor, Jay Leyda, makes no comments of his own; there have been too many comments on Melville. What we need now is exactly what Leyda has given us: the facts from which to compose our own picture of the man and his work.

It will be a slightly different picture from the sentimental or psychoanalytical portraits that have lately been popular. Here, to state them briefly, are some notions about Melville suggested, not by any one of the documents that Leyda has collected, but by all of them in their interrelationship:

1. Melville was preeminently a family man. During much of his life he was the head of a household that included his mother, his wife (born Elizabeth Shaw, of Boston), two or three of his sisters and his four children, not to mention hordes of visiting relatives. Outside the immediate household his closest friends were his three brothers, Gansevoort (till his death in 1846), Allan and Thomas, his uncle, Peter Gansevoort, his brother-in-law, John C. Hoadley, and his father-in-law, Judge Lemuel Shaw.

In these recent days when uncles, aunts and cousins have disappeared from the narrowing family circle, especially in the North, it is hard for us to realize the extent and variety of the Melville connections or of their importance in the author's life. On the one hand, it was a strain on his emotions and his purse to live surrounded by relatives; on the other hand, the family was always coming to his help. Elizabeth, or Lizzie, and his sisters copied his manuscripts (besides correcting their spelling and grammar).

Two of his brothers acted as his literary agents. Judge Shaw lent him money when he needed it, without pressing for repayment, and Peter Gansevoort paid for the publication of his long poem, "Clarel," which nobody bothered to read. When relatives died they left legacies, sometimes large ones, to Herman or Elizabeth Shaw Melville.

2. His marriage was more successful than we would gather from reading some of the recent biographies. It has become the custom to describe Melville as a victim of mother fixation and to imply that he had a barely suppressed feeling of hostility for all other women, including poor Lizzie. The truth seems to have been that he was passionately in love with her until their second child was born and that he remained a loyal and reasonably devoted husband. There was a period of some years after 1853 when Melville was threatened with insanity; there was a later period when Lizzie was close to becoming a neurotic invalid; but their troubles were followed by calmer years. His last two collections of poems were both dedicated to his wife—the very last, "Weeds and Wildings," with a dedicatory letter of sincere praise that any woman would be proud to read.

3. Melville's central difficulty was professional, not sexual. The problem he never solved and finally abandoned as impossible of solution was that of finding a public prepared to read what he wanted to write. The American public of his time was at first not unfriendly. It was glad to read *Typee, Omoo, White Jacket* and his other narratives of adventure; it was even willing to read *Moby Dick* for its account of life on a whaler; but it had no sympathy whatever for the ideas he expressed in *Moby Dick*. When he returned to some of the same ideas in *Pierre*, which was a still more fantastic story, the public refused to open the book. *Pierre* in its first year had a sale of only 283 copies.

Writing books that would earn enough to keep him alive was part of Melville's professional problem. At first he had seemed to be solving that part of the problem with reasonable success. During six years as a professional author he had been paid more than $8,500 as royalties on his books; it was a reasonable income for the time and was nearly as much as was earned by Edgar Allan Poe in his whole literary career. On the other hand, Melville had a larger household than Poe and couldn't live in a cottage; he liked to patronize the booksellers, entertain his relatives and play the country gentleman. The result was that he tried to earn more money in the most dangerous fashion for a writer, by turning out too many books, in too short a time, at too great an expenditure of emotion.

Pierre, for example, was started before he had recovered from the enormous strain of writing *Moby Dick* and was finished in two or three months of unbroken labor. A neighbor said of him in a letter, "I hear that he is now engaged in a new work as frequently not to leave his room till quite dark in the evening—when he for the first time during the whole day partakes of solid food—he must therefore write under a state of morbid excitement which will soon injure his health." The fact seems to be that *Pierre* was a turning point in his life. Not only did its failure with the public almost destroy his earning power, but the labor of writing it drove him into what we now call a nervous breakdown.

4. The documents suggest a new interpretation of his estrangement from Hawthorne. Their close friendship in 1850–1852, when Melville was writing *Moby Dick* and *Pierre* and Hawthorne was writing *The House of the Seven Gables,* is one of the dramatic episodes in the history of American literature. For a time each man had a deep effect on the other. Hawthorne is usually blamed for the coolness that followed; the story is that he was disturbed by Melville's warmth and enthusiasm and retired into an icy solitude. A more likely explanation now seems to be that it was Melville who allowed their friendship to lapse, just as he stopped seeing another close friend, Evert Duyckinck; in his exhausted and dispirited state he was withdrawing into himself. The record helps us on this point as on so many others: it shows that for the rest of his life Melville had no friends outside his own family.

The Melville Log, to say a final word for it, can be recommended to everyone interested in the history of American literature. For students of Melville it is indispensable.

1950, 1951

Whitman

The Poet and the Mask (excerpts)

❧ I haven't always been an admirer of Whitman's poetry. In the past when I tried to read *Leaves of Grass* from beginning to end, I always stopped in the middle, overcome by the dislike that most of us feel for inventories and orations. Even today, after reading all the book as Whitman wished it to be preserved and after being won over by what I think is the best of it— till I am willing, if not for the usual reasons, to join the consensus that regards him as our most rewarding poet—I still feel that *Leaves of Grass* is an extraordinary mixture of greatness, false greatness, and mediocrity. Whitman designed it as his monument, but he made the book too large and pieced it out with faulty materials, including versified newspaper editorials, lists of names from the back pages of a school geography, commencement-day prophecies, chamber-of-commerce speeches, and sentimental ballads that might have been written by the Sweet Singer of Michigan, except that she would have rhymed them. The fire bells ring in his poems, the eagle screams and screams again, the brawny pioneers march into the forest (décor by Currier & Ives), and the lovely Italian singer gives a concert for the convicts at Sing Sing, her operatic voice

> Pouring in floods of melody in tones so pensive sweet and
> strong the like whereof was never heard.

In no other book of great poems does one find so much trash that the poet should have recognized as trash before he set the first line of it on paper. In no other book, great or small, does one find the same extremes of inspiration and bathos. It is as if Whitman the critic and editor of his own work had been so overawed by Whitman the poet that he preserved even the poet's maunderings as the authentic record of genius. He did not succeed—though he worked on the problem all his life—in giving an organic form to the book as a whole. It doesn't grow like a tree or take wing like a bird or correspond in its various sections to the stages of the poet's life; instead it starts with a series of twenty-four "inscriptions," or doctrinal pronouncement, almost like twenty-four theses nailed to a church door. It reaches an early climax, with the "Song of Myself." It continues through celebrations of "women-love," as Whitman called it a little coldly, and passionate friendship for men. Then, after a series of set-pieces—some of them magnificent, like the "Song of the Open Road"—after the Civil War sketches and the big symphonies of his Washington years, it dwindles away in occasional verses and old-age echoes.

The poems are grouped by their ostensible themes rather than by their underlying moods. Thus, a section or, as Whitman would say, a "cluster" of poems called "Sea-Drift" starts with the two great meditations he wrote during his period of dejection in 1859–1860 ("Out of the Cradle Endlessly Rocking" and "As I Ebb'd with the Ocean of Life"), but it ends with a collection of minor and chiefly optimistic pieces that happen also to mention the sea. Another cluster called "Autumn Rivulets" consists in large part of late and occasional poems, like Whitman's bread-and-butter letter to the Seventeenth Regimental Band ("Italian Music in Dakota"), yet it also contains the marvelous "There Was a Child Went Forth" and other examples of his earlier and freshest work. In such an arrangement the man is lost, with his organic development; and the best poems are likely to be overshadowed, like young pines in a thicket of big-leaf poplars.

Almost all the American critics of Whitman's poetry have failed in their task of separating the pines from the poplars, the lasting values from what is trivial or sententious or weedy. It is true that Tennyson, Swinburne and William Michael Rossetti were among his early English readers, that they were good critics as well as poets, and that, in general, they admired his work for its literary qualities instead of approaching it as a political or religious text. In this country, however, the poets of his time were hostile to Whitman; almost the only exception was Emerson in the very beginning. The hostility has vanished, but without giving way to enthusiasm. As a group the poet-critics of our time pay less attention to Whitman than to any other American author of the first magnitude. More and more Whitman studies are crowding the library shelves, but they are chiefly the work of two other groups: the liberal or nationalistic historians and the teachers or graduate students of American literature.

These latter groups are interested not so much in the poetry as in the historical or mythical figure of the poet. They *need* that figure; they need an author to represent in himself the vastness and newness of the country and the unity it achieved; they need someone in literature to play the same role as Daniel Boone in the forests or Davy Crockett in the canebrakes or Lincoln saving the Union. Whitman is there, dressed and bearded for the part, and they cannot fail to accept him as the literary archetype of the pioneer. But other readers, a little more familiar with the ways of authors, find something ambiguous in Whitman's portrait of himself. When he talks too much about loving every created person, they feel that he is indiscriminate in his affections, and that it is only a step from loving to hating everyone. When he talks too much about comradeship, they suspect him—not without reason—of being self-centered and lonely. When he celebrates the life of trappers and woodsmen or cries, "O pioneers!" they read his biography and are not surprised to learn that he was chiefly a stroller through city streets. And if they come to value his work far, far above that of the other nineteenth-century American poets, it is because of the poems in which he did not boast or posture, but spoke with marvelous candor about himself and his immediate world.

To find those poems in the mass of his work is like wandering without a guidebook from room to room of a French provincial museum and searching for pictures to admire. After looking at scores of stiff portraits and dozens of landscapes rightly rejected (or hung, it doesn't matter) by the French Academy, one suddenly finds a Corot, a Courbet with its clean lines, or a fifteenth-century Virgin with the colors still as tender as the day they were painted. Whitman's best poems—and most of them are early poems—have that permanent quality of being freshly painted, of not being dulled by the varnish of the years. Reading them almost a century after their publication, one feels the same shock and wonder and delight that Emerson felt when opening his presentation copy of the first edition. They carry us into a new world that Whitman discovered as if this very morning, after it had been created overnight. "Why, who makes much of a miracle?" the poet keeps exclaiming. "As to me I know nothing else but miracles."

There is no other word but miracle to describe what happened to Whitman at the age of thirty-six. The local politician and printer, the hack writer who had trouble selling his pieces, the editor who couldn't keep a job, quite suddenly became a world poet. No long apprenticeship; no process of growth that we can trace from year to year in his published work; not even much early promise; the poet materializes like a shape from the depths. In 1848, when we almost lose sight of him, Whitman is an editorial writer on salary, repeating day after day the opinions held in common by the younger Jacksonian Democrats, praising the people and attacking the corporations (but always within reasonable limits); stroking the American eagle's feathers and pulling the lion's tail. Hardly a word he published gives the impression that only Whitman could have written it. In 1855 he reveals a new character that seems to be his own creation. He writes and prefaces and helps to print and distributes and, for good measure, anonymously reviews a first book of poems not only different from any others known at the time but also different from everything the poet himself had written in former years (and only faintly foreshadowed by three of his experiments in free verse that the New York *Tribune* had printed in 1850 because it liked their political sentiments). It is a short book, this first edition of *Leaves of Grass*; it contains only twelve poems, including the "Song of Myself"; but they summarize or suggest all his later achievements, because in his first book

Whitman was a great explorer, whereas he later became a methodical exploiter and at worst an expounder by rote of his own discoveries.

At some point during the seven "lost years" Whitman had begun to utilize resources deep in himself that might have remained buried. He had mastered what Emerson calls "the secret which every intellectual man quickly learns"—but how few make use of it!—"that beyond the energy of his possessed and conscious intellect he is capable of a new energy (as of an intellect doubled on itself), by abandonment to the nature of things; that beside his privacy of power as an individual man, there is a great public power on which he can draw, by unlocking, at all risks, his human doors, and suffering the ethereal tides to roll and circulate through him; then he is caught up into the life of the Universe, his speech is thunder, his thought is law, and his words are universally intelligible as the plants and animals." Whitman himself found other words to describe what seems to have been essentially the same phenomenon. Long afterwards he told one of his disciples, Dr. Maurice Bucke: "'Leaves of Grass' was there, though unformed, all the time, in whatever answers as the laboratory of the mind. . . . The *Democratic Review* essays and tales [those he published before 1848] came from the surface of the mind and had no connection with what lay below— a great deal of which, indeed, was below consciousness. At last the time came when the concealed growth had to come to light, and the first edition of 'Leaves of Grass' was published."

Whitman in those remarks was simplifying a phenomenon by which, it would seem, he continued to be puzzled and amazed till the end. The best efforts of his biographers will never fully explain it; and a critic can only point to certain events, or probable events, that must have contributed to his sudden discovery of his own resources. His trip to New Orleans in 1848 was certainly one of them. It lasted for only four months (and not for years, as Whitman later implied), but it was his first real glimpse of the American continent, and it gave him a stock of remembered sights and sounds and emotions over which his imagination would play for the rest of his life.

A second event was connected with his interest in the pseudoscience of phrenology. The originators of this doctrine believed that one's character is determined by the development of separate faculties (of which there were twenty-six according to Gall, thirty-five according to Spurzheim and forty-three according to the Fowler brothers in New York); that each of these faculties is localized in a definite portion of the brain; and that the strength or weakness of each faculty can be read in the contours of the skull. Whitman had the bumps on his head charted by L. N. Fowler in July 1849, a year after his return from the South. In these phrenological readings of character, each of the faculties was rated on a numerical scale running from one to seven or eight. Five was good; six was the most desirable figure;

seven and eight indicated that the quality was dangerously overdeveloped. Among the ratings that Whitman received for his mental faculties (and note their curious names, which reappeared in his poems) were Amativeness 6, Adhesiveness 6, Philoprogenitiveness 6, Self-esteem 6 to 7, Benevolence 6 to 7, Sublimity 6 to 7, Ideality 5 to 6, Individuality 6, and Intuitiveness 6. It was, on the whole, a highly flattering report, and Whitman needed flattery in those days, for he hadn't made a success of his new daily, the Brooklyn *Freeman,* and there was a question whether he could find another good newspaper job. Apparently the phrenological reading gave him some of the courage he needed to follow an untried course. Seven years later he had Fowler's chart of his skull reproduced in the second or 1856 edition of *Leaves of Grass.*

Another event that inspired him was the reading of Emerson's essays. Later Whitman tried to hide this indebtedness, asserting several times that he had seen nothing of Emerson's until after his own first edition had been published. But aside from the Emersonian ideas in the twelve early poems (especially the "Song of Myself") there is, as evidence in the case, Whitman's prose introduction to the first edition, which is written in a style that suggests Emerson's, with his characteristic rhythms, figures of speech, and turns of phrase. As for the ideas Whitman expressed in that style, they are largely developments of what Emerson had said in "The Poet" (first of the *Essays: Second Series,* published in 1844), combined with other notions from Emerson's "Compensation." In "The Poet" Emerson had said:

I look in vain for the poet whom I describe. . . . We have yet had no genius in America, with tyrannous eye, which knew the value of our incomparable materials, and saw, in the barbarism and materialism of the times, another carnival of the same gods whose pictures he so much admires in Homer; then in the Middle Ages; then in Calvinism. . . . Our log-rolling, our stumps and their politics, our fisheries, our Negroes and Indians, our boasts and our repudiations, the wrath of rogues and the pusillanimity of honest men, the northern trade, the southern planting, the western clearing, Oregon and Texas, are yet unsung. Yet America is a poem in our eyes; its ample geography dazzles the imagination, and it will not wait long for meters.

. . . Doubt not, O poet, but persist. Say "It is in me, and shall out." Stand there, balked and dumb, stuttering and stammering, hissed and hooted, stand and strive, until at last rage draws out of thee that *dream*-power which every night shows thee is thine own; a power transcending all limit and privacy, and by virtue of which a man is the conductor of the whole river of electricity.

Whitman, it is clear today, determined to be the poet whom Emerson pictured; he determined to be the genius in America who recognized the value of our incomparable materials, the Northern trade, the Southern planting, and the Western clearing. "The United States themselves are the greatest poem," he wrote, he echoed, in his 1855 introduction, conceived as if in answer to Emerson's summons. He abandoned himself to the nature of things. At first balked and dumb, then later hissed and hooted, he stood there until he had drawn from himself the power he felt in his dreams.

There was, however, still another event that seems to have given Whitman a new conception of his mission as a poet: it was his reading of two novels by George Sand, *The Countess of Rudolstadt* and *The Journeyman Joiner*. Both books were written during their author's socialistic period, before the revolution of 1848, and both were translated from the French by one of the New England Transcendentalists. *The Countess of Rudolstadt* was the sequel of *Consuelo,* which Whitman had described as "the noblest work left by George Sand—the noblest in many respects, on its own field, in all literature." Apparently he gave *Consuelo* and its sequel to his mother when they first appeared in this country, in 1847; and after her death he kept the tattered volumes on his bedside table. It was in the epilogue to *The Countess of Rudolstadt* that Whitman discovered the figure of a wandering musician who might have been taken for a Bohemian peasant except for his fine white hands; who was not only a violinist but a bard and a prophet, expounding the new religion of Humanity; and who, falling into a trance, recited "the most magnificent poem that can be conceived," before traveling onward along the open road. *The Journeyman Joiner* was also listed by Whitman among his favorite books. It is the story—to quote from Esther Shephard, who wrote an interpretation of Whitman based on his debt to the two novels—"of a beautiful, Christlike young carpenter, a proletary philosopher, who dresses in a mechanic's costume but is scrupulously neat and clean. He works at carpentering with his father, but patiently takes time off whenever he wants to in order to read, or give advice on art, or share a friend's affection."

There is no doubt that both books helped to fix the direction of Whitman's thinking. They summarized the revolutionary current of ideas that prevailed in Europe before 1848, and his early poems would be part of that current. But the principal effect of the two novels was on Whitman's picture of himself. After reading them he slowly formed the project of becoming a wandering bard and prophet, like the musician in the epilogue to *The Countess of Rudolstadt*. He no longer planned to get ahead in the world by the means open to other young journalists: no more earning, saving, calculating, outshining. He stopped writing for the magazines and, according to his brother George, he refused some editorial positions that were offered him; instead he worked as a carpenter with his father, like the hero of *The Journeyman Joiner*.

About this time there is an apparent change or mutation in his personality. Whitman as a young editor had dressed correctly, even fastidiously; had trimmed his beard, had carried a light cane, had been rather retiring in his manners, had been on good but not at all intimate terms with his neighbors, and, whenever possible, had kept away from their children. Now suddenly he begins dressing like a Brooklyn mechanic, with his shirt open to reveal a red-flannel undershirt and part of a hairy chest, and with a big felt hat worn loosely over his tousled hair. He lets his beard grow shaggy, he makes his voice more assured, and, in his wanderings about the docks and ferries, he greets his friends with bear hugs and sometimes a kiss of comradeship. It is as if he has undertaken a double task: before creating his poems he has to create a hypothetical author of the poems. And the author bears a new name: not *Walter* Whitman, as he was always known to his family and till then had been called by his newspaper associates, but rather *Walt* Whitman,

> . . . a kosmos, of Manhattan the son,
> Turbulent, fleshy, sensual, eating, drinking and breeding.

The world is his stage and Whitman has assumed a role that he will continue to play for the rest of his life. Reading his letters we can sometimes see him as in a dressing room, arranging his features to make the role convincing. In 1868, for example, he sent his London publisher a long series of directions about how his portrait should be engraved from a favorite photograph (he was always having his picture taken). "If a faithful presentation of that photograph can be given," he said, "it will satisfy me well— of course it should be reproduced with all its shaggy, dappled, rough-skinned character, and not attempted to be smoothed and prettified . . . let the costume be kept very simple and broad, and rather kept down too, little as there is of it—preserve the effect of the sweeping lines making all that fine free angle below the chin. . . . It is perhaps worth your taking special pains about, both to achieve a successful picture and likeness, something characteristic, and as certain to be a marked help to your edition of the book." There is more in the same vein, and it makes us feel that Whitman was like an actor-manager, first having his portrait painted in costume, then hanging it in the lobby to sell more tickets.

He had more than a dash of the charlatanism that, according to Baudelaire, adds a spice to genius. But he had also his own sort of honesty, and he tried to live his part as well as acting it. The new character he assumed was more, far more, than a pose adopted to mislead the public. Partly it was a side of his nature by social conventions, by life with a big family of brothers and sisters, and by the struggle to earn a living. Partly it represented a real change after 1850: the shy and self-centered young man was turning outwards, was trying to people his loneliness with living comrades. Partly it was an attempt to compensate for the absence in himself of qualities he admired in others; for Whitman had already revealed himself as anything but rough, virile, athletic, savage, or luxuriant, to quote a few of what were now his favorite adjectives. Partly his new personality was an ideal picture of himself that he tried to achieve in the flesh and came in time to approximate. You might call it a mask or, as Jung would say, a *persona* that soon had a life of its own, developing and changing with the years and almost superseding his other nature. At the end one could hardly say that a "real" Whitman existed beneath the public figure; the man had become confused with his myth.

2

I am not trying to write a biographical sketch of Whitman but merely to mention some of the events that marked or hastened his readjustment. The Civil War was the greatest of those events, in the poet's life as it was in American history. It put an end to which he could devote himself. At first he wrote newspaper articles and a long poem, "Beat! Beat! Drums!" which he hoped would encourage others to enlist; then he heard that his brother George was wounded and, in December 1862, he paid a visit to the Army of the Potomac. He found when he reached the front that George had recovered; but it was just after the slaughter at Fredericksburg and the hospital tents were crowded with other wounded soldiers lying on the frozen ground. Whitman did the little he could for them; "I cannot leave them," he wrote in his diary. Instead of going back to New York he decided to stay in Washington as a hospital visitor. He said of himself in the best of his Civil War poems, "The Wound-Dresser":

> Arous'd and angry, I'd thought to beat the alarum, and
> urge relentless war,
> But soon my fingers fail'd me, my face droop'd and I
> resign'd myself
> To sit by the wounded and soothe them, or silently
> watch the dead.

Afterwards Whitman liked to imply that he had served among the soldiers during the whole war and that, besides nursing the wounded in Washington hospitals, he had been for long periods at the front. His actual war work was briefer—perhaps two years in all—and less official; it consisted of writing letters for the wounded, making them lemonade in summer, giving them newspapers and small sums of money collected from benevolent persons, and sitting for hours beside the dying. Perhaps his greatest service was simply to be *there,* with his look of large health, at a time when most of the wounded had no visitors and no feeling that their life or death mattered to others. Whitman tried consciously to give them the will to live; and he may have been right in thinking that he had kept scores or hundreds of men from giving up the fight. If they were beyond saving, their last moments were rendered a little less painful by the presence of the red-faced, gray-bearded stranger who looked like the spirit of Fatherhood, but spoke to them as tenderly as their mothers.

Whitman had found a useful and socially recognized expression for the impulses that set him apart from other men. At times he saw Lincoln almost daily as the President rode in a little procession from his summer lodgings to the White House, and they often exchanged bows and glances; so that Whitman felt there was a wordless sympathy between them. "I love the President personally," he wrote in his diary. He had never loved his father in that fashion and had always felt half-orphaned; but now he had found a spiritual father. That was a step in his readjustment; and so too was his friendship with the young horsecar conductor Peter Doyle, whom he met every day after work; for years they lived on terms of calm affection. It was as if, after the unhappy love affair hinted at in some of the "Calamus" poems, Whitman had entered into a sensible marriage.

"I give here a glimpse of him in Washington on a Navy Yard horse car, toward the close of the war, one summer day at sundown," John Burroughs says in *Birds and Poets*. "The car is crowded and suffocatingly hot, with many passengers on the rear platform, and among them a bearded, florid-faced man, elderly but agile, resting against the dash, by the side of the young conductor, and evidently his intimate friend. The man wears a broad-brim white hat," and is Whitman, of course, while the young conductor is probably Peter Doyle. As for Burroughs, the spectator, he describes the scene as if he were taking snapshots with a candid camera:

Among the jam inside the door, a young Englishwoman, of the working class, with two children, has had trouble all the way with the youngest, a strong, fat fretful, bright babe of fourteen or fifteen months, who bids fair to worry the mother completely out, besides becoming a howling nuisance to everybody. As the car tugs around Capitol Hill the young one is more demoniac than ever, and the flushed and perspiring mother is just ready to burst into tears with weariness and vexation. The car stops at the top of the Hill to let off most of the rear platform passengers, and the white-hatted man reaches inside and gently but firmly disengaging the babe from its stifling place in the mother's arms, takes it in his own, and out in the air. The astonished and excited child, partly in fear, partly in satisfaction at the change, stops its screaming, and as the man adjusts it more securely to his breast, plants its chubby hands against him, and pushing off as far as it can, gives a good long look squarely in his face—then as if satisfied snuggles down with its head on his neck, and in less than a minute is sound and peacefully asleep without another whimper, utterly fagged out. A square or so more and the conductor, who has had an unusually hard and uninterrupted day's work, gets off for the first meal and relief since morning. And now the white-hatted man, holding the slumbering babe also, acts as conductor the rest of the distance, keeping his eye on the passengers inside, who have by this time thinned out greatly. He makes a very good conductor, too, pulling the bell to stop or go as needed, and seems to enjoy the occupation. The babe meanwhile rests its fat cheeks close on his neck and gray beard, one of his arms vigilantly surrounding it, while the other signals, from time to time, with the strap; and the flushed mother inside has a good half hour to breathe, and cool, and recover herself.

That is Whitman seen as Proust's narrator saw the Baron de Charlus crossing the courtyard and momentarily assuming the features, expression, and smile of a woman. It is, however, one of the last intimate glimpses we obtain; for another event of his Washington years had made Whitman much more cautious about revealing himself. In January 1865 he had been appointed to a clerkship in the Indian Bureau of the Department of the Interior, a sort of political sinecure. In June of that year the Secretary of the Interior, a professional Methodist named James Harlan, read a copy of *Leaves of Grass* that he found in Whitman's desk, and discharged his clerk as the author of an indecent book. Whitman's friends not only wrote letters and published a pamphlet in his defense, but found him another clerkship, in the Attorney General's office, which he was to hold for the next eight years. Thus, he did not suffer financially from the scandal and it helped in a way to bring his work before the public; but Whitman was frightened, as many other government clerks and administrators have been when they were discharged for their outside activities. After 1865 the prudent side of his nature was uppermost, and he no longer felt, or no longer indulged, his passion for public confession. He became more discreet in his dress, his actions, his language, and even the ideas expressed in his poems. He couldn't ever be a conventional bureaucrat, but nobody seemed to feel any more that he was out of place in a government office.

The stroke of paralysis that he suffered in January 1873 was the end of his active career. His "inexpressibly beloved" mother died four months later, and Whitman in his grief relapsed into a complication of diseases from which he never fully recovered, although he lived on for nineteen years. They were bitter years at first, when he was still hoping to regain his physical strength and his imaginative powers; but then he resigned himself to old age and indolence. He reread his favorite books, he rearranged his poems and wrote new ones on occasional themes; chiefly he occupied himself with the defense of his literary reputation. Camden, where he now lived, had a ferry like Brooklyn and he liked to ride back and forth on it. As his strength declined he assumed a new role, that of the seated Buddha, serene and large in the midst of his infirmities.

When we consider the fate of other poets like Poe, Baudelaire, Nerval, and Hölderlin who tried to explore the subconscious and dreamed immoderate dreams, Whitman in his last years seems amazingly well adjusted. He was now conscious at all times of the social limitations on human conduct. "Be radical, be radical, be not too damned radical" he said to his young friend Horace Traubel. He was shrewd about people, a little sharp in his financial dealings—like an old Long Island farmer—and strong in his family ties; he spent a great deal of time and other people's money in designing a tomb for all the Whitmans. And he enjoyed a sort of success: he lived on a mean street, but in a house he owned; he had money in the bank; his rich admirers sent him barrels of oysters in season and baskets of champagne (he was fond of both); and although his work was still not officially recognized in his own country, he was famous in Europe and had his American disciples to compare him with "a greater than Socrates." Speaking for the last time, I hope, from the clinical point of view, one can say that Whitman in his age had effected a cure of himself and had moved from his private world into a stable relation with society. He is a reassuring, even an inspiring figure: good and gray, but not so much a poet as the effigy on a poet's tomb.

1947

The Buried Masterpiece (excerpts)

The first edition of *Leaves of Grass*, as placed on sale July 4, 1855, bears little outside or inside resemblance to any of the later editions, which kept growing larger as Whitman added new poems. The original work is a thin folio about the size and shape of a block of typewriting paper. The binding is of dark-green pebbled cloth, and the title is stamped in gold, with the rustic letters sending down roots and sprouting above into leaves. Inside the binding are ninety-five printed pages, number iv–xii and 14–95. A prose introduction is set in double columns on the roman-numeraled pages, and the remaining text consists of twelve poems, as compared with 383 in the final or "Deathbed" edition. The first poem, later called "Song of Myself," is longer than the other eleven together. There is no table of contents, and none of the poems has a title.

Another calculated feature of the first edition is that the names of the author and the publisher—actually the same person—are omitted from the title page. Instead the opposite page contains a portrait: the engraved daguerreotype of a bearded man in his middle thirties, slouching under a wide-brimmed and high-crowned black felt hat that has "a rakish kind of slant," as the engraver said later, "like the mast of a schooner." His right hand is resting nonchalantly on his hip; the left is hidden in the pocket of his coarse-woven trousers. He wears no coat or waistcoat, and his shirt is thrown wide open at the collar to reveal a burly neck and the top of what seems to be a red-flannel undershirt. It is the portrait of a devil-may-care American workingman, one who might be taken as a somewhat idealized figure in almost any crowd.

His full name, though missing on the title page, appears twice in the first edition, but in different forms. On the copyright page we read, "*Entered according to Act of Congress in the year 1855, by* WALTER WHITMAN. . . ." On page 29, almost in the middle of the long first poem, we are introduced to "Walt Whitman, an American, one of the roughs, a kosmos." When a law-abiding citizen, even one of the roughs, changes his name even slightly, it is often because he wishes to assume a new personality. A reader might infer that *Walter* Whitman is the journeyman printer who had become a hack journalist, then a newspaper editor, before being lost to sight; whereas *Walt* Whitman is the workingman of the portrait and the putative author—but actual hero—of this extraordinary book.

No other book in the history of American letters was so completely an individual or do-it-yourself project. Not only did Whitman choose his idealized or dramatized self as subject of the book; not only did he create the new style in which it was written (working hard and intelligently to perfect the style over a period of six or seven years), but he also created the new personality of the proletarian bard who was supposed to have done the writing. When a manuscript of the poems was ready in the spring of 1855, Whitman's work was only beginning. He designed the book and arranged to have it printed at a job-printing shop in Brooklyn. He set some of the type himself, not without making errors. He did his best to get the book distributed, with the lukewarm cooperation of his friends the Fowler brothers, whose specialty was not bookselling but water cures and phrenology. He was his own press agent and even volunteered as critic of the book, writing three—or a majority—of the favorable reviews it received.

In spite of his best efforts not many copies were sold, and the first edition has not been widely read, except in the special world of literary scholars. The author himself might have been forgotten, if it had not been for a single fortunate event. One copy—not in pebbly green cloth, but paperbound—had been sent to Emerson, who was the most widely respected American of letters and the man best qualified to understand what the new poet was saying. Emerson wrote a letter of heartfelt thanks. When the letter was printed in the New York *Tribune*—without the writer's permission—it amazed and horrified the little American republic of letters. Nobody agreed with Emerson except a few of the extreme Transcendentalists, notably Thoreau and Alcott. Whitman was almost universally condemned, at least for the next ten years, but he would never again be merely a call in the midst of the crowd.

Concord   21 July
Masstts 1855

Dear Sir,

I am not blind to the worth of the wonderful gift of "Leaves of Grass." I find it the most extraordinary piece of wit & wisdom that America has yet contributed. I am very happy in reading it, as great power makes us happy. It meets the demand I am always making of what seemed the sterile & stingy Nature, as if too much handiwork or too much lymph in the temperament were making our western wits fat & mean. I give you joy of your free & brave thought. I have great joy in it. I find incomparable things said incomparably well, as they must be. I find the courage of treatment, which so delights us, & which large perception only can inspire. I greet you at the beginning of a great career, which yet must have a long foreground somewhere, for such a start. I rubbed my eyes a little to see if this sunbeam were no illusion; but the solid sense of the book is a sober certainty. It has the best merits, namely, of fortifying & encouraging.

I did not know until I, last night, saw the book advertised in a newspaper, that I could trust the name as real & available for a post-office. I wish to see my benefactor, & have felt much like striking my tasks, & visiting New York to pay you my respects.

R. W. Emerson

Mr. Walter Whitman.

Emerson was being impulsive for a Concord man, but he was also trying to make his phrases accurate. Later, disapproving of Whitman's conduct, he would change his mind about the "great career." He would not and could not feel that most of the poems written after 1855 contained "incomparable things said incomparably well." But his praise of the first edition was unqualified, and it tempts me to make some unqualified statements of my own, as of simple truths that should have been recognized long ago.

First statement: that the long opening poem, later miscalled "Song of Myself," is Whitman's greatest work, perhaps his one completely realized work, and one of the great poems of modern times. Second, that the other eleven poems of the first edition are not on the same level of realization, but nevertheless are examples of Whitman's freshest and boldest style. At least four of them—their titles in the Deathbed edition are "To Think of Time," "The Sleepers," "I Sing the Body Electric," and "There Was a Child Went Forth"—belong in any selection of his best poems. Third, that the text of the first edition is the purest text for "Song of Myself," since many of the later corrections were also corruptions of the style and concealments of the original meaning. Fourth, that it is likewise the best text for most of the other eleven poems, but especially for "The Sleepers"—that fantasia of the unconscious—and "I Sing the Body Electric." And a final statement: that the first edition is a unified work, unlike any later edition, that it gives us a different picture of Whitman's achievement, and that—considering its very small circulation through the years—it might be called the buried masterpiece of American writing.

All that remains is to document some of these statements, not point by point, but chiefly in relation to "Song of Myself."

2

The poem is hardly at all concerned with American nationalism, political democracy, contemporary progress, or other social themes that are commonly associated with Whitman's work. The "incomparable things" that Emerson found in it are philosophical and religious principles. Its subject is a state of illumination induced by two (or three) separate moments of ecstasy. In more or less narrative sequence it describes those moments, their sequels in life, and the doctrines to which they give rise. The doctrines are not expounded by logical steps or supported by arguments; instead they are presented dramatically, that is, as the new convictions of a hero and they are revealed by successive unfoldings of his states of mind.

The hero as pictured in the frontispiece—this hero named "I" or "Walt Whitman" in the text—should not be confused with the Whitman of daily life. He is, as I said, a dramatized or idealized figure, and he is put forward as a representative American workingman, but one who prefers to loaf and invite his soul. Thus, he is rough, sunburned, bearded; he cocks his hat as he pleases, indoors or out; but in the text of the first edition he has no local or family background, and he is deprived of strictly individual characteristics, with the exception of curiosity, boastfulness, and an abnormally developed sense of touch. His really distinguishing feature is that he has been granted a vision, as a result of which he has realized the potentialities latent in every American and indeed, he says, in every living person, even "the brutish koboo, called the ordure of humanity." This dramatization of the hero makes it possible for the living Whitman to exalt him—as he would not have ventured, at the time, to exalt himself—but also to poke mild fun at the hero for his gab and loitering, for his tall talk or "omnivorous words," and for sounding his barbaric yawp over the roofs of the world. The religious feeling in "Song of Myself" is counterpoised by a humor that takes the form of slangy and mischievous impudence or drawling Yankee self-ridicule.

There has been a good deal of discussion about the structure of the poem. In spite of revealing analyses made by a few Whitman scholars, notably Carl F. Strauch and James E. Miller, Jr., a feeling still seems to prevail that it has no structure properly speaking, that it is inspired but uneven, repetitive, and especially weak in its transitions from one theme to another. I suspect that much of this feeling may be due to Whitman's later changes in the text, including his arbitrary scheme, first introduced in the 1867 edition, of dividing the poem into fifty-two numbered paragraphs or chants. One is tempted to read the chants as if they were separate poems, thus overlooking the unity and flow of the work as a whole. It may also be, however, that most of the scholars have been looking for a geometrical pattern, such as can be found and diagramed in some of the later poems. If there is no such pattern in "Song of Myself," that is because the poem was written on a different principle, one much closer to the spirit of the Symbolists or even the Surrealists.

The true structure of the poem is not primarily logical but psychological, and is not a geometrical figure but a musical progression. As music "Song of Myself" is not a symphony with contrasting movements, nor is it an operatic work like "Out of the Cradle Endlessly Rocking," with an overture, arias, recitatives, and a finale. It comes closer to being a rhapsody or tone poem, one that modulates from theme to theme, often changing in key and tempo, falling into reveries and rising toward moments of climax, but always preserving its unity of feeling as it moves onward in a wavelike flow. It is a poem that bears the marks of having been conceived as a whole and written in one prolonged burst of inspiration, but its unity is also the result of conscious art, as can be seen from Whitman's corrections in the early manuscripts. He did not recognize all the bad lines, some of which survive in the printed text, but there is no line in the first edition that seems false to a single prevailing tone. There are passages weaker than others, but none without a place in the general scheme. The repetitions are always musical variations and amplifications. Some of the transitions seem abrupt when the poem is read as if it were an essay, but Whitman was not working in terms of "therefore" and "however." He preferred to let one image suggest another image, which in turn suggests a new statement of mood or doctrine. His themes modulate into one another by pure association, as in a waking dream, with the result that all his transitions seem instinctively right.

In spite of these oneiric elements, the form of the poem is something more than a forward movement in rising and subsiding waves of emotion. There is also a firm narrative structure, one that becomes easier to grasp when we start by dividing the poem into a number of parts or sequences. I think there are nine of these, but the exact number is not important; another critic might say there were seven (as Professor Miller does), or eight or ten. Some of the transitions are gradual, and in such cases it is hard to determine the exact line that ends one sequence and starts another. The essential point is that the parts, however defined, follow one another in irreversible order, like the beginning, middle, and end of any good narrative. My own outline, not necessarily final, would run as follows:

First sequence (chants 1–4): the poet or hero introduced to his audience. Learning and loafing at his ease, "observing a spear of summer grass," he presents himself as a man who lives outdoors and worships his own naked body, not the least part of which is vile. He is also in love with his deeper self or soul, but explains that it is not to be confused with his mere personality. His joyful contentment can be shared by you, the listener, "For every atom belonging to me as good belongs to you."

Second sequence (chant 5): the ecstasy. This consists in the rapt union of the poet and his soul, and it is described—figuratively, on the present occasion—in terms of sexual union. The poet now has a sense of loving brotherhood with God and with all mankind. His eyes being truly open for the first time, he sees that even the humblest objects contain the infinite universe—

> And limitless are leaves stiff or drooping in the fields,
> And brown ants in little wells beneath them,
> And mossy scabs of the wormfence, and heaped stones,
>   and elder and mullen and pokeweed.

Third sequence (chants 6–19): the grass. Chant 6 starts with one of Whitman's brilliant transitions. A child comes with both hands full of those same leaves from the fields. "What is the grass?" the child asks—and suddenly we are presented with the central image of the poem, that is, the grass as symbolizing the miracle of common things and the divinity (which implies both the equality and the immortality) of ordinary persons. During the remainder of the sequence, the poet observes men and women—and animals too—at their daily occupations. He is part of this life, he says, and even his thoughts are those of all men in all ages and lands. There are two things to be noted about the sequence, which contains some of Whitman's freshest lyric. First, the people with a few exceptions (such as the trapper and his bride) are those whom Whitman has known all his life, while the scenes described at length are Manhattan streets and Long Island beaches or countryside. Second, the poet merely roams, watches, and listens, like a sort of Tiresias. The keynote of the sequence—as Professor Strauch was the first to explain—is the two words, "I observe."

Fourth sequence (chants 20–25): the poet in person. "Hankering, gross, mystical nude," he venerates himself as august and immortal, but so, he says, is everyone else. He is the poet of the body and of the soul, of night, earth, and sea, and of vice and feebleness as well as virtue, so that "many long dumb voices" speak through his lips, including those of slaves, prostitutes, even beetles rolling balls of dung. All life to him is such a miracle of beauty that the sunrise would kill him if he could not find expression for it—"If I could not now and always send sunrise out of me." The sequence ends with a dialogue between the poet and his power of speech, during which the poet insists that his deeper self—"the best I am"—is beyond expression.

Fifth sequence (chants 26–29): ecstasy through the senses. Beginning with chant 26, the poem sets out in a new direction. The poet decides to be completely passive: "I think I will do nothing for a long time but listen." What he hears at first are quiet familiar sounds like the gossip of flames on the hearth and the bustle of growing wheat; but the sounds rise quickly to a higher pitch, becoming the matchless voice of a trained soprano, and he is plunged into an ecstasy of hearing, or rather of Being. Then he starts over again, still passively, with the sense of touch, and finds himself rising to the ecstasy of sexual union. This time the union is actual, not figurative, as can be seen from the much longer version of chant 29 preserved in an early notebook.

Sixth sequence (chants 30–38): the power of identification. After his first ecstasy, as presented in chant 5, the poet had acquired a sort of microscopic vision that enabled him to find infinite wonders in the smallest and most familiar things. The second ecstasy (or pair of ecstasies) has an entirely different effect, conferring as it does a sort of vision that is both telescopic and spiritual. The poet sees far into space and time; "afoot with my vision" he ranges over the continent and goes speeding through the heavens among tailed meteors. His secret is the power of identification. Since everything emanates from the universal soul, and since his own soul is of the same essence, he can identify himself with every object and with every person living or dead, heroic or criminal. Thus, he is massacred with the Texans at Goliad, he fights on the *Bonhomme Richard,* he dies on the cross, and he rises again as "one of an average unending procession." Whereas the keynote of the third sequence was "I observe," here it becomes "I am"—"I am a free companion"—"My voice is the wife's voice, the screech by the rail of the stairs"—"I am the man. . . . I suffered. . . . I was there."

Seventh sequence (chants 39–41): the superman. When Indian sages emerge from the state of samadhi or absorption, they often have the feeling of being omnipotent. It is so with the poet, who now feels gifted with superhuman powers. He is the universally beloved Answerer (chant 39), then the Healer, raising men from their deathbeds (40), and then the Prophet (41) of a new religion that outbids "the cautious hucksters" by announcing that men are divine and will eventually be gods.

Eighth sequence (chants 42–50): the sermon. "A call in the midst of the crowd" is the poet's voice, "orotund sweeping and final." He is about to offer a statement of the doctrines implied by the narrative (but note that his statement comes at the right point psychologically and plays its part in the narrative sequence). As strangers listen, he proclaims that society is full of injustice, but that the reality beneath it is deathless persons (chant 42); that he accepts and practices all religions, but looks beyond them to "what is untried and afterward" (43); that he and his listeners are the fruit of ages, and the seed of untold ages to be (44); that our final goal is appointed: "God will be there and wait till we come" (45); that he tramps a perpetual journey and longs for companions, to whom he will reveal a new world by washing the gum from their eyes—but each must then continue the journey alone (46); that he is the teacher of men who work in the open air (47); that he is not curious about God, but sees God everywhere, at every moment (48); that we shall all be reborn in different forms ("No doubt I have died myself ten thousand times before"); and that the evil in the world is like moonlight, a mere reflection of the sun (49). The end of the sermon (chant 50) is the hardest passage to interpret in the whole poem. I think, though I cannot be certain, that the poet is harking back to the period after one of his ten thousand deaths, when he slept and slept long before his next awakening. He seems to remember vague shapes, and he beseeches these Outlines, as he calls them, to let him reveal the "word unsaid." Then turning back to his audience, "It is not chaos or death," he says. "It is form and union and plan. . . . it is eternal life. . . . it is happiness."

Ninth sequence (chants 51–52): the poet's farewell. Having finished his sermon, the poet gets ready to depart, that is, to die and wait for another incarnation or "fold of the future," while still inviting others to follow. At the beginning of the poem he had been leaning and loafing at ease in the summer grass. Now, having rounded the circle, he bequeaths himself to the dirt "to grow from the grass I love." I do not see how any careful reader, unless blinded with preconceptions, could overlook the unity of the poem in tone and image and direction.

3

It is in the eighth sequence, which is a sermon, that Whitman gives us most of the doctrines suggested by his mystical experience, but they are also implied in the rest of the poem and indeed in the whole text of the first edition. Almost always he expresses them in the figurative and paradoxical language that prophets have used from the beginning. Now I should like to state them explicitly, even at the cost of some repetition.

Whitman believed when he was writing "Song of Myself"—and at later periods too, but with many changes in emphasis—that there is a distinction between one's mere personality and the deeper Self (or between ego and soul). He believed that the Self (or atman, to use a Sanskrit word), is of the same essence as the universal spirit (though he did not quite say it *is* the universal spirit, as Indian philosophers do in the phrase "Atman is Brahman"). He believed that true knowledge is to be acquired not through the senses or the intellect, but through union with the Self. At such moments of union (or "merge," as Whitman called it) the gum is washed from one's eyes (that is his own phrase), and one can read an infinite lesson in common things, discovering that a mouse, for example, "is miracle enough to stagger sextillions of infidels." This true knowledge is available to every man and woman, since each conceals a divine Self. Moreover, the divinity of all implies the perfect equality of all, the immortality of all, and the universal duty of loving one another.

Immortality for Whitman took the form of metempsychosis, and he believed that every individual will be reborn, usually but not always in a higher form. He had also worked out for himself something approaching the Indian notion of karma, which is the doctrine that actions performed during one incarnation determine the nature and fate of the individual during his next incarnation; the doctrine is emphatically if somewhat unclearly stated in a passage of his prose introduction that was later rewritten as a poem, "Song of Prudence." By means of metempsychosis and karma, we are all involved in a process of spiritual evolution that might be compared to natural evolution. Even the latter process, however, was not regarded by Whitman as strictly natural or material. He believed that animals have a rudimentary sort of soul ("They bring me tokens of myself"), and he hinted or surmised, without directly saying, that rocks, trees, and plants possess an identity, or "eidólon," that persists as they rise to higher states of being. The double process of evolution, natural and spiritual, can be traced for ages into the past, and he believed that it will continue for ages beyond ages. Still it is not an eternal process, since it has an ultimate goal, which appears to be the reabsorption of all things into the Divine Ground.

Most of Whitman's doctrines, though by no means all of them, belong to the mainstream of Indian philosophy. In some respects he went against the stream. Unlike most of the Indian sages, for example, he was not a thoroughgoing idealist. He did not believe that the whole world of the senses, of desires, of birth and death, was only maya, illusion, nor did he hold that it was a sort of purgatory; instead he praised the world as real and joyful. He did not despise the body, but proclaimed that it was as miraculous as the soul. He was too good a citizen of the nineteenth century to surrender his faith in material progress as the necessary counterpart of spiritual progress. Although he yearned for ecstatic union with the soul or Oversoul, he did not try to achieve it by subjugating the senses, as advised by yogis and Buddhists alike; on the contrary, he thought the "merge" could also be achieved (as in chants 26–29) by a total surrender to the senses. These are important differences, but it must be remembered that Indian philosophy or theology is not such a unified structure as it appears to us from a distance. Whitman might have found Indian sages or gurus and even whole sects that agreed with one or another of his heterodoxies (perhaps excepting his belief in material progress). One is tempted to say that instead of being a Christian heretic, he was an Indian rebel and sectarian.

Sometimes he seems to be a Mahayana Buddhist, promising nirvana for all after countless reincarnations, and also sharing the belief of some Mahayana sects that the sexual act can serve as one of the sacraments. At other times he might be an older brother of Sri Ramakrishna (1836–1886), the nineteenth-century apostle of Tantric Brahmanism and of joyous affirmation. Although this priest of Kali, the Mother Goddess, refused to learn English, one finds him delivering some of Whitman's messages in—what is more surprising—the same tone of voice. Read, for example, this fairly typical passage from *The Gospel of Sri Ramakrishna,* while remembering that "Consciousness" is to be taken here as a synonym for Divinity:

The Divine Mother revealed to me in Kali temple that it was She who had become everything. She showed me that everything was full of Consciousness. The Image was Consciousness, the altar was Consciousness, the water-vessels were Consciousness, the door-sill was Consciousness, the marble floor was Consciousness—all was Consciousness. . . . I saw a wicked man in front of the Kali temple; but in him I saw the Power of the Divine Mother vibrating. That was why I fed a cat with the food that was to be offered to the Divine Mother.

Whitman expresses the same idea at the end of chant 48, and in the same half-playful fashion:

> Why should I wish to see God better than this day?
> I see something of God each hour of the twenty-four,
>   and each moment then,
> In the faces of men and women I see God, and in my
>   own face in the glass;
> I find letters from God dropped in the street, and every
>   one is signed by God's name,
> And I leave them where they are, for I know that others
>   will punctually come forever and ever.

Such parallels—and there are dozens that might be quoted—are more than accidental. They reveal a kinship in thinking and experience that can be of practical value to students of Whitman. Since the Indian mystical philosophies are elaborate structures, based on conceptions that have been shaped and defined by centuries of discussion, they help to explain Whitman's ideas at points in the first edition where he seems at first glance to be vague or self-contradictory. There is, for example, his unusual combination of realism—sometimes brutal realism—and serene optimism. Today he is usually praised for the first, blamed for the second (optimism being out of fashion), and blamed still more for the inconsistency he showed in denying the existence of evil. The usual jibe is that Whitman thought the universe was perfect and was getting better every day.

It is obvious, however, that he never meant to deny the existence of evil in himself or his era or his nation. He knew that it existed in his own family, where one of his brothers was a congenital idiot, another was a drunkard married to a streetwalker, and still another, who had caught "the bad disorder," later died of general paresis in an insane asylum. Whitman's doctrine implied that each of them would have an opportunity to avoid those misfortunes or punishments in another incarnation, where each would be rewarded for his good actions. The universe was an eternal becoming for Whitman, a process not a structure, and it had to be judged from the standpoint of eternity. After his mystical experience, which seemed to offer a vision of eternity, he had become convinced that evil existed only as part of a universally perfect design. That explains his combination of realism and optimism, which seems unusual only in our Western world. In India, Heinrich Zimmer says, "Philosophic theory, religious belief, and intuitive experience support each other . . . in the basic insight that, fundamentally, all is well. A supreme optimism prevails everywhere, in spite of the unromantic recognition that the universe of man's affairs is in the most imperfect state imaginable, one amounting practically to chaos."

Another point explained by Indian conceptions is the sort of democracy Whitman was preaching in "Song of Myself." There is no doubt that he was always a democrat politically—which is to say a Jacksonian Democrat, a Barnburner writing editorials against the Hunkers, a Free Soiler in sympathy, and then a liberal but not a radical Republican. He remained faithful to what he called "the good old cause" of liberty, equality, and fraternity, and he wrote two moving elegies for the European rebels of 1848. In "Song of Myself," however, he is not advocating rebellion or even reform. "To a drudge of the cottonfields," he says, "or emptier of privies I lean. . . . on his right cheek I put the family kiss"; but he offers nothing more than a kiss and an implied promise. What he preaches throughout the poem is not political but religious democracy, such as was practiced by the early Christians. Today it is practiced, at least in theory, by the Tantric sect of Buddhism.

The promise that Whitman offers to the drudge of the cottonfields, the emptier of privies, and the prostitute draggling her shawl is that they too can set out with him on his perpetual journey—perhaps not in their present incarnations, but at least in some future life. And that leads to another footnote offered by the Indian philosophies: they explain what the poet meant by the Open Road. It starts as an actual road that winds through fields and cities, but Whitman is doing more than inviting us to shoulder our duds and go hiking along it. The real journey is toward spiritual vision, toward reunion with the Divine Ground; and thus the Open Road becomes Whitman's equivalent for all the other roads and paths and ways that appear in mystical teachings. It reminds us of the Noble Eightfold Path of the Buddhists, and the Taoist Way; it suggests both the *bhakti-marga* or "path of devotion" and the *karma-marga* or "path of sacrifice"; while it comes closer to being the "big ferry" of the Mahayana sect, in which there is room for every soul to cross to the farther shore. Whitman's conception, however, was even broader. He said one should know "the universe itself as a road, as many roads, as roads for traveling souls."

I am not pleading for the acceptance of Whitman's ideas or for any other form of mysticism, Eastern or Western. I am only suggesting that his ideas as expressed in "Song of Myself" were bolder and more coherent than is generally supposed, and philosophically a great deal more respectable.

1959

The Real Horatio Alger Story

There is a myth embodied in the very name of Horatio Alger, Jr. It is of course the myth of the poor boy Struggling Upward from Rags to Riches by Luck and Pluck, goaded on by a boyish determination to Strive and Succeed. Anyone born in the slums who becomes a captain of industry or merchandising is sure to be labeled an Alger hero. But the myth embodied in Alger's name, the American dream of success, is not the myth we find in his books for boys—if we read them attentively—and it is certainly not embodied in the career of the author.

About that career we find surprisingly little that is known beyond question. The biography of Alger by Herbert R. Mayes (1928) was written when Mayes was a very young man and is full of errors at the few points where it can be compared with dependable information from other sources. Much of it is based on Alger's private diaries, which have vanished since Mayes used them. Nobody knows how many books Alger wrote. Mayes compiled a list of 119 titles, and there are later lists of 135 and 143.* But the only volume of *Who's Who in America* that appeared during Alger's lifetime tells a different story. Presumably Alger himself—or, if he was too ill at the time, his married sister, who was nursing him—had a chance to correct the entry that follows his name, and part of it reads:

Author: Ragged Dick series, Tattered Tom series, Luck and Pluck series, Atlantic and Pacific series, etc., in all about 70 books, mostly juveniles, of which nearly 800,000 have been sold.

Alger died in 1899, the same year that the entry appeared, but dozens of books attributed to him were published afterward, in some cases as late as 1909. The explanation seems to be that a publisher bought the right to use Alger's name, then signed it to other juveniles that were actually the work of men he employed on a weekly salary. Nobody knows which, if any, of the later books are Alger's. Nobody knows how many copies were printed of the whole aggregation. "More than 100,000,000 copies sold!" exclaims

---

*The standard bibliography by Frank Gruber (The *Antiquarian Bookman,* November 13, 1948) lists 106 Alger books that Gruber thinks are his own work, plus eleven others presumably written by Edward Stratemeyer (although Stratemeyer once denied their authorship), and 17 books of which the authorship cannot be traced, although they were published under Alger's name—a grand total of 134.

the jacket of *Struggling Upward and Other Works,* a collection of four Alger novels that appeared in 1945. "They sold close to 200,000,000 copies, I am told," says Russel Crouse in his introduction to the same volume. Both figures are wildly implausible. It is true that Alger's books and those attributed to him were intensively merchandised after his death; they were priced as low as ten cents in paper and thirty-five cents in cloth; but it seems unlikely that their total sale was more than fifteen million, at a generous estimate.

No, Alger was not "the most widely read author of the ages," as his biographer insists on calling him, but he was faithfully read by a very wide audience. There must have been at least a million American boys who pictured themselves as Alger heroes. Over a period of forty years or more, boys collected Alger books and swapped them back and forth like tops or jackknives; his dreams had become a standard currency. Thousands of boys wrote to the author for advice, since they had come to regard him as a model of business acumen and avuncular wisdom. They would have been surprised to learn that Mr. Alger, in life, had been a most unhappy boy and that he had never grown up.

He was born in Revere, Massachusetts, on January 13, 1832 (to follow Mayes, who I suspect is right in this case; reference books give the year as 1834). He was the son of a Unitarian minister whose church was in neighboring Chelsea. "His name will be Horatio, after me," the father said, "not as a concession to any vanity of mine, but rather as a reminder to him that I shall expect him to continue the religious endeavors I have begun." Horatio Sr. tyrannized over the boy, made him read Plato and Josephus in translation at the age of eight (besides *Jack the Giant Killer*), and taught him Latin at nine. When visitors came to the parsonage, the father would ask him, "What are you going to be, Horatio?" The boy would bring his heels together and recite, "I shall be a t-teacher of the ways of God, a p-preacher of His commandments, a wiberal thinker, a woyal citizen." His schoolmates at Gates Academy called him Holy Horatio.

At Harvard he was the smallest man (five feet two) in the class of 1852, ranked tenth in his studies—he excelled in French and the classics—and wrote the class ode. He fell in love with a girl named Patience Stires, but Horatio Sr. persuaded her to break the engagement. During his senior year, Horatio Jr. noted in his diary, "Am reading *Moby Dick,*" which had been published in November, "and find it exciting. What a thrilling life the literary must be! . . . Would it be possible for me to take up writing as a life work? The satisfaction resulting from the beautiful story must be inspiring—a story that rouses readers to a new sense of the fine things of life." From that moment Alger determined not to follow his father into the pulpit.

His first steps toward a literary career were teaching in boys' schools, writing pieces for the Boston papers, then helping to edit a new magazine that lasted only a few weeks. Left without resources, he surrendered to his father and entered the Harvard Divinity School. But he rebelled again on graduation day; having received a legacy from an eccentric old gentleman whom he had once befriended, he hurried off to Paris. There he became the lover of a cabaret singer named Elise Morgue. Elise had literary tastes: she worshiped the godlike Hugo and adored the author of *Scènes de la Vie de Bohême*. When Murger died at an early age—that was in January 1861— she and her lover sat in a café holding hands, the tears streaming down their cheeks.

Soon Alger sailed home, partly because his legacy was spent, but also to escape his second mistress, an English harpy who had snatched him away from Elise. On three occasions he tried to enlist in the Union army; twice he broke his arm before being enrolled, and the third time he nearly died of pneumonia. He was rescued by his father, who finally prevailed on him to be ordained. In December 1864, he became pastor of the little Unitarian church at Brewster, on Cape Cod, where his congregation regarded him as "gentle, solicitous of the welfare of others, and humble as it behooves one of the Lord's servants to be." But he hadn't forgotten literary ambitions, and he spent much of his time writing novels for boys—his Campaign Series—instead of sermons. After less than two years he resigned his pastorate and went to New York to dream of unfading laurels while leading the life of a needy hack.

His next novel for boys, *Ragged Dick,* deals with the rise to respectability of a homeless bootblack. There were thousands like him in New York after the Civil War, when drummer boys and war orphans ran wild in the city streets, much as the little *besprizorni* did in Moscow after the Russian Revolution. Alger's book attracted wide attention when it was serialized in a boys' magazine edited by the famous Oliver Optic. The superintendent of the Newsboys' Lodging House, Charles O'Connor, sought him out, gave him a room in the House, and became his closest friend for thirty years, besides providing him with what he regarded as his real home. A Boston publisher, A. K. Loring, offered him a contract for six books about Ragged Dick and his friends, all to be written in twenty months. After that, Alger thought, he would stop writing juveniles. "It will not be long," he told a Cambridge acquaintance in 1871, "before I get started on a novel that I hope will find a place in the company of fine writing." Ten years later he wrote to his Harvard classmate Addison Brown, "I must separate myself from juvenile fiction long enough to write a lasting work. As soon as a suitable theme appears, you may be certain I will seize it and permanently give up the line in which I have till now been engaged."

Meanwhile Alger was trying to live in the fashion of the romantic novelists he had seen from a distance in Paris. He sometimes disguised himself in a long cape and a tousled wig and wandered through the Manhattan streets—looking for material, he said. In his room with a thick carpet on the floor—not the room in the Newsboys' Lodging House—with reams of paper and dozens of sharp pencils on the desk, and a little bust of Shakespeare on the mantelpiece, he paced the floor in an artist's smock and waited for inspiration like Captain Ahab on the lookout for the white whale. One spring evening during his second visit to Paris, the inspiration came, and Alger worked on his great novel most of the night. In the morning he sent an urgent message to Una Garth, a married woman with whom he had fallen in love. She wrote in her diary, as transcribed by Mayes, "I spent the afternoon with Horatio and read the opening paragraphs of his *Tomorrow.* May the Lord spare the man from a knowledge of his own incapacity!" Mrs. Garth did not completely spare him that knowledge, and Alger put aside the great book while he wrote another juvenile, *Struggling Upward,* which turned out to be the dead mean and average of all his books for boys. Then, tired of wrestling with the Muse and rejected by Mrs. Garth, he temporarily lost his mind and was carried screaming to a hospital.

When Alger recovered, he once again took refuge with Charles O'Connor and continued writing books for boys. At the Newsboys' Lodging House he acted as chaplain and also, within his limited resources, as a general patron of the institution. He helped to set hundreds of homeless boys up in business by giving each of them a blacking box or a bundle of newspapers. A very few of his novels were written with a social purpose. Thus, *Phil the Fiddler,* one of the four reprinted in 1945, is a memorial to the crusade that Alger led against the *padrone* system, by which hundreds of street musicians brought to New York from southern Italy were kept as virtual slaves. Their parents sold them to a *padrone,* who fed them scantily, lodged them in cellars, beat them, and took their earnings. The book helped to make the system illegal. *Jed, the Poorhouse Boy,* also reprinted in 1945, was intended to call attention to the plight of pauper children, and its early chapters bear a wraithlike resemblance to *Oliver Twist.* Jed himself is something of a scapegrace and has a sharper tongue than Alger's other heroes, besides an even greater talent for finding rich protectors. Skeptical readers might call the book *A Fagot's Progress.* But Phil and Jed are his boldest experiments in character, and most of his other heroes are stamped from the same metal with the same patented Alger die.

As the books tumbled out, they attracted wide attention; letters for Alger poured into the Newsboys' Lodging House from all parts of the country. But the books did not earn much money for their author, who, at the height of his reputation, still had to piece out his income by tutoring schoolboys in French and Latin. (A future justice of the Supreme Court, Benjamin N. Cardozo, was one of his pupils.) The trouble seems to have been that Alger never learned to be a businessman on the model of his heroes, and that he sold many of his books outright for modest sums instead of demanding royalties. Finally he made what might be called the ultimate sacrifice for an author by selling the right to use his name. There is no record of the transaction, except the dozens of Alger books that appeared after his death, most of which are obviously the work of other imaginations. One would guess, however, that the sale took place during a period of ill health and despondency that followed the death of Charles O'Connor; perhaps in 1896, before Alger retired to Natick, Massachusetts, to be nursed by his married sister. Together with the use of his name, he was selling his dream of being inspired to produce a novel "that I hope will find a place in the company of fine writing."

What he left behind him was his bartered name—that and his own books for boys, which can be read with some interest even today. Boys of the new generation never ask for them, but like them well enough if they come across a stray copy. The style is formal to the point of burlesque, but correct except for a few Yankeeisms ("considerable" as an adverb, for example) and absolutely clear; it shows the results of Alger's classical training. The chapters are short and consist chiefly of dialogue, which is sometimes so innocent that it acquires a double meaning. ("I want to show you some engravings," says the rich Miss Davenport to the hero of *Tom Temple's Career.*) Still, the dialogue moves rapidly and is not without conscious humor of the sort one used to hear when boys were talking together outside a village store. Here is a fair sample from *Ragged Dick*:

One of the boys, a rather supercilious-looking young gentleman, genteelly dressed, and evidently having a very high opinion of his dress and himself, turned suddenly to Dick and remarked:
"I've seen you before."
"Oh, have you?" said Dick, whirling around; "then p'r'aps you'd like to see me behind."
At this unexpected answer all the boys burst into a laugh with the exception of the questioner, who evidently considered that Dick had been disrespectful.
"I've seen you somewhere," he said in a surly tone, correcting himself.
"Most likely you have," said Dick. "That's where I generally keep myself."

Humor apart, the Alger books offer a curious picture of American culture after the Civil War. In the rather bleak world to which they introduce us, there is no art whatever, except that sometimes a young girl plays "Hearts and Flowers" on a square piano. There is no learning beyond the ability to read and cipher and, as all his heroes do, to write a flowing hand. There is no history: it is as if New York and the whole country from New

England to the California diggings had been created overnight, with the excavations raw and the scaffolding still in place. Though Alger was an ordained clergyman, there is hardly a trace of religious feeling in his novels. Some of the heroes go to Sunday school, like Ragged Dick, but that is only because one of the teachers is a rich merchant who might help them to rise in the world. Here, from a book called *Hector's Inheritance,* is a sample of Alger's moral teaching:

> "Have you any taste for any kind of liquor?"
> "No, sir," answered Hector promptly.
> "Even if you had, do you think you would have self-control enough to avoid entering saloons and gratifying your tastes?"
> "Yes, sir."
> "That is well. Do you play pool?"
> "No sir," answered Hector, wondering whither all these questions tended.
> "I ask because playing pool in public places paves the way for intemperance, as bars are generally connected with such establishments."

Playing pool is also a form of idleness, which leads to stealing, which sometimes leads to jail, but more often to poverty, the hell to which villains are assigned by his Yankee theology. His heaven is simply earning or being given a fortune (but always a modest one, for Alger himself had simple desires and a perfect ignorance of financial practices). Still, everything in his world has its cash value, and a boy who earns ten dollars a week rightly considers himself twice as good as a boy who earns five dollars a week. When the hero of *Tom Temple's Career* loses his inheritance of forty thousand dollars—Alger always gives an exact figure—he isn't in the least surprised that his guardian turns him out into the world or that his rich friends the Davenports ask him never to enter their house again. "Tom had always understood that they cared for him only because he was rich," the author explains, "and he was neither astonished nor disappointed at the change which had come over them." Elsewhere the author exclaims, "How gold reveals the virtues of those about us!" Even a beloved child has its price in gold. When Mr. Rockwell's only son falls overboard from the Brooklyn ferry (in *Ragged Dick*), he cries from the depths of his anguish, "My child! Who will save my child? A thousand—ten thousand dollars to anyone who will save him!" Dick plunges into the East River, thus achieving fame and what Alger regarded as a fortune.

The world of his novels is full of bullies, petty thieves, and confidence men. Even in the New England villages where most of his heroes are born, the leading citizen is likely to be a dishonest banker who steals the property of widows and orphans. Yet the same villages have their benevolent doctors, their self-sacrificing mothers; and the sturdy little hero, left homeless in the streets of New York, is certain to find a kind old merchant who buys him clothes and a watch. For all its bleakness, Alger's world is suffused with the optimism and faith in human nature of America in the Gilded Age. It is also suffused with a deep feeling of equality: family doesn't matter, trade or profession doesn't matter, national origin matters a little, but not a great deal; in the end nothing matters but money, and the honest newsboy has a better chance to earn it than a banker's idle son. Said A. K. Loring, his early publisher: "Alger is the dominating figure of the new era. In his books he has captured the spirit of reborn America. The turmoil of the city streets is in them. You can hear the rattle of pails on the farms. Above all you can hear the cry of triumph of the oppressed over the oppressor. . . . What Alger has done is to portray the soul—the ambitious soul—of the country."

Mayes, his biographer, has a different judgment. He explains Alger's success by saying, "He did not write down to boys. He never had to, for he was never above them."

It is true that Alger presents an obvious case of arrested development. During the Civil War he played at being a soldier and drilled a squad of Cambridge boys armed with broomsticks. Later, as if conscious of being only a boy in size, he preferred the company of bootblacks and match sellers to that of grown persons. At fifty he still liked to play with blocks, building one tower after another so high that it toppled over, and his other amusement was beating the big drum in the newsboys' band. The tower and the drum are obvious sexual symbols, but they would seem to suggest masturbation rather than the pedophilia one is always expecting to find in his life and work. He never married. Mayes tells us that he had in all three mistresses, but each of these in her own fashion was a figure of maternal authority. Thus, Elise first lured him to her door and then, as Alger hesitated, stamped her foot and gave him an order: "Don't stand here talking." Alger obeyed like a good-bad little boy.

In his novels the close personal relations are not sexual. They are sometimes fraternal—many of his heroes have beloved younger sisters—but more often they are parental and filial. The boldest approach to sexual passion is in the next-to-last chapter of *Sink or Swim,* which tells how Harry Raymond came back from the Australian gold fields with a fortune of $11,525—"which, for a boy of his age," Alger says, "was certainly a very comfortable capital." Little Maud Lindsay, "a bright, handsome girl of thirteen," was so glad to see him that she flung her arms around him. "Harry was rather embarrassed," Alger says, "at the unexpected warmth of his reception, but felt that it would be impolite not to kiss Maud in return, and accordingly did so." That is the only nonmaternal kiss in the twenty Alger books I have read and possibly in all the books he wrote (though not, I believe, in the posthumous books signed with his name).

No, Alger did not write down to boys. All the emotions in his novels are those proper to a preadolescent stage of development: rivalry with other boys, shame at wearing patched clothes, daydreams of running away (and of coming back to mother with a fortune), a possessive love for the mother, and rebellion against the wicked squire, who becomes a father symbol. Apparently these are Alger's emotions, obsessively relived instead of being merely remembered. The heroes are compensatory projections of the author, who dreamed of being as resolute as each of them, but who never disengaged himself from a painful family pattern—never, that is, except in the books he wrote for eternal boys like himself. "The cry of triumph of the oppressed over the oppressor" that A. K. Loring mentioned was, in reality, Horatio Jr.'s cry of triumph over a tyrannical father.

Every popular novel is also, on one level, a myth or a fairy tale, and most often a very old one. The myth or tale is especially clear in the Alger novel (which is of course one book with seventy or more different titles). But it is not the tale one expects it to be: not *Jack the Giant Killer*, which Alger read when he was eight years old and which presents the eternal fable of the poor boy who became immensely rich—as Andrew Carnegie did and John D. Rockefeller, Sr.—partly by luck but mostly by using his own sharp wits. Carnegie and the other robber barons were too grasping to be Alger boys—except in copydesk language—and the tale that Alger compulsively repeats is very different from theirs. Essentially it is the Greek myth of Telemachus, the supposed orphan who is forced to leave home and who sets out in search of a father. It is eventually the father's power, not his own, that restores him to his rightful place.*

In Alger's version of the myth, the hero is always fatherless and is always a boy of noble principles. Though he plays the part of a bootblack, a newsboy, or a fiddler, his open and prepossessing features betray his princely nature. Usually he comes from a New England village that takes the place of rocky Ithaca, and his widowed mother is besieged by a wicked squire who assumes the joint role of Penelope's suitors. Through the machinations

---

*As an example of how the Alger story is almost universally misconceived by journalists and even scholars, one might take Kenneth S. Lynn's introduction to his book *The Dream of Success* (1955). The book is concerned with the mythology of success as it affected the work of five American novelists. Lynn says in his introduction, "the Alger hero is the key to the meaning of the success mythology. Alone, unaided, the ragged boy is plunged into the maelstrom of city life, but by his own pluck and luck he capitalizes on one of the myriad opportunities available to him and rises to the top of the economic heap. Here, in a nutshell, is the plot of every novel Alger ever wrote; here, too, is the quintessence of the myth." Lynn seems to be confusing the Alger hero with Dick Whittington. Of course the Alger hero is not unaided; the opportunity he seizes is that of finding an adoptive father; and he never rises to more than a safe niche on the slope of "the economic heap." Though Lynn was writing a book about the effects in fiction of the Alger myth, it would seem that he never read an Alger novel with attention.

of the squire, or of his idle and snobbish son, the hero is forced to run away. He somehow keeps alive in New York until the day when he meets and befriends a stranger, perhaps by rescuing his only child from drowning or from a runaway horse. The stranger, always a widower or a bachelor, turns out to be a rich and kindly merchant. He buys new clothes for the boy— dressing him, as it were, in princely robes—then sends him on a mission, a sort of knightly quest. On the boy's triumphant return, the merchant settles on him a little fortune, usually of ten or twelve thousand dollars, and adopts him as a son or nephew or ward. It is the moment in almost any Alger novel when the childless and truly fatherless author seems to be writing with a sob in his throat. "I am rich and lonely, and without near relatives," says the invalid Mr. Stoddard to the hero of *Tom Temple's Career*, "and I want you to come and live with me. Call me uncle. I shall be proud of such a spirited young nephew."

"All right, uncle," says Tom, smiling from an open heart.

Moralists used to complain at the turn of the century that the Alger hero did not earn his fortune by hard work, but had it drop into his lap. What they missed was the fairy-tale logic of the story. The hero is of course a prince in disguise, and he gains his little fortune by discovering the place and parentage that are his by right. Then he once again displays his princely character by rushing home to help his mother. Sometimes the adoptive father or uncle comes with him. "You need be under no anxiety about Luke and his prospects," the merchant says to the mother at the end of *Struggling Upward*. "I shall make over to him $10,000 at once, constituting myself his guardian, and will see that he is well started in business." Sometimes—for example, in *Sink or Swim*—the hero arrives on the very morning of the day when his mother is to be married to the wicked squire, but then he takes out a roll of greenbacks and Squire Turner slinks away. As for the end of Alger's story—

My readers [he says] may like to know how James Turner turned out in life. [James is the squire's idle and malicious son.] A year since, he obtained the situation of teller in a bank, his father standing surety for him. He soon developed expensive tastes, and finally disappeared, carrying away thirty thousand dollars of the funds of the bank. This loss his father had to make good, and in consequence he has become a comparatively poor man, and a very sour, morose man at that. . . . So the wheel of fortune has turned and those who were once at the top are now at the bottom.

Virtue has been rewarded, vice punished, and the whole operation has been pecuniary. In that preoccupation with exact sums in dollars, and in that alone, the Alger fable resembles the typical American success story as enacted in fiction or life. There is, however, a difference even here. The robber barons loved money for its own sake and each was determined to have more of it than anyone else. "I'm bound to be rich! *Bound to be rich!*" John D. Rockefeller, Sr. once exclaimed. The Alger hero will never be truly rich, since he has a generous spirit that makes him incapable of clawing and gouging his way into a palace on Fifth Avenue. Money in the Alger novel is chiefly a symbol of other things: emotional security, for example, and affection (as of the adoptive father for his ward, or of the hero for his mother), and manly power. Money is the bow of Ulysses that slays the wicked suitor—though instead of being slain, in the Alger version, the suitor loses his money and hence his virility. The real theme of the Alger novel is not pecuniary but filial and paternal. Alger is revenging himself on his own father three times: first he kills him before the story opens by making the hero an orphan; then he gives Horatio Sr.'s worst traits to the wicked squire; and finally he provides the hero with a father-by-choice to love and understand him.

Journalists have always misinterpreted the story he told, but it would seem that many of his young readers understood it instinctively. Among the thousands of letters written to Mr. Alger, one after another said in effect, "My father is like Squire Tarbox in your story. He never lets me have money to spend. He makes me . . ." and the letter would continue the list of the boy's real or fancied grievances. Often it would end with the question, "Should I run away?" How Alger answered such letters is not on record, but his books themselves are a sort of answer. "The father who mistreats you is not a real father," they say, "but a wicked impostor. Yes, run away if you must. Go to New York and earn your living as a bootblack or a newsboy, but never play pool in public places and always be kind to strangers. Some day one of the strangers will turn out to be a father in spirit, a real father, and he will give you a little fortune."

The real message of the Alger books had a deeper appeal to preadolescent boys than the mere prospect of becoming a money baron. What I cannot understand is how the author of the message—that timid bohemian, that failure by his father's standards and double failure by his own, since he neither wrote a great novel nor amassed even a modest fortune—should come to be regarded as the prophet of business enterprise; nor why the family melodrama that he wrote and rewrote for boys like himself should be confused with the American dream of success.

1945, 1970

The Two Henry Jameses

There is a rough justice in the fate of literary reputations, if we follow them through a period of years. Most—not all—of the true ones survive, even when they have been buried and must be exhumed from a mountain of trash. The false and fabricated reputations are eventually winnowed out and blown away; often without a single hot blast from the critics, they crumble like very old newspapers. Do you remember the days when *Jurgen* was regarded as a profound and devilishly clever work, the lasting ornament of American letters? Or the days when Dreiser *and* Joseph Hergesheimer were described in the same breath as the two living masters of the novel? Or the somewhat later days when Hemingway *and* Louis Bromfield were coupled by the critics as the two giants of a new generation? A short time ago in the *New Yorker,* Edmund Wilson wrote an essay ridiculing Bromfield, and most people wondered why he devoted so much space to proving what even the little children and professors knew. Where are the debunking biographers now, who won such easy triumphs over the bearded New England worthies? Where are the proletarian geniuses flung upward from the working class like Venus from the waves, all garlanded with college degrees and Brooks Brothers ties? Some of them were honest talents and have been unjustly forgotten, but in that case they need not worry too much; the world that neglected them may end by overwhelming them with praise.

Emerson's law of compensation seems to operate in such matters. If an author is overvalued during his lifetime, he will be blamed and overblamed after his death. If a great author goes unread, like Blake or Melville, he will end by being raised above his contemporaries. That was the fate of Donne, who was seldom mentioned for two centuries after his death and whose work was at one time unobtainable except in the big libraries; by 1930 the wheel had turned and he was not only valued at his own great worth but exalted as a greater poet than Milton. Some reputations climb imperceptibly, reach what appears to be their proper level, and hold it through decades or even centuries. Others are thrown out of balance at the very beginning and never regain it; they come down through the years like a skier down a slope that frightens him, making wild sweeps from shadow into sun.

Henry James is the great example in our time of an author whose reputation fluctuated during his life, declined before his death, and has now reached a higher point than ever before. Out of all the books he wrote—and he was almost as prolific as Horatio Alger—there was only one short novel, *Daisy Miller,* that became what we should now call a best seller. Only two of his novels—*The Portrait of a Lady* in 1881 and *The Ambassadors* in 1903—were greeted, in publishers' cant, "with a chorus of critical approval." These two dates twenty years apart marked the high points of his career. James thought it had reached its lowest point in 1895, when he was hissed and hooted from the stage after the first performance of *Guy Domville.* He wrote to his old friend Howells: "I *have* felt, for a long time past, that I have fallen upon evil days—every sign or symbol of one's being in the least *wanted,* anywhere or by anyone having so utterly failed." But a worse blow was to strike him twelve years later, with the publication of the New York Edition of his novels and tales, for which he had revised the style of his earlier work and had written a preface to each novel or volume of stories. The whole was intended to serve as "a sort of comprehensive manual or *vade-mecum*" for students of fiction, besides preserving his work in lasting form, and it didn't quite go unnoticed. The *Nation* and the *New York Times Book Review* faithfully and briefly mentioned each successive volume; but there was, says Richard Nicholas Foley, who has written a thesis on the treatment of James's work by American periodicals, little or no serious discussion of the edition as a whole. It might as well have been buried in a vault in Kentucky, like the American stock of gold.

Today the New York Edition is out of print and practically unobtainable; when a book dealer manages to find a set, he can put almost any price on it that he has the courage to ask.* All of James's books in their original editions are collectors' items, even the critical works and the travel sketches. His work is more widely discussed and has more admirers than during his lifetime. It has become a commonplace remark to call him the greatest or even the only American novelist.

Of course there are other reasons for this posthumous glory besides the quality of his work and besides the law of literary compensation. The return of Henry James is also the almost mathematical result of two tendencies among American readers. The first is a literary nationalism that has been growing from year to year; one sign of it is the new courses in American literature that were being offered, before the war, in all our universities. After a century and a half of living in the future, we suddenly faced about and began the search for a "usable past"; and very soon we discovered that James, in spite of being an expatriate, was the most usable of all the dead American novelists. He was the only novelist (except for Cooper and Simms

*Much later the New York edition was reissued by Scribner's, the original publisher.

and Howells, all far beneath him in talent) who planned and executed his life work on the scale of the masters; he was the only one to achieve a continuous, unified, organic career.

The second tendency that contributes to James's reputation today is the general reaction against political or social standards in literature. It began simply as a reaction against proletarian novels and Marxian criticism, but by now it has developed much further, into a reaction against historical or genetic criticism of any type. Nothing satisfies its leaders except absolute, permanent, unchanging moral and esthetic values. Works of art are being judged in and for themselves, as if independent of any social background; and the works most likely to be praised are those most widely removed from any social movement and least contaminated with ideas. There seems to be no taint of them in James's novels. He never mentions social forces, although they figure in his work indirectly and almost secretly. He is the great example in his country of the "pure" novelist.

His working notebooks, as quoted by F. O. Matthiessen, abound in expressions of priestly or soldierly devotion to his craft. "A *mighty will,*" he wrote for his own eyes while working on *The Bostonians,* "there is nothing but that! The integrity of one's will, purpose, faith!"—"Oh art, art," he wrote a few years later, "what difficulties are like thine; and, at the same time, what consolation and encouragements, also, are like thine? Without this, for me, the world would be, indeed a howling desert."—"But courage, courage, and forward, forward," he wrote before starting *The Tragic Muse.* "If one must generalize, that is the only generalization. There is an immensity to be done, and, without being presumptuous, I shall at the worst do part of it. But all one's manhood must be at one's side." His two younger brothers had served in the Civil War, and Henry apparently had felt a sense of inadequacy or even guilt at being physically unable to join them. It was in the act of writing that he discovered a moral equivalent for the hardships and dangers of the military life. And a new generation of brave but quite unwarlike soldiers has come to admire him as a hero of art.

2

Nevertheless a debate continues among James's readers and critics, with those who admire or at least concede the virtues of his early stories, but hold that his later work shows a rootlessness, a snobbishness, an unreality that might well be explained by his divorce from American life, standing against the others who believe that the three long novels he wrote when he was turning sixty are the high and frosty summits of American fiction. The debate goes back to the first publication of *The Wings of the Dove* (1902),

The Ambassadors (1903), and *The Golden Bowl* (1904). William Dean Howells tried hard to end it in 1903, when he wrote his dialogue on "Mr. Henry James's Later work"; he spoke of course for the devoted Jacobites. In 1905 William Crary Brownell answered Howells in a longer essay that expressed his adverse moral judgments and his distinguished lack of comprehension. Van Wyck Brooks succeeded Brownell as leader of the anti-Jacobite faction, the Whig gentry. The simple thesis he advanced in *The Pilgrimage of Henry James* (1925) and still more forcefully in *New England: Indian Summer* was that the later novels could not be so good as the early ones because James had lived too long in England. That was for some time the accepted opinion, in the years when James wasn't being read, although it was combated by Matthew Josephson in his *Portrait of the Artist as American* (1930) and was roundly denied by Stephen Spender, who seemed to be saying in *The Destructive Element* (1936) that James was the central writer of our time.

Henry James: The Major Phase, by F. O. Matthiessen, might be approached as merely another episode in these Jacobite wars, but it has one great advantage over the earlier forays and incursions. It is better armed; it is equipped with new evidence. Recently James's working notebooks from 1878 to 1914, in which he recorded his intimate thoughts and the slow growth of his novels, were presented by his nephew and namesake to the Houghton Library at Harvard. Mr. Matthiessen, with Kenneth B. Murdock, is now preparing them for publication.* He quotes from them extensively in the present volume; and they show that James regarded his later work as more ambitious than anything attempted in the past.

They also show that the year 1895 was the turning point in his career. Feeling that his novels would never be popular, he had been writing a succession of plays—to make money, as he flatly said, but also in the effort to overcome a sense of solitude. He seems to have resembled one of his characters—Mortimer Marshal in "The Papers"—to the extent of nursing a secret: "that to be inspired, to work with effect, he had to feel he was appreciated, to have it all somehow come back to him." Not much came back of the effort James put into his plays. One of them, a dramatized version of his early novel *The American,* had been indifferently received in London after a mild success in the English provinces. Four others had been printed without being produced. A sixth, *Guy Domville,* closed in London after thirty-one performances that earned eleven hundred dollars for the author, as he wrote to his brother William; there had been many worse

*This volume, *The Notebooks of Henry James,* was published in New York, 1947, by the Oxford University Press, which had published *Henry James: The Major Phase* in 1944. Later the most extreme of the anti-Jacobite statements was to be Maxwell Geismar's *Henry James and the Jacobites* (Boston, 1963), which most critics condemned as intemperate. From the other side, the most persuasive defense of James is of course Leon Edel's many-volumed life of the Master.

failures on the stage. But the first night of the play—January 5, 1895—had been worse than a failure; it was an international scandal. Some of the well-dressed people in the stalls approved of the play and cried, "Author, author!" The crowd in the pit hated it and bore a grudge against the producer on this and older counts. When the author appeared before the curtain, they greeted him with hoots and jeers and roars—James wrote to his brother—"like those of a cage of beasts at some infernal 'zoo.'" Newspapers in London and New York carried the story of how the uproar continued for fifteen minutes while the author stood there cowering under the storm.

Deeply humiliated, so that he could never bear to be reminded of that night, James abandoned for all practical purposes his attempt to win a larger public. It is true that he would later publish several stories described by him as "shameless potboilers"—including one great story, "The Turn of the Screw," but also including others that were genteelly romantic in the tone of the popular magazines and almost as mechanical in plot as if they had been signed by O. Henry. For the most part, however, his next years would be devoted to the sort of work he regarded simply as "the best." He wrote in his notebook just after the great fiasco:

I take up my *own* old pen again—the pen of all my old unforgettable efforts and sacred struggles. To myself—today—I need say no more. Large and full and high the future still opens. It is now indeed that I may do the work of my life. And I will.

A month passed and he felt more confident:

I have my head, thank God, full of visions. One has never too many—one has never enough. Ah, just to let oneself go—at last; to surrender oneself to what through all the long years one has (quite heroically, I think) hoped for and waited for—the mere potential and relative increase of quantity in the material act—act of appreciation and production. One has prayed and hoped and waited, in a word, to be able to work *more*. And now, toward the end, it seems, within its limits, to have come. That is all I ask. Nothing else in the world. I bow down to Fate, equally in submission and in gratitude.

That notebook entry of February 14, 1895, foreshadows James's later period, though there was still to be some fumbling before the major works of the period were under way. Of one thing James was already certain: those works would utilize "the divine principle of the Scenario" that he had learned from his costly experience in the theatre. They would follow the scenic method, in other words, and would be as tightly constructed as plays. As for the "potential and relative increase of quantity in the material act," it was not to be long delayed. During the first five years that James spent in the little town of Rye, from 1898 to 1903, he produced a volume of work that was unprecedented even in his own generally fruitful career. He wrote two short novels, *The Awkward Age* and *The Sacred Fount*; two collections of stories, *The Soft Side* and *The Better Sort*; and a two-volume life of the sculptor William Wetmore Story, besides his three most richly elaborated novels. Nobody should doubt after rereading them that they are his best novels too. Mr. Matthiessen has every right to describe that period in James's life as "the major phase."

In his critical essay, each of the three great novels receives a chapter of outline and analysis, in the light of James's working notes, and each is assigned its rank. Mr. Matthiessen has many reservations about *The Golden Bowl* and a few about *The Ambassadors*; he believes that *The Wings of the Dove* is James's masterpiece, "that single work where his characteristic emotional vibration seems deepest." *The Ivory Tower*, which also receives a chapter, might possibly have been as good, he says, if James had lived to finish it. There is an introductory chapter, extremely interesting, on "the art of reflection" that James applied to all his work; and there is a long appendix analyzing the changes James made in *The Portrait of a Lady* twenty-five years after its first appearance, when he was preparing the New York Edition of his collected works. Simple in structure and temperate in expression, *Henry James: The Major Phase* is almost a model of the critical monograph.

There is, however, one fault or omission to be noted that does not greatly affect the quality of the book, but that does have a bearing on the debate about Henry James. Mr. Matthiessen has not so much answered the arguments of the anti-Jacobites as he has introduced totally different arguments. Almost everything he says about the later James is true, but it is not quite the whole story. A great deal that Van Wyck Brooks says about him is also essentially true, even though overstated at times and written in the style of a highly cultured prosecuting attorney. It is true, for example, that James's later novels are rather thin in subject matter, considering their length and enormous elaboration. It is true that they reveal an ignorance of America and, even more strikingly, an ignorance of European life outside the international set. And it is true that they are novels about adultery (or something close to it, in *The Wings of the Dove*) that show a curious want of passion, almost as if James had written *War and Peace* without the battle scenes.

James himself, in the little book on Hawthorne that he wrote in 1879, gave us a sort of license to prefer his early work. He praised *The Scarlet Letter* in terms that might be applied to the first version of *The Portrait of a Lady*. Coming first among Hawthorne's novels, he said, it was simpler and more complete than the others. "It achieves," he continued, "more perfectly what it attempts, and has about it that charm, very hard to express, which we find in an artist's work the first time he has touched his highest mark—a sort of straightness and naturalness of execution, an unconsciousness of his public, and freshness of interest in his theme." James also admired *The Scarlet Letter* for its style. "It is admirably written," he said. "Hawthorne afterwards polished his style to a still higher degree, but in his later productions—it is almost always the case in a writer's later productions—there is a touch of mannerism. In *The Scarlet Letter* there is a high degree of polish, and at the same time a charming freshness; his phrase is less conscious of itself."

James's phrase, in his later novels, is extremely conscious of itself, and that is by no means its only fault. With its endless sentences dotted thickly with commas, it gives the impression of being both long-winded and short-breathed, as if the author were panting while he climbed an interminable flight of steps. He says in one of his prefaces, "This, amusingly enough, is what, on the evidence before us, I seem critically, as I say, to gather," and we feel that his words are uttered in little gasps. Most of them, in the sentence just quoted, add hardly a shade to the meaning he is trying to convey. Sometimes his famous density is little more than verbosity, and the reader feels himself to be fumbling for ideas, with sticky fingers, in a tub of very old hen-feathers.

Mr. Matthiessen believes that James's revisions in the New York Edition were generally an improvement over his early style; but after reading the discussion carefully I am not so sure that I agree with him. Some of his retouches made the characters more vivid and others introduced effective figures of speech. There were many changes, however, that merely complicated the style. When Madame Merle faces her former lover, in the first version of *The Portrait of a Lady*, she says to him, "How do bad people end? You have made me bad." In the revised version she says, "How do bad people end?—especially as to their *common* crimes. You have made me as bad as yourself." That is more definite, if a little harder to grasp; but it lacks the classical finality of the original statement. In his revisions, James was proud of the way he handled the "he said—she said" problem. But why should it be a problem at all? Why not, like Hemingway, write "he said" and "she said" whenever they are necessary for the sense, instead of looking for elegant variations? The later James was obsessed with finding elegant variations: "she returned," "he just hung fire," "she gaily engaged," and it reminds one of reading a play with too many stage directions.

But the worst feature of James's later style is the inversions that are most noticeable in very short phrases. "Will that so much matter?" he says, instead of, "Will that matter so much?" Very often he forces the verb to the end of the sentence, as in German. He writes: "Maud a little more dryly said"—"Had he had time a little more to try his case"—"What in the world's that but what I shall be just *not* doing?"—"But what are they either, poor things, to do?"—"I suppose that's what I horribly mean"—"I'll go to him then now"—"He wonderfully smiled." English is becoming more and more an uninflected language like Chinese, in which the function of words is shown chiefly by their position in the phrase. To change that position arbitrarily; to write, "He wonderfully smiled," instead of "smiled wonderfully" (and what does "wonderfully" mean in that connection: "for a wonder"?—"wonderingly"?—"in a wonderfully pleasant fashion"?) is to violate the spirit of the language as shaped by all the living and dead millions who speak or have spoken it. Not only is it a symbol of James's separation from the public; it directly expresses and, in a real sense, it *is* that separation.

The anti-Jacobites are right to say that James's later work shows the bad results of exile and expatriation; but they explain his problem in much too simple terms. James was not merely, as they believe, expatriated in the sense of making his home in England. He was self-exiled from England too, until the First World War; he spent most of his life in the world of creation. He wrote in his notebook: "To live *in* the world of creation—to get into it and stay in it—to frequent it and haunt it—to *think* intensely and fruitfully—to woo combinations and inspirations into being by a depth and continuity of attention and meditation—this is the only thing." It was the only thing that James really desired; and it explains the great virtues of his later novels as well as their vices. The virtues and the vices were interrelated and intermingled. In order to become a great novelist, he made himself purely a spectator of life; he denied himself the luxury of holding opinions "even on the Dreyfus case," as he said; and thereby he lost his sense of participation in life and the sort of understanding gained by those who act on their opinions. In the pursuit of combinations and inspirations, he divorced himself from the public, and the divorce made him feel, "well, blighted to the root." At the same time, however, the liberty gained through being unpopular helped him to create independent and self-sustaining works of art. In his "major phase," to follow Matthiessen, or in his decadent period, to rephrase Brooks, there are not two Henry Jameses, one of them a hero in the world of creation, the other a fussy old snob in a fawn-colored vest. There is one Henry James who must be accepted in his strength and weakness.

If we accept him so, the strength far outweighs the weakness. What we remember in his later novels is not their narrowness or their awkward style, but rather their rare quality of self-dependent life. James said in his preface to *Roderick Hudson* that the novelist's subject was like the painter's: it consisted in "the related state, to each other, of certain figures and things." His emphasis falls on the word "related"; and we note that everything in his later novels exists, develops, declines, is extinguished or transformed, *in relation* to something else in the book—not in relation to something outside, to the reader's supposed knowledge of historical incidents or social forces. Everything is bathed in the same consciousness as in some transparent medium; the characters move like swimmers seen from below in utterly clear water. The whole pattern they form, in its complexity, possesses and keeps an inner balance like that of a painting or a symphony; and that explains the permanence of his novels. Their subject matter is not only limited, but in many cases it is fatally out of fashion: for example we feel that Lambert Strether's late discovery of life in Paris, in *The Ambassadors*, was not so much tragic as pathetic. There is no longer the contrast that James described at such length, between the innocent American and the sophisticated European. In these days, however, when innocent and direct Europeans are likely to be confronted with cynical Americans; when the moral standards of New York are more lax than those of Paris; when the millionaire and the nobleman have lost the high position that James assigned to them in his novels—even now, the best of those novels have an inner life that illuminates the life about us and will continue to illuminate our children's lives.

1945, 1970

THE TWENTIETH CENTURY

Robert Frost

A Dissenting Opinion

Robert Frost has been more heaped with academic honors than any other American poet, living or dead. Although he was never graduated from college, having left Dartmouth after two months and Harvard after two years—more credit to his dogged independence—he holds by a 1944 count no less than seventeen honorary degrees. He was twice made a Master of Arts (by Amherst and Michigan), three times a Doctor of the Humanities (by Vermont, Wesleyan, and St. Lawrence), and twelve times a Doctor of Letters (by Yale, Middlebury, Bowdoin, New Hampshire, Columbia, Williams, Dartmouth, Bates, Pennsylvania, Harvard, Colorado, and Princeton). He has been chosen as Phi Beta Kappa poet by Tufts, William and Mary, Harvard (twice), and Columbia. He has been a professor at Amherst; a poet in residence and a fellow in letters at Michigan; a Charles Eliot Norton professor, a Ralph Waldo Emerson fellow, and a fellow in American civilization at Harvard, all these being fairly lucrative appointments. He has been awarded four Pulitzer prizes, one more than E. A. Robinson and two more than Stephen Vincent Benét, the only other poets to be named more than once. He has also received the Loines award for poetry, the Mark Twain medal, the gold medal of the National Institute of Arts and Letters, and the silver medal of the Poetry Society of America. His work has been the subject of at least two full-length critical studies, many brochures, pamphlets, dissertations, bibliographies, and a memorial volume, *Recognition of Robert Frost,* not to mention hundreds of essays which, with some discordant notes in the early years, have ended as a vast diapason of praise.

And Frost deserves all these honors, both for his poetry in itself and for a long career devoted to the art of verse. In a country where poets go to seed, he has kept his talent ready to produce perfect blossoms (together with some that are misshapen or overgrown). It is a pleasure to name over the poems of his youth and age that became more vivid in one's memory with each new reading: dramatic dialogues such as "The Death of the Hired Man" and "The Witch of Coös," among half a dozen others; descriptions or narrations that turn imperceptibly into Aesop's fables, as do "The Grindstone" and "Cow in Apple Time"; and, best of all, short lyrics such as "The Pasture," "Now Close the Windows," "The Sound of the Trees," "Fire and Ice," "Stopping by the Woods on a Snowy Evening" (always a favorite with anthologists), "To Earthward," "Tree at My Window," "Acquainted with the Night," "Neither Out Far Nor In Deep," "Beech," "Willful Homing," "Come In" . . . and I could easily add to the list. One of his best lyrics was written in 1892, when Frost was a freshman at Dartmouth; three or four others were included in his recent book, *The Witness Tree,* published just fifty years later; and these recent lyrics show more skill and density of expression than almost anything he had written before.

The same volume and the one that preceded it—*A Further Range,* published in 1936—also contain bad poems that have been almost equally admired: long monologues in pedestrian blank verse, spoken as if from a cracker barrel among the clouds, and doggerel anecdotes directed (or rather, indirected) against the New Deal; but a poet has the right to be judged by his best work, and Frost at his best has added to our never sufficient store of authentic poetry. If in spite of this I still say that there is a case against him and room for a dissenting opinion, perhaps I chiefly mean that there is a case against the zealous admirers who are not content to take the poet for what he is, with his integrity and his limitations, but insist on regarding him as a national sage. Still worse, they try to use him as a sort of banner for their own moral or political crusades.

We have seen the growth or revival in this country of a narrow nationalism that has spread from politics into literature (although its literary adherents are usually not political isolationists). They demand, however, that American writing should be affirmative, optimistic, not too critical, and "truly of this nation." They have been looking round for a poet to exalt; and Frost, through no effort of his own—but more through the weakness than the strength of his work—has been adopted as their symbol. Some of the honors heaped upon him are less poetic than political. He is being praised too often and with too great vehemence by people who don't like poetry, especially modern poetry. He is being presented as a sort of Sunday-school paragon, a saint among miserable sinners. And the result is that his honors shed little of their luster on other poets, who in turn feel none of the pride in his achievements that a battalion feels, for example, when one of its officers is cited for outstanding services. Frost's common sense and his "native quality" are used as an excuse for belittling and berating all his contemporaries, who have supposedly fallen into the sins of permission, obscurity, obscenity, and yielding to foreign influences; we even hear of their treachery to the American dream. Frost, on the other hand, is depicted as a loyal, autochthonous, and almost aboriginal Yankee. We are told not only that he is "the purest classical poet of America today"—and there is truth in Gorham B. Munson's early judgment—but also that he is "the one great American poet of our time" and "the only living New Englander in the great tradition, fit to be placed beside Emerson, Hawthorne and Thoreau."

But when he is so placed and measured against them, his stature seems diminished; it is almost as if a Morgan horse from Vermont, best of its breed, had been judged by the standards that apply to Clydesdales and Percherons. Height and breadth and strength: he falls short in all these qualities of the great New Englanders. And the other quality for which he is often praised, his utter faithfulness to the New England spirit, is hardly a virtue that they tried to cultivate. They realized that the New England spirit, when it stands alone, is inclined to be narrow and rigid and arithmetical. It has reached its finest growth only when cross-fertilized with alien philosophies. Hinduism, Sufism, Fourierism, and German Romanticism: each of these contributed its share to the New England renaissance of the 1850s. Even Thoreau, who died almost in sight of his birthplace, said that he had traveled much in Concord; he spoke of bathing his intellect "in the stupendous and cosmogonal philosophy of the Bhagvat-Geeta. . . . The pure Walden water," he went on to say, "is mingled with the sacred water of the Ganges." And even Hawthorne, who told us that "New England is quite as large a lump of earth as my heart can really take in," was eager for any new ideas that might help to explain the nature of New Englanders as individuals or as members of society. The books he borrowed from the Salem Athenaeum, during the twelve lonely years he spent at home after his graduation from college, included the complete works, in French, of Rousseau, Voltaire (several times), Pascal, Racine (several times), the *Essais* of Montaigne and, in English translation, the works of Machiavelli, as well as a great number of volumes on science, philosophy, government, general history, and the past of New England. Some of his weaker contemporaries were quite unbalanced by the foreign learning with which they overloaded their minds; but the stronger ones assimilated everything and, in the end, reasserted their New England natures, which had become immensely richer as a result of what they had learned.

Even Frost, as purely Yankee as his character seems today, was partly formed by his three years abroad. The turning point in his life was the moment when he was able to sell his first New Hampshire farm—which his grandfather had bought for him on condition that he live there for at least ten years—and when his wife said, "Let's go to England and live under thatch." In England after 1912 he made the reputation that enabled him to live by poetry and teaching. In England, too, he had the experience of meeting other poets who understood what he was trying to say: Lascelles Abercrombie, Rupert Brooke, Wilfred Wilson Gibson, and Edward Thomas. They were willing to learn from him, and Frost, in a sense, learned even more from them: that is, he learned to abandon the language of genteel verse and to use his own speech without embarrassment. It is interesting to compare *A Boy's Will*, published in London but written in New Hampshire before his English journey, with *Mountain Interval,* published in 1916 after his return to this country, but written chiefly in England. The poems in *A Boy's Will* gave his own picture of the world, but the picture was over-laid with conventional decorations: with phrases like "maidens pale," "sweet pangs," "airy dalliance," and "thine emulous fond flowers." On the other hand, the poems written in the English countryside used the language spoken by educated farmers north and east of Boston. Their speech had formerly been regarded as a mere dialect, to be misspelled for quaint or comic effects and to be used only in homely ballads like "Skipper Ireson's Ride" or in satirical comments like "The Biglow Papers"; but Frost in England had done what Hemingway would later do in Paris: he had refined his native idiom into a literary language capable of expressing the whole range of his emotions.

It was after his return that he carried the process further. Having learned to write as well as speak New Hampshire, he chose to think New Hampshire, in the sense of accepting its habits and customs as immutable laws. Unlike the great Yankees of an earlier age, he expressed hostility toward innovations in art, ethics, science, industry, or politics. He bridled when he heard "a New York alec" discussing Freudian psychology, which Frost for his part dismissed as "the new school of the pseudo-phallic." In his later poems he objects to researches in animal behavior (which he calls "insti-tuting downward comparisons"), to new inventions (saying that ingenuity should be held in check), and even to the theory of evolution—or at least he ridicules one farmer who speaks of it admiringly, whereas he sympathizes with another who stops him on the road to say:

> The trouble with the Mid-Victorians
> Seems to have been a man named John L. Darwin.

New ideas seem worse to him if they come from abroad, and worst of all if they come from Russia. He is continually declaiming against Russians of all categories: the pessimistic Russians, the revolutionary Russians, the collectivistic Russians, the regimented Russians, the five-year-planning Russians; he seems to embrace them all in a global and historical dislike that extends from Dostoevsky to Dnieperstroy. He is horrified by the thought that New England might be exposed to the possibility of adopting any good or bad feature of the Russian program. Thus, after reading about a project for rural rehabilitation, he was quick to write:

> It is in the news that all these pitiful kin
> Are to be bought out and mercifully gathered in
> To live in villages next to the theatre and store
> Where they won't have to think for themselves any more;
> While greedy good-doers, beneficent beasts of prey

Swarm over their lives, enforcing benefits
That are calculated to soothe them out of their wits,
And by teaching them how to sleep the sleep all day,
Destroy their sleeping at night the ancient way.

Sometimes Frost decides that it would be a relief "To put these people at one stroke out of their pain"—these people being the marginal farmers; then next day he wonders how it would be if someone offered to end his own troubles. The upshot is that he proposes to do nothing whatever, being satisfied with the New England countryside as it is—or rather, as it was in his early manhood—and outraged by anyone who tries to improve it. Yet there are other poems in which he suggests that his faithfulness to "the ancient way" is more a matter of habit than conviction. In "The Black Cottage," he speaks of an old woman who had lost her husband in the Civil War, and who believed that the war had been fought for some deeper principle than freedom for the slaves or an inseparable union:

She wouldn't have believed those ends enough
To have given outright for them all she gave.
Her giving somehow touched the principle
That all men are created free and equal.
And to hear her quaint phrases—so removed
From the world's view today of all those things . . .

It is a Protestant clergyman who is telling us about her life, in one of Frost's dramatic monologues; but the poet seems to repeat his words with approval and to share his belief that freedom, union, and equality are all quaint words "so removed from the world's view today." The old woman was an orthodox Christian, and her presence in church kept the minister from changing any phrases in the creed. He goes on to say:

I'm just as glad she made me keep hands off,
For, dear me, why abandon a belief
Merely because it ceases to be true.
Cling to it long enough, and not a doubt
It will turn true again, for so it goes.

And that, too, seems to express Frost's attitude toward the old New England standards. He is more conventional than convinced, more concerned with prudence than with virtue, and very little concerned with sin or suffering; one might say that he is more Puritan, or even prudish, than he is Christian. All the figures in his poems are decently draped; all the love affairs (except in a very late narrative, "The Subverted Flower") are etherealized or intellectualized; and although he sometimes refers to very old adulteries, it is only after they have been wrapped in brown paper and locked away in cupboards. On the other hand, there is little in his work to suggest Christian charity or universal brotherhood under God. He wants us to understand once and for all that he is not his brother's keeper:

> I have none of the tenderer-than-thou
> Collectivistic regimenting love
> With which the modern world is being swept.

One of his narratives, "Two Tramps in Mud Time," has often been praised for the admirable lesson with which it ends; and yet a professor told me not long ago that his classes always seemed vaguely uncomfortable when they heard it read aloud. It was first published in 1934, and it deals with what seems to have been an incident of the depression years. The poet tells us how he was working in his dooryard on an April day between winter and spring; he was splitting great blocks of straight-grained beech with a lovely sense of satisfaction. Two tramps came walking down the muddy road. One of them said, "Hit them hard," and then lingered by the roadside, suggesting wordlessly that he might take the poet's job for pay. The poet assumed that they had spent the winter in a lumber camp, that they were now unemployed, and that they had slept "God knows where last night." In life the meeting may have had a different sequel. Perhaps the poet explained to the homeless men that he liked to split his own wood, but that he had other work for them to do; or perhaps he invited them into the kitchen for a slab of home-baked bread spread thickly with apple butter. In the poem, however, he lets them walk away without a promise or a penny; and perhaps that explains why a college class—west of the Alleghenies, at least—cannot hear it read without feeling uneasy. Instead of helping these men who wanted to work, not go on relief, Frost turns to the reader with a sound but rather sententious sermon on the ethical value of the chopping block:

> But yield who will to their separation,
> My object in living is to unite
> My avocation and my vocation
> As my two eyes make one in sight.
> Only where love and need are one,
> And the work is play for mortal stakes,
> Is the deed ever really done
> For heaven and the future's sakes.

The meter and tone of the passage remind us of another narrative poem written in New England almost a hundred years before; but "The Vision of Sir Launfal" came to a different conclusion:

> Not what we give but what we share,
> For the gift without the giver is bare;

> Who gives himself with his alms feeds three,
> Himself, his hungering neighbor and me.

What Frost sets before us is an ideal, not of charity or brotherhood, but of separateness. "Keep off each other and keep each other off," he tells us in "Build Soil." "We're too unseparate out among each other. . . . Steal away and stay away." In some of his poems he faintly suggests Emerson, and yet he is preaching only half the doctrine of self-reliance, which embraced the community as well as the individual. Emerson said, for example, "He only who is able to stand alone is qualified for society," thus implying that the self-reliant individual was to use his energies for social ends. Frost, on the other hand, makes no distinction between separateness and self-centeredness. In his poems, fine as the best of them are, the social passions of the great New Englanders have been diverted to smaller goals. One cannot imagine him thundering against the Fugitive Slave Law, like Emerson; or rising like Thoreau to defend John Brown after the Harper's Ferry raid; or even conducting a quietly persistent campaign against brutality on American ships, as Hawthorne did when he was consul at Liverpool. He is concerned chiefly with himself and his near neighbors, or rather with the Yankees among his neighbors—for although his section of New England is largely inhabited by Poles and French Canadians, there are only two poems in which these foreigners are mentioned. He says when splitting his straight-grained beech blocks:

> The blows that a life of self-control
> Spares to strike for the common good
> That day, giving a loose to my soul,
> I spent on the unimportant wood;

And one feels that the blows might symbolize the inward turning or backward turning of energies in a region that once had wider horizons. In another poem, the rambling monologue called "New Hampshire," Frost asks his readers:

> . . . How are we to write
> The Russian novel in America
> As long as life goes so unterribly?
> There is the pinch from which our only outcry
> In literature to date is heard to come.
> We get what little misery we can
> Out of not having cause for misery.

But the truth is that life in this country goes terribly and unterribly, depending on the point of view; we have more than our share of property and comfort, but also more than our share of suicides, nervous breakdowns in middle age (among the prosperous), and violence among all classes. Life doesn't go unterribly for Frost himself when he is writing his best lyrics; but at other moments he seems to suffer from nearsightedness or want of imagination. During his public career as a poet, there have been two crises in this country that went as deep as the conflict over slavery that engaged the best energies of the earlier New England writers. To the depression of the early 1930s, his answer was a group of poems in which he preached his doctrine of separateness, advising each of us to be a "Lone Striker." To the rise of fascism in Europe and the war spreading over the world, he also had a sort of answer; at least he wrote a philosophical poem called "The Lesson for Today," in which he undertook to discuss contemporary problems—but in what a curious fashion!

The poem was read before the Phi Beta Kappa Society of Harvard University on June 20, 1941, a year after the fall of France, nine months after the battle of England, and two days before the invasion of Russia. It is addressed, however, to a poet of Charlemagne's court, with whom Frost proposes to argue the question which century is darker, the ninth or the twentieth. "You and I," he says to this forgotten poet:

> As schoolmen of repute should qualify
> To wage a fine scholastical contention
> As to whose age deserves the lower mark,
> Or should I say the higher one, for dark.

After briefly noting the fact that every age has something to be sorry for, "A sordid peace or an outrageous war," Frost then picks out as the worst and sorriest feature of our own age, what?—not tyranny or heartlessness or insecurity, not invasions or massacres, but something, as he thinks, far deeper:

> Space ails us moderns; we are sick with space.
> Its contemplation makes us out as small
> As a brief epidemic of microbes.

And so, lost in space, he manages to overlook the misfortunes under his eyes. There is something appealing in the notion of a poet or philosopher retiring to his mountain farm and musing over the eternities; but when his musings in time of civil and universal war lead him to such a coldly inadequate conclusion, one decides that something is wanting in him, if not as a lyric poet, then certainly as a prophet (for he has his pretensions to prophecy) and even more as a literary idol to be set before the American nation—some absent quality, one might call it breadth or sympathy or imagination or simple curiosity about the fashion in which two-legged featherless creatures live and die.

Unlike some of his predecessors and contemporaries in New England,

Frost does not strive for greater depth to compensate for what he lacks in breadth; he does not strike far inward into the wilderness of human nature. It is true that he often talks about the need for inwardness. He says, for example, in "Build Soil," which with all its limitations is the best of his long philosophical poems and perhaps the only one worth preserving:

> We're always too much out or too much in.
> At present from a cosmical dilation
> We're so much out that the odds are against
> Our ever getting inside in again.

And yet he sets limits on the exploration of himself, as he sets them on almost every other human activity; here again he displays the sense of measure and decorum that puts him in the classical, or rather the neoclassical, tradition. He is always building defenses against the infinite, walls that stand "Between too much and me." In the woods, there is a pile of rocks and an iron stake to mark the limit of his land; and here too,

> One tree, by being deeply wounded,
> Has been impressed as Witness Tree
> And made commit to memory
> My proof of being not unbounded.

The woods play a curious part in Frost's poems: they seem to be his symbol for the uncharted country within ourselves, full of possible beauty, but also full of horror. From the woods at dusk, he might hear the hidden music of the brook, "a slender, tinkling fall"; or he might see wood creatures, a buck and a doe, staring over the stone fence that marks the limit of the pasture lot. But he doesn't cross the fence, except in dreams; and then, instead of brook or deer, he is likely to meet a strange Demon rising "from his wallow to laugh." And so, for fear of the Demon, and also because of his moral obligations, he merely stands at the edge of the woods to listen:

> Far in the pillared dark
> Thrush music went—
> Almost like a call to come in
> To the dark and lament.
>
> But no, I was out for stars;
> I would not come in.
> I mean not even if asked,
> And I hadn't been.

But Hawthorne before him, thin and conventional as he was in many of his tales, still plucked up his courage and ventured into the inner wilderness; and Conrad Aiken's poems and stories (to mention only one example of New England work today) are written almost solely from within that haunted mid-region. To explore the real horrors of the mind is a long tradition in American letters, one that goes back to our first professional novelist, Charles Brockden Brown. It was continued by Poe and Melville and Henry James, and it extends in an almost unbroken line into the late work of Hemingway and Faulkner. But Frost, in several of his finest lyrics, is content to stop outside the woods, either in the summer dusk or on a snowy evening:

> The woods are lovely, dark and deep.
> But I have promises to keep,
> And miles to go before I sleep,
> And miles to go before I sleep.

If he does not strike far inwards, neither does he follow the other great American tradition (extending from Whitman to Dos Passos) of standing on a height to observe the panorama of nature and society. Let us say that he is a poet neither of the mountains nor of the woods, although he lives among both, but rather of the hill pastures, the intervales, the dooryard in autumn with the leaves swirling, the closed house shaking in the winter gales (and who else has described these scenes more accurately, in more lasting colors?). In the same way, he is not the poet of New England in its great days, or in its catastrophic late-nineteenth-century decline (except in some of his earlier poems); he is rather a poet who celebrates the diminished but prosperous and self-respecting New England of the tourist home and the antique shop in the old stone mill. And the praise heaped on Frost in recent years is somehow connected in one's mind with the search for authentic ancestors and the collecting of old New England furniture. One imagines a saltbox cottage restored to its original lines; outside it a well-sweep preserved for its picturesque quality, even though there is also an electric pump; at the doorway a coach lamp wired and polished; inside the house, a set of authentic Shaker benches, a Salem rocker, willow-ware plates and Sandwich glass; and, on the tip-top table, carefully dusted, a first edition of Robert Frost.

1944

Edwin Arlington Robinson

Defeat and Triumph

I

It was in October 1902, not long before his thirty-third birthday, that Edwin Arlington Robinson's third book of poems appeared. He counted on it to rescue him from the furnished room on West Twenty-third Street, in Manhattan, where he lived in fear of meeting his landlord.

His first book, or rather pamphlet, had been printed at his own expense in 1896, when he was still in Gardiner, Maine, the "Tilbury Town" of his poems. The second, called *The Children of the Night,* had been issued in 1897 by one of the "vanity publishers" who earn their profits by charging authors for the privilege of having their work appear between stiff covers. Robinson was by then nearly penniless, the family fortune having trickled away in speculations by an older brother, and it was one of the poet's Harvard friends who paid for the edition of 550 copies. It received some praise from a handful of reviewers.

This third book had traveled in manuscript to six or seven publishers. One of them—Small, Maynard of Boston—had first accepted it, then withdrawn the acceptance after a change in management, but a long time had passed before it was returned to the author. Later he learned the reason why. A junior editor had left it behind in a Boston brothel, where the kind madam took charge of it until his next visit to the brothel three months afterwards. The manuscript had then resumed its travels. Finally it was to be published at the expense of the author's friends, like *Children of the Night,* but the respected house of Houghton Mifflin had agreed to distribute it, and the friends had laid plans to assure its favorable reception. Presentation copies would be sent to famous writers of the day. Various Harvard professors would be asked to review the book, and it would be priced at only a dollar to encourage a wide sale.

The author of the book was a big-framed, lean young man with a high narrow forehead, a luxuriant brown mustache and glowing brown eyes behind spectacles. He was shy and almost speechless in company until he had taken half a dozen drinks and could say, "Now I'm up where you people are." Drunk or sober he had a sense of his incapacity for practical work. "If I could have done anything else on God's green earth," he told a friend, "I never would have written poetry. There was nothing else I could do, and I had to justify my existence." He had spent years on the new book, with special attention to the title poem, "Captain Craig," which was the longest, most defiant work he had so far undertaken. With a mixture of realism, eloquence and mischief it describes the death of a pauper who is more to be admired than all the rich men of Tilbury Town. Emery Neff has the right phrase for it, in his book on Robinson, when he calls it "a twofold assault upon conventional conceptions of beauty and conventional ideals of success." For the time when it was written, Robinson himself was not exaggerating when he called the poem "revolutionary."

But his revolution was like one of those Central American plots that end with a few shots fired and some junior lieutenants in the guardhouse. The book appeared and nothing in the literary world was changed. The presentation copies mostly went unread. The favorable reviews by Harvard professors were never written or never published, except for Trumbull Stickney's friendly lines in the *Harvard Monthly*, which appeared after a long delay. Most of the other reviews were short as well as belated; the longer ones attacked the book as a threat to ideality. "Can the lesson be lost?" said the *Independent*. "Shall not the many merits of the book . . . rather emphasize than conceal the dangers to which poetry is exposed at present?" "Worse than Browning . . . a mistake rather than a failure," said the famous poet Bliss Carman. Then silence fell. It was as if Robinson and his friends had painfully rolled a boulder to the edge of the Grand Canyon, pushed it off and waited breathlessly. After a while there was the echo of a pebble-sized splash far below, and then they were alone in the desert.

The desert for Robinson was the fourth-story room where he sat in a rocking chair always facing the door, as if he expected someone to appear and change his life. Creaking back and forth the chair complained for him; the poet said nothing. He was tired of sending contributions to the magazines, which accepted very few of his poems and hadn't paid for one since 1895. He was tired of borrowing money from his friends. He had to refuse dinner invitations because his clothes were too shabby; often he ate his meals at the free-lunch counters of the neighborhood saloons, where he could load his plate with pig's feet after buying a schooner of beer. He looked so forlorn that once when he was eating alone at the Old Homestead, on Ninth Avenue, the waiter offered to lend him two dollars. Finally a friend almost as poor as himself offered to find him a job, and he went to work as a timekeeper for a subway construction gang, at twenty cents an hour for a ten-hour day.

He was sharing in the general defeat of almost all the serious writers who had come forward during the 1890s. Dreiser, for example, went through similar experiences at exactly the same time. Disheartened by the failure of *Sister Carrie* and by the refusal of magazine editors to print his work, he sat brooding in a furnished room like Robinson's and wondered whether he shouldn't commit suicide. His brother Paul Dresser rescued him and sent him to a sanitarium. There he was told that he should spend his days outdoors until his full recovery, and so he went to work for a railroad construction gang for $1.20 a day. Among the novelists of the time who had tried to write about American life in the naturalistic fashion, Dreiser was the only one to survive into another era. The others had either died prematurely, like Crane, Norris, and Harold Frederic, or else they had gone over to the enemy like Hamlin Garland, who had been the prophet of a new American literature and who by 1900 was writing Western romances to be read in porch swings.

2

Robinson would be almost the only survivor among the poets, and eventually he would become the lonely spokesman for a generation that had vanished. When he attended Harvard as a special student, from 1891 to 1893, the poets there had been a brilliant band which Robinson envied from a distance. Some of the names were William Vaughn Moody, Philip Savage, Hugh McCulloch, Trumbull Stickney—the most talented—and George Cabot Lodge. Santayana, another survivor, said of them when they were gone, "All these friends of mine, Stickney especially, of whom I was very fond, were visibly killed by the lack of air to breathe. People were very kind and appreciative to them, as they were to me, but the system was deadly and they hadn't any alternative tradition (as I had) to fall back upon; and, of course, they hadn't the strength of a great intellectual hero who can stand alone." Robinson would have felt ashamed if anyone had called him an intellectual hero, but he had a single-minded devotion to poetry that was lacking in most of the others, besides a stubborn capacity to endure. If asked what he did during the bleak years for American literature after 1902, he might have given the same answer that Abbé Sieyès gave when asked what he had done during the Reign of Terror: "I lived." He lived without writing much verse, but also without betraying his ideals. During the eight months that he worked in the subway he went underground, literally, as serious American writing had figuratively gone underground.

He emerged slowly, as if he had become afraid to live in the sun. The story of his reappearance begins late in 1903 at Groton School, where Kermit Roosevelt was then a student; he asked one of the instructors for a good book to read. The instructor, who had known Robinson in Maine, suggested *The Children of the Night*. Kermit was so impressed by it that he ordered several copies from the publisher and sent one of them to his father in the White House. The President was equally impressed; he read some of Robinson's poems aloud at a Cabinet meeting and carried the book along with him on his campaign tour that fall. "What shall we do with Robinson?" he asked Richard Watson Gilder of the *Century,* who had come to interview him on "The President as a Reader." The editor suggested a post in the consular service, but Roosevelt didn't believe that poets should live abroad. In June 1905 he made Robinson a "special agent" in the New York Custom House at a salary of two thousand dollars a year and with the understanding that he should spend his time writing poetry. It was one of the few occasions—Hawthorne's appointment to the Custom House in Salem, and later as consul at Liverpool, was another—on which an American administration has come to the aid of a talented man of letters.

Still the poetry refused to be written. Robinson was recovering very slowly from the failure of *Captain Craig,* and he was spending more time in "shopping"—as he called his nightly tour of the neighborhood saloons—than he was at his writing table. It wasn't until he lost his post in the Custom House, at the beginning of the Taft Administration, that he gathered up courage to write a new book. *The Town Down the River,* as he called this group of poems chiefly about New York, was a little more conventional than his early verse and it would be more favorably reviewed. It was published by Scribner's in 1910, a year before Harper's published Dreiser's *Jennie Gerhardt.* Dreiser and Robinson never met, but they emerged from obscurity together after suffering the same defeat.

In the poetry revival that began in 1912, "the lyric year," Robinson played only an indirect part; he was bored by the arguments and out of sympathy with many aims of the younger poets. "Do you write free verse?" a stranger asked him, and Robinson answered, "No, I write badly enough as it is." He owed a debt, however, to the crusaders for free verse and especially to Amy Lowell, who greatly admired his work. As a result of their campaigns the magazines were printing more poems, including more of Robinson's, and the public was buying more of his books. His prospects seemed so encouraging that he stopped drinking after a long struggle, during which he told his friend Ridgely Torrence that he felt like "scratching down the stars." He also abandoned the attempt to write plays and novels on which he had wasted three years; once more he gave all his time to verse.

By 1920 the younger poets regarded him as a figure to be revered from a distance. He had two distinctions in their eyes; the first was that, in spite of the wasted years, he had devoted more time to poetry than any other American and had become, except for Robert Bridges in England, the finest technician writing conventional verse in the English language, with few rivals in France or Germany. But the second distinction seemed more important: Robinson was then the only American poet who had achieved an integrated career and one that was marked by complete absorption in his art. For poetry he had sacrificed everything else: marriage, home, the respect of his neighbors and the hope of rising in the world. Poetry was his vocation, his avocation, and his livelihood, such as that was, for he lived without teaching or book reviewing or lecturing or reading from his books; he simply worked and expected to be fed like Elijah by the ravens.

Actually it was his friends who fed him after he lost his post in the Custom House. They were not too rich themselves, but they clubbed together and, beginning in 1916, gave him an income of twelve hundred dollars a year, sometimes increased by special gifts; it was equivalent to the salary, at the time, of a junior instructor in a small college. Not until 1922, when he was fifty-three years old and had published his *Collected Poems,* did he become completely self-supporting. The gifts he received before that time didn't wound his Yankee pride because he felt that they were being given not to him as a person, but through him to poetry. Having taken vows of poverty, chastity and obedience to his art, he could accept donations as if he were a whole monastic order.

3

But he paid a price for his defeats and renunciations, in his work as in his life. After the failure of *Captain Craig* he never again displayed the resilience and high spirits of that volume. His humor became a subdued irony and he lost his eagerness for making experiments. What was worse, he seems to have lost most of his intellectual curiosity. He continued to admire the authors he had read at Harvard in 1891–1893 and he showed no interest in the new ideas that were sweeping over the world. One finds little trace of them, for example, in his famous philosophical poem "The Man against the Sky," written in 1915. His biographer Emery Neff says that the poem, "bringing to bear upon the supreme problem of human destiny consummate qualities of intellect, human understanding and art, towers above any other . . . written upon American soil." Does it tower above Whitman's "Song of Myself"? or above Hart Crane's "The Bridge"? or even above several of Robinson's shorter poems? To me it seems to be written with an eloquence that is not Robinson's style at its laconic best; sometimes it suggests the high fuzziness of his friend William Vaughn Moody. The consummate ideas to be found in the poem are largely complaints against scientific materialism in the forms it assumed during the 1890s:

> Are we no greater than the noise we make
> Along one blind atomic pilgrimage
> Whereon by crass chance billeted we go
> Because our brains and bones and cartilage
> Will have it so?

Robinson's answer is simply that we *must* have a grander destiny. For, if the materialists are right about us—

> If there be nothing after Now,
> And we be nothing anyhow,
> And we know that,—why live?

For himself he had first been forced and then had deliberately chosen to live obscurely and almost surreptitiously. He avoided famous persons instead of seeking them out; the company he preferred was that of his friends, and later of his disciples. He traveled only from New York to New England at the beginning of each summer and back again in the fall. He never saw the South or the West, and it was not until 1923 that he made his first trip across the Atlantic. It lasted three months and he came back without crossing the Channel, a little disappointed by the fact that he was not more widely known in England.

Having existed for years in miserable surroundings, he became indifferent to his surroundings; any room would do if it had a bed, a table, and a rocking chair. From 1918 to 1922, when he could have afforded a better home, he lived in an old-fashioned railroad flat in Brooklyn. The dining-room was Robinson's study, and there he received his guests, including two poets from Harvard. He worked on a golden-oak pedestal table covered with a heavy vomit-colored cotton cloth; behind him was a built-in china closet painted a hideous brown and containing, instead of dishes, neat piles of Sweet Caporal cigarettes in pasteboard boxes. Later I learned that he lived in the flat through kindness for a boyhood friend whose wife had deserted him; but I still wondered why Robinson and the friend hadn't moved, as they could easily have done, to a less dismal lodging. The truth seems to have been that he didn't notice the objects around him and wasn't impressed by their shapes or colors.

He was cut off from any functional relationship with the community, as husband, father, employer, or employed; he wasn't even a taxpayer until the success in 1927 of his Arthurian epic *Tristram* earned him a small fortune and enabled him to pay his old debts with New England scrupulosity. He was loyal, modest, full of compassion, and yet his separation from society threw him back on himself and forced him to create characters out of his own mind. He gave them wonderful names—John Evereldown, Luke Havergal, Miniver Cheevy—and curious fates, but in his later years he sometimes forgot to give them faces. Some of the long poems that he wrote after *Tristram* are like the conversations of ghosts in unfurnished rooms. But twenty or more of the shorter poems are unforgettable, not only for their subtlety, not only for their sober diction, but also for their moments of splendor that burst like thunderstorms in the desert, as at the end of "Eros Turannos":

> Meanwhile we do no harm; for they
>   That with a god have striven,
> Not hearing much of what we say,
>   Take what the god has given;
> Though like waves breaking it may be,
> Or like a changed familiar tree,
> Or like a stairway to the sea
>   Where down the blind are driven.

1948

Eugene O'Neill in Connecticut

Back in the early 1920s, Eugene O'Neill was the animating spirit of a group that surrounded the Provincetown Players. His success as a dramatist had enabled the Players to move to New York and had kept their venture alive in bad seasons. It had kept me alive, too, during a hard year when I was paid ten dollars a week to be a black ghost in *The Emperor Jones* and a white ghost in a revival of *Where the Cross Is Made*; I never aspired to play the part of any living person. Although I hadn't been eating much that year, I made a rather substantial wraith, even with streaks of aluminum paint over my ribs to make them look as if the flesh had rotted away. Then Gene stopped writing plays with ghosts in them and my stage career came to an end. It was a minor example of how his decisions affected all of us.

If the Provincetown Players drank at the Hell Hole—officially known as the Golden Swan—which stood at the southeast corner of Fourth Street and Sixth Avenue in Greenwich Village, that was also because of Gene. Before it became a speakeasy, the Hell Hole was a Raines Law hotel, which means that there were furnished rooms upstairs and that, in theory, it furnished meals to travelers. As legal proof of the theory, the same mummified sandwiches appeared Sunday after Sunday on the round tables in the back room. Not even the unfed stumblebums who slept there on winter nights would dust off the sandwiches and eat them. The Hell Hole before the First World War, when it stayed open all night, was one of the principal models that Gene copied for Harry Hope's saloon in *The Iceman Cometh*. It was the grubbiest drinking parlor west of the Bowery—the No Chance Saloon, Bedrock Bar, the End of the Line Café, the Bottom of the Sea Rathskeller, as Larry Slade calls it in the play. "Don't you notice the beautiful calm in the atmosphere?" he continues. "That's because it's the last harbor. No one here has to worry about where they're going next, because there is no farther they can go."

Larry Slade in life was Terry Carlin, a gaunt, benign Irishman who had retired from gainful occupation after a working career that lasted one day. It was a Saturday, Terry explained, and the gainful occupation was that of helping behind the bar, where he had slaved from noon to midnight in order to empty the till after the saloon was closed. But the proprietor emptied it first, and Terry, disillusioned, had sworn never to do another day's work in his life. He kept the oath and lived to be nearly eighty, on a chiefly liquid diet. During Prohibition he used to drink canned heat, strained through a not very clean blue bandanna—that is, till the afternoon when I heard him say dreamily, "I'll have to stop drinking wood alcohol. It's beginning to affect my eyesight." Terry was a mystic of sorts who had been a radical syndicalist in his early days and then a philosophical anarchist. He had also been a patron of the Hell Hole when anyone would buy him a drink, as Gene often did. At Provincetown in the summer of 1916, Terry had repaid the debt by introducing his desperately shy friend to the Players as a young man with a trunkful of unperformed plays.

Outside of a few drunken radicals or ex-radicals like Terry and Hippolyte Havel (Hugo Kalmar in *The Iceman Cometh*), the denizens of the Hell Hole were more practical than the characters in Gene's play. Some of the latter were invented and others were carried over from Jimmy the Priest's, a waterfront dive that had been one of Gene's earlier haunts. At the Hell Hole, the regular patrons included sneak thieves and shoplifters, touts, a square-shooting Negro gambler down on his luck, and a few bedraggled prostitutes—until 1917, that is, when "us girls" were driven off the streets and saloonkeepers were told not to serve them. There was a famous West Side gang known as the Hudson Dusters. Not many of the antisocial characters at the Hell Hole had spunk enough to be gangsters, but Hudson Dusters or simply Dusters was what we always called them. Gene had been drinking with them since 1915, when he first lived in the Village. The Dusters pitied him, sometimes fed him when he was starving, and one of them offered to steal him an overcoat when he was shivering with cold. "Tell you what, Gene," said an amiable shoplifter, "You make a trip up Sixth Avenue right away. Go to any store, pick out any coat you like, and tell me where it hangs on the rack. I bring you the coat tomorrow."

Gene hadn't accepted the offer, but he liked to tell about it, and anyone could see that he was proud of being accepted by the Dusters as one of the crowd. He had earned a place there by his apprenticeship in raggedness and drunkenness and near starvation, as well as by his unfailing good manners. He felt—and perhaps the Dusters felt—that he was leagued with them in a sullen rebellion against property and propriety. To a lesser extent he was also leagued with the Greenwich Villagers, particularly if they were poor and eccentric and a little outside the law. I think that for him the world was divided into downtowners and uptowners, as for a later generation of rebels it would be divided into hipsters and squares. For some time after becoming a successful playwright, he entered the uptown world with trepidation and in disguise, almost like a scout in enemy country, fearful of being caught and condemned to death, or forced to abandon his loyalties. He wouldn't even go to see his own plays when they were produced on Broadway. In the plays he depicted uptowners as hypocritical and sex-obsessed, and also as representatives of the paternal authority that he defied. He wanted to fling the truth about them into their smug faces. He wanted to show the uptowners, including his father, what he could do to enforce his dreams, but he didn't want to win them over; he wanted to impress and overawe, not persuade. In the back room of the Hell Hole, which was lighted by two flickering gas jets, with the corners of the room in darkness so that it looked like an expressionistic setting for *The Lower Depths,* among the honest sneak thieves and panhandlers at the very end of the line, he was safe from his father's reproaches; he could take off his mask and be understood.

That was what I felt about O'Neill, but what did I really know about him? Today how much do I really remember? I had seen him perhaps a dozen times, in the street, in the back room of the Hell Hole, at the Provincetown Playhouse, and once in the cold-water flat of Spanish Willie Fernandez, a bootlegger and small-time politician who worshiped him. I had heard some of his stories about life on shipboard and in a tuberculosis sanitarium, but it seems to me now that I heard them from others, his good friends and mine. I know that he liked to sing chanteys, omitting the obscene stanzas, and that his favorites were "Whisky for My Johnny" and "Blow the Man Down." When ordering another round of drinks, he might sing in a low voice,

> Whisky is the life of man,
>   (Whisky—Johnny),
> Oh, I drink whisky when I
>   ca-a-an
>   (Whisky for my Johnny).

In humming the other chantey, he would pause to say that the slow rise and fall of the refrain, "Way-O, blow the man down," was like the movement of a ship on an ocean swell, and he would illustrate his meaning with a wavelike gesture of his right hand. But did I really see him make the gesture or was it someone else who made it in telling me about an evening spent with Gene? Often we fall into the illusion that the good friends of our friends are our good friends too.

Searching through my mind, discarding the questionable pictures and the stories told by others, I find that most of what I truly remember about Gene is connected with a visit to the O'Neills' country house at the beginning of November 1923, when the other guests were Hart Crane, whom we had met that summer, and my first wife, Peggy Baird. And what remains is not a continuous memory but a series of pictures, as if one's mind were a theatre, and a spotlight moved to illuminate one corner of the stage and then another while leaving the intervening spaces in blackness.

. . .

Hart Crane and I are climbing out of a nearly empty Harlem Division local at Purdy's Station on a Friday evening just after dark. Nobody else gets off the train. Gene's second wife, Agnes Boulton, had taken Peggy to the country earlier in the week, and now they are waiting for us on the dimly lighted platform. There are hugs, twitters, and Hart's boom of greeting. Shivering a little in the country air, I look up at the shadowy presence of big trees to the south of the station. Just north of it a sinister-looking bridge crosses the railway. A very bright electric bulb is burning at the top of the embankment, against a starless sky. A long flight of steps rises through shadows toward the single light. It is a stage setting by Robert Edmond Jones and makes me feel like a ghost again in one of Gene's early plays.

Carrying our bags, we struggle up the steps to where the O'Neills' new touring car is waiting under the light. The chauffeur, whose name is Vincent Bedini, drives us eastward by narrow roads lined with stone walls. From time to time, far back from the road, we catch glimpses of big houses among the trees, sailing past us like brilliantly lighted wooden ships. At some point we cross the Connecticut state line.

The O'Neills have recently bought one of the big houses in Ridgefield, I think with part of a legacy from Gene's brother Jim, or Jamie, though there have also been big royalties from *Anna Christie* and smaller ones from *The Hairy Ape*. The house is an 1890-ish affair called Brook Farm by its former owners, with a wide tree-dotted lawn and more than forty acres of land. Gene meets us in the hallway and so does his new dog—an Irish wolfhound, we are informed, the color and texture of coarse sandpaper and the size of a three-month-old calf. "He's extinct," I say, patting his head. "The *Encyclopaedia Britannica* tells us that Irish wolfhounds are an extinct breed." Offstage the telephone rings. With his hind paws slipping a little on the pale yellow hardwood floor, the dog rises to his full height, which is greater than mine, puts his forepaws on my shoulders, and looks down into my eyes. Enter Mrs. Fifine Clark, the housekeeper, known as "Gaga" by the family; she says there is another call from New York, from the Theatre Guild. "I'll take it," Gene murmurs. He comes back with a brief report, "I said no." There aren't any other guests and we sit down to an excellent dinner without being offered a drink. The door to the hallway is closed against Finn, the dog, who hasn't learned table manners.

After luncheon on Saturday, Gene and I are alone in a window nook at the left rear of the enormous living room. Hart has disappeared, I don't know where, and the girls are in Agnes's bedroom exchanging confidences over glasses of whisky and water, I suspect, but there is no liquor downstairs.

Gene picks up a heavy green medical-looking book from the table beside us; it is one of Wilhelm Stekel's treatises on sexual aberrations—perhaps *The Disguises of Love,* which has recently been translated from the German. There are enough case histories in the book, Gene says, to furnish plots to all the playwrights who ever lived. He turns the pages and shows me the clinical record of a mother who seduced her only son and drove him insane. Then he talks about the German Expressionists, Toller and Kaiser and Hasenclever, whose plays he has read because they are said to resemble his own. Gene thinks their work is bold and interesting, but much too easy. The word "easy," which seems to be his strongest expression of disapproval, reminds him of *Anna Christie.* "I never liked it so well," he says, "as some of my other plays. In telling the story I deliberately employed all the Broadway tricks I had learned in my stage training. Using the same technique, and with my early experience as a background, I could turn out dozens of plays like *Anna Christie,* but I won't ever try. It would be too easy."

Nodding politely, I look down at the polished beech floor, with tiny eyes here and there in the wood. I think it is the handsomest floor I have ever seen.

Gene has taken me upstairs to the room where he works, a big bedroom so meagerly furnished that it looks like an abbot's cell. (Croswell Bowen, who wrote one of the books about O'Neill, tells me there was a crucifix over the bed, but I don't remember seeing it.) There are no books or pictures in the room. Between the two north windows is a dark mahogany secretary with drawers at the bottom, a cabinet at the top, and a drop-leaf table for writing. There are no papers on the writing surface. Gene opens the doors of the cabinet and takes out two or three medium-sized bound ledgers: "I write in these," he says. Each ledger contains several plays. Opening one of them, he shows me the text of *The Emperor Jones,* written with a very fine pen, in characters so small that they are illegible without a reading glass. There are no blank lines, and the text of the whole play fills only three pages of the ledger—or is it five? I think of the Lord's Prayer engraved on the head of a pin.

Gene tells me he is writing a play about New England, but he doesn't want to discuss it until it is finished. He is being extraordinarily kind to a shabby young man without a reputation. Partly that is because I am a friend of his friends, definitely not an uptowner, but there is something else involved—perhaps a need to explain himself to a new generation of writers, to a representative of the future by which he will be judged. I listen but do not respond, as I might well have done if he were French or English. In this country, as a result of the First World War, there has come to be a gulf between literary generations, besides that older gulf between fame and obscurity. Although Gene is only ten years older than I, he had come of age in a different world, and I feel we have very few admirations or even interests in common. Gene is trying to cross the two gulfs, but, in my defensive pride and foolish reticence, I do nothing to help him.

Rather late in a dry evening, Gene takes Hart and me down to the cellar, the only part of the house that seems to arouse his pride of ownership. He shows us the big coal furnace, with pipes radiating in all directions like the arms of an octopus. Standing under a bare electric light, he points to the cement floor and says that Vincent keeps it as clean as the living room. Vincent is a European who can't stand the way Americans let things go to waste. Last month he had gathered apples from the old orchard and made three barrels of cider. There they are—Gene points a finger into the shadows, where three fifty-gallon casks stand on a rack.

As a country boy I offer a disquisition on the virtues of hard cider, the wine of the Puritans, the interior sunlight of New England. "Let's broach a cask," Hart says. Gene demurs, but hesitantly; Vincent mightn't like it, he says, the cider is only three weeks old, and besides he doesn't know how a barrel should be tapped. Here I interrupt with my country knowledge. There is a spigot lying on the rack, I say, with a maul beside it. Cider doesn't have to ferment all winter; sometimes it tastes even better when the sugar hasn't quite worked out.

Gene goes upstairs to Gaga's kitchen and comes back with a white china pitcher and three glasses. By that time I have tapped a barrel, spilling more than a little cider on Vincent's clean floor. We stand with our full glasses under the bare electric light. "I can see the beaded bubbles winking at the brim," Hart says. Gene takes a sip of cider, holds it in his mouth apprehensively, gives his glass a gloomy look, then empties the glass in two deep nervous swallows. After a while we fill the pitcher again. When I go upstairs to bed, long after midnight, Gene is on his knees drawing another pitcher of cider, and Hart stands over him gesturing with a dead cigar as he declaims some lines composed that afternoon.

Soliloquy. I am lying awake while the clear gray morning light pours in through the bedroom windows. I am saying to myself that the O'Neills rattle around in this big country house like the last dried peas in a box— or better, like castaway sailors who have blundered into a deserted palace on the shore. But the sailors would laugh if they found wine in the cellar, where Gene hardly even smiles.

Peggy and I are running over the immense lawn in pursuit of the wolfhound. He mustn't be allowed to cross the road because, in spite of his amiable temper, the mere size of him terrifies the neighbors; he has developed a bad habit of killing chickens, and there have been threats that he would be shot. Finally he lets us catch him and lead him, or be dragged by him, back to the house. "The O'Neills—were kings in Ireland," I pant as we go. "It's like Gene—to buy—a dog of an extinct breed—the royal hunting dog of Irish kings—that kills the neighbors' chickens."

The big round table has been set for luncheon, with a plateful of hors d'oeuvres at each place. I look through the glass doors of the dining room and see the extinct dog walking gravely round the table, lowering, not raising, his head to empty each plate in turn. At luncheon Mrs. Clark gives soup to us instead. We are told at the last moment that Gene won't be down because he's working.

That evening we are in Woodstock, New York, sixty miles from Ridgefield as the crow flies. I know from one of Hart's published letters that we had been taken there in the O'Neills' touring car, which means that Vincent was at the wheel, but I don't remember by what roads, or how we crossed the Hudson, or anything that was said. A sort of curtain had fallen, to rise on another scene. My one intervening impression, a faint one, is that Agnes came along for the ride, then left rather hurriedly before dinner.

Now we are in a sort of eviscerated farmhouse, where ceilings and partitions have been ripped out to make an immensely high living room, with a balcony at one side and bedrooms opening out of it. There are six of us, all of an age except Niles Spencer's kid sister, who is pretty and sixteen. We have organized a game of hide-and-seek and go storming in and out of doors, up and down the balcony stairs, in alternate troughs and crests of laughter—first laughter pushed down, as into the hollow of a wave, then laughter splashing over us in breakers, with Hart's voice booming above them. For the Ridgefield pilgrims, it is as if a thin but perceptible mist of constraint, of jokes not made and differences of opinion that mustn't be aired, had suddenly been laughed away.

Hart stayed at the Woodstock farmhouse until after Christmas. Peggy and I went back to New York, where on Thursday of that week I wrote a letter to one of my literary friends. I told him briefly about the trip and said, "Eugene O'Neill, Mr. O'Neill the playwright, Gene . . . speaks a language so different from ours that we seemed to converse from different worlds." So the trip had ended for me in a failure of communication that was largely my fault.

There was, however, a sequel. All that Sunday, instead of working, Gene had kept on drawing pitchers of cider from the tapped barrel. While Agnes was away from Brook Farm he had called a taxi that took him to Purdy's, where he vanished. Agnes went to New York and spent a frantic week in search of him. Afraid of what the newspapers might say, she avoided the Bureau of Missing Persons; instead she made telephone calls to his friends and kept visiting his old haunts, including the Hell Hole.

On the last of her visits there, the proprietor confessed to her that Gene had sat in the back room and drunk himself into a coma. To avoid trouble with the police, he had been stashed away in the mysterious upstairs that none of us had seen, where Gene said that a crazy old woman wandered through the hallways, opening and closing doors. Agnes had him driven to Ridgefield, where in a few days he went back to work on *Desire Under the Elms*. That was not the last of his alcoholic misadventures, but his need to write plays proved stronger than his impulse toward self-destruction. A few years later, faced with the choice between writing and drinking, he stopped drinking for the rest of his life.

1957

Hart Crane in Search of a Home

A Memoir

I knew him for nearly a year before we felt any great sympathy for each other. We had first met on a warm evening in August 1923. I had lately come back to New York after two years in France and was working again as a copywriter for Sweet's Catalogue Service. Hart, who had arrived from Cleveland in March of that year, was in the copywriting department of the J. Walter Thompson agency. We had written for the same little magazines, including *Broom* and *Secession,* and had exchanged letters about poetry. At last he paid me a visit in the old house on Dominick Street, almost in the shadow of the downtown skyscrapers, where my first wife and I were living in two upstairs rooms.

He was twenty-four years old, a solidly framed and apple-cheeked young man dressed in a brown suit to match his prominent eyes. Gesturing with a dead cigar, he tramped up and down the living room announcing that he was sick of being a copywriter; that advertising appealed to nothing but the acquisitive instinct. I had never liked that sort of sweeping declaration. Advertising, I said, appealed to a whole collection of human characteristics or weaknesses or whatever you wanted to call them: sex and greed and social emulation and romantic dreams of the future. I doubted whether there was any such thing as a human instinct.

Hart flushed and his mouth turned down at the corners. "You don't know what you're talking about," he growled in a Midwestern voice. He shook hands on leaving, after shifting the dead cigar to his mouth, but he stamped out of the house almost as if he were shaking the dust of it from his feet.

I saw him several times that fall. At the end of October he resigned from J. Walter Thompson's, saying that he was caught there like a rat in a trap, and we spent a weekend together at Eugene O'Neill's country house, with disastrous results for O'Neill when we tapped a cider barrel and set him to drinking again. In the spring of 1924 Hart was jobless, roomless, and dependent on the hospitality of friends. I told him about an opening at Sweet's Catalogue Service and he got the job—at forty dollars a week, or ten dollars more than he had previously been earning. Our desks were beside each other and we had lunch together two or three times a week, yet still there was a shadow of constraint between us.

"Hart isn't very bright," I told Peggy one evening at dinner.

I meant that he hadn't the quick competence I had come to expect of my friends, most of whom had been scholarship boys in college. Hart had not finished high school, and although he read intensely, rather than widely, there were immense gaps in his knowledge of things we took for granted. When one explained to him how a certain piece of copy was to be handled, he sometimes had a look of sullen incomprehension. I hadn't yet learned to appreciate his single-minded devotion to writing poems, or his capacity for working at each of them week after week until it had assumed the exact new shape of which he dreamed.

It was Allen Tate who brought us together. He had been exchanging letters with Hart, and when he made what I think was his first visit to New York, in June 1924, it was Hart who introduced him to most of my friends. I had forgotten the circumstances of my first meeting with Allen until he mentioned them in a letter. There was a party, he says, in the Greenwich Village apartment of James Light, a director of the Provincetown Playhouse. "I remember," the letter continues, "that I appeared neatly dressed in a dark suit, carrying a preposterous walking stick and wearing a Phi Beta Kappa key. I was completely unsophisticated. You were already a man of the world—had been to France and known the Dadaists, etc. You remarked, 'We no longer wear our Phi Beta Kappa keys.' And you picked up somewhere an old stick—not a cane—and carried it the entire evening."

That is Allen's story, not mine, for I didn't feel then like a man of the world and he never impressed me as being unsophisticated. I thought, then or later, that he had the best manners of any young man I had known, in America or France. I thought he used politeness not only as a defense but sometimes as an aggressive weapon against strangers. But he couldn't have been offensively polite to me that evening, in spite of my jibes, and we must have arranged to meet again at Hart Crane's on the following Tuesday.

That second meeting with Allen I do remember, and I even found the date of it in a letter: June 24, in the late afternoon. Hart had recently moved to Brooklyn Heights, where he had rented a back room with a magnificent view of Brooklyn Bridge. After exclaiming at the view, we talked about poetry. Hart gestured, as always, with a dead five-cent cigar while he declaimed against the vulgarity of Edgar Poe. Allen and I had reservations. Seeing a volume of Poe on the shelf, I opened it and read "The City in the Sea":

> While from a proud tower in the town
> Death looks gigantically down.

Hart exclaimed that it was good to hear a poem read aloud. We left his room, all three of us talking excitedly, and wandered through the streets lined with red-brick warehouses until we came to the end of a scow at the end of a pier at the Brooklyn end of the bridge. There we sat talking, more slowly now, while we looked across the river at an enormous electric sign— WATERMAN'S FOUNTAIN PENS—and all those proud towers beyond it with the early lights flashing on. Suddenly we felt—I think we all felt—that we were secretly comrades in the same endeavor: to present this new scene in poems that would reveal not only its astonishing face but the lasting realities behind it. We did not take an oath of comradeship, but what happened later made me suspect that something vaguely like that was in our minds.

It must have been late in the summer that Allen moved to New York. William Slater Brown was there too, Cummings' fellow prisoner in the Enormous Room. Bill had lately married one of my high-school friends, Sue Jenkins, who was capably editing a pulp magazine called *Telling Tales*. Allen became her assistant at a salary of thirty dollars a week, then the beginning rate for assistant editors. I think that was after he married Caroline Gordon, who was introduced to us as a newspaper woman from Tennessee; "You'll like her," Sue said. Matthew Josephson, who had been the editor of *Broom*—at no salary whatever, in the last months of the magazine—was now a customer's man in Wall Street, but he found a good deal of time for his impecunious friends. Even Kenneth Burke had deserted his New Jersey farmhouse to spend a winter in the Village. That was the good winter, or so I have always thought of it, when we met after work at the Poncino Palace to drink hot rum toddies at the kitchen table, and when we had dinner together once or twice a week at John Squarcialupi's restaurant, then on Perry Street.

> All of an age, all heretics,
> all rich in promise, but poor in rupees,
> I knew them all at twenty-six,
> when to a sound of scraping shovels,
> emerging from whatever dream,
> by night they left their separate hovels
> as if with an exultant scream,
> stamped off the snow and gathered round
> a table at John Squarcialupi's,
> happy as jaybirds, loud as puppies.

At the time we were planning the first (and last) issue of an angry little magazine to be called *Aesthete 1925*, and that gave a sort of direction to the dinners, with contributions to be shouted up and poems to be read aloud, but soon the evenings would dissolve into anecdotes and horseplay. Kenneth Burke was the arguing man and the noisy analyst of human follies, including his own. Allen revealed a gift for comic inventions and pure impishness. Hart, after banging away at the big upright piano while shaking his bristly head to the beat of "Too Much Mustard," always made more than his share of the jokes, laughed louder, if possible, than anyone else, and drank more of John Squarcialupi's red wine. Later in the evening, though, he might be as morose as a chained bear in a Russian tavern. Once he upset a bottle of wine on the tablecloth, pushed back his chair, and plunged out of the door without saying a word.

"Where is he going?" I asked.

"Don't you know?" said one of the girls, who made a point of knowing almost everything. "He's going to Brooklyn to pick up a sailor."

I had indeed known that he was homosexual, though I forget how I learned about it; probably Hart himself had told me, as he usually ended by doing with a new friend; or he had told someone else who passed the news along. I regarded it as an item of personal gossip, as if I had been told that he had a birthmark on his back or suffered—as he did—from constipation. He did not look or talk like a homosexual; he looked like a country boy masquerading in a business suit, and his speech was northern Ohio except for a few big words and a larding of waterfront obscenities. "I never could stand much falsetto," he used to say. Instead of being delicate, his poems were solidly built and clumped on heavy feet, like Hart himself; and his social behavior—as much of it as I had a chance to observe—seemed aggressively masculine. Hart liked women, and his favorites were not of the thwartedly maternal type sometimes known as fairy godmothers; he liked girls of his own age, the prettier the better, and usually they liked him in return. Some of them made laudable attempts on his vice, and Hart abetted them, up to a point. The situation became comic when, as sometimes happened, he snatched a girl from the roving hands of a heterosexual friend. But most of his friends were intensively married, and Hart seemed happy in their company.

There was, however, one obvious sign of alienation to be noted even in that best of winters. At some moment in the evening, after the hilarious stage and the stage at which he repeated one phrase obsessively, Hart's face would assume that sullen look, and he would begin glancing toward the door. It may have been that, as Gorham Munson said, he felt subtly excluded from the domestic concerns of the others. Kenneth Burke once told me: "I remember a party at the Browns'. Party had got to humming, and Hart had got to the stage where he felt it was time for him to become angry. I happened to be near the door when I saw him stamping across the room, all ready to leave in a huff. I said, 'What's the matter, Hart?' He began muttering about how awful 'all these people' were. Whereat I, being in a good-naturedly impish stage, decided to spoil his rhythm. I pointed out that he had no reason to be indignant. Everybody here was his friend, we all thought him a great poet, nobody's fighting—so what more did he want? He turned back, muttering, and got lost in the general turmoil. A little later, the same pattern, Hart storming toward the door in a mighty rage. So I went through my part of the routine again. I said I simply could not understand why he felt so resentful when everybody thought so highly of him, etc. Why 'these awful people'? Hart went back a second time. Of course there was a third time too, with Hart storming out and my plaintive, mollifying interruption, 'Now wait a minute, Hart, what's the matter now?'

"Hart turned, pointed, and shouted at the top of his voice, 'I can't stand that damned dog!'"

Always there was something Hart couldn't stand, people or dogs or "all those cats tramping up and down the stairs," and during the spring of 1925 his particular aversion was working for Sweet's Catalogue Service. This time I was more than a little offended, for I had found him the job and regarded it as a pleasant sort of refuge. If I was planning to leave the refuge too, that was because I could earn a living by free-lance writing. Hart, on the other hand, was a poet with no facility in writing prose for publication. His letters were marvelous if he dashed them off, but he suffered from writer's block when faced with the simplest book review. The only trade he knew was copywriting, at which he never acquired great competence, but he was safe at Sweet's as long as he cared to stay. The copy chief liked him and accepted his implausible excuses when he stayed home with a hangover. The salary was low even for those days, but most of us felt that a poet shouldn't demand much money; what he should look for was a job that kept him alive without consuming his ambition or his vital energy. Copywriting for Sweet's Catalogue was merely stating the facts about honest products, and except for two months before the annual publication date, there was no feeling of pressure. Hart was able to write some fine poems during his year at Sweet's, including all but the first and last of the six "Voyages"; he even found time to work on them in the office. It was a friendly office too, but still he began talking again of being caught like a rat in a trap.

At the end of May he demanded that his salary should at once be doubled. When the demand was refused, as Hart expected it to be, he resigned on two weeks' notice, without money saved or much prospect of earning it. Meanwhile Bill Brown, who had received a small legacy, was buying land in the hills seventy-five miles north of Greenwich Village. On the land was an old house that had to be painted, and Hart offered his services as a painter's helper. That was the beginning of a new era for all of us.

2

I first saw the Browns' house at the Fourth of July party they gave that summer. It was an eighteenth-century cottage facing the two stone fences of a post road that had been abandoned for at least a hundred years. Beyond the fences was an old orchard and then a wilderness of overgrown fields. The Browns' land, eighty acres of it, lay in the township of Pawling, New York, near the southern end of a high ridge that paralleled the Connecticut state line. Later when I moved into the neighborhood—as Allen Tate did for a time, and Robert M. Coates the novelist, and Matthew Josephson— I learned something about its history. The ridge along the state border had always been the haunt of outlaws and hermits; during the Revolution it was the last refuge of the local Tories, called "robbers" by the farmers. A band of them had been surrounded and shot down or captured at Robbers' Rocks, a jumble of boulders near the Browns' property. Tory Hill, as the Browns called the neighborhood, still had its share of men who lived outside the law. There were several bootleggers, including a Wall Street bankrupt and a cashiered army officer named Wiley Varian, and there was a character known as the Russian Wolf, who used to brew himself glasses of tea while robbing an unoccupied house.

Most of the houses on the back roads were inhabited by childless couples or old bachelors or widows living alone. The second-growth woods crept over the stone fences and crowded into the dooryards. Tory Hill was a decaying, even desolate neighborhood, but it had dirt roads for walking, blueberries in the unpastured fields, deer in the woods, trout in the brooks that tumbled through secret glens, and never a game warden or a No Trespass sign. October and November were the season when wagonloads of apples went jolting across the state line to the cider mill in Sherman. There was the smell of fermenting cider on all the back roads, and before the deep snows fell, old people came out of their houses for a sort of saturnalia. One passed groups of them by the roadside, hairy men in rags who sang in cracked voices or shouted obscenities. Once I saw Hart among them, reeling and shouting with the others.

We newcomers in the neighborhood—"Dear Tories," as Hart addressed us in his letters—had our saturnalias too, usually on national holidays when friends could join us from the city. The first of our big parties was on that Fourth of July in 1925. The Fourth was a Saturday, but the festivities started the day before, as Hart described them in a letter to his mother. "Nothing could beat the hilarity of this place," he told her, "—with about an omnibusful of people here from New York and a case of gin, to say nothing of jugs of marvelous hard cider from a neighboring farm. You should have seen the dances I did—one all painted up like an African cannibal. My makeup was lurid enough. A small keg on my head and a pair of cerise drawers on my legs!" I remember his pagan ecstasy as he capered on a stone fence built by God-fearing Yankee farmers. "We went swimming at midnight," he continued, "climbed trees, played blind man's buff, rode in wheelbarrows, and gratified every caprice for three days."

It was on Saturday that Hart did his cannibal dance. Afterward, with the nail keg still perched on his head, he sat by the lilacs in the dooryard, med- itatively emptying a box of salt on the phonograph. Sometimes he glanced up at a tree that seemed to be rooted in the dazzlingly blue sky. Caroline Tate, pregnant and stark sober, heard him repeating time and again: "Where the cedar leaf divides the sky . . . where the cedar leaf divides the sky . . . I was promised an improved infancy." On Sunday afternoon, the third day of the party, Hart finally attained the state of exultation in which he was able to write, or put together, one of his more difficult poems. A drizzling rain had driven us indoors from the hummocky lawn that served as an obstacle course, or law court, for our hard-argued games of croquet. Hart went into his room, next to the big kitchen where we were telling stories, and for the next hour we could hear him pounding the typewriter while his phonograph, now cleaned of salt, blared away at full volume. Sometimes the phonograph ran down, the pounding stopped, and Hart fell to declaiming what seemed to be lines of verse, although we couldn't hear the words through the closed door. At last the door opened. Hart came stamping out, his eyes blazing, with a dead cigar in one hand and two or three sheets of heavily corrected typescript in the other.

"Rread that," he growled exultantly, like a jungle cat standing over its kill. "Isn't that the grreatest poem ever written?"

It was "Passage," an intoxicated vision that is hard to understand even in its final draft. That early form of it was nearly incomprehensible, except for a few magical phrases, but we nodded our heads and said yes, yes, it was marvelous, it was a great poem; any milder praise, at the moment, would have driven Hart into a sullen anguish. An hour later most of us started back to the city. Hart stayed on Tory Hill to finish painting the house—"That old dry wood just *drrinks* it up," he kept repeating—and also to revise the poem, a process that required days or weeks of sobriety. "Aside from this one blowout," he told his mother, perhaps truly, "I have not had a drop since I have been here."

That summer Mrs. Crane sold the big house in Cleveland where Hart had passed most of his boyhood and adolescence. She summoned him there to help dispose of the furniture, and he was gone for two months. From his tower room he gathered all his possessions—"5 cases of books; 1 trunk (filled with blankets, china, pictures, etc.); 1 desk; 1 chair."—and shipped them by freight to the Browns'; but Hart didn't follow them, since the cottage was too small to accommodate a permanent lodger. Instead he spent most of the autumn in New York, not writing much and looking desper- ately, by then, for any sort of job.

Meanwhile the Tates had moved to Tory Hill. They couldn't buy a farm- house, not having received a legacy, but they rented eight semifurnished rooms from Mrs. Addie Turner, who lived with her aunt in a barnlike house half a mile from the Browns' cottage by a path that wound through abandoned fields. As compared with the cottage it had conveniences: a pump in the kitchen, a mailbox outside the door, and a telephone less than a mile away. The rent for the rooms was only eight dollars a month, but I wondered how the Tates were going to keep warm and pay for their groceries. Much later Allen told me that while they were living at Addie Turner's the monthly income of the family—mostly from book reviews—was forty dollars or less. But potatoes were cheap that year, and Allen warmed himself twice, in Thoreau's phrase, by sawing and splitting his own firewood.

They were living as cheaply as possible in order to buy time. For Caroline—whose mother had offered to take the baby—it was time to finish a novel, the second she had attempted. Allen had no such definite project, and I think he was trying to preserve something precious to poets; Scott Fitzgerald called it an "inner hush," but it is closer to being an inner monologue, a trickle of words directed to an inner audience, which silently approves the words or demands that they be repeated and revised. Sometimes new conceptions or magical phrases occur in the midst of the monologue, and then it is time to seize upon them, to work over them patiently, to shape them into a poem. But I know Allen felt, as I did too, that real poems did not come from a delicately chosen subject; they had to be waited for; they could not be willed into being. The problem was how to achieve a continual readiness to accept and shape the poems when they did appear, while refusing to commit oneself to any lesser and time-consuming purpose such as earning more money, for example, or eating meat every day.

In the midst of their poverty the Tates were planning to solve Hart's financial problem and thus make it possible for him to finish the long poem he had been talking and dreaming about for nearly three years. Hart had a greater thirst for fame than the rest of us, and it made him less patient in the face of hardship. "For the last six weeks I've been tramping the streets," he said in a letter to his wealthy father, from whom he was estranged, "and being questioned, smelled and refused in various offices. . . . My shoes are leaky, and my pockets are empty; I have helped to empty several other pockets, also. In fact I am a little discouraged." The Tates wrote to New York and invited him to share their living quarters. He would need very little money, they told him; there would be no distractions from writing, and he would have a big room to himself. Hart eagerly accepted their offer, but before he took the train to Patterson, New York, which was the nearest station to Addie Turner's, there was a dramatic change in his fortunes. He had written to the financier Otto Kahn, asking for the loan of a thousand dollars to help him write *The Bridge,* and Kahn—after consulting with Waldo Frank and Eugene O'Neill—not only gave him the money but promised him another thousand if he needed it. Hart finally reached the Turner house on Saturday, December 12, after several nights of celebration. Instead of being despondent and empty-handed, he arrived with liquor, fancy groceries, a new pair of snowshoes, and extravagant plans of work for the coming year.

Considering the strongly marked personalities of all three writers and the cramped quarters in which they were living—only three of the eight rooms could be heated above freezing—and considering the difference in economic status, with Hart now spending six times as much on himself as the Tates were spending together, anyone might have predicted that his visit would end in a quarrel; the proof of good will on both sides is that everyone lived in comparative harmony for nearly four months of a hard backcountry winter. There is a pretty full record of those months in *The Letters of Hart Crane*, which of course should be read with the understanding that the letters present only one side of the story. For two or three weeks Hart was happy putting his room to order and collecting his old and new books in one place for the first time in years. January proved to be colder than usual, even for the hill country along the Connecticut border, and he complained of chillblains from sleeping alone in a frigid room. He said that his hands were so stiff from chopping wood that he could scarcely hold a pen, but nevertheless he was "at work in an almost ecstatic mood" on the last or "Atlantis" section of *The Bridge*. Downstairs at the kitchen table, Caroline was working at her novel hour after hour. Allen was meditating poems as he tramped through the woods with a single-barreled shotgun called the White Powder Wonder; once he shot a squirrel. Hart finished a draft of "Atlantis" toward the end of the month and made a hasty visit to his mother in Cleveland. Soon after his return the deep snows fell, and the Turner house was as effectively isolated as a lighthouse on a Maine island. There were six weeks when the mailman couldn't get through and when Hart used his snowshoes to carry home mail from the farmhouse a mile away that had a telephone. Still, everything was harmonious because everyone was working. Hart had started on the first section of *The Bridge*; then he formulated a new scheme for the whole cycle of poems. "One's original ideas has a way of enlarging steadily," he said, "under the spur of concentration on minute details of execution."

The trouble with that sort of minute concentration is that it can be continued only for a certain time. The trouble with back-country winters is exactly the opposite: they go on and on without consulting the calendar. Hart had finished his new outline for *The Bridge* by the middle of March and had summarized it in a letter to Otto Kahn, but snow was still falling at the end of the month. When it melted at last, the roads were deep in mud, and the Turner house was as effectively isolated as it had been in February. For the first time Hart's letters assumed a querulous tone, now

that he found himself incapable of working. "A life of perfect virtue, re-
dundant health, etc.," he said, "doesn't seem in any way to encourage the
Muse, after all. . . . I drone about, reading, eating and sleeping." But Hart
was never able to drone about for days on end. He would feel a sudden
need to unburden himself, or would think of a funny story that had to be
told, and a moment later he would come bursting into the room where
Allen was trying to finish a review, or else he would clump across the kitchen
while Caroline was puzzling over a difficult scene, and then, if he was
greeted with something less than heartfelt warmth, he would clump back
to sulk in his study. There had to be an explosion, and it came in the middle
of April, before the first spring weather. After that the only communication
between "Mr. Crane's part," as Addie Turner called his rooms, and "the
Tates' part" was by means of notes slipped under doors.

The Tates stayed in the Turner house all summer and raised a garden.
Then, having been offered a basement on Perry Street, they went back to
the place where money had to be spent, but where it was a great deal easier
to earn. Hart had left at the end of April, bound for the Isle of Pines with
Waldo Frank, but his possessions remained at Mrs. Turner's, in his own
quarters. No matter how far he wandered during the next few years, he
always came back to Tory Hill. Mrs. Turner's house was the nearest thing
he had to a home.

Addie Turner was a grass widow of sixty with a whining voice and a
moderately kind heart. Her barn of a house had once served as a dormitory
for a boys' academy that briefly existed in the neighborhood. Besides "Mr.
Crane's part" and "the Tates' part" (later occupied as a studio by Peter
Blume), it also included "*my* part," as Addie called it, and "my aunt's part."
The aunt was a woman of eighty who never spoke to strangers; she spoke
to God. Once we heard her saying as she washed her two dishes, "*Great
Expectations*—I've read that book twenty times and I still don't like it." "Mr.
Crane's part" was two rooms on the second floor, one of them a big study.
It was always neat when I saw it, the drop-leaf oak desk bare of papers, the
books on their shelves, and the snowshoes crossed on the wall, not far from
a carved wooden panoply of African arms that Hart had also bought with
his check from Otto Kahn. Mrs. Turner "did" for him and cooked most of
his meals, which they ate together. Sometimes when Hart felt good and the
phonograph was playing, he put both arms around her oversize waist and
whirled her across the room until she dissolved in simpers.

Hart was at home in the country without belonging to the country. He
did not go trouting in the spring, or plant a garden, or have a dog to follow
him, or gather apples for his own cider, or saw and split a winter's supply
of wood. Sometimes he helped the Browns with their country chores, but
only as a child might help them, for the fun of it. Like Addie Turner and

the hairy old men, he never owned a car or learned to drive one. He spent the mornings in his study, then late in the afternoon he tramped the roads, perhaps with an empty cider jug to be filled on Birch Hill. In the evening he usually visited the Browns, but sometimes he roamed much farther. When we were living five miles from Tory Hill, Hart came to see us fairly often. I remember one occasion when Peggy and I drove home from a fairly gay evening at the Browns' and went to bed at midnight. It must have been hours later when I woke to find a heavy arm resting on my shoulder. Hart was lying face downward between my wife and me, embracing both of us. Without saying a word, we disengaged ourselves. Hart rose, also without a word, and dressed in the faint glow of starlight from the window; then he groped and grumbled his way down the breakneck stairs. We never asked him how he got home.

Hart, Hart. . . . He did so much that was outrageous, but so much that was unaffectedly kind or exuberant and so much that kept us entertained. Nobody yawned when Hart was there. He liked to dance—aggressively, acrobatically, without much knowledge of steps, but with an unerring sense of rhythm; he swept his partner off her feet and usually she followed him with a look of delicious terror. He liked to do solo dances too, including one that he called the Gazotsky because it was vaguely Russian. He liked anything sung by Sophie Tucker or Marlene Dietrich and burst into admiring chuckles as he listened. He liked to hear nonsense poems, the bawdier the better, and wrote a few of them. I remember one about Sappho that he used to recite:

> Said the poetess Sappho of Greece,
> "Ah, better by far than a piece
>   Is to have my pudenda
>   Rubbed hard by the enda
> The little pink nose of my niece."

Somebody repeated Hart's lines to Norman Douglas, in a slightly altered version, and he promptly included them in his famous anthology of dirty limericks. I forget what Hart said when he saw the book.

There is so much I forget about him, as if part of my own life had been erased, and so much I remember too. Hart, Hart. . . . He had a streak of puritanism and liked to punish himself for his vices. He also had a snobbish streak that was revealed when he talked about rich or titled acquaintances. Sometimes he promoted a friend—Harry Crosby, for instance—to the status of millionaire without consulting Dun and Bradstreet's. In spite of a robust constitution he suffered from a number of recurring ailments, including acidosis, urethritis, urticaria (or plain hives), constipation, crabs, and rose fever. These he treated with home remedies, chiefly canned tomatoes, larkspur lotion, and an enema bag. He tried to stay away from doctors, possibly because he was afraid of being given the obvious advice: Stop drinking.

Much as he liked plays, he did not go to see them unless somebody gave him free tickets. He seldom went to movies, and I do not remember seeing him with a newspaper in his hand; in fact I never heard of his reading for entertainment. He read classical authors, slowly and intently; his favorites were Dante, Rabelais, Marlowe, Shakespeare, Melville, Whitman, and Rimbaud. I think he approached them almost as if they had written the standard textbooks of advanced engineering; he was looking for models that would help in designing his Bridge. When he dipped into magazines, it was chiefly to see what other poets of the time were doing. Almost everything in his life was directed toward one end, that of writing great poems, and he permitted himself few distractions. Working in advertising agencies was a distraction from poetry, so he couldn't stand much of it. But drunkenness, dancing, frenzied conversation, and sexual orgies were not distractions for Hart, since he regarded them as means of attaining a heightened consciousness and hence as essential parts of the creative process.

3

As I think back on his brief career and its bitter end, they seem to me as foreordained as the results of a demonstration in a laboratory: take this and that, do this and that, and here is what happens. Hart, of course, had special gifts combined with liabilities, and there was something in the mood of the age that encouraged special types of frenzy, but otherwise the operation might almost have proceeded in a vacuum. Philip Horton was mistaken in the subtitle he chose for his fine early biography of Hart: "The Life of an American Poet." Hart was a poet and an American, but putting the two words together produces a sentimental effect, as if Horton were saying, "This is what happens to poets in America; they are driven to madness and suicide." Or again it is as if he were saying to Hart's relatives (most of them dead), and the magazines that did not print his work (but many of them did), and the publishers who hesitated over his books, and the critics who attacked them, and Hart's friends who had patience with him, but perhaps not enough (or too much)—as if he were saying, "You failed to understand him, all of you, and hastened his end."

The fact is that Hart might have lived in any country and the result would have been the same: for example, he might have been called Mayakovsky or Yesenin. When he went to France in 1929, he met with less comprehension from the *agents de police* than he ever did from Irish cops in Brooklyn.

The French kicked and beat him, threw him into jail, and "the dirty skunks in the Santé wouldn't give him any paper to write poems on, the bastards," as Harry Crosby wrote in his Paris diary. Hart didn't talk much about the experience. What he wouldn't admit to others or even to himself—except in moments of cold self-knowledge that he never ceased to have—was that he could scarcely have written the poems even if the bastards had given him plenty of paper and a private cell. By 1929 the operation had gone beyond the point of fruitful returns.

John Untermeyer's later and more circumstantial biography (*Voyager: A Life of Hart Crane,* 1969) makes it clear that family circumstances—the divorce of his parents and, in particular, the mother's neurotic demands on him—were largely responsible for launching him on the course he would follow. But once he was launched on the course, I doubt whether any amount of understanding could have done more than delay the end of it. The immediate forces that led to the tragedy were more internal than external, and they were literary before they were moral. They had their source in Hart's single-minded determination to write great poems of a special type, and even more in the process he found for writing them.

The process started when Hart chose, or was chosen by, the subject for a poem. We do not know exactly how or when that happened—whether it was in a moment of drunken exaltation or during lonely hours at his desk—but almost everything that followed has become a matter of record. His first step, after the subject imposed itself, was to make a collection of words and phrases that might be used in the poem. He liked words that had an unusual sound or shape, and "thesaurized" them, as the French say, almost like a magpie collecting bits of glass. Some of the best words came from his rereading of Melville and Whitman. Almost all the phrases were invented—with what a heaped-up wealth of images—but a few of them were overheard in waterfront speakeasies or in the Seventh Avenue subway: "I'm a Democrat, I know what time it is." "Fandaddle daddy, don't ask for change. If you don't like my gate, why do you swing on it?" He made note of the phrases, whether invented or overheard, on the backs of envelopes he carried in his pockets, and sometimes he tested their effect by reciting them to a group of friends. "One must be drenched in words, literally soaked in them," he told Gorham Munson, "to have the right ones form themselves into the proper pattern at the right moment."

That first stage in the creative process might last for weeks or months—it lasted five years with "Cape Hatteras"—or the words might be collected for a poem that would never be written, as in the case of a projected "Calgary Express" for which he was still taking notes in 1929. Once the right words had formed themselves into something like the proper pattern, there came a stage of revision that again might last for weeks or months. Hart was like the sorcerer of a primitive tribe; he was trying to produce not poems only, but incantations or mantras that would have a magical power, evoking in the reader the same hallucinated visions that the poet had seen. Such incantations cannot exert their full effect unless every pause is calculated and every word is in its inevitable place; not a syllable can go to waste; everything has to be patiently tested, sharpened, enriched, and clarified. "What made the first part of my poem so good," Hart said truly in another letter to Munson, "was the extreme amount of time, work and thought put on it."

But that was the third stage, not the second, and something had to intervene between the collection of shining phrases and their assignment, one by one, to their final places in a pattern. The pattern itself had to take shape, at the right moment—or rather, for Hart, there had to be a "new level of consciousness," as he called it, at which he saw a vision of what the poem should be as a structure in time. The vision might be a momentary thing, but it was absolutely essential to Hart, and he would make any sacrifice to achieve it. When he was a boy writing his first poems, he found that smoking strong cigars was one means of inducing visions—"I used to feel myself being wafted right out of the window," he said. Later he decided that drinking wine was an easier way. "If I could afford wine *every* evening," he said in a letter written from Cleveland in 1922, "I might do more"—that is, write better poems. "My carousing on New Year's Eve," he said a few months later, "had one good outcome; it started the third part of 'Faustus and Helen' with more gusto than before." "The Wine Menagerie," which grew out of a similar experience, begins with the lines:

> Invariably when wine redeems the sight,
> Narrowing the mustard scansions of the eyes,
> A leopard ranging always in the brow
> Asserts a vision. . . .

The first drafts of almost all his poems, after 1922, were composed in the same fashion, sometimes after years of waiting for the right moment. That moment, on which he pounced like a leopard, was a state of nervous exaltation usually induced by alcohol, but also provoked at times by rage or sexual frenzy; and it could be prolonged and intensified—so he soon discovered—by listening to music with a heavy beat (usually blues or rumbas or Ravel's *Bolero*). Therefore he got drunk night after night, always hopefully; therefore his typewriter stood close to an Orthophonic Victrola, then the newest thing in portable wind-up phonographs; and therefore he cruised the waterfront looking for obliging sailors. All his carousals had an element of self-sacrifice, almost of self-flagellation; they were undertaken partly and primarily as a means of driving himself to write great poems. As

Rimbaud had done half a century before him, he was trying to make himself a seer "by a long, immense, and calculated derangement of all the senses."

Rimbaud abandoned the effort at the age of twenty; he said of it afterward, "All *that* was bad." For the rest of his life, which was somewhat longer than Hart's, he wrote nothing but letters and a few travel articles. How many other poets have tried that method of self-induced frenzy—and how many sham poets, each pretending to believe in his talent as an excuse for his vices, or simply for cadging drinks. I used to watch their performances at the Café du Dôme, and later I would see them slumped over the sidewalk tables with their long hair dribbling in a sticky pool of rum; they were a troupe of bogus failures, all hating one another. But the method has been followed by genuine poets too, and sometimes it has led to remarkable achievements, as in Hart's case and a very few others; the trouble is that nobody has enough talent or a strong enough constitution to follow it for more than a few years. Dissipation, which has been a means to an end, soon becomes an end in itself. The critical sense, which is a sober faculty, has little chance to be exercised. There is less capacity for sustained revision, and therefore the incantations lose the rightness on which they depended for their magical power. As regards the essential visions, they can no longer be evoked by a strong cigar or a flask of wine in an Italian tenement; they must be aroused by more brutal stimulants—and are they visions then, or merely hallucinations? The "leopard ranging always in the brow" asserts itself in acts of destruction or self-destruction.

That was Hart's story in brief. His recipe for writing poems was relatively successful for only five years—from 1923 to 1927—and it was completely successful for only five weeks, in the summer of 1926, when he was on the Isle of Pines. During those weeks of frenzied labor he completed more than half the poems in *The Bridge,* including all but one of what nobody should hesitate to call the great poems. The following summer, on Tory Hill, he wrote "The River," which seems to me the greatest of all, and soon afterward a draft of "The Hurricane," which was his last attempt to create a new idiom; but that was close to the end of his development as a poet. The three long poems that he wrote in the fall of 1929 in a desperate effort to finish *The Bridge*—they were "Indiana," "Cape Hatteras," and "Quaker Hill"— proved to be sentimental or bombastic and, as I think Hart realized, they weakened the effect of the work as a whole. He would have done anything to revive his talent, and he even tried the expedient of staying sober for three months, while visiting his father at Chagrin Falls, near Cleveland, but it was not a success. "If abstinence is clarifying to the vision, as they claim," he wrote to Waldo Frank during that period, "then give me back the blindness of my will. It needs a fresh baptism." It received not only a baptism, in the following year, but a total immersion in folly.

During that final year in Mexico, Hart told Katherine Anne Porter "that he was no longer capable of feeling anything except under the most violent and brutal shocks: 'and I can't even then deceive myself that I really feel anything,' he said." Nevertheless he proved capable of having one completely new experience, a tender and passionate love affair with a woman, and under that stimulus he stayed sober long enough to finish a poem about Mexico, "The Broken Tower," that was almost worthy to be placed with the best of the poems he had written in 1926. In other circumstances it might have been the beginning of a new symphonic cycle. But he no longer had enough confidence in himself to be sure the poem was good without assurance from friends, which was slow in coming; and it had required such exhausting efforts that he doubted whether he could write another.

Hart lived for only a month after finishing "The Broken Tower" at the end of March 1932. There were many reasons for his suicide, including his frenzied drinking, his sexual quandary, his lack of money—or prospects of earning it—and his feeling that poets had no place in American life, at least during those early years of the Depression. He used to fling up his arms and shout, "What good are poets today! The world needs men of action." But the mood would have passed if only he could have been sure that he was still a poet. Writing poetry—not poems written, but those to come— was the motive and justification for all his vices, for life itself. He would never be an old man using his picturesque decay as an excuse for getting drinks on the house. With no more poems he could be confident of writing, now that his method had betrayed him, he had no reason for being. Wherever he turned or ran, he was caught like a rat in a trap, and the trap was himself.

4

The last time I saw Hart was six miles from Tory Hill, on the next-to-last Sunday of March 1931. Peggy and I had separated, painfully but amicably, and she was planning to go to Mexico for a divorce. I was living in New York, working hard for *The New Republic*. Peter and Ebie Blume, who were spending the winter in Sherman, in the Josephsons' not-much-remodeled farmhouse, had asked me up for the weekend. When I arrived on Saturday afternoon I was surprised to find Hart there. He greeted me shyly at first, as if he thought I might be angry at him, and then with boisterous good humor.

"They've given me a Guggenheim, what do you think of *that*?" he said.

I thought it was splendid, but wondered what would happen next. Since his return from Paris, Hart had been running through friends and admirers like an heir through his rich estate. One usually tolerant companion had said of him, "People will love Hart when he's dead." They loved him when he was living, too, but he was making it hard for them. After a famous Labor Day at Amawalk in 1929, his friends had stopped inviting him to big parties. That was when he smashed Montgomery Schuyler's collection of records and tried to throw the phonograph out of a second-story window. Then he shouted to Monte, "My father is a millionaire. Who is *your* father?" Matty Josephson had a story to tell from New York. "All right, so we give a party," he said, "and Hart is there, and along about one o'clock he gets to the violent stage where he wants to smash the furniture. So we throw him out. We don't hold it against him, it's just the way he was. But we were in a rented place and we couldn't have the furniture smashed. When the party is finally over, we go to bed. Then along about four in the morning Hart has progressed to the contrite stage. So he phones, waking you up to apologize. That's the stage you can't forgive."

In the spring of 1930 Addie Turner had become terrified of his violence. Once when he stormed into the night to buy another jug of cider, she locked the door against him, but he broke it down when he got back and broke a window too; then he went reeling from room to room with a lighted lamp. "Oh, Mr. Crane," she wailed. At the beginning of July Addie told him to take what he owned and leave the house. "Mr. Crane's part" stood empty that summer, and Hart stayed in neighboring farmhouses, wherever he was invited for a week or a month. There were two weeks when he lived in a tent, but not in sin, with a girl he called Little Miss Twidget. His possessions were scattered in two or three places. Now in March, after his sober but unproductive winter in Chagrin Falls, he was back to collect the possessions, by which he set great store—the snowshoes, the books, the panoply of African arms, and a silver-bronze "Sea Gull" by Gaston Lachaise—and leave them in charge of the Blumes, with whom he was on good terms. He had decided that this would be his last visit to the neighborhood.

That afternoon he passed out gifts to everybody, with a warmth and thoughtfulness that made them precious. To Peter he gave a suit of evening clothes, handed down from his father; to Ebie, a pea jacket and a striped French sailor shirt; to Muriel Maurer—a friend of the Blumes—the broad red-flannel sash he had never dared to wear; and to me, a belt embossed with a large brass anchor. I felt as though we were Roman soldiers casting lots for his garments. At dinner the Blumes served one drink to each of us, then took the bottle away. Hart watched it go in unaccustomed silence.

Sunday, the last of the days I spent with Hart, might have been the epitome of many other days. In the morning, while Peter worked on a painting—it was "South of Scranton," now at the Metropolitan—Hart and I went for a walk on the frozen road, under the gray March sky. Hart was thoughtful; he seemed to have acquired the tired wisdom about himself that is sometimes revealed by dissipated men (as notably in Byron's letters). He talked without bitterness about the critics who had condemned *The Bridge* and wondered if they weren't partly right; "But—" he said, and left the word hanging. His difficulty now was that he didn't know what to do next. In asking for the Guggenheim he had spoken of going to France, but he was dismayed by the thought of the months he had wasted there.

"What about Mexico?" I said.

I had spent October in Mexico, and I talked about its somber landscapes, its mixture of Spanish and Indian cultures, and its cheapness as compared with Europe. Cheap rum, cheap cigars that were good to smoke, houses that rented for practically nothing, and a man to take care of the house— a *mozo*—for ten dollars a month. Some of the *mozos* were said to offer additional services, and I had heard that the sexual customs of the Aztecs were much like those of the Arabs.

Hart took a few steps in silence. "Maybe I'll go to Mexico," he said, "if the Guggenheim people don't mind."

Suddenly he started talking about the long poem on Cortez he had planned to write. He recited four lines of the poem—I think they were the only ones ever written, but they seemed to open gates for him. At lunch there was nothing to drink and Hart didn't complain. His face, instead of being pale as it was in the morning, had gone beet red under his now completely gray hair. He talked excitedly about Mexico and then, without a pause, about Marlene Dietrich, whose voice, he said, came straight from Tutankhamen's tomb. Ebie, usually attentive to her guests, made only a pretense of listening. Once she went out to the pantry and came back with a worried look. I learned afterward that Hart had found and carried off the bottle that the Blumes had produced at dinner. It wasn't the first time he had displayed the drunkard's talent for finding hidden liquor and hiding it somewhere else.

That afternoon was a party for Hart, even if the rest of us were sober, and it proceeded like all his parties, by inexorable phases. First came the hour when he was full of honest warm affection for everyone present and had so many good things to say about each of us that we must have all been blushing. He spoke with the same affection of his friend Harry Crosby, publisher of *The Bridge,* who had committed suicide while on a visit to New York the year before; then he insisted on reading us one of Harry's long poems, which described a voyage down the Nile in a dahabeah. The poem had a refrain, and Hart shouted it at the top of his voice, pounding his fist on the table:

> Let the sun shine!
> And the sun shone.

It seemed the dark living room was flooded with hot Egyptian sunlight. Hart excused himself for a moment, I suppose to visit the hidden bottle. When he returned, he was in the second phase, that of brilliant monologue. Everything reminded him of something else: landscapes, of musical compositions; poems, of skyrockets or waterfalls; persons, of birds, animals, or piles of grimy snow; he could abstract the smile from a woman's face and make us see it in the design of the mantelpiece. His now immense eyes glowed in the first lamplight; they seemed to have burned the vitality from his other features and turned his hair to ashes. Soon he was launched on a stream of words repeated more for their sound than for their meaning. I was going to say that nobody ever made a record of Hart's monologues, but that isn't quite true: Hart himself recorded a few of them when he was drinking alone, and there were times when he must have hammered away at his typewriter as if he were addressing a crowded room. I found one of those jottings among my papers. Part of it reads: "They say my digits fidget, that I'm but a follicle of my former fratricide. . . . What shall I do? I masticate firmly and bite off all my nails. I practice invention to the brink of intelligibility. I insult all my friends and ride ostriches furiously across the Yukon, while parrots berate me to the accompaniment of the most chaste reticules. By all the mysteries of Gomorrah, I ask, what can a gaping gastronomist gather in such a gulch of simulation?"

That was how he talked for part of the late March afternoon, but then there began to be periods of silence, while Hart glared into the shadows as if in search of enemies. I may have heard him utter the word "betrayal." It was the phase at which one might have expected broken furniture, but luckily he was a little afraid of Peter, who had put an end to one of his drunken rages by throwing him down and sitting on his chest, until Bill Brown came to sit on his thrashing feet. This time the dangerous moment passed and dinner was served. Hart said little during the meal, and less while he was packing, although there was an interlude when he had us searching the house for his bottle of larkspur lotion. We found it sitting on the mantelpiece, where he had left it; then we set out in an open touring car for the twenty-mile drive to the station. Hart crouched against Muriel's thick-piled coat and shivered violently, while his eyes followed the headlights as they picked out now a white farmhouse, now a line of heavy white posts at a curve in the road. He began wailing, "Oh, the white fences . . . oh, the interminable white Connecticut fences"—as if he were giving voice to some inner anguish, buried for years, and as if the fences were an expression of everything that had hindered him from creating a myth for America.

Hart slept in the train, then roused himself as it crawled into Grand Central Station. He said good-by to me in the concourse, warmly but decisively, while his eyes kept glancing away. He had entered the last phase of his party—a familiar phase, though I never saw more than the start of it—when he cruised the waterfront looking for sailors and sometimes ended by being beaten or jailed. As I watched him almost running with his two bags toward the taxi stand, I thought that he was obeying the iron laws of another country than ours, and I felt that his weekend had been a sort of furlough from the dead.

1973

Van Wyck Brooks's "Usable Past"

After Van Wyck Brooks finished the last volume of *Makers and Finders,* the most important work of his later years was his three books of memoirs. The first of these was *Scenes and Portraits* (1954), the second and liveliest was *Days of the Phoenix* (1957), and the third, more discursive, was *From the Shadow of the Mountain,* which appeared in 1961 when Brooks was seventy-five. Not one of them has received the attention that each deserves. It is a convenience and a pleasure to have them available in this one big volume.

I think of them together as Brooks's memoirs rather than his autobiography in the strict sense. Of course the work is autobiographical too; it tells us candidly what we need to know about the author's family, education, career, and guiding purposes. Still, it is less concerned with these or with his inner world—except in one moving chapter of *Days of the Phoenix*—than it is with the outer world, which for him consisted mostly of writers and painters. He looked at them all with an observant and hopeful eye. *Scenes and Portraits,* the title of the first book, might be applied to the work as a whole.

In rereading it we note again what we might have forgotten, that Brooks was a painterly writer, with a gift for rendering character by costume or gesture and atmosphere by his choice of images. One of the best of his many interiors painted in the Dutch style is Petitpas' restaurant in the Chelsea district of Manhattan, where old J. B. Yeats, the poet's father, used to preside over a tableful of writers without publishers and artists without a gallery. Among the occasional guests was Blaikie Murdoch, a Scotsman of wide and curious learning, who "followed his own personal notions of style," Brooks says, "sprinkling commas over his writing as a Parsee sprinkles red pepper over meat. . . . Bald as a tonsured monk, with a mind as ripe as old Roquefort cheese, Blaikie Murdoch was living in a basement somewhere, cooking his meals on a gas-jet, not far away; and, as he talked, he would stealthily manoeuvre stray crusts of bread on the table into the yawning pockets of his old brown jacket."

We remember Murdoch by those crusts of bread, as we remember old Yeats by his impractical wisdom and his delight in fine words, including the name of the disease from which he was to die. When he heard that he was an "antique cardiac arteriosclerotic," he said to Brooks, "I would rather be called that than the King of the South of Egypt." Among the other guests at Petitpas', we recognize Alan Seeger by "the long black Paris student's cape" that he borrowed one winter when he had no overcoat, and Brooks himself, then in his early twenties, by his splendid waistcoats and the holes in the bottoms of his shoes. Every detail helps to recreate the atmosphere of a time when young writers were poor by choice as well as necessity and when many of them wore poverty as a uniform, but with a flower in the buttonhole.

Old Yeats, poor as the youngsters who surrounded him, was a portrait painter without commissions, and he was also Brooks' tutelary spirit. Once he said that the genius of his art was "largely a genius for friendship." The best portraits are painted, he explained, when friendship governs the relation of the sitter to the painter. Brooks took the principle to heart, and perhaps that is why he has devoted less space in this volume to himself than to his friends. He gives us heroic portraits of Max Perkins, Ned Sheldon, that brilliant playwright crippled and blinded by arthritis, Waldo Frank, Sherwood Anderson, and many others, including most of the rebels who surrounded him when he was writing the early essays that announced a second American renaissance. Meanwhile the author himself is revealed not so much directly as by reflection, with his friendships serving as mirrors of his own idealistic, shy, loyal, dogged, scrupulous, but not unworldly spirit. As for his career, we see again that it had logical consistency and, almost to the end, a continued growth of a sort not often found in the lives of American writers.

For himself Brooks had only one ambition from the days when he went to high school in Plainfield, New Jersey. He wanted to be a writer, and he knew almost from the beginning what kind of writer: not a novelist, not a poet—though he wrote some early verses—but a critic. At first he thought of becoming an art critic on the model of Ruskin, but soon he began writing about books. "I was convinced," he says, "that criticism in some form was the most delightful activity one could dream of in this world. I even felt that everything might be expressed in criticism, as others have felt about music or fiction or sculpture." Gradually this private ambition developed into a public and largely unselfish one. That was for two good reasons: because he couldn't hope to become a critic of stature unless he had new, important, preferably native works to criticize, and because he couldn't succeed in his personal aim unless he helped to create an atmosphere in which other young writers might succeed. Thus, his career would depend in two ways on the general fate of American letters.

The fate seemed dubious in the years from 1904 to 1907, when Brooks was an undergraduate at Harvard. It was a time when the Eastern universities regarded themselves as trading posts beleaguered on the edge of Indian country, where they offered a stock of cultural goods to the younger natives. Almost all the goods had been freighted in from Europe. Students received the impression that there had once been an American literature of sorts, but that it lay "a generation or more behind us," as the poet George E. Woodberry told his Columbia classes. He expressed only a tempered admiration for the older literature, which had produced, he said, not one poet who was even of the rank of Thomas Gray. His judgment was echoed at other universities. When Barrett Wendell of Harvard wrote a book about American literature, he made his readers feel—so Howells said—that the subject was "not worth the attention of people meaning to be critical." Our past was thus abolished as a field of study, and hardly a course was offered at Harvard or elsewhere that dealt at length with American writers. As for the present, Woodberry disposed of its claims to attention in the article on American literature that he wrote for the eleventh edition (1910) of the *Encyclopedia Britannica*. He concluded the article by saying that the social tradition and culture of the American people

. . . make them impenetrable to the present ideas of Europe as they are current in literary forms. Nor has anything been developed from within that is fertile in literature. . . . The intellectual life is now rather to be found in social, political and natural science than elsewhere, the imaginative life is feeble, and when felt is crude; the poetic pulse is imperceptible.

Yet Harvard in those days was full of aspiring writers, some of whom would become Brooks's lifelong friends. They all wanted to produce enduring works, but they saw little hope of producing them in their native land where all the fruits seemed blighted. One of the aspirants, who looked forward to being an art critic, told Brooks in a letter that American criticism was virtually all "broken meat from the European table." The moral he drew was that one should "Sit at the first table, not the second," and he hurried off to Italy, where he planned to emulate Bernard Berenson. Other Harvard friends went to Paris or London or a German university; any city in Europe seemed to have a better climate for writing than New York. In those days Brooks himself believed "that the only chance an American had to succeed as a writer was to betake himself [to Europe] with all possible speed." He raced through college in three years, then traveled by steerage to England, where he nearly starved as a free-lance journalist and published his first book at the age of twenty-three.

As soon as the book appeared he went back to New York, in obedience to another and opposite belief that he held at the same time. "I was convinced as well," he says, "that a man without a country could do nothing of importance, that writers must draw sustenance from their own common flesh and blood and that therefore deracination also meant ruin. For me, at that time, the American writer could neither successfully stay *nor* go—he had only two alternatives, the frying-pan and the fire; and the question was therefore how to change the whole texture of life at home so that writers and artists might develop there."

His early ambition, without changing in essence, had found a new goal that would be retained for the rest of his life—though at different times he would follow different paths toward the same destination. Happily the question he tried to answer was not so broad and futile as it sounds. As a critic, a single dissenting voice, he realized that he couldn't do much "to change the whole texture of life at home." He might, however, do something to change our conception of the writer in America, and the writer's conception of his own task, always with the aim of encouraging himself and others to do better work, the best that was in them. To this aim he devoted himself with admirable consistency and—let it be recorded—with an amazing degree of success.

There is one field in which the success can be measured. When we think of the contempt for American authors, mixed with ignorance about them, that prevailed in universities during the reign of Barrett Wendell; when we contrast it with the reverence for many of the same authors that is now being proclaimed in hundreds of scholarly monographs each year, as well as being revealed statistically by the multiplication of courses in American literature—while living writers share in the glory reflected from the past by being invited to the campus as novelists or poets in residence—we might also remember that Brooks had more to do with creating the new attitude than anyone else in the country. Not a few of the academic critics who attacked him in later years were men whose careers would have been impossible if Brooks had not found them a subject and broken a path they could follow.

I said that he tried different methods of approaching what remained the same goal. In reality there were only two of the methods, and each of them belonged to a different stage of his career. In the early stage, which lasted from 1909 to 1926, he was the prophet of a new literature, and his method was a combination of exhortation, admonition, and holding up to scorn. America in 1915, he said, was "like a vast Sargasso Sea—a prodigious welter of unconscious life, swept by ground-swells of half-conscious emotions." Ideally the country might have looked for direction to its poets and novelists and critics, who serve as "the pathfinders of society; to them belongs the vision without which the people perish." But the writers themselves were lost. "What immediately strikes one, as one surveys the history of our literature during the last half century, is the singular impotence of its creative spirit. That we have always had an abundance of talent is, I think, no less evident: what I mean is that so little of this talent really finds its way. . . . The chronic state of our literature is that of a youthful promise which is never redeemed."

I am quoting from three of Brooks's early essays: *America's Coming-of-Age* (1915), *Letters of Leadership* (1918), and *The Literary Life in America* (1921). Together they composed a manifesto for the new generation of writers, one that has been compared in its effects with Emerson's address "The American Scholar," delivered at Harvard in 1837. Emerson did more than anyone else to produce what was afterward known as the American renaissance. There was something Emersonian in Brooks's tone, and writing in the early days of a second renaissance, he found as many eager listeners.

He did not merely utter lamentations, which were justified at the time; he also diagnosed the weakness of American writing and offered a prescription for making it stronger. As compared with the writing "of almost any European country"—and the comparison with France and England was never far from Brooks's mind—its principal weakness was that "Our writers all but universally lack the power of growth, the endurance that enables one to continue personal work after the freshness of youth had gone." Instead of developing into great men of letters, they had surrendered easily to commercialism and convention, largely—Brooks told us in italics—because they had lacked "the sense that one is *working in a great line*." His prescription followed from the diagnosis: we should develop a tradition in American literature and, by studying its history, we should try to discover what he was the first to call a "usable past."

The two famous biographies that he wrote during this period were part of the search for that past, but they were also cautionary tales; they showed the consequences resulting from two different answers to his old question, whether American writers should live abroad or stay at home. *The Ordeal of Mark Twain* (1920) presented the example of a great American author who stayed at home and crippled his talent by yielding to native conventions. In later years Brooks revised the book to incorporate new facts, but he never changed his central judgment of Mark Twain's career. *The Pilgrimage of Henry James* (1925) told the story of another great author, one who lived abroad and who suffered equally—so Brooks insisted—through losing touch with his own people. About James he was never sure of having been completely fair. "I was to realize, looking back," he says, "that I had been quarreling with myself when I appeared to be quarreling with Henry James. For, like many of my friends, I too had been enchanted with Europe, and I had vaguely hoped to continue to live there. It struck me that if I was always 'straining to read the face of America,'—Paul Rosenfeld's phrase for my obsession—it was because of an over-determination, and perhaps the question of expatriation had so possessed my mind because this mind itself had been divided."

There was a time when "I was pursued especially," Brooks also says, "with nightmares in which Henry James turned great luminous menacing eyes upon me." That was during the prolonged nervous breakdown that he suffered after 1926, when his life became a succession of doctors, nursing homes with barred windows, and dreams of self-annihilation. "I could no longer sleep," he says, "I scarcely sat down for a year, I lived in a Plutonian psychical twilight." When he emerged from this "season in hell," as he calls it in that moving chapter of *Days of the Phoenix,* he was ready at the age of forty-five to start a new career.

Its goal would be the same as in his earlier career, that is, to give us a new picture of the American writer, of what he had done in the past and of what he might achieve. But Brooks had changed during his season in hell, and he was now temperamentally unable to follow his earlier method of combining exhortation with admonishment like a prophet in Israel. As for holding up to scorn or writing cautionary tales, both seemed alien to his new character, for the wound in himself had made him loath to expose the wounds in others. He looked eagerly now for things he could praise, especially in the lives of earlier American writers who had been long neglected. At the same time his experience in sanitariums had given him—or helped to give—more patience, a stronger sense of discipline, and a new habit of rising early in the morning, never later than six, and going straight to work. He was ready now to move toward his goal by a second method based on patient scholarship.

The five volumes of *Makers and Finders* took him nineteen years to write, or about four years for each volume. During that time he worked ten or twelve hours a day and read five thousand American books, some of which had not been opened by anyone else for more than half a century. What seems remarkable in this age of collective undertakings is that he did the work unaided by collaborators, research assistants, or even a secretary. He copied out all the quotations, and "I have not found one error in transcription," he said in a letter to a Harvard classmate, Samuel Eliot Morison, who had questioned some statements in *The Flowering of New England.* Besides Brooks's passion for the sort of accuracy that one couldn't demand of a hired assistant, he had another passion for being his own copyist. "It's the only way to get the feel of an author," he explained. "Passages copied by someone else don't have the same meaning." The manuscript of each volume was written in his small, nervous, angular, hard-to-decipher hand at the rate of never more than a page of three hundred and fifty words each day. It was the sort of purely individual project on a grand scale that has seldom been carried out since the days of Prescott, Parkman, and the other great New England historians.

The work as it progressed had an interesting critical reception. For *The Flowering of New England,* which was the first volume to appear, in 1936, though it came second in Brooks's plan for the series, there was something close to universal praise. Almost the only discordant voices were some of those on the political left, where one heard complaints that Brooks was no longer a leader and prophet, but had turned to "scholarly storytelling." The stories of course had a purpose, but the left-wing critics were slow to grasp it. Among the academic reviewers, Morison was the only one who thought that Brooks had been reckless with his facts. Brooks was disturbed by the charge and wrote his classmate a seven-page letter, not for publication, a copy of which was found among his own papers marked "*Important*—to keep."

So far [one page of it reads], in going over my book, and the various criticisms of it, I have detected 14 mistakes. This includes two mistakes (the same mistake repeated) regarding the Franconia Notch, also the error about the sloop Harvard, and about H. G. Otis, who was not a merchant. . . . Some of these errors are exceedingly slight, and even on the ragged edge of truth. Observe, I am not defending this ragged edge. I did not say that Otis's punch-bowl held ten gallons. I had, and thought I conveyed, a different visual image in saying that "ten gallons of punch evaporated out of it," i.e., that the punch-bowl was refilled. Again, regarding the sloop Harvard, I did not specifically say that it was moored at the port, and I certainly thought it was, and I gladly accept the blame for my misstatement. (On looking through my notes, I find that I got this impression from Lowell's *Cambridge Thirty Years Ago*: "Cambridge has long had its port, but the greatest part of its maritime trade was, thirty years ago, entrusted to a single Argo, the sloop Harvard," etc.) The error was not in the transcription, but in a faulty inference from it. It seems to me, in the case in question, the inference was not unnatural, but I freely confess my error in 14 cases.

Now why do I dwell on this? To show that I am not disinclined to be careful about "pesky facts" and to ask you how you justify the charge that I "throw my facts about."

In truth the charge, though made in good faith, could not be justified except by adducing some inconsequential errors that Brooks was glad to correct, and it was seldom repeated in reviews of later volumes. The first of these, *New England: Indian Summer* (1940), had an autumnal rather than a springlike charm as compared with *The Flowering,* but this other quality was equally appreciated by its reviewers, some of whom babbled in a delirium of praise. There were attacks, however, in three or four scholarly journals, and there were more of these after *The World of Washington Irving* (1944), which Brooks regarded as the best of his books. Dealing as it did with the early writers of the Republic, many of whom had been forgotten even by scholars, it conveyed a happy feeling of exploration and rediscovery; but academic critics complained about Brooks's method. They said that he was wasting his time on minor figures, that he wasn't truly critical, and that in fact he wasn't writing a history of American literature of the sort that could be assigned to their students. The complaints were louder after *The Times of Melville and Whitman* (1947), and loudest after the series was completed with *The Confident Years* in 1952. By that time, moreover, the attacks on Brooks's method were being accompanied by others on his conception of American literature as a whole.

It has always seemed to me that the critics had reason, not for rushing into battle against Brooks, but for discussion and disagreement with him about that last grand question. At the end of *The Confident Years* he tries to define the American tradition that he has been presenting in narrative form all through the five volumes. It is, he tells us, a belief in the inherent goodness of men and in their capacity to govern themselves; it is "the tradition of Jefferson, Paine and Crèvecoeur and the roundhead side in the English civil war,—with all the typical American institutions . . . and it was this that Europeans had in mind when they complained that American writers had never been 'American enough.'"

From this [he continues] had sprung the great body of writers from Benjamin Franklin down to a regiment of poets, romancers, historians and thinkers who had given the country, in literature, a character of its own, and to deny this was to deny that America had a character, that it was anything but a congeries of exiles from Europe. This was the core of America, in fact,—to the world America meant this or nothing,—it was what the "Latin genius" was to France; and where else could one find the American "uniqueness" to fit the prescription of Eliot himself that "the culture of each country should be unique"?

But is Brooks defining the only American tradition in literature? One notes in this final chapter of *Makers and Finders* that he seems obsessed with T. S. Eliot, whom he accuses, in effect, of having betrayed the essential spirit of the nation. Might it not be more accurate to say that Eliot has followed one American tradition in preference to another? Brooks himself has earlier made it clear that Eliot had many American predecessors, both in choosing to live abroad and in his attitude toward the art of letters. Other critics have traced his lineage as a writer through Henry James back to Hawthorne or, more circuitously, back to Poe by way of the French symbolists, who were proud of having adopted many of Poe's ideals. I am not the first to suggest that there are at least two traditions in American literature; perhaps there are several. If we prefer to have only two, there is the tradition that Brooks extols as being essentially American, the tradition of the sunny, expansive writers who believed in human improvability, and beside it another tradition that is dark, intensive, pessimistic about human nature, and preoccupied with form rather than message. Both have been long established in this country. If Brooks's tradition goes back to Franklin and Emerson, the other might be traced to Charles Brockden Brown, at the end of the eighteenth century, or even to Jonathan Edwards.

It was Brown who said in a letter: "An accurate history of the thoughts and feelings of any man, for one hour, is more valuable for some minds than a system of geography; and you, you tell me, are one of those who would rather travel into the mind of a ploughman than into the interior of America. I confess myself of your way of thinking." That suggests another way of distinguishing the two traditions: there are the writers in breadth and the writers in depth; there are the morning writers and—thinking of Brown and his successors—the twilight or nocturnal writers. In Philip Rahv's famous distinction, somewhat different from the one I have been suggesting, the literary Redskins are at war with the Palefaces. Most but not all of the writers whom Brooks praises for being essentially American are Redskins. The great men in his tradition are Emerson, Thoreau, Whitman, and after them Mark Twain (in *Huckleberry Finn,* but not later), William James, Parkman, Howells, Dreiser, and, among the general of the 1920s, Thomas Wolfe. In the other tradition the great names are Hawthorne, Melville, Henry James, Henry Adams, and Faulkner.

And must we choose one side or the other? If there *are* two sides, that is, and only two—a questionable proposition—must we vote that only one of them is truly American, thus abandoning the writers on the other side to Europe or the feudal past or simple neglect? I have to confess that by temperament and training I feel more drawn to the writers in depth than to the expansive morning writers in the Emersonian line. But our literature is not so rich that it can afford to surrender any of its great men, Emerson *or* Hawthorne, Whitman or Melville, Parkman or Henry Adams, Brooks or Eliot; we need them all. By defining the American tradition restrictively, Brooks makes it seem poorer than it was in fact—and also poorer than he has made it seem in his five volumes of narrative. The academic critics had reason to argue with him on this point. Most of them, however, made the same sort of mistake as Brooks by rejecting another group of authors, exactly the ones that Brooks admires in his final chapter.

I have said too much about that one chapter and thus have neglected his real achievement in *Makers and Finders.* It was not to define the American tradition, but rather to present it as a Tolstoyan novelist might do, in a grand historical pageant that flows on author by author, scene by scene, and volume after volume. For the first time he proved by narration, description, and quotation, rather than argument, that this country has had a continuous life and character in literature.

.   .   .

I have never been impressed by the academic complaints about Brooks's method, most of which were based on various misconceptions of his purpose as a historian. Academic critics like to feel that a work on American literature can be assigned to some familiar type; that its orientation is social or political or biographical or psychological, or that it is a history of ideas, or that it chooses the major authors and studies their work in depth. *Makers and Finders* belongs to none of these types, and in fact there is no real parallel in American or foreign scholarship for Brooks's attempt to recover a literary tradition where none had been thought to exist. Since the goal was new, he had to find a new method of reaching it, and this is what most of the critics have failed to understand.

Part of his method was to suggest, as a landscape painter might do, the special atmosphere of cities and sections where literary movements started or flourished or declined. One remembers particularly his pictures of Boston after the Civil War, in *New England: Indian Summer,* and of Philadelphia at the end of the eighteenth century, in *The World of Washington Irving,* but there are dozens of these effectively painted literary landscapes. A more important part of the method was to emphasize the interconnections among writers, the points at which they came together to form a field of radiating forces that was almost like a magnetic field. For an example of such emphasis, one might turn to *The Times of Melville and Whitman* and consider his treatment of Bayard Taylor, the flimsy poet and entertaining traveler who was long regarded as a rival of the great New Englanders. Brooks devoted eight pages to his literary career, about the same space that would be assigned to him by an old-fashioned literary historian. The new-fashioned historians, in their preoccupation with major writers, would give him no space whatever; perhaps they wouldn't mention his name. But men like Taylor are essential to Brooks's purpose, for, as he tells us in his memoirs, "It is the minor books or writers that body forth a culture, creating the living chain that we call tradition."

The facts to be mentioned about this minor but once famous writer are chosen with the "living chain" in mind. Brooks doesn't tell us the date of Taylor's birth (1825) or give us the titles of his principal works in verse or prose. What we learn about him is chiefly:

1. That he belonged to the staff of the New York *Tribune,* like many other talented authors of his time (and elsewhere in the book Brooks lists them by name).

2. That he made his reputation by walking through Europe and sending back letters to the American press. On his return he was invited to dine with Bancroft, Cooper, and Melville, while N. P. Willis wrote an introduction to his book of travels.

3. That he had grown up in southern Pennsylvania, which in some ways resembled rural New England as described in the novels of Harriet Beecher Stowe—"which the novels of Bayard Taylor in turn resembled,—though the people were less keen and their interests were narrower and simpler, as Taylor's novels were dimmer than Mrs. Stowe's." (One notes that Brooks's critical comments on his authors are often expressed as comparisons with other American authors of the same period.)

4. That Taylor was first inspired to travel by reading Washington Irving, N. P. Willis, and Longfellow's *Outre Mer*, and that later it was Irving who advised him to visit the Orient.

5. That he lectured on American literature in Weimar, Goethe's city, and introduced a distinguished audience to the works of Emerson, Longfellow, and Bryant.

There is no need to cite other facts of the same nature from the eight-page passage on Taylor, or to list the forty-two pages on which his name is mentioned elsewhere in the book, always in connection with other names, for I think that by now the nature of Brooks's emphasis is clear. What interests him in Taylor, as in many authors of second or third rank, is not their books primarily or their private lives, but chiefly their points of contact with fellow authors. I think it was Bernard DeVoto who complained that Brooks's subjects never fall in love and never have children unless the children are authors too. The omission of family matters weakens some of his portraits, but families are unessential to his purpose. He is trying to show that American writers, besides existing in the social world, also moved in a closed system of their own. By revealing their points of contact he creates, as it were, a medium in which the writers existed and in which they transmitted energy by collision, like so many planets or atoms. Many critics, including Eliot and his followers, have talked about the value of a literary tradition, but they have left its nature a little vague. Brooks was the first author in any language to make a tradition real and almost palpable by presenting it as a rich texture of meetings, readings, and ideas passed from one writer to another.

For all the critical attacks it had to withstand, *Makers and Finders* effected a deep change in our judgment of the American past and hence, I think, in our vision of the future. It will remain for a long time our greatest sustained work of literary scholarship. But Brooks's story doesn't end with the completion of the last volume a few days after his sixty-fifth birthday in February 1951. During the next twelve years he wrote ten other books, all conceived in the same spirit as *Makers and Finders*, though not, of course, on the same grand scale. He was continuing to revive our memories of neglected heroes.

Except for the memoirs, my favorite among his later books is the one about that peppery, corncob-pipe-smoking Scotch Irishman, his old friend the painter John Sloan, who, in his good early work, was a novelist in color, just as Brooks himself is here again a landscape painter and portraitist in words. The landscapes are chiefly those of the New York art world in the pioneering days of the Armory Show.

After *John Sloan* I should place Brooks's defense and appreciation of William Dean Howells, a book that complements his earlier biographies of Mark Twain and Henry James in a way that *The Life of Emerson* had failed to do. Howells was a lifelong friend and rival of James, as well as the closest friend of Twain, and his career reveals still another approach to the provincial narrowness and iron conventions that had ruined so many American writers. Instead of fleeing to Europe with James, or letting himself be partly crippled by the conventions as Twain had been—or rising serenely above them with Emerson—Howells had flourished within the conventions while somehow preserving an integrity of purpose. He had also done more for his fellow writers, including the rebels of the 1890s, than anyone else of his time.

Brooks felt instinctively drawn to Howells and, in his later years, even came to resemble him. They were both short, solid men (though Brooks never let himself develop the paunch that Howells carried with dignity); they both had quite good manners and dressed quietly well (Brooks with a half-inch of white cuff showing at the end of his sleeves); they both had very high foreheads and white soup-strainer mustaches (though Brooks's features were less old-Roman than Howells' and gave an impression of shy benignity). Both men were utterly devoted to the art and profession of writing books, and both suffered at the end from neglect. "I am comparatively a dead cult," Howells said in a letter, "with my statues cut down and the grass growing over them in the pale moonlight." Brooks for his part complained more than once of being "an infrared type" surviving in an ultraviolet era of pessimism. Remembering the Chinese proverb, "A man is more the child of the age he lives in than he is of his own father and mother," he sometimes felt that the changing times had made him an orphan.

But the neglect was less harsh in Brooks's case than in that of Howells. It was softened by many public honors and, in a more gratifying fashion, by a stream of visits and letters from young writers who had been heartened by his work. One of them wrote, "I feel less like a nomad whenever I finish one of your books. Even at my loneliest, I feel sustained by the record of men before me who have struggled toward consciousness." A novelist said, "My work grows out of what went before. I feel I'm in the line." Another added, "One gains a real feeling of participation. . . . Our struggles of today fall into a new perspective." Brooks listened to these new voices as old J. B. Yeats had listened to Brooks, in the years when they sat together at the long table in Petitpas' garden.

Old Yeats's confident spirit pervades this volume of memoirs. Because of his wisdom, Brooks says, "J. B. Yeats was to leave behind him a great and lasting memory in many minds, for, whatever the virtues of Americans may be, wisdom is not one of them and most of his friends had never seen a wise man. . . . Who had ever heard of an American sage since the days of Emerson and Thoreau?" It becomes clear in retrospect that Brooks was trying to lead a sage's life. The story indirectly told but vividly suggested in his memoirs is that of an author who has followed a single line of development with complete integrity. It was in 1921 that Brooks asked a famous question: "Of how many of our modern writers can it be said that their work reveals a continuous growth, or indeed any growth, that they hold their ground tenaciously and preserve their sap from one decade to another?" Clearly there were no such American writers at the time, since Howells had died the year before and the new men were still too young for their careers to be judged. If there were a few such writers by 1960—Brooks himself among them—the change was partly owed to the work he had done for the literary profession in this country, by restoring its traditions and giving its members a past on which to build.

1965

Two Views of George Santayana

At Harvard

❧ Jorge Agustín Nicolás Ruiz de Santayana—as I think his name appears on his still Spanish passport—was born in Madrid on December 16, 1863. Less than nine years later he reached Boston, as the result of several unlikely and even preposterous events that he describes at length in his autobiography, *Persons and Places: The Background of My Life*. Imagine that his mother met Don Agustín de Santayana when they were the only two Europeans on a little island in the Philippines. Imagine that a year or two later she married a New England merchant named George Sturgis, on a British frigate in Manila harbor. Imagine that Sturgis died in the midst of a disastrous business venture and that she transported her four children to Boston, losing one of them on the way. And there were other curious events to follow. Mrs. Sturgis went to Spain for a visit, met Don Agustín again and married him. When little Jorge, the child of this second union, was five years old, she traipsed back to Boston with her Sturgis children. Jorge was sent to follow them three years later, because a series of family misfortunes had left his father alone in the house and unable to care for him. All these accidents—or in philosophical terms, these inevitabilities—were the necessary background of Santayana's career.

If he had remained in Spain, I cannot imagine that he would have become a distinguished philosopher. He would have gone into government service like his father, and he would have written rather florid verse—for his early style showed a tendency toward softness, toward decoration, and in Spain it would have lacked the discipline furnished by writing in a foreign language. There was nothing essentially new in his principles. He said in the fifty-year report of his Harvard class—it was '86—"I think I have changed very little in opinion or temper. I was old when I was young, and I am young now that I am old." Intellectually he was almost two thousand years old when he entered college: he was a Roman of the early empire, a disciple of Lucretius and Democritus. His philosophy was the common sense of the Mediterranean world, which is very different from common sense in New England. Essentially it was a philosophy of submission—first of all to nature, then to the weakness of the human body and mind, then finally to constituted governments, even if they are evil, and to the recognized church, even if it is based on a myth.

Although Spain is only in part a Mediterranean country, there are thousands of Spanish intellectuals who agree at heart with these ideas. In Spain, lacking opposition, Santayana might never have bothered to express his common sense as a systematic philosophy. In Boston he seemed a rank heretic, and so he talked and wrote and philosophized to defend his position. Idealism had begun to grow morbid in Boston, and Santayana's pagan ideas were a valuable tonic. They flourished like many importations to a new continent; almost like rabbits and foxes in Australia.

And Santayana himself flourished at Harvard. He was poor but brilliant, handsome in a not too foreign way and socially vouched for by his Sturgis relatives. As a sophomore, he played the leading lady in Institute theatricals. His class records show that he was on the staff of "The Lampoon"; that he helped to found "The Harvard Monthly"; that he belonged (in alphabetical order) to the Art Club, the Chess Club, the Everett Athenaeum, Hasty Pudding, the Institute of 1770, the O. K. Society, Phi Beta Kappa, the Philosophical Club (president) and the Shakspere Club. Apparently he joined almost everything open to undergraduates—except Porcellian, which was not in reach of his pocketbook, the Christian Brethren and the Total Abstinence League, from both of which he was barred by his principles. He was graduated *summa cum laude,* with honors in philosophy; he received a traveling fellowship and, in due time, he was given a teaching appointment.

During the next ten years, Don Jorge repaid with interest his debt to New England. The 1890s were a dull period there for literature; the great figures had disappeared and nobody had come forward to replace them except genteel imitators; it was what Van Wyck Brooks calls the Age of the Epigoni. Harvard College, however, was in a state of intellectual ferment, to which Santayana contributed more than his share of yeast. Men now in their seventies talk wistfully about the dinners of the O. K. Society, where Santayana often read one of his lighter poems and where his table talk became a legend. Among the younger members of O. K. were Philip Littell, Hutchins Hapgood, Robert Morss Lovett, William Vaughn Moody, Learned Hand, Ellery Sedgwick, Winthrop Ames, Charles M. Flandrau (who gave the best contemporary picture of the period in his "Harvard Episodes"), George Cabot Lodge, and Trumbull Stickney. These last two, except perhaps for Moody, had more creative fire than any of their colleagues, but the fire languished and they died very young—"visibly killed," as Santayana said in a letter, "by the lack of air to breathe. People individually were kind and appreciative to them, as they were to me, but the system was deadly, and they hadn't any alternative tradition (as I had) to fall back upon." In spite of the system, Lovett and his college friend Robert Herrick became great teachers of the next generation. The others had less to say, and Santayana could not give them much to supply that deficiency, since his own work is not characterized by vigor or freshness of ideas. What he could and did teach them, chiefly by example, was to talk well and to write in the tone of men used to good conversation. By combining two provincial cultures—for Madrid was even more of a backwater than Boston—he achieved a real cosmopolitanism; and he played somewhat the same role at Harvard that Pater had been playing at Oxford. Then, in 1912, he went back to Europe and eventually settled in Rome, the capital and shrine of the Mediterranean mind.

This first volume of *Persons and Places,* which carries Santayana's story down to his graduation from Harvard, contains not a hint or a personal reflection to show that it was written during the present war; even the style is detached, ironic and, in its manner, perfect. Indeed, the coolness of the book is a little ostentatious. It is almost as if someone had asked him, "What should writers do in wartime?" and as if, instead of giving a theoretical answer—a manifesto or a call to arms—Santayana had produced this volume which might have been written at any time, at any place, but only by a stylist and a man of wisdom.

Because of its contrast with the shoddy literature that we are being given today, one is tempted to exaggerate the merits of Santayana's prose. *Persons and Places,* judged by this first volume, is an admirable work that is far from being the greatest autobiography of our time; it has the art but not the human complexity of Yeats's story. It seems as cold, bare and drafty as a Venetian palace in winter. Santayana warns us that he has "a very short memory, except for such things as I absorb and recast in my own mind." A few of his anecdotes are unforgettable, especially those dealing with his father, who was deaf, skeptical and a hypochondriac. Once, when convinced that he was dying, he was assailed at the same moment by hunger; and his voice boomed through the house as he tried to whisper, *"La Unción y la gallina!"*—"Extreme Unction and a boiled chicken." Santayana's mother refused to join the Roxbury Plato Club on the ground that she had no time. "What do you *do*?" asked the persistent visitor. "In winter," said the Spanish lady, "I try to keep warm, and in summer I try to keep cool." But there are too few of these revealing episodes (which abound in Yeats) and most of Santayana's characters seem wordless and disembodied.

He has a tendency, in talking about people, to pass rapidly from personality to philosophy, so that we seem to be moving in a realm of abstract essences. Moreover, he shows a disturbing lack of affection. There are only two of his many friends whom he praises unreservedly; he met both of them in the Boston Latin School and hasn't bothered to see them since 1882. About the others he makes curiously niggling comments. It is as if, dwelling among ideas, he greeted the world of men with a limp handclasp and a somewhat chilly eye.

In Society

❦ The second volume of George Santayana's memoir—he calls it *The Middle Span*—is shorter than the first, and the substance of it seems thinner, too. He is dealing now with the quarter-century between his graduation from Harvard in 1886 and his sudden resignation as a professor in 1912. This is the ground that he has gone over before: he wrote about some of his students in his one novel, *The Last Puritan,* and about James and Royce, his two great colleagues of the Philosophy Department, in a volume of lectures, *Character and Opinion in the United States*. But there was more to be said concerning his own connection with Harvard in those years, and Santayana has omitted too much of it. He tells us almost nothing, for example, about the young writers who were students in his courses or visitors to his various rooms in the Yard. Some of them would play a considerable part in the abortive renaissance of the 1890s, or in the literature of political protest during the early 1900s, or in the revolt against the genteel tradition that began about 1910. During all three decades, Harvard continued to serve as a nursery for American writers, as it had served in the greater days of New England; and it was not until 1917 or thereabouts that poets and novelists in throngs began to appear from other colleges: first Princeton and Yale, in the war years; then Chicago, Vanderbilt, California, Michigan. . . . As long as Santayana remained at Harvard, he helped to set the tone for writing there, not only by his lectures, which were very popular with the literary set, but also by his poems, his poetry readings, his philosophical essays and his legendary conversation at the dinners of the O. K. Society. Yet there is so little mention of literature in his memoirs that at one point he stops to apologize.

"I have commemorated many American friends," he says, "and not one man of letters, not one poet." By way of atonement, he then devotes three lonesome pages to his friend Trumbull Stickney, who might have been a great poet except that he lived in the wrong age and died too soon. There were other poets at Harvard in those years: Edward Arlington Robinson and Robert Frost, to mention only two; but both of these were poor boys, socially unrecognized, and they were not likely to attract Santayana's attention. As a young instructor, he liked to associate with the college swells. He was pleased when the O. K., which had been started as a literary society, began to admit athletes and Gold Coast politicians. He said in the first volume of his memoirs: "I liked to feel a spark of sympathy pass from those sound simple active heirs of the dominant class to my secret philosophy: and sometimes the spark did pass, and in both directions." He was a snob in those days, to put the matter bluntly, and later he tried to excuse himself. "It might seem," he said, "that all my life I have been 'sponging' on my rich friends, or even that I have sought rich friends for that purpose. This was not the case: there were plenty of rich people about that I fled from. But with people with whom I was otherwise in sympathy, friendship was naturally more easily kept up and cemented if they had a house where they could ask me to stay, or could invite me to be their guest, partly or wholly, for trips or entertainments that I couldn't afford if left to my own resources." Elsewhere he often praises the simple life—"Anything suffices," he says, "if nothing else is demanded"—and he makes you think of Oscar Wilde's remark that his own tastes were simple, he wanted only the best.

He valued kind hearts, and valued them all the more if they beat under coronets. The highest moment in his undergraduate career was when he received a visit from the second Earl Russell, who had been directed to Santayana's room by one of his rich friends. As the young earl looked out of the window, Santayana says, "at the muddy paths and shabby grass, the elms standing scattered at equal intervals, the ugly factory-like buildings and the loud-voiced youths passing by, dressed like shop assistants, I could well conceive his thoughts, and I said apologetically that after Oxford all this must seem to him rather mean; and he replied curtly, 'Yes, it does.'" Santayana was not in the least offended. He went on to explain, so he says, "our manner of life, our social distinctions, our choice of studies, our sports, our food, our town amusements. He listened politely, obviously rather entertained and not displeased to find that, according to my description, all I described might be dismissed forever without further thought." It was the beginning of a friendship that lasted forty-five years, until John Stanley Russell died and the earldom passed to his younger brother Bertrand, the philosopher. Santayana had only two complaints against his friend. The first was "that being the heir to so many privileges he should appreciate them so little, and should use the strength that he derived from tradition in deriding tradition and destroying it"—in brief, that he joined the Labor Party. The second wasn't that he got himself involved in curious love affairs—with two sisters at once, Santayana implies, and again with a mother and a daughter—but rather that he couldn't keep his wives and mistresses out of court. "A young man with a brilliant career open to him in the world is a fool to flout public opinion," Santayana says, "even if he secretly despises it. Peace with the polite world is all-important for one's comfort and euphoria so long as one lives in the polite world."

Peace with the polite world and the political world and all the reigning powers is a central point in Santayana's philosophy. He describes himself as "a materialist, cynic and Tory."—"Regal and priestly grandeur," he says, "even dimly suggested, has always impressed me." He wept at one of Queen Victoria's processions, and when he first trod the steps of Windsor Castle, it was "not without profound emotion." For all his Anglomania, he also admired the provincial nobility of Boston; and he was even willing, as an instructor, to accept and observe the social judgments of Harvard undergraduates. The proudest moment of his teaching career seems not to have been the publication of *The Sense of Beauty,* his first philosophical work, and neither was it his formal appointment to the faculty; instead of these, it was his election as a graduate member of the Gas House, then the most elegant of the so-called "waiting clubs." In his rooms he used to give poetry readings, chiefly to club members. Once he tried to introduce his friend Trumbull Stickney to these readings—"But no," he says, "it wouldn't do. Julian confidentially informed me that 'the others didn't like him.' Why not? Because he had mentioned the sunset and called it 'gorgeous.'" Santayana bowed to their judgment and excluded the one gifted poet who might have attended their poetry evenings. Their standards were false and foolish, he felt, but it would also be foolish to object to them. Precisely by not objecting, he confirmed and strengthened the false standards. Those were the days when Harvard was afflicted with a multiplicity of caste distinctions: Yard against Gold Coast; clubs against fraternities against the great mass of the unaffiliated. And unrecognized. Santayana had nothing to do with founding the system, but in one sense he bears a little of the responsibility for it: that is, he approved it, followed its rules, and gave it the support of his prestige as a philosopher.

That is part of the story he tells between the lines of his memoirs; but besides this comedy of manners there are also hints of a private drama with painful overtones. Apparently the year 1896 marked a crisis in Santayana's life. "My young friends," he says, "had become too young for me and I too old for them; I had made a private peace with all religions and philosophies; and I had grown profoundly weary of polite society and casual gayeties." After taking a year's leave of absence, which he spent at the English Cambridge, he returned to Harvard; but he had lost his belief in teaching together with most of his social ambitions; indeed, he suggests that the next fifteen years were a somnambulistic period in his life and one he would like to forget. On receiving a legacy in 1912, he at once resigned his professorship and sailed for Europe, never to return.

The period that followed will be described in the third volume of his memoirs. On the whole it was happier and more productive than his last years at Harvard; and yet there seems to be something forced and almost inhuman in its serenity. He says: "For the future, I desired nothing fixed, no place in society, no circle of prescribed friends and engagements. . . .

For constant company I had enough, and too much, with myself." Again he says: "The intellectual world of my time alienated me intellectually. It was a Babel of false principles and blind cravings, a sociological garden of the mind, and I had no desire to be one of the beasts. I wished to remain a visitor, looking in at the cages." Santayana had always regarded himself as a visitor; he had been a Spaniard in America, an American in England, an Englishman in Rome, and even his relatives in Avila, his birthplace, had regarded him as a transatlantic cousin. Now the process of alienation would be carried still further, as he watched the death struggles of Europe with little interest and less understanding. When he mentioned them at all, it would be in the voice of a Martian on earth, or rather—so little likeness do his observations bear to our own picture of events—in the voice of a strayed earthling on Mars.

1944, 1945

E. E. Cummings

One Man Alone

Gertrude Stein who had been much impressed by The Enormous Room said that Cummings did not copy, he was the natural heir of the New England tradition with its aridity and its sterility, but also with its individuality.   *—The Autobiography of Alice B. Toklas*, p. 208

I

❧ It was a curious background for a rebel poet. Edward Estlin Cummings was born (1894) and brought up on a quiet street north of the Harvard Yard, one where distinguished professors lived. William James and Josiah Royce were neighbors, and Charles Eliot Norton had a wooded estate nearby that bordered on Somerville and its Irish tenements. Cambridge in the early 1900s . . . good manners, tea parties, Browning, young women with their minds adequately dressed in English tweeds. I think it was T. S. Eliot who said that life there was so intensely cultured it had ceased to be civilized. The younger poet's family was part of that life. Edward Cummings, the father (Harvard '85), had been an instructor in sociology, but then had become a clergyman, preaching in Boston as the assistant, the colleague, and finally the successor of Edward Everett Hale at the South Congregational Society, Unitarian. Sometimes on Sundays little Estlin, as the family called him, passed the plate. The father, famous for rectitude, was also president of the Massachusetts Civic League and was later executive head of the World Peace Foundation.

The son attended a public high school, Cambridge Latin, where he tells us that the admired principal was a Negro.* Sending Estlin there was apparently one of his father's democratic ideas and another—when the son went on to Harvard, class of '15—was to have him live at home for the first three years. That encouraged his bookish habits and also cut him off from college life, including the club system with its societies, waiting clubs, and final clubs—always something ahead to make students act with propriety for fear of being blackballed. Cummings joined nothing but the Musical Society and the board of a literary magazine that had published some of his early poems. There were two such magazines at Harvard in those days,

*Cummings' biographer, Charles Norman, says that the black principal, a woman, was at a grade school the boy attended.

The Monthly and *The Advocate,* and they looked down on each other—or, to be accurate, they nodded to each other coldly from the facing doors of their respective sanctums on the dusty third floor of the Harvard Union. The Monthlies thought that the board of *The Advocate,* which then appeared fortnightly, was composed of journalists, clubmen, athletes, and disciples of Teddy Roosevelt, a former editor, with not a man of letters among them. The Advocates suspected that the Monthlies were aesthetes (as indeed most of them came to be called), scruffy poets, socialists, pacifists, or worse. It was for *The Monthly* that Cummings chose to write.

In his last undergraduate year he took a room at college and became a gossiped-about figure in the groups that surrounded *The Monthly.* It was the only time in his life that he formed part of a group, but even then he stood apart from most of the others and preferred to keep his relations one to one. He was intensely shy and private in the Cambridge fashion. Still, among the ones he saw often were Dos Passos, Robert Hillyer the conservative poet (though with some distrust on both sides), S. Foster Damon ("who opened my eyes and ears," Cummings was to write, ". . . to all ultra, at that moment, modern music and poetry and painting"), and two very rich young men, James Sibley Watson and Scofield Thayer, who greatly admired his poems and drawings. Cummings decided to stay at Harvard for a year of postgraduate work. At commencement he was awarded a degree *magna cum laude,* with honors in Literature, Greek and English. He was also chosen to give the Disquisition and shocked his classmates and their parents—those who listened—by speaking on "The New Art," with examples from Amy Lowell and Gertrude Stein.

At the time he was in full revolt against almost everything—except personal integrity—that Cambridge and his father stood for. Cleanliness, godliness, decorum, public spirit, then chastity went by the board. Cummings developed a taste for low life, something that teemed in Boston. One night the Boston police were embarrassed to find his father's car, with its clergyman's license plates, parked outside a joint near Scollay Square. Cummings and Dos Passos, both virgins at the time, were not "upstairs"; they were drinking in the parlor while holding a polite conversation with the madam.

> When you rang at Dick Mid's Place
> the madam was a bulb stuck in the door.

In the autumn after his postgraduate year, Cummings went to New York, where he spent three months at the only office job he was ever to hold. The experiment having failed by reason of pure boredom, he went to work seriously on his drawing and painting (the drawing was often inspired; the paintings were impressionistic and weak in color). He took no part in the debate over preparedness for war, one which shook the country in the winter of 1916–1917 and which, as a minor effect, disrupted the board of *The Harvard Monthly*. Four of the editors were pacifists, the other four were superpatriots, all eight were impractical, and they couldn't agree on what to print. In April 1917, when Congress declared war, *The Monthly* disappeared from Harvard, but not from memory. An editorial that carefully didn't mention the war explained that publication was being suspended because of "existing circumstances." Cummings by that time was on his way to France as a volunteer in the Norton-Harjes Ambulance Corps.

On the old *Touraine* of the French Line, a tub that wallowed its way through the submarine zone, he met William Slater Brown, another New Englander. Brown, lately a student at Columbia, was a pacifist proud of knowing the anarchist Emma Goldman. Cummings was mildly patriotic, but he didn't allow opinions, at the time, to interfere with his friendships. Through a mistake at headquarters, the two young men were not immediately assigned to an ambulance unit and had a month to spend in Paris. They roamed the streets in all the glow of youth, went to the Russian Ballet, and learned to speak passable French, apparently with the help of Paris ladies ("little ladies more / than dead exactly dance / in my head"). Finally they went to the front in Section 21, whose commanding officer, Lieutenant Anderson, distrusted them because they wore dirty coveralls and were too friendly with the French mechanics. An artillery company quartered in their village had mutinied that spring, and Brown talked about war weariness in letters to friends (as well as in one to Emma Goldman). A French censor reported his remarks to Lieutenant Anderson, who said that Brown was a dangerous character and that Cummings should be arrested too. Cummings might have been cleared—of what charge? there was none—but a sense of personal honor kept him from assuring the military examiners that he detested all Germans. Together the friends were shipped off to La Ferté, to a detention barracks that Cummings was later to celebrate as "the Enormous Room."

The three months he spent there were another watershed, after the rebellion of his last two years at college. Confined with men of all nations, mostly illiterate, even inarticulate, all used to living outside the law, Cummings found that he liked some of them—especially those he called the Delectable Mountains—vastly more than he liked his college classmates. They gave him a new sense of human values: individuals could be admired for their generosity and courage, but social authority was always and everywhere stupid. By example they encouraged him to exalt feeling over knowledge, and they also gave him a new aesthetic. He was soon to say, on page 249 of *The Enormous Room*, "that there is and can be no such thing as authentic art until the *bons trucs* (whereby we are taught to see and imitate on canvas and in stone and by words this so-called world) are entirely and thoroughly and perfectly annihilated by that vast and painful process of Unthinking which may result in a minute bit of purely personal feeling. Which minute bit is Art."

The honors student in Literature, Greek and English was busy unthinking his five years at Harvard and was getting ready to write poems that would each, he hoped, embody a moment of intensely alive and personal feeling. Meanwhile Dr. Edward Cummings, having learned of his son's disappearance, made vigorous efforts first to find where he was, a difficult task in itself, and then to obtain his release. As pastor of the South Church, he was not without friends in Washington. When the French received official inquiries, they gave the son another farcical hearing and finally set him free. Brown, with his letters as evidence, was condemned to the military prison at Précigny, from which nobody had come out living since the first days of the war. There he fell victim to scurvy, but Dr. Cummings was busy with his problem, too, and he was released before the disease had crippled him.

After the Armistice, Brown and Cummings rented a Greenwich Village apartment that became a model of squalor. Cummings liked to roam through the Lower East Side and the Syrian quarter near the southern tip of Manhattan. He was painting "all the time," Brown says, but was also writing scores, even hundreds of poems in many new manners. Meanwhile the death of *The Harvard Monthly* had an unexpected sequel. Scofield Thayer and Sibley Watson had bought a moribund political fortnightly, *The Dial*, which they set about transforming into the most distinguished magazine of the arts that had appeared in this country. In some ways and in some contributors it carried on the tradition of *The Monthly*, this time with a national audience. The first issue, for January 1920, featured the poems and drawings of E. E. Cummings. I remember how they provoked indignant remarks from more conservative poets and, in particular, how Bobby Hillyer fumed.

In the autumn of that year Cummings wrote *The Enormous Room* at his father's house near Silver Lake, New Hampshire. He wrote it at the father's suggestion and partly to keep Dr. Cummings from suing the French government for a million dollars; also he wrote it very fast, in a style close to the spoken idiom he had fashioned for himself over the years. Dr. Cummings had the manuscript copied by his secretary, then went over it with a blue pencil, crossing out the bad words and making other minor changes (for example, a character whom the son called Jesus Christ was renamed Judas). It was hard to find a publisher, but the new firm of Boni and Liveright was more venturesome than others, and Dr. Cummings persuaded them to accept the book. When it appeared in 1922, it was read with enthusiasm by younger writers, and the free-ranging, partly colloquial, partly involved style had a lasting effect on American prose. *The Enormous Room* was not a commercial success. Horace Liveright, who thought he had been fooled, came to dislike the book so much that he wouldn't allow the unsold copies of the first edition to be remaindered; he sold them for wastepaper.*

2

In the years from 1923 to 1926 Cummings published four books of poetry: *Tulips and Chimneys,* *&* (he wore his titles cut short), *XLI Poems,* and *Is 5.* Many or most of the poems in all four were written either at college or during the burst of activity and experiment that followed his release from the detention barracks at La Ferté, but the first and the last book stand somewhat apart from the other two. In *Tulips and Chimneys* there are some of his recent experiments, but there are also earlier long pieces full of oriental or medieval color, and these seem utterly traditional in their effort to be exotic. Only one of them has life in it, "All in green went my love riding," a lyrical ballad that is a gifted exercise in Preraphaelitism. The fourth book, *Is 5,* contains many satirical pieces written in what seems to have been a new manner for Cummings. "Poems, or Beauty Hurts Mr. Vinal," "she being Brand-new," "workingman with hand so hairy-sturdy," "my sweet old etcetera": these and others deal mostly with contemporary subjects, using catch phrases and advertising slogans that are strictly of the time (as note "pretty littleliverpill–hearted-Nujolneeding-There's-A-Reason americans" in the diatribe against Harold Vinal, a harmless lyric poet from Maine); yet their wit and their headlong rhythms give them an inner life that makes them nearly indestructible. Among all the books of poetry that Cummings published, *Is 5* is still the liveliest.

None of the first four books was a popular success. The audience for poetry was even smaller at the time than in earlier and later periods, and most of it shared Mr. Vinal's tastes for conventional beauty. With Cummings the critics were severe: they condemned his fleshly realism, his experiments with typography, and his custom of using a small "i" for the first-personal pronoun. "e. e. cummings" they called him, with a visible curl of the lip. But the more his work was condemned by critics, the more it was admired by many of the younger writers and the more he was adopted as one of their spokesmen, along with Dos Passos and Hemingway. Fitzgerald had been the first spokesman, but rebels lost faith in him when he appeared too often in *The Saturday Evening Post*. Cummings too was making a keep-

---

*Later he must have regretted the gesture, when he found that there was a revived demand for the book. *The Enormous Room* was reprinted three or four times during the 1920s.

alive compromise, by writing prose pieces for *Vanity Fair*, but most of these were signed with a pseudonym. As for his private life, he kept it private, and that added to his prestige.

He wasn't often seen at parties in the middle 1920s, though hostesses tried to capture him and though he had overcome his shyness to the point of liking to have an audience. "I've watched him operating among strangers," another poet said rather envyingly. "He starts talking to one person in a low confidential voice and the person starts laughing. Then another person drifts up, glass in hand, and bends forward to hear what is being said. Cummings talks lower, faster, and funnier, without cracking a smile, and a third person appears. Pretty soon the whole room is grouped around Cummings, everybody laughing, everybody with eyes on him so as not to miss a word." "Jesus, he was a handsome man," as he had written of Buffalo Bill. He had large, well-shaped features, carved rather than molded, eyes set wide apart, often with a glint of mischief in them, and in those days a good deal of fine khaki-colored hair. "Doesn't he look like a faun!" I heard a young woman say. "Or like a bad boy," another said, also admiringly. In later years, when he had lost most of the hair and the rest was clipped off, he looked more like a bare-skulled Buddhist monk.

He was the most brilliant monologuist I have known. What he poured forth was a mixture of cynical remarks, puns, hyperboles, outrageous metaphors, inconsequence, and tough-guy talk spoken from the corner of his wide, expressive mouth: pure Cummings, as if he were rehearsing something that should afterward appear in print. Sometimes it did: "His Royal Highness said 'peek-a-boo' and thirty tame fleas left the prettily embroidered howdah. . . . Thumbprints of an angel named Frederick found on a lightning-rod, Boston, Mass." Perhaps the style of those harangues is better suggested by his *i: six nonlectures* as these were delivered at Harvard in the early 1950s. The second nonlecture, for instance, starts by praising the world in which he grew to manhood: "a reckless world, filled with the curiosity of life herself; a vivid and violent world welcoming every challenge; a world worth hating and adoring and fighting and forgiving: in brief, a world which was a world." Then, after ridiculing the later ideal of "quote security unquote," he tells a story that has to be repeated in his own words.

Back in the days of dog-eat-dog [he says] . . . there lived a playboy; whose father could easily have owned the original superskyscraper-de-luxe; a self-styled Cathedral of Commerce, endowed with every impetus to relaxation; not excluding ultra-elevators which (on the laudable assumption that even machinery occasionally makes mistakes) were regularly tested. Testing an ultraelevator means that its car was brought clean up, deprived of safety devices, and dropped. As the car hurtled downward, a column of air confined by the elevator shaft became more and more compressed; until (assuming that nothing untoward happened) it broke the car's fall completely—or so I was told by somebody who should know. At any rate, young

Mr. X was in the habit not only of attending these salubrious ceremonies, but of entering each about-to-be-dropped car, and of dropping with it as far as the laws of a preEinsteinian universe permitted. Eventually, of course, somebody who shouldn't know telephoned a newspaper; which sent a reporter; who (after scarcely believing his senses) asked the transcender of Adam point-blank why he fell so often. Our playful protagonist shrugged his well-tailored shoulders—"for fun" he said simply; adding (in a strictly confidential undertone) "and it's wonderful for a hangover."

Here, I feel, we have the male American stance of my adolescence; or (if you prefer) the adolescent American male stance of what some wit once nicknamed a "lost generation"; whereof—let me hastily append—the present speaker considers himself no worthy specimen. My point, however, isn't that many of us were even slightly heroic; and is that few of us declined a gamble. I don't think we enjoyed courting disaster. I do feel we liked being born.

In Cummings' published work, that passage is one of the very few in which he used the pronoun "we" as referring to any group larger than the one composed of the poet and his love. Usually other groups were "they," alien and hostile. But "we," meaning his generation, were reckless persons who liked to accept a challenge, and "we" sometimes gambled with death simply "for fun" and to reaffirm our joy in being alive. That is surely a theme or feeling that pervaded the 1920s; an adolescent feeling, if you will—Cummings makes that concession to critics—but one to which he looked back in the 1950s with a continuing sense of we-ness.

The 1920s had other favorite themes and one is amazed, in rereading his early work, to find out how often Cummings expressed them. Of course he was a lyric poet in the bad-boy tradition, broadly speaking, of Catullus and Villon and Verlaine. Of course he kept returning to the standard lyrical subjects of love, death, April, and the special quality of a moment. But traditional as he was on one side of his work, and determinedly unique on another, he was also a man of his generation. Much oftener than one might expect, he said what other young writers were saying at the time, or would soon be saying, and he usually said it with more ingenuity and morning freshness.

I won't revert to themes directly connected with his adventures in war-time: the feeling that death was omnipresent and life all the more to be enjoyed; the other feeling, for American ambulance drivers, that they were spectators of the greatest show on earth; and the notion that everyone in authority was stupid and that only common soldiers deserved sympathy. All this one finds in his early poems, together with other war-connected themes. More than other postwar writers, Cummings made fun of the big words, especially when spoken by politicians. Better and more amusingly than others he expressed his mistrust of almost everyone over thirty: "o the sweet & aged people who rule this world(and me and you if we're not very careful) . . . OH the bothering dear unnecessary hairless old." But Cummings also wrote poems on other themes that were popular with a whole generation of rebel writers, and here I might give a few examples.

There is first of all the revolt against Victorian standards, especially those prescribing chaste language and chaste behavior. Cummings made himself a leader in the revolt by describing, explicitly and often, the act of sex. Thus, in his second book of poems, *&*, there are nine rather labored sonnets recording visits to various prostitutes, including "Cecile . . . Alice . . . Loretta, cut the comedy, kid . . . Fran Mag Glad Dorothy."

There is the expatriate theme of praise for "superb and subtle" Paris, with its churches at twilight, its cafés, its streets that "turn young with rain," and its little ladies.

There is the tourist without Baedeker wandering beside his mistress among Roman ruins. "Ponder, darling, these busted statues," he tells her; but then he exhorts her to turn aside from the unimportant past and "instigate constructive horizontal business."

There is the spectator's report on New York as another such Greatest Show as the war had been. Dos Passos embodied the report in a long novel, *Manhattan Transfer,* but Cummings was more succinct:

> by god i want above fourteenth
>
> fifth's deep purring biceps, the mystic screech
> of Broadway, the trivial stink of rich
>
> frail firm asinine life

There is the supercilious delight in advertising slogans and the habit of using them in poems. Cummings used them only for satire—"what's become of Maeterlinck / now that April's here / (ask the man who owns one / ask Dad, He knows)"—but later Hart Crane and others began to exploit them seriously.

There is the contempt for citizens who lead ordinary lives, "impersons" who accept the slogans at face value.

There is the utter scorn for conventional poets still feeding on the past:

> if we are to believe these gently O sweetly
> melancholy trillers amid the thrillers
> these crepuscular violinists among my and your
> skyscrapers—Helen & Cleopatra were Just Too Lovely,
> The Snail's On The Thorn enter Morn and God's
> In His andsoforth.

There is the respect for rebels of all sorts, even for Communists in those early days. Thus, in his report of a Paris demonstration broken up by the police, Cummings says that "the communists have fine Eyes . . . none look alike," whereas the police, "tidiyum, are very tidiyum reassuringly similar."

There is compassion for outcasts, not excluding the drunk lying in his pool of vomit as people carefully step around him, and there is the feeling that poets are outcasts too, for all their pride. "why are these pipples taking their hets off?" Cummings asks in an idiom borrowed from Krazy Kat of his favorite comic strip. He answers:

> the king & queen
> alighting from their limousine
> inhabit the Hôtel Meurice(whereas
> i live in a garret and eat aspirine)

There is finally the deep strain of anti-intellectualism that I have already mentioned. Among its manifestations is a prejudice against scientists and "prurient philosophers" who poke and prod the earth, combined with praise for a child's direct vision that sees the earth as "mud-luscious" and "puddle-wonderful."

There is, in fact, almost every theme that was to be widely treated by new writers in the 1920s, except for Hemingway's theme of giving and accepting death, and Fitzgerald's theme of the betrayed suitor for the very soul of money. Cummings spoke of money not often and then with the disdain of a barefoot friar. Besides the themes he treated, his poems embody various attitudes that lay behind them: the passion for reckless experiment in life and art, the feeling that a writer's duty was to be unique, and the simple determination to enjoy each moment and make the most of having been born. In spite of his aloofness, it is no wonder at all that the rebel writers had come to regard him as an indispensable spokesman for their cause.

The question in the middle 1920s was what Cummings would do next.

3

His next work, to their surprise, was for the theater and it was not so much a play as a brilliant vaudeville. *Him* (1927) was abused by the drama critics, but it was deliriously enjoyed by the younger people in the audience. Once again Cummings had spoken for them, and *Him* is in fact so much "of the twenties"—in the attitudes it reveals toward women, politics, Negroes (here admired for their sexual freedom), and the life of art—that it has seldom or never been revived. During the original production by the Provincetown Players, the very small auditorium was crowded every night, but the production was expensive, the Players were losing money they didn't have, and the piece had to be withdrawn after a few weeks. Cummings went back to painting and writing verse.

A new book of poems, *VV* (which he also called "*ViVa*"), appeared in 1931 and was a mild disappointment to his readers. Mostly the book deals with the same themes as his earlier work, but it is less exuberant than *Is 5*—much less of a hurrah than the title promises—and it speaks less directly for the poet's generation. There is a growing bitterness in the satires directed against politicians, generals, and run-of-the-mine people. The bitterest of all has proved to be the most enduring: it is the ballad of blond Olaf, the conscientious objector who is prodded with bayonets, then beaten to death while repeating "I will not kiss your f.ing flag." As a general thing, however, the development revealed in the book is a matter much less of tone than of technique.

Although Cummings' technique is a confusing subject, one argued back and forth since his poems first appeared in *The Dial,* much of it depends on the elaboration of a few devices that are fairly simple in themselves. Too much of it so depends, a reader may end by feeling. The two principal devices employed in *VV* had appeared at times in his earlier work, but here he carries them both to extremes. One is the calligram—or picture writing, to use a more general term—and the other is the word scramble, which might also be called the cryptogram. Cummings' use of the two devices has been discussed more than once, and I do not propose to resume the discussion here. It is enough to say that when he combines calligram with cryptogram, as he sometimes does in *VV,* the result in three or four cases is something beyond my ability to decipher. Even worse, a deciphered statement may be one that Cummings has made elsewhere, in plainer words, and thus it leaves a reader with the impression that his time and the poet's have both been wasted. *VV* is the most ingenious of Cummings' books, but—aside from the ballad of blond Olaf, a tribute to the poet's mother, and a few other moving poems—it is by far the least successful.

On the technical side, however, *VV* gives more than a hint of two additional devices that the poet was to cultivate more intensively in his later books. One of these is his use of negative terms—especially those formed by the prefixes "un-," "im-," and "not-" and the suffix "-less"—to imply special shades of meaning. In Poem XLII, for instance, he speaks of an "upward deep most invincible unthing," which I should take to be a spiritual essence. Poem LXVII tells of watching "unhands describe what mimicry," and here I don't know exactly what he means, although "unhands" would be a sinister word in Cummings' idiom. In later books one finds a host of such expressions: "an undream of anaesthetized impersons," "a notalive undead too-nearishness," "unfools unfree / undeaths who live," "till unwish returns on its unself," and the adjective "whereless," one that might pass into general usage. The poet says of politicians who want to save the world, "scream, all ye screamers, till your if is up / and vanish under prodigies of un." If such prodigies do not unexist, it is because Cummings has performed them.

The other device is the game he was beginning to play with parts of speech. It is a game with elastic rules or none at all: roughly, any part of speech can be transformed into any other. Verbs, adjectives, pronouns, even some adverbs and conjunctions, are used instead of nouns. Nouns become verbs ("but if a look should *april* me"), or they become adverbs by adding "-ly," or adjectives in the superlative by adding "-est" (thus, instead of writing "most like a girl," Cummings has "girlest"). Adjectives, adverbs, and conjunctions, too, become participles by adding "-ing" ("onlying," "softlying," "whying"); participles become adverbs by adding "-ly" ("kneelingly"). Some of those practices are foreshadowed in *VV*, where one finds, for instance, "footprints on the sands of was"—of time, obviously, though "was" in later books becomes "the past." Also in *VV* one finds "the smallening World" and "laughtering blocks"—the latter a hideous phrase—as well as "togethering" and "foreverfully," both more effective. In the later books—which include *50 Poems* (1940), *1 × 1* (1944), *XAIPE* ("Rejoice!" 1950), and *95 Poems* (1958)—such coined words and transposed parts of speech come close to being a new language. An example in *50 Poems* is Poem 29, of which the first stanza reads:

> anyone lived in a pretty how town
> (with an up so floating many bells down)
> spring summer autumn winter
> he sang his didn't he danced his did.

A translation—omitting the second line, which means whatever it means—might be, "The poet lived year by year in an ordinary town, where he sang his negations and danced his affirmations." Need one say that Cummings' new language has a marvelous way of lending strangeness to sometimes rather commonplace statements? It also serves as a means of avoiding various words that he detested. Later in the same poem, when he says that "noone loved him more by more," it is obvious that "noone" is the poet's wife. After his second divorce, Cummings was happily married for nearly thirty years, a fact attested by some of his finest poems, but the word "wife" appears in none of them.

Any words involved in his game with parts of speech acquired a plus or a minus value. Thus, "was" as a noun is minus; "is" and "am" and "become" are plus. "Who" is plus, but "which" is minus, especially when it refers to impersons, and so is the adjective "whichful." "It," another neuter, seems to be the negative of "he" or "him" and leads to "itmaking," a term of utter condemnation. "Where" and "when" are both minus as nouns; "where-lings" and "whenlings" are pitiable people, "sons of unless and children of almost"—one might say the Jukes and Kallikaks of Cummings' world. The honorifics are "here" and "now." "beautiful most is now," he says, and else-where, in a fine tribute to his father,

> this motionless forgetful where
> turned at his glance to shining here.

All such words have become abstractions, and the meanings they imply are ethical and metaphysical. Usually ethics and ontology are fatal subjects for modern poets, but Cummings was feeling impelled to venture into them. The anti-intellectual was about to become, in limited ways, an ide-ologist. There had been changes in his life and they had led to a number of ideas that were partly new for him and were completely opposed at the time to those held by "mostpeople," as he called the American public. When one looks back at his career, it would seem that he had to invent his new language as the only fresh and serviceable means of expressing the ideas in poetry.

4

Changes in his life. . . . His father had been killed in a motor accident (at a grade crossing in a blinding snowstorm), his second marriage had broken up, and in 1931 he had made a trip to Russia. This last was a shattering experience, much on the order of Dos Passos' visit to Loyalist Spain in 1937. Cummings wrote a prose book about the trip (*Eimi*, 1934), which is hard to read because of its pointillist style, but in which the conclusions are forth-right. Russia, he reported, was a country racked by fear and suspicion. Liv-ing under the shadow of Stalin, Communists were the bigoted defenders of a system that destroyed individuals. Soon the same conclusions were being stated in his poems:

> every kumrad is a bit
> of quite unmitigated hate
> (travelling in a futile groove
> god knows why)
> and so do i
> (because they are afraid to love

Cummings was not afraid to love, but he hated, too, and his hatred (or call it his feeling of revulsion) circled out from Stalin and his "kumrads" to wider and wider social groups. First to be encompassed were politicians who abetted communism by making appeals to the same public yearning for a better life. Cummings had always detested politicians, but now he raged against them:

> a politician is an arse upon
> which everyone has sat except a man

Reformers and crusaders, especially those who supported the New Deal, came next into the circle of aversion:

> then up rose pride and up rose pelf
> and ghibelline and guelph
> and ladios and laddios
> (on radios and raddios)
> did save man from himself

Growing still wider, the circle was drawn about salesmen of every type: "a salesman is an it that stinks . . . whether it's in lonjewray or shrouds"—a salesman in shrouds being anyone in favor of entering World War II on Stalin's side. Labor unions were still another abomination:

> when serpents bargain for the right to squirm
> and the sun strikes to gain a living wage—
> when thorns regard their roses with alarm
> and rainbows are insured against old age

—then, Cummings says, "we'll believe in that incredible unanimal mankind." At this point the circle of those rejected has become so wide that it includes almost everyone living except "you and me," that is, the poet, his love, and perhaps a handful of friends.

Not since the trip to Russia had Cummings been a spokesman for his literary generation. Most of its other members—with almost all the younger writers—had been moving in an opposite direction from his. During the 1930s a dream that haunted many was that of joining forces with all the dispossessed and of moving forward shoulder to shoulder into a brighter future. Even Hemingway shared the dream for a time. *To Have and Have Not,* published during the Spanish Civil War, has a hero who lives by his own law, but his dying words are "No matter how a man alone ain't got no bloody fucking chance." "It had taken him a long time to get it out," Hemingway adds in his own voice, "and it had taken him all his life to learn it." Steinbeck, a younger man, was more affirmative in *The Grapes of Wrath* (1939): he tells how the mistreated Okies in California acquired a sense of collective purpose, until each of them—as Preacher Casy prophesies before his death—was on the point of becoming only a little piece of "one big soul." Cummings had no patience with this religion of humanity, or with humanity itself. He was to write during World War II:

> pity this busy monster,manunkind,
>
> not. . . .
>
>   listen:there's a hell
>
> of a good universe next door;let's go

Long before that other war, his statements of opinion had begun to seem inopportune and embarrassing. *Eimi*, for instance, appeared at a moment when much of the book-reading public was entranced by the Russian Five Year Plan, and it proved to be a commercial disaster. Its publisher rejected Cummings' next book of poems. After extensive travels in manuscript, and with a change in title, this was finally printed at his own expense as *No Thanks* (1935). It was dedicated, with no thanks, to fourteen publishers: Farrar and Rinehart, Simon and Schuster, Coward-McCann, Limited Editions, Harcourt Brace, Random House, Equinox Press, Smith and Haas, Viking, Knopf, Dutton, Harpers, Scribners, and Covici Friede. Cummings' first *Collected Poems* (1938) had less trouble in finding a home, and the books that followed had none at all, but I can't remember that they were widely discussed. In the left-wing press, hardly anyone excoriated Cummings or pleaded with him sorrowfully, as some did with Dos Passos; the books were mostly passed over in silence, as if they were social blunders. Perhaps it was the feeling of simply not being heard that made the poet's voice too shrill in some of the later diatribes.

Most of the poems, however, didn't suffer in themselves from his changed opinions, as the later novels of Dos Passos undoubtedly suffered. Dos Passos had different problems, having cast himself in the role of contemporary Gibbon. One of his self-imposed tasks was to report events in such a way as to reveal underlying forces. If he had been wrong about those forces during his early career, mightn't he be equally wrong after his loss of faith in the workers' revolution? That question must have nagged at him—though he didn't mention it to others—and it would help to explain the discouraged tone of his later fiction. Cummings took no interest in historical forces. He was essentially a lyric poet, and in the best of his later work he continued to deal with the traditional lyric themes of love and death, of spring-time and the ineffable quality of moments. There was less exuberance than in the early poems, less inventiveness in spite of the game he played with parts of speech, but there was at times more depth, combined with the effort I mentioned to express a coherent attitude, almost a metaphysic.

This last was something that Dr. Edward Cummings would have understood, and indeed it represented, in some measure, a return to the father. Such returns can be traced in the lives of many writers: Dos Passos is one of them but there are scores of examples from which to choose. How often rebellion against the father—perhaps under the sign of the mother—is revealed in early works, and how often the father's image looms behind the later career! A younger poet, Wendell Berry, has written about such a change in his own life. Of his father he says:

> Now he speaks in me
> as when I knew him first,
> as his father spoke
> in him . . .
>   and I have grown
> to be brother to all
> my fathers, memory
> speaking to knowledge,
> finally, in my bones.*

If Cummings too admired his father more and more, it was obviously not for the social doctrine one assumes that the father preached to his congregation at the South Church, Unitarian. It was for personal qualities: love, kindness, utter independence, and faith based on an inner rightness of feeling:

> Scoring the pomp of must and shall
> my father moved through dooms of feel;
> his anger was as right as rain
> his pity was as green as grain

The New England tradition to which the poet returned was not that of the Unitarians or of the Calvinists, much less of the Come-outers, but that preached by Emerson in the years after he left the pulpit and before he became an Abolitionist. It was the tradition of the autonomous individual standing before God (or the Oversoul), living by universal laws in harmony with nature, obeying an inner voice, and letting society take care of itself. Emerson . . . there is no record that Cummings ever read his essays, yet his ideas had once pervaded the Cambridge air, and Cummings' later poems are Emersonian in more respects than one.

Thus, Emerson in the flush of his thought was an individualist to such an extent that he could not conceive of history as a process involving social systems and masses of people. "An institution," he wrote, "is the lengthened shadow of one man . . . and all history resolves itself into the biography of a few stout and honest persons." He regarded events of the past as mere decorations of the contemporary mind. "This life of ours," he said, "is stuck round with Egypt, Greece, Gaul, England, War, Colonization, Church, Court and Commerce, as with so many flowers and wild ornaments grave and gay. I will not make more account of them." For Cummings too, history was supremely unimportant:

*From "The Gathering" (*The Nation,* January 31, 1972, p. 151).

> all history's a winter sport or three:
> but were it five,i'd still insist that all
> history is too small for even me;
> for me and you,exceedingly too small.

Here "me and you" are of course the poet and his love, the only group to which Cummings proclaimed his loyalty. He could do so because "me and you" were really not a group; they were "wonderful one times one." For him almost every group of more than two was either mythical or malevolent, or both. "swoop(shrill collective myth)into thy grave," he exclaimed in that same poem. In other poems we read that the state is an "enormous piece of nonsense" and that its citizens (or "sit-isn'ts") are a huge "collective pseudobeast / (sans either pain or joy)." Emerson wrote, and Cummings would have agreed, that "Society everywhere is in conspiracy against the manhood of every one of its members." As a rule, however, Emerson expressed less hostility to groups than Cummings did; he simply disregarded them in his scheme of things (while acknowledging the existence of "races," as he called the English and the French; of course what he meant was nations). He was interested in the moral character of each nation, but not at all in its politics. I am sure he would have assented when Cummings said:

> a state submicroscopic is—
> compared with pitying terrible
> some alive individual

Cummings also wrote that "there are possibly 2½ or improbably 3 individuals every several fat thousand years," and here the echo seems unmistakable. Emerson had said in "The American Scholar," "Men in history, men in the word of to-day, are bugs, are spawn, and are called 'the mass' and 'the herd.' In a century, in a millennium, one or two men; that is to say, one or two approximations to the right state of every man." I can imagine that Emerson would have nodded happily—as Whitman would have nodded too—when Cummings suggested that any man truly alive contains the universe within himself:

> (his briefest breathing lives some planet's year,
> his longest life's a heartbeat of some sun;
> his least unmotion roams the youngest star)

Emerson was more of a mystic, in the technical sense of the word, than most critics have realized, and some of his essays refer explicitly to an "ecstatical state" in which the soul is reunited with the Oversoul.* Such a state

---

*He is most explicit in "The Method of Nature," an address delivered at Colby College in 1841. The address, not often read today, is almost a handbook of "the perennial philosophy."

is to be understood in a famous passage near the beginning of *Nature*: "Standing on the bare ground—my head bathed in the blithe air and uplifted into infinite space—all mean egoism vanishes. I become a transparent eyeball; I am nothing; I see all; the currents of the Universal Being circulate through me; I am part and parcel of God." Time and space being abolished at such moments, the soul is bathed in a higher Reason to be distinguished from mere Understanding. The distinction in Cummings' later poems is between "know" or "because," both contemptuous nouns in his language, and "feel," which is something to be honored ("my father moved through dooms of feel"). As for the states of ecstasy, they are possibly foreshadowed in the early poems by Cummings' effort to render the special quality of moments. In later poems that sense of the moment, the now, is so intensified that it comes close to being a mystical vision. "ten centuries of original soon"—that is, of history—are "plunged in eternal now." "dimensionless new alls of joy" flood over the poet as he perceived the 'illimitably spiralling candy of tiniest forever." "now the ears of my ears awake," another poem ends, "and now the eyes of my eyes are opened." In passages like these Cummings appears to be writing as the latest—though I suspect not the last—of the New England Transcendentalists.

The parallel can be carried too far. Where Emerson was essentially a Neoplatonist, Cummings was a scoffer in his youth, then more and more a Christian. He does not think of Christ as the most perfect man, in Emerson's way of speaking, but rather prays to him as a divine intercessor. In theological terms his God is less immanent than Emerson's and more transcendent. He says in a poem addressed to God—here I translate into prose—"How should any tasting, touching, hearing, seeing, breathing, merely human being—lifted from the no of all nothing—doubt unimaginable You?" As regards a future life, one of the subjects on which Emerson remained ambiguous, Cummings lets us infer that he believes in the resurrection of the flesh. "our now must come to then," he tells his love in a late sonnet—

> our then shall be some darkness during which
> fingers are without hands;and i have no
> you:and all trees are(any more than each
> leafless)its silent in forevering snow
>
> —but never fear(my own,my beautiful
> my blossoming)for also then's until

Other poems of the time make it clear that "until," for Cummings, was the moment when lovers shall rise from the grave.

5

Cummings lived into the late summer of 1962 and continued working to the last day. His career, if not his opinions, had been remarkably self-consistent. Except for his painting, carried on through the years, and except for a few lively incursions into prose—of which *The Enormous Room* is the most durable—he had never worked at any trade except that of writing verse. "*Peintre et poète,*" he had told a French policeman who asked his profession before arresting him; I think that was in 1923. Poet and painter—and nothing else—he remained to the end.

He wrote twelve books of poetry, including one that appeared after his death (*73 Poems,* 1963), but not including collected or selected works. The books contain 770 poems in all, an impressive output for a lyric poet and one recalling that of another New Englander, Emily Dickinson. Most of the poems are as short as hers, with perhaps one-fourth of them variations on the traditional fourteen-liner. After the early romantic pieces in *Tulips and Chimneys,* Cummings never ventured again into longer forms. Not all the poems are on the same level, and some of the more ingenious ones remind me that there is a drawer in our house full of kitchen gadgets made of stamped tin and wire, all vastly ingenious—U.S. patent applied for—but many of them unworkable and most of them seldom used. Cummings' inventions, too, are sometimes gimcrack and wasted, but the best of them have enriched the common language. The best of his lyrics, early and late, and not a few of the sonnets—more, it seems to me, on each rereading—have a sweep and music and underlying simplicity that make them hard to forget. And where does he stand among the poets of our time? He suffers from comparison with those who built on a larger scale—Eliot, Aiken, Crane, Auden among others—but still he is unsurpassed in his special field, one of the masters.

One may feel that in his later years, when he was groping his way back toward Emerson, Cummings wrote rather more new poems than he had new things to say. He might have been more severe with his work, and with his acolytes, but he had earned the privilege, after all, of being a little self-indulgent. He did not abuse the privilege. Except for those six nonlectures at Harvard, his only concession to the public, and to the need for earning money, was reading his poems aloud to mostly undergraduate audiences in all parts of the country. It required physical courage, for by that time he was partly crippled by arthritis, wore a brace on his back that jutted out two inches from his shoulderblades, and had to read while sitting in a straight-backed kitchen chair. After reading for half an hour, he had to rest for ten minutes; then he came back to finish the program. Nevertheless he held and charmed the audience, which was usually acquainted with his work and well prepared to listen.

He was speaking in the McCarthy years to what had come to be known as the silent generation. Sometimes he scolded the youngsters, as at Harvard, for being obsessed with security. "What is that?" he asked them. "Something negative, undead, suspicious and suspecting; an avarice and an avoidance; a self-surrendering meanness of withdrawal; a numerable complacency and an innumerable cowardice. . . . How monstrous and how feeble seems some unworld which would rather have its too than eat its cake!" The youngsters, cautious as they were at the time, liked to dream about the romantic freedom of the 1920s. They specially enjoyed his early poems, with their recklessness and brio, but they did not object to the conservative Christian anarchism of the later poems. Once again Cummings, the man stubbornly alone, found himself accepted by others as a spokesman.

1973

A Farewell to the Last Harvard "Dandy"

After the shock of hearing that a great writer is dead, one goes back to his early years, if lucky enough to have known about him then. It is something done partly for solace and partly, if one is a critic, in an effort to place his work in context.

E. E. Cummings' early years were spent in Cambridge, Massachusetts, at home and at Harvard. When he was at Harvard, from 1911 to 1916, a poetic tradition there was drawing to a close, although some of the poets who represented it were still to become famous. The tradition had started about 1890, and it includes such distinguished names as those of Trumbull Stickney—our most neglected major poet—Edwin Arlington Robinson, Wallace Stevens, Conrad Aiken, and T. S. Eliot, among a score of others.

It has never been given a name, and an accurate one would be hard to find for a movement that comprehended so many diverse talents, but simply for convenience we might call it the tradition of the Harvard dandies. Of course these poets weren't dandies in the sense that they dressed or acted with any precious sort of refinement. The dandyism went into their poems, which were as proudly discriminating and as free from vulgarity (except of a deliberate sort, introduced for effect) as the costume of a Regency gentleman.

All the Harvard dandies had a cold, dry, sharp New England wit of the kind that stabs you with icicles. As distinguished from other poets of the period, they all had a sense of fact that sometimes became brutal realism. Almost all of them were pagans, in the sense that they invoked Greek deities—especially goat-footed Pan—more often in their poems than they invoked Christian saints, and also in the sense that all except Robinson started as fleshly poets, in revolt against Christian austerity.

Including Robinson this time, they had all received sound classical educations, and almost all of them read and admired modern French poetry. That double pattern of influence, Greek and French, was set by Trumbull Stickney, who was the first American to be awarded a doctorate by the Sorbonne, after writing a thesis in French about axioms in Greek poetry. But they also worshiped the Elizabethans and believed somewhere in their minds that poetic drama was the highest form of art, so that sooner or later they all wrote or tried to write poetic plays.

I mention these men as a group, which they never were, because they help us to recognize the antecedents of another poet. For all his rebellions and innovations, Cummings was, in another sense, the last and youngest of the poets in a rich tradition. He was the last of the dandies because the Great War changed the literary atmosphere at Harvard and elsewhere. The poets who appeared after 1920 had a different set of values and aspirations—some of which, incidentally, they learned from Cummings as his work changed with the years.

I didn't know him when he was in college. By the fall of 1915 Cummings was already a graduate student, outside the horizon of a freshman, but I must have seen him at two or three meetings of the Harvard Poetry Society, which he helped to found later in the academic year. Already he was famous in college literary circles for his wit and his escapades. He had taken his degree magna cum in the classics and English, he had quoted Amy Lowell and Gertrude Stein in a commencement address, and, the son of a famous minister, he was in revolt against ministerial standards. On one occasion his father's car, with its clergyman's license plates, was found parked outside a famous joint near Scollay Square, to the embarrassment of the Boston police. Some of the poems he published in the *Harvard Monthly*, of which he was secretary, had made the Cambridge ladies squirm deliciously with horror.

In those days there were two literary magazines at Harvard, the *Monthly* and the *Advocate*, which were not on good terms with each other. There was a feeling among editors of the *Monthly* that editors of the *Advocate* were clubmen, athletes, journalists, disciples of Teddy Roosevelt, and not truly devoted to the art of letters. The feeling on the *Advocate* was that editors of the *Monthly* were art-for-art's-sakers, long-haired aesthetes, socialists, pacifists, or worse. The daily *Crimson* kept urging them both to amalgamate into one really good literary magazine, but they showed no disposition to follow this apparently sound advice.

As a matter of fact, they gained something from their rivalry. The editors of both magazines, glaring at each other from facing doorways on the dusty third floor of the Harvard Union, were inspired to "show those people over there that we can put out a better paper." The *Advocate* had more success in being liked by undergraduates, but the *Monthly* in Cummings' time had more soon-to-be-famous contributors. Some of his editorial colleagues were Gilbert Seldes, Robert Nathan, John Dos Passos, and Robert Hillyer.

In the winter of 1916–1917, after Cummings had taken his M.A. and moved to New York, the issue that divided the two magazines was that of preparedness and pacifism. The *Advocate* was as hot for preparedness as the most famous of its one-time editors, Theodore Roosevelt. The *Monthly* was of divided mind or minds: four of the editors were pacifists and four were superpatriots. That division on the staff led to the end of the brilliant but impractical *Monthly* in the spring of 1917, when this country entered the war. In an editorial that didn't mention the war, the editors explained that they were suspending publication on account of "existing circumstances."

But the story of the *Monthly* had a sequel. In January 1920, a former editor of the magazine, Sibley Watson, and another rich young Harvard graduate named Scofield Thayer brought out the first issue of the monthly *Dial*. It proved to be the most distinguished literary magazine that has so far appeared in this country, and it was also, in some of its aspects, the *Harvard Monthly* revived for readers over the nation. The featured contributor, whose verse and drawings in the first issue caused an almost nationwide scandal, was E. E. Cummings.

His career from that time was remarkably self-consistent. Except for his painting, carried on over the years, and some brilliant excursions into prose, he applied himself exclusively to writing verse. Of how many other American poets could that be said? There is Conrad Aiken, of course, but how many others, if asked their profession, could truthfully answer "poet," and not teacher, critic, lecturer, anthologist, publisher, or journalist writing poems in his spare time? How many could say that they have never sacrificed their poetry to their public enthusiasm or administrative duties or to the simple desire for getting themselves talked about? Cummings' poems were talked about, and his aberrant punctuation, but not his private life. He spent much of it in poverty, most of it in deliberate obscurity—as regards his person—and all for the sake of getting his work done.

During his later years his one concession to the public, and to the need for earning money, was reading his poems aloud, mostly to college audiences in all parts of the country. It required physical courage, for by that time he was partly crippled by arthritis, wore a brace on his back that jutted out two inches from his shoulder blades, and had to read while sitting on a straight-backed kitchen chair. Nevertheless he held and charmed the audience, and I found that students were more familiar with his work than with that of any other contemporary poet except Robert Frost. They all knew Frost, but many of them had learned two or three of Cummings' poems by heart.

One of the last times I saw him was at the University of Michigan in 1957. The hall in which he was reading had eight hundred seats, and it was full long before the reading began. Then the doors were locked, and more than a thousand other students milled about in the streets. It was the first and last time in this country that I heard of students almost rioting to hear a poetry reading, and Cummings must have enjoyed that tribute to the magic of his verse.

1962

S. Foster Damon

The New England Voice

In the matter of reputation, S. Foster Damon was as different from Hemingway as any two authors can be. Although he produced a considerable body of work, he never had to be destroyed by his successors or forgotten by the public, since he was never sufficiently known. His influence, less broad than intensive, was exerted chiefly on his friends.

I was one of the friends for fifty years. He disapproved of my first marriage and we saw less of each other after 1919, but still we kept in touch. At the end of a letter written the day after Thanksgiving 1966, I asked Foster a question. "Did you introduce me to Laforgue," I said, "or was I already Laforguing when I used to come out to Newton and drink tea in your room, in the spring of 1918? I remember your copy of *Tender Buttons,* but there is so much I forget." Foster waited a month, then answered frugally on a New Year's card. "Mal—" he said, using a nickname that everyone else has forgotten. "Yes, I remember showing you the poems of Jules Laforgue. We went over them together. Happy New Year to you both!"

So Laforgue was one more of my debts to Foster.

I have tried to make a list of the others. They include the early works of Ezra Pound, especially *Ripostes,* the poems of Stephen Crane, and the prose of Herman Melville, who as late as 1918 was an unknown writer in this country: I don't know where Foster had found his copy of *Moby Dick.* He was a specialist in hard-to-find books by unknown authors. Blake, of course, was not forgotten; almost everyone had read *Songs of Innocence* and *Songs of Experience*; but it was Foster who introduced me to the poems in the Rossetti and Pickering Manuscripts and to *The Marriage of Heaven and Hell.* He couldn't persuade me to follow him into the later prophetic books, and there were other gifts he offered that I was unwilling to accept: Gertrude Stein and Thomas Holley Chivers, for example, whom I always placed in the same category of might-be-interesting-to-others. His gift to me of Amy Lowell was not of her poems, on which I reserved judgment, but of her vivid and overwhelming personality; it was Foster who had her invite me to Sevenels, her big house in Brookline. I forget how many times we went there together to read our poems aloud and then to be praised and scolded by Miss Lowell as we puffed away at her Manila cigars.

Many others have owed the same sort of debts to Foster, who was "invariably an opener of doors," as the composer Virgil Thomson remarks in his autobiography. The remark comes after some memories that greatly resemble my own. Thomson says:

I came to know S. Foster Damon, slender, pale poet with a blond mustache, at that time [1921] instructing in English A while preparing privately, since Harvard would have none of it, the book that was to open up the language of William Blake. Foster was a composer as well as a poet and a scholar—also a close associate of Amy Lowell, whose biographer he became in the 1930s. I do not remember how I first knew him; but I do remember long walks and talks; and I remember his bringing me music and books that he thought I ought to know. Some of these, such as the critical writings of T. S. Eliot and the Irish tales of James Stephens, I found merely informative or charming. Others changed my life. Among these last were the piano works of Erik Satie, a pile of them four inches high, and a thin small volume called *Tender Buttons,* by Gertrude Stein. I returned these favors by introducing him to peyote, which we would take together, sometimes with another poet and English A instructor, Robert Hillyer. Foster has often re-appeared in my life and almost always with gifts in hand.

Among those who have acknowledged the gifts was E. E. Cummings, a close friend of Foster's when both were undergraduates. We read in his *i: six nonlectures* that "S. Foster Damon . . . opened my eyes and ears not merely to Domenico Theotocopuli [El Greco] and William Blake, but to all ultra (at that moment) modern music and poetry and painting." Cummings told his biographer, Charles Norman, "Practically everything I know about painting and poetry came to me through Damon." I wonder how many other poets might have ground for making a similar acknowledgment. Also I wonder, after more than fifty years, how it was that Foster opened so many doors for others while inveterately standing in the shadows to let them pass.

2

Poets abounded at Harvard, and would-be poets, when I went there in the fall of 1915. Foster was the ancient among them, for he belonged to the class of '14 and was starting his second year as a graduate student. I saw him for the first time at a meeting of the Harvard Poetry Society, which had just been organized. The poets were seated round a huge table in the dimly lighted sanctum of *The Harvard Monthly.* Pale in the lamplight, with straight ryestraw-colored hair, Foster read some poems that were chaste in form, but rather less chaste in sentiment. The reading was almost apologetic, with a notable lack of drama. When Foster came to a line that was shocking, for those days, his flat New England Seaboard voice would become flatter and more noncommittal. Still there were a few gasps of indignation. I don't remember whether I spoke to him after the meeting—that would have been a presumptuous act for a freshman—or whether we were introduced on some later occasion. But it seems to me, as I go poking among my memories, that more than once in my sophomore year, when poems of mine were beginning to be printed in *The Advocate,* we went into Boston together to drink seidels of dark beer at Jake Wirth's German saloon. One of my new literary friends warned me against Foster's pernicious influence.

It was in 1918 that I saw more of him than in any other year. In February I had come back to Harvard after six months as assistant driver of a munitions truck for the French Army, and another month with two Pittsburgh friends, Jimmy Light and his wife Sue Jenkins, who had moved on to Greenwich Village, where Jimmy was soon to become a director of the Provincetown Players. Foster, still in Cambridge, was continuing his graduate studies after trying to enlist in the army. Many times he appeared at my door with a green baize bag full of books. He would open the bag, select a book, and read about a passage that had struck his fancy; then we would talk about the usually forgotten or disparaged author. Once he had me visit the family's big suburban house in Newton for the weekend, and once or twice he took me to the rooms above the Western Club, where he lived with Philip Hillyer Smith, now my neighbor in Connecticut, and a group of noisy seniors. Smith tells me that Foster used to prowl up and down the study, smoking a long-stemmed German porcelain pipe, then dart to the table and write either a line of verse or a bar of music—or perhaps a sentence about Blake's prophetic books; one could never be sure which it would be.

At that time his poetry was better known than his scholarship, as a result of his appearance the previous year in *Eight Harvard Poets,* a volume that included the best of his early work along with that of Cummings, Dos Passos, Robert Hillyer, and others. I don't know what he saw in an awkward and acne'd boy of nineteen with country manners; it must have been our interest in poetry that brought us together. We were both enlisted in another war that raged simultaneously with the war in Europe: this one between the Ancients and the Moderns in poetry. Of course we were on the Modern side, and I ridiculed the Ancients for believing—or so I said—that poetry should express the daydreams of a twelve-year-old girl in words of one syllable. Foster attacked them for artlessness and timidity.

In April of 1918 I was, to my amazement, elected president of *The Harvard Advocate.* It was not a tribute to my brilliance, as I thought for a dizzy moment, but simply a recognition of the fact that I planned to wait a few months before going into the army. Most of my former colleagues on the editorial board were already in uniform. To keep the paper alive in their absence, I enlisted the help of such friends as Foster and John Brooks

Wheelwright, that tall, quizzical, High Church Anglican poet, whose sister Louise was later to become Foster's wife. Also I struck a blow for the Moderns by inviting Amy Lowell to read her new poems at an *Advocate* smoker on May 2. In his biography of Miss Lowell, Foster quotes her as saying, "I was, as usual, smuggled into an upper chamber, and kept quiet with cigars"—which I had been careful to provide—"while they heckled me in true undergraduate fashion." Miss Lowell, wreathed in smoke, crushed the hecklers as if with bolts from a fat thundercloud. But she made no answer of record to Jack Wheelwright's quite earnest question: "What do you do when you want to write a poem and haven't anything to write about?"

In June Foster and I took a walking trip that ended in a shack on a hilltop near the village of Candor, New York. A Greenwich Village friend had told me about the shack, for which we paid in advance a month's rent of three dollars. On our first evening there, over a supper of trout and wild strawberries (with bread and milk from a farm in the valley), we began talking about the *Spectra* hoax. It had lately been a front-page story in several newspapers: "Poet Unmasks Huge Joke on World of Art." The joke was a widely reviewed book called *Spectra* (1916) that presented the work of a new literary school purportedly founded by two Pittsburgh poets: Emanuel Morgan, just home from Paris, and a tempestuous Hungarian beauty, Anne Knish. In reality Morgan was Witter Bynner, who had at last revealed the imposture, and Knish was his friend Arthur Davison Ficke, another lyric poet of moderate skill and immense conservatism. Foster and I agreed that the joke was not only a good one but also a victory for the Ancients. It was time, we told each other, for the Moderns to stage a counterattack. Why couldn't we hoax the hoaxers?

On the following day, June 15, we produced almost the entire *opus poeticum* of Earl Roppel, later to be known as "the plowboy poet of Tioga Country" and "the bard of the rushing Catatonk." We also composed a letter to Bynner that served to introduce the poems. We said in part, or had Earl Roppel say, "I got your book out of the free library at Owego and read it all through that night and I like it very much though I do not understand it all. It gives you such a picture of life. Now, Mr. Bynner, what I want to say is this: I write some and I feel I write different from most. . . . And now I am drafted and have to leave next week. This seems to cut off all that my life has been. Before I go I would like to have the opinion of someone I feel knows what poetry is on my poems which enclosed please find."

I had supplied the name Earl Roppel and most of his country background. In writing his poems we tried to adumbrate the utterly inane, but our particular purpose was to burlesque what we thought was the false innocence of lyric poets like Witter Bynner. We each wrote about half of the poems, by count, though I have to admit that Foster's were better than

mine; he showed a gift for mischievous parody that he should have cultivated in his later career. A good example of his work was the precious qua-
train "Moon Light," to which he appended a note for Bynner: "This one
I wrote after reading your book."

> Last night when I was in our surrey,
>   Driving home with my best girl,
> I saw the moon run down the fence-row
>   Like a fat squirrel.

Soon after the birth of our plowboy poet, Kenneth Burke arrived at the
hilltop shack with a stubbornly chaste young woman from Ohio (later she
went to Paris and became an admired photographer). We saw a sample of
her handwriting and thought it had exactly the unformed, ingenuous look
that Earl Roppel's might have had. After providing ourselves with a ruled
school tablet, we persuaded her to copy out the poems and the letter to
Bynner. Then, thinking that the joke was too good to drop after a week—
and forgetting our primary purpose of striking a blow for the Moderns—
we made a few changes in the letter and had her copy it out for Amy Lowell
(with an additional poem that Foster had written as a pastiche of Miss Lowell's style: "Oh Venice! Masks! Stilettos!"). Revised once again, the letter
and the poems were also copied for my friend Conrad Aiken, but then we
had to stop; the young woman from Ohio was complaining that she had
no time to enjoy the countryside. I was enjoying it hugely; every morning
I set out with a can of worms and every afternoon I came back with a string
of trout. Foster would match them with a sonnet and a lard bucket half full
of wild strawberries. In the evening we argued about God knows what,
Kenneth and I laughing boisterously, Foster chuckling, while our aman-
uensis toiled away at our only table, under the only lamp.

A few days later we scattered from the shack on a hilltop: I was taking
a summer course in military science (mostly sham battles and bayonet drill),
Foster had an assignment from the Red Cross, and Kenneth was going to
work in a shipyard. We left word with the postmaster in Candor that letters
for Earl Roppel should be forwarded to Kenneth's address in Greenwich
Village. The letters were slow in reaching us. First to arrive by that roundabout course was the one from Conrad Aiken; it expressed a measured
appreciation of young Roppel's poetic gift and advised him to read Keats
and Tennyson. Aiken also sent him an inscribed copy of Palgrave's *Golden
Treasury*, which I have kept to this day. Amy Lowell was less restrained in
her enthusiasm. She offered to submit some of Roppel's verse to *Poetry* and
felt sure that it would be printed. "He has the modern spirit," she told
Foster when he next came out to dinner at Sevenels. "I don't know where
he got it, but he has it."

No letter arrived from Bynner, and for a long time we thought that our joke had missed its principal target. Two years later, however, I wrote a short article about the plowboy poet, and Bynner, when he read it, was sporting enough to tell me the whole story. He had been teaching at the University of California when he received Earl Roppel's little sheaf of verses. He had shown them to his colleagues in the English department at Berkeley, who had agreed with him that even Robert Burns might have admired their simplicity and freshness. Of course he had written to Roppel—more than once, as a matter of fact—and he had offered to help him publish a volume of poems, but the letters had been returned from an address in New York City (Kenneth had moved) with a note on the envelopes: "No such person." At Berkeley Professor Arthur Farwell of the music department had seized upon one of the poems (Foster's masterpiece of parody) and had set it to a stirring tune. It was sung before a huge audience in San Francisco by a chorus of three thousand trained voices. Professor Farwell told the newspapers that "Sun-set" (as Foster had entitled it) was the best patriotic song-poem in America:

> Flag of our country, strong and true,
>   The sky is rosy with your bars;
> But as they fade it turns to blue
>   And radiant with your stars.
>
> And as I watch the setting sun,
>   I call to God apart,
> "Give me the soul of Washington,
>   And give me Lincoln's heart!"

Meanwhile Bynner had written a letter of inquiry to the public library at Owego, ten miles from Candor. The librarian answered that nobody named Earl Roppel had ever been there to borrow books. Bynner began to suspect that someone had duped him: "Could it be Edna Millay?" he asked his friends. Others in the Bay Area maintained their faith in the plowboy poet. In his amusing book *The Spectra Hoax* (1961), William Jay Smith quotes from an article that appeared after the Armistice in *The San Francisco Bulletin*. The author was Zoë Burns, and she said: "Ever since I read the story and some of the work of Witter Bynner's lost poet, I've been wondering about the lad who had such a freshly interesting outlook on life from the narrow confines of a little New York hamlet and to whom the great dreams came thronging while he plowed the fields. . . . And I'm wondering if the war took that fresh fine almost-girlish sweetness out of him and made him bitter as it has so many of our youths." (Foster and I had worked hard to parody that twelve-year-old-girlish tone.) "Was the heart of him smitten by the thunder of war?" Miss Burns continued. "And the melody of his spirit silenced by its horrors? Was perchance his very life blown out like a candle in the blast?" Of course she was correct in her surmise that Earl Roppel had been a wartime casualty; he died because his only begetters had been separated by military service. Still, he had enjoyed his moment of glory, which might have been Foster's moment, too, if he could have been there to accept the applause. In the next fifty years S. Foster Damon was to receive many honors, if not a tithe of those he rightly earned. Harvard never acknowledged him. Nothing he signed with his own name was ever to be sung by a chorus of three thousand trained voices.

3

Thinking back on Foster's bogus anthem and how it was glorified as the work of another poet, I felt that it might have served as a portent of his career. Always he displayed (or concealed) a talent for being unrecognized and, in relation to the public taste, untimely. In that age of celebrities, the 1920s, he remained the obscure and usually unacknowledged background of celebrities. His first scholarly work, *William Blake: His Philosophy and Symbols* (1924), was an illustration of that singular gift. It was written too soon and it opened too many doors, with the result that Harvard did not accept it "in partial fulfillment," as the phrase used to run, "of the requirements for the degree of doctor of philosophy." It was to inspire many doctoral dissertations. All the subsequent Blake scholars have made use of it; some have written successful books that depended on it; but meanwhile Foster's book, which had appeared in an edition of only a thousand copies, was to remain out of print for twenty years or more.

That early example of his talent for anonymity was to be followed by others. He next wrote what is still the only extended study of Thomas Holley Chivers (1809–1858). The book appeared in 1930 and, so far as I remember, attracted no attention whatever. In that first year of the Depression, nobody was interested in the question whether Poe had copied Chivers in some of his poems—or had it been Chivers who copied Poe? The Depression continued year after year, always breeding new crises, and Foster continued to stand aloof from the issues it raised. His new undertaking was a biography of Amy Lowell, an authoritative record of all the picturesque, outrageous, or illuminating episodes in her Napoleonic career. In 1935, when the book was published, the literary world had turned away from Miss Lowell and everything she stood for.

Foster's next published work was for once more timely; it was a facsimile collection, with editorial notes, of a hundred American popular songs from the years before the Civil War. It appeared in 1936, at a moment when American history was becoming a popular subject, and composers were to use Foster's book as a source of background music for some highly successful motion pictures. But the book itself had a limited sale, and again Foster received little credit as a pioneer. He was busy for several years with other projects, including plays and a very long narrative poem that nobody wanted to publish. In 1952 I gave a lecture at Brown, where Foster had been teaching since 1927. After having breakfast with the Damons, I sent him a perturbed letter:

"Dear Foster: I'm addressing the letter to you because, in addition to its serving as a bread-and-butter, or buttered-toast, letter to you and Louise, it also has to touch on the great question of your unpublished manuscripts. They worry me. I don't know any writer of our time who has had so little recognition for what he has done. . . ."

The letter continued with what I hoped were some practical suggestions for publication. Having the professional point of view, I was given to making practical suggestions—except in regard to my own work—but in this case they had no practical results. Foster told me at the time—or was it a little later?—that he had set to work on a complete edition of Chivers' prose and poetry. "Chivers, Chivers," I said to myself in despair. Only the first of three projected volumes was published (1957), in the midst of a silence that shattered one's ears.

But Foster's masterpiece of anonymity was the last book of poems he wrote, *Nightmare Cemetery* (1964). He had published two much earlier collections, and they had earned him some of the usual honors, including the presidency of the New England Poetry Society and its Golden Rose. *Astrolabe* (1927) was the more impressive of the early volumes, by virtue of two rather long mystical poems, both with the same title, "Apocalypse"; they seemed to promise further visions and experiments. The promise was not fulfilled by the poems in *Tilted Moons* (1929), which were mostly decorative and indebted to Foster's reading, with pervasive echoes of Verlaine and Laforgue. Except for that long narrative, I doubt whether he wrote many poems in the next twenty or thirty years. In his late sixties, however, he struck a new vein and worked on it until he had completed *Nightmare Cemetery*, a double sequence of seventy-three sonnets that is, among other things, a remarkable technical achievement.

That is not its principal claim to being remembered, but still the virtuosity should not be overlooked. The work includes examples, and good ones, of orthodox Petrarchan and Shakespearean sonnets, with other examples of almost every possible variation, new and old, from those two basic patterns. Foster does omit a few. Thus, he gives us a sonnet in hexameter, but none in tetrameter or trimeter, none in "sprung rhythm," and none in syllabic verse. Those metrical experiments, however, are hardly missed in the diversity of stanzaic forms he offers. To list a few, there are sonnets in which the conventional octave and sestet are replaced by two seven-line stanzas. There are two double sonnets. There is one sonnet in rhyming couplets, one in rhyming tercets, and one in *terza rima*. There is a sonnet in five stanzas of two, three, four, three, and two lines respectively; of course they add up to fourteen. All but two of the sonnets are of that conventional length, but there is also a thirteen-line sonnet with a compli-cated rhyme scheme and an extended sonnet in which one line, the twelfth, bursts indignantly into six lines, all rhyming in "-ation." In still another sonnet, the word "myself" replaces the rhyme in each of eight lines:

> Yes, even the scenery (not too bad): myself.
> And you, the disgusted audience,—myself.

It is a statement of philosophical idealism carried to the point of solip-sism, as with many New England poets of the last century. In Foster's case, however, the dependence of the outer cosmos on the inner cosmos is expressed not only in a variety of measures but also in a candid, self-deprecatory fashion (the world is a play written by "myself," he says, but "badly written") and in a tone of voice sustained from the first sonnet to the last. He must have felt, and rightly, that the book was immensely better than anything he had written in his early years.

And what did he do to bring *Nightmare Cemetery* to public attention? Did he submit the separate poems to a hierarchy of magazines, beginning with most prestigious and running down the scale (but not too far, since printing them in the littler magazines would be a tactical error)? Did he read them for radio programs or make those personal appearances on the poetry circuit that are now so easy to arrange? After those preliminary steps, did he keep sending the manuscript to big trade publishers until he found an editor with taste enough to admire it and authority enough to get it accepted? And then did he write to famous colleagues who might be per-suaded to review the book or at least to furnish a few adulatory words for the jacket? Those are the usual shifts to which poets are driven by their thirst for glory and their recognition that poetry is not a popular art. I doubt whether they even occurred to Foster, burdened as he was with New England shyness and seventy years of accumulated ignorance about the technique of becoming a famous poet. Perhaps "incapacity" would be a better word. In 1918 he had known what steps to take in order to create the reputation of Earl Roppel, but neither then nor later had he been able to regard his own reputation in the same impersonal way, as a problem in literary mechanics. At any rate, he chose the most effective means of not recapturing an audience. He had the book published, if one can use the word, by friends at the Rhode Island School of Design, in an edition of two hundred numbered and expensive copies. Then, having sent out a few dozen copies for review and some others as gifts to friends, he simply waited for recognition.

Two years later he was still waiting. He said in a mildly querulous letter (October 13, 1966), "*Not one* of the copies of my *Cemetery* sent to poetry and other literary magazines so much as got listed in 'Books Received.' And of course no reviews. I guess that one peek showed my poems to be sonnets, and sonnets are not worth noticing any more."

Sonnets are out of fashion, but there was another reason for the universal oversight. Foster had presented *Nightmare Cemetery* under a pseudonym—Samuel Nomad—and with a prefatory note that read: "All the characters in this book are entirely imaginary including the author." He must have regarded the pseudonym and the note as a transparent literary device, since, as he explained in another letter, the author's identity is revealed in the thirteenth line of the sonnet on page ten: "the clumsy letters of my name reversed." Samuel Nomad and S. (for Samuel) Foster Damon: any reader could see the connection. But where were the readers? Foster did not realize that hardly anyone, these days, would even open a book by a pseudonymous author half-published in a small edition by a school of design. Hardly anyone, that is, took the peek that would have shown the poems to be sonnets, let alone reading as far as the thirteenth line of the sonnet on page ten. In the glut and gurry of contemporary writing, there are too many nominated poets wailing for attention. Hardly any editor thinks of assigning a completely unknown book for review.

Or did the author realize all this and was he obeying his instinct for self-obliteration?

What *Nightmare Cemetery* needed and still needs is the sort of adventurous reader that Foster was in his Harvard years. But is there such a reader today?—I mean with Foster's knight-errantry in riding to the rescue of neglected books as if they were maidens immured in a donjon keep. Some of those books had languished so long unread that they had become the equivalent of maiden great-aunts before he freed them from dusty shelves and displayed them to his friends. "Look at this, Estlin (or Jack, or Virgil)," he would say a little proudly, as if he had returned from a knightly quest with Sleeping Beauty riding on his crupper. But who will go questing after *Nightmare Cemetery*?

If Samuel Nomad were a person and if his book had been written fifty years ago—as in some ways it might have been, for it does not propose to be timely—I can imagine what Foster might have said about it, after producing it from that enormous green baize bag. "Look at this, Mal," he would have begun in his flat voice, but with an edge of excitement: "here's something I found today. The author calls it a Halloween prank, but it's a grisly and labored one, a double sequence of sonnets about death. Is it great poetry? No, it doesn't even try to be, and yet it belongs in a great line: Emerson, Jones Very, Emily Dickinson, all the New England metaphysicals. Yes, and let's add Edward Rowland Sill and E. A. Robinson for a touch of pessimism. Here's why it impresses me: it's at the very end of the line."

I would open the book and read a sonnet. "This one doesn't sound like Emerson," I would say.

"Oh, you mean the one where Nomad compares his own death to pulling the chain and going down the toilet? That sonnet will prove my point as well as another. It's pure New England in its self-absorption—the wrong word; it makes me think of toilet paper—and in its identification of the self with the universe. But it's Emerson upside down, Emerson turned pessimist and raging cynic, Emerson's great tides of universal Being transformed into 'the gulp of the celestial watercloset.' I tell you, it's the end of the line."

Foster would snatch the book from my hand and go pacing up and down the room. "This Nomad fellow," he would say, "is evidently an old man telling what he thinks is the shameful truth about himself. He isn't a celebrity, he isn't popular and outgoing, and he faces what he calls 'the time when I am slowly, horribly, killed.' His dim hope of an afterlife depends on finding readers for his poetry, yet some deep compulsion makes him insult them and drive them away. He can make jokes about his shameful truths or dress them in Halloween masks from a children's party, but he hasn't time left to be bothered with telling lies. He hasn't time to be decorative in his language or to grope for figures of speech; one metaphor set forth in simple words, sometimes in slang, is all he finds room for in one sonnet. Listen:

> "'Life is the big neighborhood party, me lad,
> to which you weren't invited. And so what.
>
> "'walk in as though you owned the place—be brash
> and grab the prettiest girl and make her dance.
>
> "'(This is one party that you cannot crash.)
> —So, go home; climb into bed and try to sleep.
> (The cold, deep bed and your long, long last sleep.)'

"He writes for the ear, not the eye," Foster would comment, "and the only liberties he allows himself are in rhyme and stanza and especially in meter. There he delights in asperities and rugosities. His iambic pentameters are sprinkled with trochees; there are two in the first line I read, besides one anapest, and the line about the cold, deep bed has three spondees. Reading such lines makes me think of New Hampshire fields that are strewn with boulders. The soil runs thin as the blood runs thin; Nomad is the last of a great line. Sometimes his voice wheezes like the hand-pumped organ in an old meetinghouse; it is the voice of New England, and yet his own voice unmistakably. Because of it his book exists in itself when so many books are the mere facsimiles of others. Listen for a last time."

Foster would page through the book and, in his own unmistakable voice, would read me six lines of "Epitaph":

> I tried to write my name: that much seemed needed.
> And I have failed if it has found a place
> only beneath the title. But I succeeded
> if in this verbal wilderness and valley
> sometimes you hear a voice you cannot place
> that speaks your own name softly, authentically.

It seems that Samuel Nomad, or rather S. Foster Damon in his last book of poems, has succeeded in that self-absorbed but self-effaced and wholly authentic fashion.

A FOOTNOTE

There was to be one more published book of poetry, *The Moulton Tragedy* (1970), but this had existed in manuscript since the beginning of World War II. It is "a heroic poem with lyrics," and it is based on the legend of a New England Faust, Jonathan Moulton, who drove a Yankee bargain with the Devil. *The Moulton Tragedy* is technically brilliant like the sonnets, it is full of local history, and it has eerie moments that continue Foster's lifelong interest in the occult. It appeared when narrative poetry was even less in fashion than the sonnet. By that time Foster had suffered a stroke, and he was probably unable to read the reviews, which, as always, were as far and few as the lands where the Jumblies live.

Foster died on Christmas Day 1971 (he had been born in 1893, on Washington's Birthday). A book of his *Selected Poems* was published in 1974 by Abattoir Editions (University of Nebraska at Omaha). Besides being handsomely printed, the book is well edited and introduced by Donald E. Stanford, but I wish it could have been much longer. *Nightmare Cemetery* still serves as Foster's epitaph.

1978

Conrad Aiken

From Savannah to Emerson

Rereading Conrad Aiken's work, one is impressed again by the unity that underlies its real mass and apparent diversity. He published some fifty books, all told, and they include novels, stories, criticism, a play, an autobiography, and thirty or more books of poems that were finally brought together in *Collected Poems: Second Edition,* a volume of more than a thousand closely printed pages. He was a poet essentially, but he was also the complete man of letters, distinguished for his work in many forms of verse and prose. The unity was there, however, and in every form he spoke with the same candid, scrupulous, self-deprecatory, yet reckless and fanciful New England voice. Yes, the voice was that of his ancestors, not of his birthplace. Aiken says of himself in his last poem, "Obituary in Bitcherel,"

> Born in beautiful Savannah
> to which he daily sang hosanna
> yet not of southern blood was he
> he was in fact a damned Yankee.

I remember first meeting him in 1918, when I was a junior at Harvard. Not long before I had read *The Jig of Forslin,* a long poem that impressed and a little frightened the apprentice poet by what it had done to achieve a symphonic form. I went to see its publisher, Edmund Brown, who ran a little bookstore near the Back Bay station, and he gave me the author's address. There was an exchange of letters and Aiken suggested that we meet in the lobby of the Hotel Touraine. I was to look for a man in an orange necktie who wasn't a fairy.

Aiken was then twenty-eight years old, was six years out of college, and was already the author of two red-haired children and four published volumes of post-Romantic poetry, besides two others waiting to appear. On that mild February evening I saw the necktie as he came in the door; it was brighter than his Valencia-orange hair. For the rest he wore the Harvard uniform of the period: white button-down oxford shirt and brown suit. His forehead was broad, his jaw was square, and his blue eyes were set wide apart. Short and solidly built, a block of a man, he had a look of mingled shyness and pugnacity.

I remember that our conversation was broken at first, but that later, over seidels of beer, we found many common interests in spite of my callowness and our nine years' difference in age. We both liked Boston in decay, we had notions about the French Symbolists, we spoke of achieving architectural and musical effects in verse (such as Aiken in fact had achieved), and we were fascinated by the political maneuvers of the poetry world without wishing to take part in them. Soon we were talking without pauses, talking with such excitement—at least on my part—that I didn't notice the streets through which we wandered before parting at the door of Aiken's lodging house, on the unfashionable side of Beacon Hill.

I was right to be excited, and elated too, since I found afterward that Aiken seldom opened himself to literary strangers. There were years when he stayed away from almost all writers and editors as a matter of principle, and I was lucky to be one of the few exceptions. He refused to attend literary dinners and could seldom be inveigled into cocktail parties. In some ways the shyest man I knew, he was also one of the best talkers. The shyness kept him from talking in company except for an occasional pun: thus, he would describe his friend Tom Eliot's notes to *The Waste Land* as a "verbiform appendix," or Frost's less successful poems as having "the artlessness that conceals artlessness"; but such phrases were spoken in a voice so low that most of the company missed them. Only quite late at night, or earlier over martinis with one or two friends, would he launch into one of those monologues that ought to be famous for their mixture of flagrant wit and complete un-self-protective candor.

In the course of time I discovered that candor was close to being his central principle as a man and a writer, particularly as a poet. The principle evolved into a system of aesthetics and literary ethics that unified his work, a system based on the private and public value of self-revelation. No matter what sort of person the poet might be, healthy or neurotic, Aiken believed that his real business was "to give the lowdown on himself, and through himself on humanity." If he was sick in mind, candor might be his only means of curing himself. "Out of your sickness let your sickness speak," Aiken says in one of his Preludes—

> the bile must have his way—the blood his froth—
> poison will come to the tongue. Is hell your kingdom?
> you know its privies and its purlieus? keep
> sad record of its filth? Why this is health.

"Look within thyself to find the truth" might have been his Emersonian motto; and it had the corollary that inner truth corresponds to outer truth, as self or microcosm does to macrocosm. Aiken believed that the writer should be a surgeon performing an exploratory operation on himself, at whatever cost to his self-esteem, and penetrating as with a scalpel through layer after layer of the semiconscious. That process of achieving self-knowledge might well become a self-inflicted torture. At times the writer might feel—so Aiken reports from experience—"the shock of an enormous exposure: as if he had been placed on a cosmic table, *en plein soleil*, for a cosmic operation, a cosmic intrusion." Let him persist, however, and he will be rewarded by finding—here I quote from a letter—"what you think or feel that is secretly you—shamefully you—intoxicatingly you." Then, having laid bare this secret self, which is also a universal self, the writer must find words for it, accurate and honest words, but poured forth—Aiken says in a Prelude—without reckoning the consequences:

> Let us be reckless of our words and worlds,
> And spend them freely as the tree his leaves.

Here enters the public as opposed to the merely private value of complete self-revelation. By finding words for his inmost truth, the writer—especially the poet—has made it part of the world, part of human consciousness. He has become a soldier, so to speak, in the agelong war that mankind has been waging against the subliminal and the merely instinctive.

But service in that war involves much that lies beyond the simple process of discovering and revealing one's secret self. The writer must divide himself into two persons, one the observer, the other a subject to be observed, and the first must approach the second "with relentless and unsleeping objectivity." The observer-and-narrator must face what Aiken calls "That eternal problem of language, language extending consciousness and then consciousness extending language, in circular or spiral ascent"; and he must also face the many problems of architectural and sequential form. The words that depict the observed self must not only be honest; they must be "twisted around," in Aiken's phrase, until they have a shape and structure of their own; until they become an "artifact" (a favorite word of his) and if possible a masterpiece that will have a lasting echo in other minds. The "supreme task" performed by a masterpiece—as well as by lesser works and deeds in a more temporary fashion—is that of broadening, deepening, and subtilizing the human consciousness. Any man who devotes himself to that evolving task will find in it, Aiken says, "all that he could possibly require in the way of a religious credo."

His name for the credo was "the religion of consciousness."* It is a doctrine—no, more than that, a system of belief—to which he gave many refinements and ramifications. Some of these are set forth, with an impressive

---

*The phrase "religion of consciousness" was I think first used in print by F. O. Matthiessen in *Henry James: The Major Phase* (New York: Oxford University Press, 1944); it serves as title for the last chapter. But the chapter has less to say about James's consciousness than one expects of such a fruitful critic as Matthiessen. Long after reading the book, I learned that he had discussed it with Aiken and had borrowed the phrase from him, after receiving Aiken's permission.

density of thought and feeling, in two long series of philosophical lyrics, *Preludes for Memnon* (1931) and *Time in the Rock* (1936); Aiken regarded these as his finest work. But the doctrine is a unifying theme in almost all the poetry of his middle years, say from 1925 to 1956, and in the prose as well. It is clearly exemplified in his novels, especially in *Blue Voyage* (1927), which brought young Malcolm Lowry from England to sit at the author's feet, and *Great Circle* (1933), which contains a brilliant, drunken, self-revealing monologue that Freud admired; he kept the book in his Vienna waiting room. Self-discovery is often the climax of Aiken's stories, and it is, moreover, the true theme of his autobiography, *Ushant* (1952). At the end of the book he says of his shipmates on a postwar voyage to England, "They were all heroes, every one of them; they were all soldiers; as now, and always, all mankind were soldiers; all of them engaged in the endless and desperate war on the unconscious."

2

Aiken's life had an intricate unity almost like that of his poetry and his fiction. Such is one's impression after reading *Ushant*, which deserves a place among the great autobiographies. In American literature there is nothing to compare with it except *The Education of Henry Adams*, which is equally well composed, equally an artifact—to use Aiken's word again—but which gives us only one side of the author. In *Ushant* the author writes in the third person, like Adams, and maintains the same objective tone, while recording not only his "education" but also his faults and obsessions, his infidelities, his recurrent dreams, his uproarious or shabby adventures: in short, while trying "to give the lowdown on himself, and through himself on humanity."

His pursuit of the essential self leads him back to his childhood in Savannah, spent in a house with a high front stoop and a chinaberry tree in the back yard. He tells of two experiences in the Savannah house that were to shape the rest of his life. One of these was lying on the carpeted floor of the nursery and reading the epigraph to the first chapter of *Tom Brown's School Days*:

> I'm the poet of White Horse Vale, Sir,
> With liberal notions under my cap.

Not understanding the word "poet," Conrad asked his father what it meant, and learned that the admired father had also written poems. From that moment the boy determined to be a poet himself, with liberal notions, and to live in England somewhere near White Horse Vale. Indeed he was to live there for many years, in a house with a big room in which he tried to re-create the parlor of the Savannah house. "The entire life," he says, "had thus in a sense annihilated time, and remained, as it were, in a capsule or in a phrase." It was the second experience, however, that confirmed the first and froze it into an enduring pattern. Since it was the last and grisliest scene of the poet's childhood in Savannah, it should be presented in his own words:

". . . after the desultory early-morning quarrel came the half-stifled scream, and then the sound of his father's voice counting three, and the two loud pistol shots; and he had tiptoed into the dark room, where the two bodies lay motionless, and apart, and, finding them dead, found himself possessed of them forever."

Perhaps it would be more accurate to say that the dead New England parents took possession of their son. Conrad was brought north to live with relatives in New Bedford, but still he was to spend the rest of his life coming to terms with his father and his mother. There was to be a third experience, however, that also helped to shape his career, though it was partly a sequel to what happened in Savannah. Conrad had spent happy years at Harvard and had made some lifelong friends, including Tom Eliot. When he was about to be graduated, in 1911, he was elected class poet. He refused the honor, resigned from college in something close to panic, and fled to Italy. "He had known, instantly," he says in *Ushant,* "that this kind of public appearance, and for such an occasion, was precisely what the flaw in his inheritance would not, in all likelihood, be strong enough to bear. . . . It was his decision that his life was to be lived *off-stage,* behind the scenes, out of view." In the next sixty years he did not change his mind. Aiken never, to my knowledge, gave a public lecture, read his poems to a women's club (or any other live audience), or appeared on a platform to accept an honorary degree.

Partly as a result of his obstinately remaining off-stage, he has been more neglected by the public than any other major American poet since Herman Melville, who was privately published, and Emily Dickinson, who didn't bother to put her poems into books. Aiken had those fifty published titles, but not one of them was a booksellers' choice. In 1934 I asked him for nominations to a list that was going to be printed in *The New Republic,* of "Good Books That Almost Nobody Has Read." He nominated Kafka's *The Castle*—that was long before the Kafka boom—then added in a postscript: "Might I also suggest for your list of Neglected Books a novel by c. aiken called *Great Circle,* of which the royalty report, to hand this morning, chronicles a sale of 26 copies in the second half year? and *Preludes for Memnon,* which I think is my best book, and which has sold about seven hundred copies in three years."

In 1946 I had the notion of trying to persuade some quarterly to publish a Conrad Aiken number. What should go into it? I asked him in a letter. He answered from England, making no suggestions whatever. "Appraisals of my work," he said, "have been rare or brief or nonexistent whether in periodicals or books on contemporary poetry: in me you behold an almost unique phenomenon, a poet who has acquired a Reputation, or a Position, or what have you, without ever having been caught in the act—as it were, by a process of auto-osmosis. At any given moment in the Pegasus Sweepstakes, in whatever Selling Plate or for whatever year, this dubious horse has always been the last in the list of the also-ran,—he never even placed, much less won, nor, I regret, have the offers to put him out to stud been either remunerative or very attractive. Odd. Very odd."

A few years later he began to receive a series of official honors,

> And Awards and Prizes of various sizes
> among them a few quite delightful surprises. . . .

as he said in his "Obituary in Bitcherel." He accepted the honors gladly, on condition that they didn't involve a public appearance. Thus, from 1950 to 1952 he served as Consultant in Poetry at the Library of Congress. He received the Bryher Award in 1952, a National Book Award in 1954, the Bollingen Award in 1956, the Fellowship of the National Academy of Poets in 1957, the Gold Medal for Poetry of the National Institute in 1958, and finally the National Medal for Literature in 1969. Meanwhile his position with the public (and with the booksellers) had improved scarcely at all; perhaps it had deteriorated. He reported in 1971 that his *Collected Poems: Second Edition,* containing the work of a lifetime, had a sale for its first half-year of 430 copies.

It is hardly surprising that some developments in his later poems went unnoticed by poetry readers, and by critics too.

3

Without in the least abandoning his religion of consciousness, Aiken's poems of the 1950s and 1960s introduced some new or partially new elements. One of these was a note of ancestral piety, with allusions to earlier Aikens, but more to his mother's connections, the Potters (who had started as New Bedford Quakers) and the Delanos. The note is already audible in "Mayflower," written in 1945. It is a poem partly about the ship (on which two of the poet's ancestors had been passengers), partly about the flower, and partly about the sandy shores of Cape Cod, where the Pilgrims had landed before sailing on to Plymouth. In other poems there is frequent mention of what might be called ancestral scenes: New Bedford and its whaling ships; the Quaker graveyard at South Yarmouth, on the Cape, where Cousin Abiel lies buried; Sheepfold Hill, also on the Cape; and Stony Brook, where the herring used to spawn by myriads. There is also talk of godfathers and tutelary spirits: among the poets Ben Jonson, Shakespeare, Li Po, and among historical figures Pythagoras and William Blackstone, the scholar and gentle heretic who built a house on the site of Boston before the Puritans came, then moved away from them into the wilderness. Blackstone becomes the hero of Aiken's cycle of poems about America, *The Kid* (1947). In "A Letter from Li Po" (1955), the Chinese maker of timeless artifacts is set beside the scoffing Quaker, Cousin Abiel:

> In this small mute democracy of stones
> is it Abiel or Li Po who lies
> and lends us against death our speech?

Another new or newly emphasized feature of the later poems is something very close to New England Transcendentalism. Its appearance should be no surprise, except to those who have fallen into the habit of regarding Transcendentalism as a purely historical phenomenon, a movement that flourished from 1830 to 1860, then disappeared at the beginning of the Civil War. On the contrary, it has been a durable property of New England thinking, a home place, one might say, to which some poets return as they grow older. In one or another of many aspects, the Transcendental mood is manifested in Robinson, in Frost, to some extent in Eliot, perhaps in Millay—see "Renascence" and some of the very late poems—then in Cummings, Wilder, S. Foster Damon, John Wheelwright, and most clearly in Conrad Aiken.

A complete definition of Transcendentalism would comprise most of Emerson's essays, beginning with *Nature*. As a shorter definition, the best I have found is a paragraph in the article "Transcendentalism" in *The Oxford Companion to American Literature*. One is grateful to the editor, James D. Hart, for bringing almost everything together in a few sentences. He says:

. . . the belief had as its fundamental base a monism holding to the unity of the world and God and the immanence of God in the world. Because of this indwelling of divinity, everything in the world is a microcosm containing within itself all the laws and meaning of existence. Likewise the soul of each individual is identical with the soul of the world, and latently contains all that the world contains. Man may fulfill his divine potentialities either through a rapt mystical state, in which the divine is infused into the human, or through coming into contact with the truth, beauty, and goodness embodied in nature and originating in the Over-Soul. Thus occurs the doctrine of the correspondence between the tangible world and the human mind, and the identity of moral and physical laws. Through belief in the divine authority of the soul's intuitions and impulses, based on the identification of the individual soul with God, there developed the doctrine of self-reliance and individualism, the disregard of external authority, tradition, and logical demonstration, and the absolute optimism of the movement.

For a brief statement of Transcendental doctrines, James Hart's paragraph—from which I have omitted a few introductory phrases—seems to me almost complete. It does omit, however, two doctrines of some importance. One is the rejection of history—at least of history conceived as an irreversible process, a causally linked series of events in which the masses as well as the "representative men" play their part. For this rejection, see Emerson's essay "History" and also many of Cummings' later poems. Thornton Wilder, a New Englander by descent and residence—though born in Wisconsin—tells us that history is not a sequence but a tapestry or carpet in which various patterns are repeated at intervals. Having spatialized time in this fashion, Wilder could never have become a social or a political historian, and the statement applies to others working in the same tradition.

One might say that Transcendentalists as a type—if such a type exists—are most at home in essays and poetry. If they turn to fiction, as Wilder did, they write novels dealing with morals rather than manners. Manners are the expression of standards prevailing in a group, and Transcendentalism denies the existence of groups except as arithmetical sums of separate persons: one plus one plus one. Only the individual is real and bears within himself a portion of the Over-Soul. That is the other doctrine omitted from Hart's admirable paragraph, and it explains why the Transcendental cast of mind is skeptical about political science and usually contemptuous of politicians. Aiken, for example, says of himself in *Ushant*: ". . . he had never found it possible to take more than a casual and superficial interest in practical politics, viewing it, as he did, as inevitably a passing phase, and probably a pretty primitive one, and something, again, that the evolution of consciousness would in its own good season take care of."

Is consciousness, for Aiken—the consciousness of mankind as shared by each individual—close to being an equivalent of the Over-Soul? That might be stretching a point, and indeed, I should be far from saying that, among twentieth-century New England writers, there is any complete Transcendentalist in a sense that might be accepted, for instance, by Margaret Fuller. It is clear, however, that there are several New England writers, most of them among the best, whose work embodies aspects of the Transcendental system (though seldom its "absolute optimism"). The aspects are usually different in each case, but two of them, at least, are shared by all the writers I mentioned. All are fiercely individual, in theory and practice, and all are moralists or ethicists, even or most of all when defying an accepted system of ethics.

Why this revival of the Transcendental spirit should be particularly evident in New England is hard to say. One is tempted to speak of something in the blood, or in the climate, or more realistically of a tradition handed down by a father or a favorite schoolteacher, rejected in the poet's youth, then reaccepted in middle age. Usually there is not much evidence of a literary derivation: for instance, Cummings and Millay were not at all interested in the earlier Transcendentalists. Aiken might be an exception here. Boldest of all in his development of certain Transcendental notions, he also, rather late in life, found them confirmed by ancestral piety and especially by the writings and career of his maternal grandfather.

William James Potter was a birthright Quaker who became a Unitarian because he felt that the doctrines of the Friends were too confining. In 1859 he was called to the Unitarian church in New Bedford, where he soon began to feel that Unitarianism was confining too. In 1866 he refused to administer the rite of communion; following the example of Emerson, he told his congregation that he could no longer do so in good conscience. In 1867 he refused to call himself a Christian and was thereupon dropped from the roll of Unitarian ministers. He was so admired, however, for being upright and unselfish and a good preacher that his congregation gave him a unanimous vote of confidence. With Emerson, Colonel Higginson, and others, he then founded the Free Religious Association, which was intended to unite all the religions of the world by rejecting their dogmas and retaining from each faith only its ethical core. Dogmas were what he abhorred.

When the poet came to read Grandfather Potter's published sermons, he was impressed by their bold speculations about the divine element in men. He wrote an admiring poem about his grandfather, "Halloween," in which he quoted from the journal that Potter had kept during his early travels in Europe. A quoted phrase was ". . . so man may make the god finite and viable, make conscious god's power in action and being." That sounds the Transcendental note, and it is also close to phrases that Aiken himself had written: for example, in the 1949 preface to one of his Symphonies, where he says that man, in becoming completely aware of himself, "can, if he only will, become divine."

There is another point, apparently not connected with Grandfather Potter, at which Aiken comes even closer to Transcendentalism. Once more I quote from that convenient definition by James Hart: ". . . everything in the world is a microcosm containing within itself all the laws and meaning of existence. Likewise, the soul of each individual is identical with the soul of the world, and latently contains all that the world contains. . . . Thus occurs the doctrine of correspondence between the tangible world and the human mind." Aiken, with his senses open to the tangible world, often speaks of this correspondence, which sometimes becomes for him an identity. Thus, he says in "A Letter from Li Po":

> We are the tree, yet sit beneath the tree,
> among the leaves we are the hidden bird,
> we are the singer and are what is heard.

Reading those lines, one can scarcely fail to think of Emerson's "Brahma":

> They reckon ill who leave me out;
>   When me they fly, I am the wings;
> I am the doubter and the doubt,
>   And I the hymn the Brahmin sings.

Aiken is still more clearly Emersonian, however, in what is almost the last of his poems, *THEE,* written when he was seventy-seven. Though comparatively short—only 250 lines, some consisting of a single word—it appeared as a handsome book, with lithographs by Leonard Baskin, and it is indeed one of his major works. First one notes that the poet has changed his style and that here—as, to a lesser extent, in some of the other late poems—he has abandoned the subtle variations and dying falls of his earlier work. *THEE* is written in short, galloping lines with rhymes like hoofbeats:

> Who is that splendid THEE
> who makes a symphony
> of the one word
> be
> admitting us to see
> all things but THEE?

Obviously THEE is being used here as the Quaker pronoun: "Thee makes," not "You make" or "Thou makest." Aiken may well have learned that usage from the Potter family. As for his question "Who?" it sends us back once more to Emerson. Just as Aiken's "consciousness" at times comes close to being the Emersonian Over-Soul, so THEE is the spirit of Nature as defined in Emerson's essay. "Strictly speaking," the essay says, ". . . all that is separate from us, all which Philosophy distinguishes as the NOT ME, that is, both nature and art, all other men and my own body, must be ranked under this name, NATURE." Aiken's name is THEE, but it has a different connotation. Whereas Emerson's Nature is admired for revealing in each of its parts the universal laws that wise men obey, Aiken's THEE is a pitiless force that nourishes and destroys with the divine indifference of the goddess Kali. Also and paradoxically, it is a force evolving with the human spirit—

> as if perhaps in our slow growing
> and the beginnings of our knowing

as if perhaps
o could this be
that we
be
THEE?
THEE still learning
or first learning
through us
to be
THY THEE?
Self-praise were then our praise of THEE
unless we say divinity
cries in us both as we draw breath
cry death cry death
and all our hate
we must abate
and THEE must with us meet and mate
give birth give suck be sick and die
and close the All-God-Giving-Eye
for the last time to sky.

When I first read *THEE,* it reminded me strongly of an untitled poem by Emerson, one that Aiken, so he told me, had never read—and no wonder he had missed it, since it does not appear in the *Complete Works,* even buried with other fragments in an appendix. One finds it in Volume II of the *Journals,* a volume including the period of spiritual crisis that followed the death of Emerson's beloved first wife, Ellen. She died February 8, 1831, and the poem was written July 6—at night? it must have been at night—immediately after a tribute to Ellen and thoughts of rejoining her in death. The poem, however, seems to announce the end of the crisis, since it is the entranced statement of a new faith. Here are two of the stanzas:

If thou can hear
Strong meat of simple truth,
If thou durst my words compare
With what thou thinkest in the soul's free youth,
Then take this fact unto thy soul,—
God dwells in thee.
It is no metaphor nor parable,
It is unknown to thousands, and to thee;
Yet there is God.

Who approves thee doing right?
God in thee.
Who condemns thee doing wrong?
God in thee.
Who punishes thine evil deed?
God in thee.
What is thine evil need?

Thy worse mind, with error blind
And more prone to evil
That is, the greater hiding of the God within. . . .

Emerson never went back to polish or even finish the poem, so that it remains a broken rhapsody—rather than an artifact like *THEE*—and yet it states bluntly the seminal idea that he would develop in his essays of the dozen years that followed. What made me think of the poem when reading *THEE* is something in the style, in the irregular lines—not all of them rhymed—and in the message, too, with its identification of outer and inner worlds and its assertion that men are potentially divine. Of course where Emerson celebrates the power of the indwelling spirit, Aiken gives a twist to Transcendental doctrine by stressing, first, the indifferent power of THEE, and then the dependence of THEE on the individual consciousness—with which it must "meet and mate," from which it learns to become more truly itself, and with which, perhaps, it must die. The speculation seems more imaginative than philosophical, and yet one feels that—with the whole religion of consciousness—it finds a place in the Transcendental line.

In Aiken's beginnings, he had been poles apart from Emerson. He had been atheistic and pessimistic, not optimistic and Unitarian. He had never been impressed by the German Romantic philosophers or by the Neoplatonists, let alone by Sufism and Brahmanism; instead his intellectual models had been Poe first of all, then Santayana, Freud, and Henry James. He would have been out of place in Emerson's Concord, since he continued all his life to be fond of women, mischief, bawdy limericks, and martinis. Nevertheless, at the end of his long career, he had worked round to a position reminiscent of that which Emerson had reached in 1831, before he had published anything. That seems to me an intellectual event of some interest, especially since it was announced in a memorable poem. But *THEE* aroused little attention when it appeared in 1967, and later it seems to have been almost forgotten.

In August 1972 I wrote Aiken to say that we had celebrated his eighty-third birthday with a little party and that I had read *THEE* to the guests. He answered wryly. My letter had arrived in the same mail as another announcing that the unsold copies of *THEE*—most of the copies, that is—had been remaindered.

4

For the neglect of his work by the public, one can give several explanations, though none of them seems adequate. In the early days when he was writing a book-length poem every year, Aiken's poetry was too modern and experimental for him to share in what was then the enormous popularity of

Amy Lowell and Vachel Lindsay. Later, in the 1920s, it seemed not experimental enough, or at least not eccentric enough. In the 1930s it was condemned as having no social or revolutionary meaning; in the 1940s it wasn't
rich enough in images (most of his work is musical rather than visual, and
music was becoming the lost side of poetry); in the 1950s it was condemned
again as not being "close enough in texture" to suit the intensive reading
methods of the new critics (but what should one say of the *Preludes*?); and
in the 1960s it was disregarded as being written mostly in iambic pentameters, a measure that had fallen out of fashion. Aiken followed his own fashion, and his work developed by an inner logic which was not that of the
poetry-reading public.

But what about the admirable prose of his novels and stories and of his
great autobiography? Two or three of the stories, including "Silent Snow,
Secret Snow," have appeared in dozens of anthologies, but in general the
prose, too, has failed to capture the public imagination.

I suspect that the long neglect of Aiken's work is due in large part to
policies more or less deliberately adopted by the author. In his heart he
didn't want to become a celebrity. Not only did he never appear on a public
platform, but also he refused to cultivate the literary powers, if such persons
exist; instead he went out of his way to offend them. Always for the best
of reasons, he bickered with editors, jeered at anthologists, rejected his own
disciples one after another, and made cruelly true remarks about fellow poets,
who would soon take their revenge by reviewing his books. He must have
expected those reviews, familiar as he was with literary folkways. They made
him angry, they wounded his pride—but did they also give him a somehow
comfortable assurance that he would continue to live "*off-stage,* behind the
scenes, out of view"? Was it all part of the same pattern as his resigning from
Harvard in preference to writing and publicly reading the class poem?

I last saw him in January 1972. By then he had made the great circle and
was living in Savannah, only a few doors from the now gutted house where
he had spent his childhood. Old Bonaventure Cemetery, where his parents
lay buried, also was quite near. Conrad himself was suffering from the ills
of human flesh, including some rare ones whose names I heard that day for
the first time, but he still made puns while his beloved wife mixed martinis.
We talked about the literary world, not so excitedly as at our first meeting
half a century before and with more bitterness on Conrad's part. Still, he
had done his work and knew it was good. He had proclaimed his religion
of consciousness and had lived by its tenets. He had never compromised—
as he was to say on his deathbed—and he could feel certain that, for all his
hatred of intruders, the great world would some day come round to him.

1978

J. P. Marquand

Anthropologist of the Boston Story

Imagine that a highly trained anthropologist had led an expedition into New England to study its native folkways. Imagine that he had become friendly with the headmen and headwomen of the aborigines and had been allowed to participate in all their peculiar rites, including the Friday Afternoon Sewing Circle. Imagine too that he had received expert advice from a former Brahmin who had become partly westernized by living in New York. As a result of his studies, he would have collected a mass of material, classified under the various heads of "Getting a Living," "Making a Home," "Training the Young," "Using Leisure," "Engaging in Religious Practices and Community Activities." Then imagine that after consulting with his colleagues he had decided not to publish a scientific report. "Robert Lynd has done that already," he might say. "There isn't any use in writing another 'Middletown.' Instead let's get hold of a skilled literary craftsman, somebody who knows how to write for the popular magazines, and have him turn our material into a novel that will be easy to read, but without sacrificing any of its value as scientific observation."

H. M. Pulham, Esquire is the novel that might have resulted from such a project, even though all the collaboration took place inside one man's head. John P. Marquand was the anthropologist; he was also the partly westernized Brahmin and the literary craftsman who fashioned the smoothly running novel. That suggests a way of solving the Marquand puzzle which several critics have lately mentioned. The question they are asking is how the same man succeeds in writing detective stories for the slick-paper magazines and novels for the Pulitzer Prize and the Book-of-the-Month Club. The answer may be that Mr. Marquand is a triply divided personality.

First, as a novelist proper, he is a thoroughly competent fiction technician. His style is easy, straightforward, economical—the sort of style that can be developed only by writing a great deal. His dialogue is always in character and keeps the story moving. His plots are efficient mechanisms, with all their bolts tightened, all their rough edges filed away; and this is true no matter whether he is telling the slick-paper story of a fabulous Japanese detective or making a serious study of a Boston man who never got over it.

The Bostonian of his latest novel (*H. M. Pulham, Esquire*) might have been the son of the late George Apley, the one who came home two weeks before the old man died. His name is Henry Moulton Pulham, and he was educated at home in Brookline, and at St. Swithin's, at Harvard, and at Lee Higginson's. Then, torn from his comfortable orbit by the war, he goes to New York and falls in love with a young woman in the advertising game. But since he can't marry her without being false to all his traditions, Harry comes back to Boston and marries one of the girls he had always known. It happens that the girl had previously fallen in love with a New York advertising man and that Harry is only her second choice, as she is Harry's; that is already neat enough. Twenty years later, just before Harry's class reunion, the two love affairs have an even neater sequel. Harry meets the New York girl again and thinks of running away with her, but discovers that they "can't go back." On the same day, at the same hour—even in the same words—Kay Pulham talks about running away with the New York man, but decides that they "can't go back." That sort of plot is like a Hotchkiss-type driving shaft with noiseless hypoid gears. It carries you through the book efficiently, but it is strictly an engineering product, bearing no relation to any event in nature.

In his second aspect, as a partly westernized Brahmin, Mr. Marquand knows both the Bostonians and the New Yorkers, and is especially good at describing the contacts between them. The trouble is that his loyalties are divided, with the result that one finds several contradictions in the character of his hero. Harry Pulham is sometimes incredibly stupid and sometimes intelligent, even subtle. He is sometimes the symbol of what the author has learned to dislike in Boston, sometimes the symbol of what he has always admired, and sometimes not a symbol at all, but a human being. The reader is confused about him because the author himself is confused.

It is in his third aspect, as a social scientist, that Mr. Marquand is at his best. The Back Bay he describes for us is as true to life and almost as complete as Mr. Lynd's Middletown, besides being more entertaining. Mr. Marquand says in a foreword that "living men and women are too limited, too far from being typical, too greatly lacking in any universal appeal, to serve in a properly planned piece of fiction." Acting on this principle, he gives us characters who are not so much people as social types, with all the inessentials stripped away from them. Bob Ridge, for example, is the disembodied essence of an insurance agent; and Bo-jo Brown is not only a college athlete but almost a Platonic Idea. As for the incidents that the author describes, they belong in any New England anthology: there is a class luncheon to end class luncheons, a really classical family quarrel, a Boston courtship while taking the dogs out walking, and a dinner party that sounds and tastes and yawns like Boston after dark. Everything is perfectly done, perfectly typed and, I suspect, more accurate than any anthropologist's description of life in the South Sea Islands.

Beyond that, Mr. Marquand has the knack of writing flat, unemphatic sentences which you read without thinking about them but which somehow stick in your mind. The headmaster of St. Swithin's says, "All that changes is the boys, and they don't change much either—not even when they're grown up." It is almost the last word about New England preparatory schools. As for Harry's college, "I always say that Harvard is the most democratic institution in the country, but secretly I do not believe it." The New York girl visits Harry's family in Boston, and "I don't know why I was continually afraid that she might say the wrong thing, because she never did." When the New York man makes fun of his classmates, Harry says to himself, "I can be amused by people when they talk that way. I am even broad-minded enough to see their point of view." Shortly afterwards the New York man and Kay Pulham go to a football game together, both very carefully dressed; Harry thinks that they "looked as though they belonged on the Yale side more than our own"; that is perfect Harvard. So too is Harry's account of his own life as written for the class history.

But at times the satire is human instead of merely local. Thus, when Harry has to bring his son and his daughter home from Maine in an uncomfortably crowded automobile, "I kept telling myself that I was fond of children." And before that, when the children were watching Harry and Kay on the tennis court, one of them had said, "They still play all right." Mr. Marquand still writes novels, and purely as fiction they are all right, which is to say all wrong. As social history, they are marvelous.

1941

Thornton Wilder

Time Abolished

🌸 Let us go back once again to the middle 1920s, which were famous years for American writing. A group of powerful novelists who had started as idol smashers were at last being accepted by the public. They would become idols themselves, but first they were producing their mature and most characteristic work as if in a burst of creative energy. *An American Tragedy, Arrowsmith, Dark Laughter, Barren Ground,* and *The Professor's House* all appeared in 1925. So did *Manhattan Transfer* and *The Great Gatsby,* but these were works by younger men who pictured what seemed to be a different world. Soon the picture would be enlarged by other members of the World War I generation. Hemingway's first book of stories was published in 1925, as I have noted, and his first novel in 1926. That same year Faulkner came forward with *Soldier's Pay,* and Hart Crane with *White Buildings,* a first collection of poems that carried a first introduction, by Allen Tate. It was the year when Cummings published *Is 5,* not a first book of verse, but his wittiest, and when Edmund Wilson wrote a series of critical dialogues, *Discordant Encounters*. In 1926 a new galaxy of writers was taking shape, with its novelists, poets, playwrights, and critics.

That was also the year when Thornton Wilder published *The Cabala*. I was lucky enough to be sent an advance copy—a young book for a young reviewer—and it became a personal discovery for me as for many others. From the opening sentence—"The train that first carried me into Rome was late, overcrowded, and cold"—it announced a new writer who was not a novice, who knew how to set a scene and how to make simple words stand cleanly on a page. "It was Virgil's country," he said at the end of the first paragraph, "and there was a wind that seemed to rise from the fields and descend upon us in a long Virgilian sigh." That had the authority of rightness; nobody could improve it by changing words or the order of words, and it also hinted that the story, although set in the present, would have something to do with the past. A circle was closed when the shade of Virgil appeared in the last chapter and spoke to the young traveler on his way back to America. The book had form, and hardly anyone doubted from the first that Wilder would be an important member of the new galaxy.

But did he really belong to it in any sense except that of being the same age as the others and hence of having lived, in some respects, the same sort of life? . . . He was born in 1897, a year after Dos Passos and Fitzgerald, two years before Hemingway and Hart Crane, and like those others he was born in the Middle West. He was the second of five children, two boys and three girls. His father, Amos P. Wilder, was a Down East Yankee and a devout Congregationalist who had taken a doctorate in economics at Yale and then had bought a newspaper in Madison, Wisconsin. As a publisher Dr. Wilder also played a part in Republican politics, and during the Taft administration he was sent to China, where he served as consul general at Hong Kong and Shanghai. He tried to instill a sense of duty into all his children and to pick a career for each of them: for example, Amos, the older son, was designed to be a theologian, and he carried out the father's plan; later he became a professor at Harvard Divinity School.

About Thornton's future there was more doubt. He read wildly, wrote plays for his sisters to act in cheesecloth robes, and used the margins of his schoolbooks for taking literary notes. "Poor Thornton, poor Thornton," his father used to say, "he'll be a burden all his life." It was decided to make him a teacher, on the theory that he would fail in any other profession. Among the schools he attended were Thacher, in Ojai, California; a missionary school at Chefoo, on the China coast; and the Berkeley, California, high school, from which he was graduated after the family returned to the States. He was sent East to Oberlin College for two years because his father thought that Yale was too worldly for an underclassman. In 1918 he enlisted in the Coast Artillery, rising, he said, "by sheer military ability to the rank of corporal." He then went back to Yale, where he wrote for the *Lit* and read his one-act plays to classmates who crowded his room. In 1920–1921 he was studying archaeology at the American Academy in Rome. Then his father summoned him home with a cablegram: "HAVE JOB FOR YOU TEACHING NEXT YEAR LAWRENCEVILLE LEARN FRENCH." Wilder knew French already, having always been quick with languages, but he set about learning to teach it.

He was launched in the profession that had been picked out for him, and he enjoyed it—at Lawrenceville, the preparatory school near Princeton where he taught for six years, as later at the University of Chicago and briefly at Harvard. He was a born teacher, and in that respect he shows more resemblance to writers of a later generation than to those of his own. Sometimes he remains a teacher even when he is writing plays and novels. At Lawrenceville, where he was a housemaster as well as an instructor, his only time for literary work was "after the lights of the House were out and the sheaf of absurd French exercises corrected and indignantly marked with red crayon." Then, writing in a bound ledger with a fountain pen, he might set down the first draft of a three-minute play for three actors—he wrote more than forty of these, and the best of them were later collected in a volume called *The Angel That Troubled the Waters* (1928)—or he might work on a more ambitious project growing out of his year in Europe and called in its first state *Notes of a Roman Student*.

He became a novelist as if by request. Friends from the Yale *Lit* wrote and asked him, "Why haven't you published a book when you were the most brilliant in your class and all your friends have published?" His answer was to copy out from his *Notes* about a hundred pages of manuscript, which afterward became the first three chapters of *The Cabala*. He finished the book during a summer at the MacDowell Colony in Peterborough, New Hampshire; almost always his writing has been done away from home, during three or four months spent in some new corner of the globe. Then, having read galley proofs of *The Cabala* not too carefully—the first edition was full of misspellings—he wrote the first sentence of a new novel: "On Friday noon, July the twentieth, 1714, the finest bridge in all Peru broke and precipitated five travelers into the gulf below."

From its publication in November 1927, *The Bridge of San Luis Rey* was a success with the public. There were six new printings in the one month of December. In May it received the Pulitzer Prize. During the year after its publication it had a sale of two hundred thousand copies (the publisher claimed three hundred thousand) without benefit of book clubs or cheap editions. It was popular in England too, and was soon transformed into most of the European languages. Its success—still a little hard to understand, for the best qualities of *The Bridge* are not those usually regarded as being popular—was one of the accidents or miracles that sometimes happen in the lives of young writers and that happened a little more frequently in the 1920s, though seldom on this grand scale. One day the author was a housemaster in a boys' boarding school with a passion for writing in his spare time, to please himself. The next morning he could read with a little incredulity that he had "already attained to the front rank of living novelists" and that his book was quite simply "a work of genius." The critic was William Lyon Phelps of Yale, who had always been given to superlatives, but in England Arnold Bennett agreed with him. "The writing," Bennett said, "has not been surpassed in the present epoch. It dazzled me by its accomplishment."

Wilder resigned his post at Lawrenceville and spent much of the next two years traveling in Europe. His third novel, *The Woman of Andros* (1930), was started in England—where parts of it, he says, were thought out during church services—and was continued on the Riviera, at New Haven, where he was planning a house in the suburbs—"the house that *The Bridge* built"—and at Oxford, Paris, and Munich. For a pastoral novel about Greece in the last century before the Christian era, it appeared at an unpropitious moment—a year after Black Thursday, in a month marked by bank failures, apple sellers at street corners, and stockbrokers jumping out of high-story windows. It was mildly praised, as a general rule, but *The New Republic* printed a famous review by Michael Gold that abused Wilder as the "Prophet of the Genteel Christ," as "this Emily Post of culture," and challenged him to write about the sufferings of his fellow Americans. Wilder accepted the challenge, in part, by writing *Heaven's My Destination* (1934), a novel in which the hero comes from the Middle West, is a traveling salesman in the Depression years, and makes laughable efforts to be a saint. This time most of the reviewers were indifferent or puzzled. It was an early sign of the coolness that has long existed between Wilder and the critics; one might speak of them as nodding distantly or respectfully when they pass him in the street, but almost never stopping to talk. His work has been crowned or clobbered with all sorts of official honors—with almost everything but the Nobel Prize—but for thirty years or more it has received less critical attention than the work of any other major American writer.

2

His life until 1930 had resembled, in most respects, the lives of other Americans born at the turn of the century who were making their way as novelists. It was distinguished from those other lives chiefly by the fact that two of his boyhood years had been spent in China—an experience that had more of a negative than a positive effect on his work—and by his professional interest in teaching. Everything else seems on the surface to be part of a familiar picture: the early delight in reading, the literary reputation gained in college, the wartime service in the army (although it was his older brother, the future theologian, who went abroad with the ambulance corps), the year in Europe as a spectator of greatness and decay, the critical recognition of a first book and the popular success of a second, followed by more wanderings abroad; all the novelists of his generation have been great travelers. On the Riviera in 1928–1929, he was one of the brilliant young men who often met at Gerald and Sara Murphy's: some of the others were Hemingway, MacLeish, Cole Porter, Dos Passos, and Fitzgerald, whose next novel, *Tender Is the Night,* would be dedicated to the Murphys. *Tender* was praised even less than Hemingway's books of the early 1930s, while Faulkner, then writing his best work, was condemned or passed over in silence. Thus, even the attacks on Wilder in the early Depression years were part of a pattern in many lives.

Yet under the surface there was an essential difference between his life and those of the others, a difference not so much in events as in the quality of experience, and it helps to explain a quality in his work. As immensely varied as that work has been, in fiction, drama, and criticism, with each new book presenting a different period and place—from the Ice Age to the Atomic Age and from Peru to the isles of Greece, passing through Omaha and Grover's Corners, New Hampshire—still it has been animated from the beginning by the same spirit, and by one that is almost unique in our time and country. Perhaps, by contrasting Wilder with the other novelists of his generation, we can find at least an approximate statement of what the spirit is.

Most of the others had a geographical starting point, a sort of rock to which their early books were attached like mussels. One thinks of Faulkner's county in Mississippi, of Hemingway's Michigan woods, of Wolfe's Asheville (or Altamont), and of Summit Avenue in St. Paul, the locus of many stories by Scott Fitzgerald. With this generation, a strong sense of place reentered American literature for almost the first time since Hawthorne and Thoreau. But the place that most of them cherished was the country of their childhood where they had felt at home. They were always thinking back on it, or saying good-by to it (as Glenway Wescott in *Good-bye, Wisconsin*), and often they complained, as Wolfe did in the title of his last novel, that *You Can't Go Home Again.*—In all his travels Wilder never had that sense of being exiled or expatriated, because there was no one place that he regarded as home. Perhaps that was the chief result of his boyhood years in China; they did not make him a citizen of the world, but they took him away forever from Madison, Wisconsin. He ceased to be a Midwesterner, and he did not become a Californian in spite of his schooling. Later he was a little more of a New Englander, but chiefly he is an American, whose home is wherever he opens a ledger, uncaps a fountain pen, and begins writing about people anywhere.

The others had a home place, but no longer had a family. That doesn't mean they had quarreled with their parents; the days of tears and final separations had ended for writers with the Great War. Now the young men simply went their way, but it was so different from the parents' way, there was such a gulf between generations (as again there would be in the late 1960s), that sons couldn't talk sincerely with their fathers and be understood. They had rejected the standards by which the fathers lived.—There was no such rejection in Wilder's early career. He never belonged to a conspiracy of youth, leagued in a moral rebellion against middle age. He had worshiped in his father's church and followed the profession his father picked out for him. In a way he represented continuity and tradition, so far as they existed in American society.

The others lived in a new world, but not one they had fashioned for themselves. They were disillusioned by the postwar reaction, cynical about politics, hostile to the institutions of society, and pessimistic about the future, while having a good time in the present and feeling a little guilty about it, or hung over. Some of them were becoming connoisseurs of decay. Fitzgerald called them "all the sad young men."—Wilder describes himself as "fundamentally a happy person." He likes to find the goodness or greatness in people and books. He is optimistic by instinct, in the fashion of an older America.

The others were new or at least tried to be new; they made experimental forays in all directions. Each of them wanted to write what might have been the first novel since the beginning of time, from a fresh vision of life, in a new language. Some of the minor writers, now forgotten, would have liked to abolish all literature before Joyce or Baudelaire or whoever might be their idol of the month. I have heard a toast drunk to Caliph Omar for burning the library at Alexandria.—Wilder is devoted to books, the older the better, and he says that his writing life has been "a series of infatuations for admired writers." He likes to acknowledge that most of his plots are borrowed and to specify their sources, as in a note that precedes *The Woman of Andros*: "The first part of this novel is based upon the *Andria*, a comedy of Terence, who in turn based his work upon two Greek plays, now lost to us, by Menander." But Wilder transforms the borrowed material, with a richness of invention that would be rare in any age, and becomes original through trying not to be.

Each of the others had an ideal of art that was allied to symbolism, or to naturalism, or to impressionism, or was a mixture of all three. In any case the ideal was an outgrowth of the romantic movement, and some of the writers tried to make their lives romantic too, most often Byronic or Baudelairean.—Wilder holds to the classical ideal of measure and decorum. Most of his infatuations have been for classical authors, including Sophocles, Catullus, Virgil, Mme. de Sévigné, and La Bruyère, as well as the severely classical Noh drama of Japan, although he has also taken lessons from Proust and Joyce. Among his models he makes little distinction of time or place, for he remembers what he was told by an admired professor at Oberlin: "Every great work was written this morning." Perhaps his tastes are more Roman than Greek, and more English Augustan than Roman. Yale in his day was a center of eighteenth-century studies, and there has always been something of that century in his habit of mind; possibly he is the one contemporary author who would subscribe to most of the axioms that Pope advanced in his *Essay on Criticism*:

> Like Kings we lose the conquests gain'd before
> By vain ambition still to make them more;
> Each might his sev'ral province well command.
> Would all but stoop to what they understand.

> Those RULES of old discover'd, not devis'd,
> Are Nature still, but Nature methodiz'd.
>
> Regard not then if Wit be old or new,
> But blame the false, and value still the true.
>
> Men must be taught as if you taught them not,
> And things unknown propos'd as things forgot.

Pope's ideal, and Wilder's, is to restate in new, but not shockingly new, language "What oft was said, but ne'er so well express'd." I doubt whether any other writer of his generation would exclaim, as Wilder did to a reporter from *Time,* that "Literature is the orchestration of platitudes."

3

But there is a more fundamental difference between his work and that of his contemporaries. The others write novels about a social group—sometimes a small group, as in *Tender Is the Night,* sometimes a very large one, as in *U.S.A.*—or they write about an individual in revolt against the group, as in *A Farewell to Arms.* The central relation with which they deal is between the many and the one. Very often—to borrow a pair of terms from David Riesman—their theme is the defeat of an inner-directed hero by an other-directed society. They feel that the society and its standards must be carefully portrayed, and these writers are all, to some extent, novelists of manners.—Wilder is a novelist of morals.

Manners and morals are terms that overlap, sometimes confusingly, but here I am using the two words in senses that are easier to distinguish. Manners would be the standards of conduct that prevail in a group, large or small, and hence they would change from group to group and year to year. Morals would be defined as the standards that determine the relations of individuals with other individuals, one with one—a child with each of its parents, a husband with his wife, a rich man with a poor man (not *the* rich with *the* poor)—and also the relations of any man with himself, his destiny, and his God. They are answers found by individuals to the old problems of faith, hope, charity or love, art, duty, submission to one's fate . . . and hence they are relatively universal; they can be illustrated from the lives of any individuals, in any place, at any time since the beginning of time.

The characters in Wilder's novels and plays are looking for such answers; his work is not often concerned with the behavior of groups. An outstanding exception might be *Our Town* (1938), in which the Stage Manager speaks with the voice of the community. But the community hasn't much to say about itself and will not admit to having local color; it might be any town, a fact that explains the success of the play in towns all over the country, and other countries. The events portrayed are coming of age, falling in love, getting married, and dying; in other words they are not truly events—except for the characters, who are not truly characters—but rather they serve as examples of a universal pattern in human lives; and they are not greatly affected, in the play, by the special manners of this one community. *The Cabala* also starts by dealing with a group, but very soon the young American narrator shifts his attention to its separate members, explaining that he is "the biographer of the individuals and not the historian of the group." The statement applies to the author himself, and in a simpler form: Wilder is not a historian. In Rome he had studied archaeology and had learned to look backward and forward through a long vista of years; that sort of vision is a special quality of all his work. But what he sees at the end of a vista is what the archaeologist often sees, that is, fragments of a finished pattern of life in many ways similar to our own. It is not what the historian tries to see: a living community in a process of continual and irreversible change.

The other novelists of his generation are all in some way historians. Their basic perception was of the changes in their own time, from peace to war, from stability to instability, from a fixed code of behavior to the feeling that "It's all right if you can get away with it." For them the Great War was a true event, in the sense that afterward nothing was the same. All of them were "haunted fatally by the sense of time," as Wolfe says of his autobiographical hero. His second novel was *Of Time and the River*. Hemingway's first book was *In Our Time* and he let it be understood, ". . . as in no other time." Faulkner saw his time in the South as one of violent decay. When Dos Passos tried to put thirty years of American life into one big novel, he invented a device called the Newsreel, intended to convey the local color of each particular year. Fitzgerald put the same sort of material into the body of his stories; he wrote as if with an eye on the calendar. *The Great Gatsby* belongs definitely to the year 1923, when the Fitzgeralds were living in Great Neck, Long Island, and *Tender Is the Night* could have ended only in 1930; no other year on the Riviera had quite the same atmosphere of things going to pieces. Both books are historical novels about his own time, so accurately observed, so honestly felt, that the books are permanent.—Wilder would never attempt to draw such a picture of his time. He is the great unsocial and antihistorical novelist, the master of the anachronism.

Like Dos Passos he gives us a newsreel, or rather two of them, to introduce the first two acts of *The Skin of Our Teeth* (1942). The contrast here is complete. Where Dos Passos recalls such episodes as the capture of the bobbed-hair bandit, the Florida real-estate boom, and the suppression of a revolt in Canton (to the refrain of "I'm Dancing with Tears in My Eyes"), Wilder presents another order of phenomena. Before the first act, when the lights go out, the name of the theater flashes on the screen and we hear the Announcer's voice:

The management takes pleasure in bringing to you—the news of the world! (*Slide 2. The sun appearing above the horizon.*) Freeport, Long Island. The sun rose this morning at 6:32 a.m. This gratifying event was first reported by (*Slide 3*) Mrs. Dorothy Stetson of Freeport, Long Island, who promptly telephoned the Mayor. The Society for Affirming (*Slide 4*) the End of the World at once went into a special session and postponed the arrival of that event for *twenty-four hours* (*Slide 5*). All honor to Mrs. Stetson for her public spirit.

New York City. (*Slide 6, of the front doors of the theater.*) The Plymouth Theater. During the daily cleaning of this theater a number of lost objects were collected, as usual (*Slide 7*), by Mesdames Simpson, Pateslewski, and Moriarity. Among these objects found today was (*Slide 8*) a wedding ring, inscribed: To Eva from Adam. Genesis 2:18. The ring will be restored to the owner or owners, if their credentials are satisfactory.

Wilder's news of the world is first what happens every day, and then what happened at the beginning. In all his work—except for that hint of the Creation—I can think of only one event that marks a change in human affairs: it is the birth of Christ, as announced on the first and the last page of *The Woman of Andros*. Perhaps another event is foreshadowed in a much later novel, *The Eighth Day* (1967): it is the birth of new messiahs, something that might resemble a Second Coming. That other Christian event, the Fall, is nowhere mentioned and seems to play no part in Wilder's theology. Everything else in his plays and novels—even the collapse of a famous bridge—is merely an example or illustration of man's universal destiny. Nothing is unique, the author seems to be saying: the Ice Age will return, as will the Deluge, as will Armageddon. After each disaster man will start over again—helped by his books, if he has saved them—and will struggle upward until halted by a new disaster. "Rome existed before Rome," the shade of Virgil says at the end of *The Cabala*, "and when Rome will be a waste there will be Romes after her." "There are no Golden Ages and no Dark Ages," we read in *The Eighth Day*. "There is the oceanlike monotony of the generations of men under the alternations of fair and foul weather." The same book says, "It is only in appearance that time is a river. It is rather a vast landscape and it is the eye of the beholder that moves."

4

At this point I think we might glimpse a design that unites what Wilder has written from beginning to end. He has published not quite a dozen books, each strikingly different from all the others in place, in time, in social setting, and even more in method, yet all the books illustrate the same feeling of universally shared experience and eternal return. *Everything that happened might happen anywhere and will happen again.* That principle explains why he is able to adopt different perspectives in different books, as though he were looking sometimes through one end of a telescope, sometimes through the other. In *The Ides of March* (1948) a distant object is magnified and Rome in 45 B.C. is described as if it were New York two thousand years later. In *Our Town* he reverses the telescope and shows us Grover's Corners as if it had been preserved for two thousand years under a lava flow and then unearthed like Herculaneum. He has many other fashions of distorting time. *The Long Christmas Dinner* (1931) is a one-act play in which the dinner lasts for ninety years, with members of the family appearing from a bright door and going out through a dark door, to indicate birth and death. *The Skin of Our Teeth* epitomizes the story of mankind in three acts and four characters: Adam, Eve, Lilith, and Cain. They are living in Excelsior, New Jersey, when the glacial cap comes grinding down on them. In Atlantic City, just before the Deluge, they launch an ark full of animals two by two from the Million Dollar Pier.

Because Wilder denies the importance of time, his successive books have proved to be either timely or untimely in a spectacular fashion—and in both cases by accident. *The Bridge* exactly fitted the mood of the moment, and nobody knows exactly why. *The Woman of Andros* was published thirty years too late or too soon. *The Skin of Our Teeth* had a more complicated history. Produced on Broadway in 1942, it was a success largely because of Tallulah Bankhead's so-jolly part of Lilith, or Lily Sabina. Hardly anyone said that the play expressed the mood of the moment, or of any other moment. But when it was staged in Central Europe after World War II, it was not only a success but a historic one, for any cast of actors that played in it. The Germans and the Austrians seem to have felt that it was a topical drama written especially for them, to soften their defeat and give them strength to live.

The Skin of Our Teeth is derived in part from *Finnegans Wake,* as *The Woman of Andros* is based in part on Terence's *Andria,* and as the plot of *The Bridge* was suggested by one of Mérimée's shorter plays. We read in a note on *The Matchmaker* (1954), "This play is based upon a comedy by Johann Nestroy, *Einen Jux Will Er Sich Machen* (Vienna, 1842), which was in turn based upon an English original, *A Day Well Spent,* by John Oxenford." There are many other acknowledged derivations in Wilder's work, from authors of many times and countries, and together they reveal another aspect of his disregard for history. He feels that a true author is independent of time and country, and he also feels, apparently, that there is no history of literature, but only a pattern consisting of books that continue to live because they contain permanent truths. Any new author is at liberty to restate those truths and to borrow plots or methods from older authors, so long as he transforms the borrowed material into something of his own. Not only was every great book written this morning, but it can be read tonight as on the first day. That principle, in two of Wilder's plays, becomes a metaphor that is a masterpiece of foreshortening. In a one-acter called *Pullman Car Hiawatha* and again in the third act of *The Skin of Our Teeth,* the great philosophers are presented as hours of the night. One of the characters explains: "Just like the hours and stars go by over our heads at night, in the same way the ideas and thoughts of the great men are in the air around us all the time and they're working on us, even when we don't know it." Spinoza is nine o'clock, Plato is ten, Aristotle is eleven, and Moses is midnight. Three thousand years of thought are reduced to four hours, which pass in less than two minutes on the stage.

This foreshortening of time becomes an opportunity for the novelist as well as for the playwright. When history is regarded as a recurrent pattern rather than as a process, it becomes possible to move a character from almost any point in time or space to almost any other. In *The Bridge* Mme. de Sévigné reappears in Peru as the Marquesa de Montemayor. Keats is presented in *The Cabala,* with his genius, his illness, his family problems; and he dies again in 1920 among a group of strange characters who might be resurrected from the *Memoirs* of the Duc de Saint-Simon, or who also might be classical gods and goddesses in modern dress. Persons can be moved backward in time as well as forward. Edward Sheldon, the crippled and blinded dramatist who lived for thirty years in retirement, dispensing wisdom to his friends, appears in *The Ides of March* as Lucius Manilius Turrinus, and one suspects that Cicero, in the same novel, is a preincarnation of Alexander Woollcott. As for the hero of the novel, he is not a historical character but a model or paradigm of the man of decision, as such a man might exist in any age. Wilder has called him Julius Caesar, much as Paul Valéry called his man of intellect Leonardo da Vinci, and much as Emerson gave the title of "Plato" to his essay on man as philosopher.

So Emerson's name comes up again. Emerson was of course the prophet who gave no importance to groups or institutions and refused to think of history as a process. When he discussed Montaigne or Shakespeare, it was not against the background of their times, but rather as "representative men" whom he might meet at any dinner of the Saturday Club. Wilder, in the brilliant series of lectures that he gave at Harvard in 1950–1951, started with Emerson, Thoreau, and other classical American writers, notably Melville and Whitman. What he tried to deduce from their works was the character of the representative American, but what he actually presented was, I suspect, partly a reflection of his own character. Here are some of his statements:

From the point of view of the European an American is nomad in relation to place, disattached in relation to time, lonely in relation to society, and insubmissive to circumstances, destiny, or God.

Americans could count and enjoyed counting. They lived under a sense of boundlessness. . . . To this day, in American thinking, a crowd of ten thousand is not a homogeneous mass of that number, but is one and one and one . . . up to ten thousand.

Since the American can find no confirmation of identity from the environment in which he lives, since he lives exposed to the awareness of vast distances and innumerable existences, since he derives from a belief in the future the courage that animates him, is he not bent on isolating and "fixing" a value on every existing thing in its relation to a totality, to the All, to the Everywhere, to the Always?

Those are perceptive statements, but I should question whether they apply to most Americans today, or to many American writers since the First World War. Their primary application is to all the big and little Emersonians, beginning with Thoreau (who is Wilder's favorite) and Whitman. In our own day they apply to Wilder himself more than to any other writer— more than to Cummings, even, whose later work revives the Emersonian tradition, but chiefly on its romantic, mystical, anarchistic side. Wilder is neoclassical, as I said. He goes back to Pope and Addison in his attitude toward the art of letters, but in other habits of thought he clearly goes back to the Transcendentalists. His work has more than a little of the moral distinction they tried to achieve, and like their work it deals with the relation of one to one, or of anyone to the All, the Everywhere, and the Always. Like theirs it looks toward the future with confidence, though not with the bland confidence that some of the Emersonians displayed. "Every human being who has existed can be felt by us as existing now," Wilder says in another of his Norton lectures, as if to explain his foreshortening of history. "All time is present for a single time. . . . Many problems which now seem insoluble will be solved when the world realizes that we are all bound together as the population of the only inhabited star."

1973

John Cheever

The Novelist's Life as a Drama

Late in the fall of 1930, John Cheever appeared in my office at *The New Republic,* where I was then a junior editor recently assigned to the book department. John was eighteen and looked younger.* He had a boyish smile, a low, Bay State voice, and a determined chin. We had just printed the first story he submitted to a magazine, a fictionalized account of why and how he got himself expelled from Thayer Academy, in South Braintree. Promptly John had come to New York to make his fortune as a writer.

The story—we called it "Expelled"—had come to us marked for my attention. I had felt that I was hearing for the first time the voice of a new generation. There were some objections by the senior editors, who pointed out that we didn't often print fiction. "It's awfully long," Bruce Bliven said; he had the final voice on manuscripts. I undertook to cut it down to *New Republic* size and it went to the printer. When John appeared we talked about the story. I didn't tell him that it had caused a mild dispute in the office. Instead I invited him to an afternoon party, the first that the Cowleys had dared to give in their bare apartment a few doors down the street.

I had forgotten that party of Prohibition days, but John remembered it fifty years later when he went to Chicago and spoke at a dinner of the Newberry Library Associates. The Library had acquired my papers and wanted to hold a celebration, with John as the principal speaker. "I was truly provincial," he said in evoking that long-ago afternoon. "Malcolm's first wife Peggy met me at the door and exclaimed, 'You must be John Cheever. Everyone else is here.' Things were never like this in Massachussets. I was offered two kinds of drinks. One was greenish. The other was brown. They were both, I believe, made in a bathtub. I was told that one was a Manhattan and the other Pernod. My only intent was to appear terribly sophisticated and I ordered a Manhattan. Malcolm very kindly introduced me to his guests. I went on drinking Manhattans lest anyone think I came from a small town like Quincy, Massachusetts. Presently, after four or five Manhattans I realized that I was going to vomit. I rushed to Mrs. Cowley, thanked her for the party, and reached the apartment-house hallway, where I vomited all over the wallpaper. Malcolm never mentioned the damages.

*John always said "seventeen" in telling the story; he was inexact about his age, since he was born May 27, 1912. He also said that his manuscript was addressed to me because he had been reading my first book of poems, *Blue Juniata,* and thought I might sympathize.

John must have walked or staggered back to what he called "the squalid slum room on Hudson Street" that he had rented for $3 a week. At the time his only dependable income was a weekly allowance of $10 from his older brother Fred, who had kept his job during the Depression and believed in John's talent. His only capital was a typewriter for which he couldn't often buy a new ribbon. That first winter in New York he had lived—so he reported—mostly on stale bread and buttermilk. As time went on he found little assignments that augmented his diet; one of them was summarizing the plots of new novels of MGM, which was looking for books that would make popular movies. John was paid $5 for typing out his summary with I don't know how many carbons. *The New Republic* couldn't help him much except by giving him unreviewed books for sale; it was "a journal of opinion," mostly political, and John wasn't given to expressing opinions; by instinct he was a storyteller. He kept writing stories and they began to be printed, always in little magazines that didn't pay for contributions.

I told Elizabeth Ames about him. Elizabeth was the executive director and hostess of Yaddo, a working retreat for writers and artists in Saratoga Springs, and I had served on her admissions committee. She invited John for one summer, liked him immensely, and later renewed the invitation several times. John would never forget his indebtedness to Yaddo, which had fed and lodged him during some of his neediest periods.

In New York I sometimes gave him advice, not about his writing, which I had admired from the beginning, but about finding a market for it. Once I told him it was time for a novel that would speak for his generation as Fitzgerald had spoken in *This Side of Paradise*. It turned out that John had already started a novel, and he showed me the first three or four chapters. They wouldn't do as the beginning of a book, I reported; each chapter was separate and came to a dead end. It might be that his present talent was for stories. . . . Then why wouldn't editors buy the stories? he asked me on another occasion. By that time I had been divorced from Peggy and had remarried, this time for good. It was a Friday evening and John had come for dinner in our new apartment. "Perhaps the stories have been too long," I said, "usually six or seven thousand words. Editors don't like to buy long stories from unknown writers." Then I had an inspiration. I suggested that he write four very short stories, each of not more than a thousand words, in the next four days. "Bring them to me at the office on Wednesday afternoon and," I said grandly, "we'll see whether I can't get you some money for them."

John carried out the assignment brilliantly. I doubt whether anyone else of his age—he was then twenty-two—could have invented four stories, each different from all the others, in only four days, but John already seemed to have an endless stock of characters and moods and situations. Although

The New Republic seldom printed fiction, one of the four could be passed off as a "color piece" about a burlesque theater. "Yes. Short and lively," was Bruce Bliven's comment when I showed it to him. The other three mini-stories, plainly fictions, I sent along to Katharine White, then fiction editor of *The New Yorker,* and she accepted two of them. That event, which I have told about elsewhere, was the beginning of John's career as a professional writer. *The New Yorker* was his principal market for more than thirty years and it would end by printing 119 of his stories.

In the course of time John became impatient with the accurate reporting that was demanded of *New Yorker* writers, especially in the days when Harold Ross was editor. It set limitations on fiction, and John always wanted to go farther and deeper into life. "This table seems real," he later said in an interview, "the fruit basket belonged to my grandmother, but a madwoman could come in the door any moment." In the stories he wrote after World War II, the madwoman appeared more often. Once she was a vampire; that was in "Torch Song." Once she assumed the shape of an enormous radio that picked up conversations from anywhere in a big apartment building. That story, his first with a touch of the impossible, was also his first to be widely anthologized.

Some future critic should trace John's development as a writer by reading his work from the beginning in its exact chronological order. The work changes from year to year and from story to story. "Fiction is experimentation," he was later to say; "when it ceases to be that it ceases to be fiction. One never puts down a sentence without the feeling that it has never been put down before in exactly the same way, and that perhaps the substance of the sentence has never been felt. Every sentence is an innovation." That is too seldom true of fiction, but it is true of John's best work, in which the sentences, apparently simple, are always alive and unexpected. Reading them makes me think of a boyhood experience, that of groping beneath roots at the edge of a stream and finding a trout in my fingers.

There were times of crisis when his purposes changed rapidly. One of these must have been during his work on *The Wapshot Chronicle,* his first novel and still his most engaging book. Perhaps it isn't a novel so much as a series of episodes connected with the imaginary town of St. Botolphs, on the south or less fashionable shore of Massachusetts Bay, and with the fortunes of the Wapshot family; John was right to call it a chronicle. The characters are presented with a free-ranging candor that must have embarrassed the Cheevers, to whom the Wapshots bore a family resemblance, but also with an affection not often revealed in his New York or Westchester stories. John felt that he couldn't publish the book until after his mother died. It appeared in 1957 while the Cheevers were spending a year in Italy. John was happy about the *Chronicle,* and this without seeing the reviews, most of which were enthusiastic. Writing it seems to have given him a new sense of scope and freedom.

Nevertheless he was having trouble with his second novel, *The Wapshot Scandal,* which was to be seven years in the writing. While work on it progressed slowly, or not at all, he published two more collections of stories (there would finally be six of these in all). One of the new collections bore a title that suggested another change in direction: *Some People, Places, & Things That Will Not Appear in My Next Novel.* In the title story he was performing what almost seems a rite of exorcism: he was presenting in brief, and then dismissing with contempt, a number of episodes that, in his former days, he might have developed at length. Not one of them, he now believed, would help him "to celebrate a world that lies spread out around us like a bewildering and stupendous dream."

He tried to present that dream in *The Wapshot Scandal,* but in writing the book he found little to celebrate. He had to record how the Wapshots, with their traditional standards, faced the new world of aimlessness, supermarkets, and fusion bombs. They died or went to pieces—all of them except Coverly Wapshot, more solid and unattractive than the others, who found himself working in a secret missile base and lost his security clearance. The book is almost as episodic as the *Chronicle,* but with the episodes more tightly woven together. Each of them starts with a scene that is accurately observed—it might correspond to Cheever's real table and his grandmother's fruit basket—but then everything becomes grotesque, as if his madwoman had come in the door. On one occasion she is followed by a screaming crowd of madwomen in nightgowns with curlers in their hair. The book has an unflagging power of invention and was praised by critics when it finally appeared; also it had a fairly impressive sale. John himself "never much liked the book," as he was to say when he was interviewed much later for *The Paris Review,* "and when it was done I was in a bad way. I'd wake up in the night and I would hear Hemingway's voice—I've never actually heard Hemingway's voice, but it was conspicuously his—saying, 'This is the small agony. The great agony comes later.'"

But first would come another agony that was not the greatest, but was not a small one either. After thirty years of intimate relations, *The New Yorker* rejected one of his longer and more treasured stories, "The Jewels of the Cabots." John sold the story to *Playboy* for twice what *The New Yorker* would have paid, but still his pride had been hurt. There were other rejections, one or two of them inexcusable, and John stopped publishing in *The New Yorker.* If one were plotting his life as a theater piece, one might say the curtain had fallen on a second act.

· · ·

A few years later John published a third novel, *Bullet Park* (1969), that was more tightly plotted than the second. It pleased him more than the *Scandal*. "The manuscript was received enthusiastically everywhere," he reported, "but when Benjamin DeMott dumped on it in the *Times,* everybody picked up their marbles and went home. I ruined my left leg in a skiing accident and ended up so broke that I took out working papers for my youngest son." John was exaggerating, as he liked to do with gullible reporters. The son, then twelve years old, never thought about working papers; in due time he went off to Andover and Stanford. But John, horrified at going into debt, wasn't making progress with his writing, and he confessed to himself that he had become an alcoholic. He had a heart attack, nearly fatal, in 1972. Having recovered, he accepted teaching assignments, first at the Iowa School of Writing and then at Boston University, where, so he said, "I behaved badly."

For the black years that might be called a third act in his life, I'm not sure about the sequence of events, and I have to depend on his later accounts. I was seeing less of John. In 1967 our only son, Robert, had been married to John's daughter Susan in a high-church ceremony at St. Mark's in the Bouwerie. The elder Cowleys played no part in the preparations for an expensive wedding. At the reception, under an outside tent in the churchyard, the Cheever connection drank their champagne on one side of the tent, while the smaller Cowley contingent sat grouped on the other. That marked a growing difference in styles of life between the two families. For ten years after *The Wapshot Chronicle* and before *Bullet Park,* John had earned a substantial income: there were Hollywood contracts and what seemed to me huge advances from publishers. The Cheevers had bought and remodeled a big stone house in Westchester County, to the disapproval of some *New Yorker* editors, who felt that authors should defend their economic freedom by living on a modest scale. The Cowleys did live modestly, farther out in the country, and spent rather less than they took in. I came to suspect that the Cheevers, who traveled widely, always in first class, now regarded us as tourist-class country cousins. Then Rob and Susan were divorced, after eight years of marriage. It was an amicable divorce, with no children to argue about (only two golden retrievers) and with no hard feelings. Still it was the end of casual family visitings.

I was always overjoyed to see John, but was a little tongue-tied even when we met at Yaddo, where we were both on the board of directors, or at various committee meetings of the American Academy; there was never much time for confidences. Later John would tell the public about his misadventures. After Boston University he went home to the big stone house, where he fell into utter depression. He used to wash down several Valium tablets with a quart of whiskey. He was trying to abolish himself—but why?

Clearly it was less a matter of his finances or his physical state than of his concern with the art of fiction; he felt that his life as a writer was at an end. He was also a sincerely religious man, though he wouldn't talk much about the subject, and he must have felt that he had fallen from grace forever. His family, deeply concerned, told him that alcohol would kill him, as it had already killed his loved and resented older brother. "So what?" he said, taking another drink. In 1975 he finally listened to the family and committed himself to Smithers, a rehabilitation center. He was to speak darkly, in later years, of going mad when deprived of liquor and of being wrapped in a straitjacket.* The treatment was prolonged, whatever it was, and it worked; after being released from Smithers, John never again took a drink. He experienced a new sense of redemption, elation, and release from bondage. Almost immediately he set to work on a novel, which he finished in less than a year.

The novel, of course, was *Falconer,* published in 1977; John was to call it "a very dark book that displayed radiance." It was the story of Ezekiel Farragut, a moderately distinguished professor who becomes a drug addict, who kills his brother with a poker, and who is sentenced to ten years in Falconer Prison. There he is redeemed, partly through a homosexual love affair, and loses his craving for Methadone. The book reads swiftly and displays John's gift for economical prose with not a misplaced word, beside his amazing and unflagging talent for invention. Some of the episodes have a touch of the miraculous. A cardinal descends from the skies in a helicopter and carries off Zeke's lover to freedom. A young priest appears in the cellblock and administers last rites to the hero. "Now who the hell was that?" Zeke shouts to the guard. "I didn't ask for a priest. He didn't do his thing for anybody else." Symbolically Zeke is about to die, be entombed, and rise again. In life his cellmate dies instead. Attendants come to put the corpse into a body bag. Farragut zips open the bag, removes the corpse, and takes its place; then he is carried out of the prison. Walking in the street a free man, his head high, his back straight, "Rejoice," he thought, "rejoice."

Those are the last words of Cheever's longest continuous fiction. Judged purely as a novel, *Falconer* has obvious faults. There are loose strings never tied up and events left unexplained. The reader is forced to wonder how Zeke Farragut will survive in his new life, considering that he has no money, no identity, and is still dressed in his prison clothes. Then one reflects that the faults don't matter much; that *Falconer* is not a novel bent on achieving verisimilitude, but rather a moving parable with biblical overtones of sin and redemption; it is Magdalen redeemed by divine grace and Lazarus raised from the dead. That is how it must have been read by thousands,

---

*The treatment at Smithers did not include a straitjacket, but John had been confined briefly in another institution.

and the book had an astoundingly wide sale, enough to pay off its author's debts for the first time in years.

And the fourth act in the drama?

The success of *Falconer* led to another change in John's character, as well as in his public image. He had always managed to keep from being a celebrity. When he was twelve years old his parents had given him their permission to earn his future living as a writer—if he could earn it—but only after he promised them that he had no idea of becoming famous or wealthy. In later years he had kept the promise, though with some latitude in the matter of income, since he liked to support the family on a generous scale. He had refused several offers that promised to make him rich, though he had always been shrewd in a Yankee fashion (and his agent was known for striking hard bargains). In the matter of fame, he had obdurately defended his privacy. Medals and honors he accepted when they came, if grudgingly, but he had done his best to avoid being interviewed—often by the simple device of getting drunk, or getting the interviewer drunk. But *Falconer* had made him a national figure as if by accident, and he found himself enjoying his new status.

For the first time in his life he gave interviews willingly—and brilliantly too, since he said without hesitation whatever was on his mind. Always the interviewers would mention his boyishness. I suppose the word was suggested by his lack of self-importance, his deprecatory smile, and his candor in speaking about intimate misadventures. In simple fact he was now an old man, wearied by the physical demands he had made on himself, so that he was older in body and spirit than his sixty-five years. He now had nothing to lose by telling the truth, so long as it made a good story. He was finding pleasure in addressing a new audience—as he explained more than once—but also he wanted to set things straight with himself and the world while there was still time.

His next book after *Falconer* would be a retrospective undertaking, *The Stories of John Cheever* (1978), collected at last in one big volume. He had chosen sixty-one stories for the book, after omitting all those printed before his army service in World War II (though some of that early work is worth preserving) as well as two or three stories written during his breakdown. Almost all the others he arranged in roughly chronological order. For the first time a wider public could note the changing spirit of his work over the years, not to mention its essential unity. John also had given the book a brief, illuminating Preface that has been widely quoted. "These stories," it says at one point, "seem at times to be stories of a long-lost world when the city of New York was still filled with a river light, when you heard the Benny Goodman quartets from a radio in the corner stationery store, and when almost everybody wore a hat. . . . The constants that I looked for in this sometimes dated paraphernalia are a love of light and a determination to trace some moral chain of being. Calvin played no part in my religious education, but his presence seemed to abide in the barns of my childhood and to have left me with some undue bitterness."

The moral element is always present, if concealed, in a Cheever story. At first the bad people, whose commonest sin is heartlessness, seem hard to distinguish from the good people, but they end by indicting themselves, and Cheever was an inexorable judge (especially when faced by women bent on expressing themselves at everybody's cost). He was not a tender judge of his own work, and there are only two sentences of the Preface that I think are in error as applied to himself. He says, "The parturition of a writer, I think, unlike that of a painter, does not display any interesting alliances to his masters. In the growth of a writer one finds nothing like the early Jackson Pollock copies of the Sistine Chapel paintings with their interesting cross-references to Thomas Hart Benton." That seems to me far from the truth. Among the important writers of this later time, Cheever reveals more alliances than others to three masters of the World War I generation.

Hemingway was his first master, as was evident in John's early and now forgotten stories. These copied many features of Hemingway's style, as notably the short sentences, the simple words, the paring away of adjectives, adverbs, conjunctions, and the effort to evoke feelings without directly expressing them, simply by presenting actions in sequence and objects seen accurately as if for the first time. I can testify that the novel John tried to write when he was twenty-one—and abandoned after three or four chapters—had as its obvious starting point a story by Hemingway, "Cross-Country Snow." It would have been the equivalent, in his case, of Jackson Pollock's attempts to copy the Sistine Chapel. Very soon Cheever developed a style of his own that became more effective than Hemingway's later style; he never parodied himself. Still, he retained what he had learned from that early master, including an enthusiasm for fishing and skiing. Hemingway as a father figure appeared in his dreams.

The resemblance to Fitzgerald was more often noted, especially during John's middle years. His characters, like Fitzgerald's, were mostly from the upper layers of American society (though Cheever didn't invest them with the glamour of great wealth). Like Fitzgerald he had the gift of double vision; he was both a participant in the revels and, at the same moment, a fresh and honest-eyed observer from a different social world. Both men were at heart romantics, even if they had different dreams. Cheever's was not the dream of early love and financial success; he was more obsessed with the middle-aged nightmare of moral or financial collapse. Sometimes, however, he wrote sentences that might grace a Fitzgerald story, as, for

252 / THE TWENTIETH CENTURY

example, "The light was like a blow, and the air smelled as if many wonderful girls had just wandered across the lawn." Both men were time-conscious and tried to recapture the feeling, the smell, the essential truth of a moment in history. One can often guess the year when a Cheever story was written by internal evidence, without looking for the date of publication. It is the same with Fitzgerald, of whom Cheever was to say admiringly, "One always knows reading Fitzgerald what time it is, precisely where you are, the kind of country. No writer has ever been so true in placing the scene. I feel that this isn't pseudohistory, but the sense of being alive. All great men are scrupulously true to their times." It was one of the things that Cheever tried to be. His stories also imply moral constants that make them relatively timeless—but then Fitzgerald, too, was a moralist, "a spoiled priest."

And Faulkner? Here it is not at all a question of early influence or the relation between explorer and settler. I'm not sure that Cheever even read Faulkner during the 1930s, although he was an enormous reader. It is rather a question of natural resemblances in writing and in character as well. The two didn't look alike, but they were both short, handsome men attractive to women and blessed from childhood with enormous confidence in their genius. (The influence of mere stature on writers' careers is a subject that calls for more study. Often the Napoleons of literature—and the Balzacs—are short men determined not to be looked at from above.) Both Cheever and Faulkner were high-school dropouts and self-educated. Like Faulkner from the beginning, Cheever was a storyteller by instinct and kept turning description into narration. Note for example the panoramic views of Bullet Park, at the beginning of the novel, and of St. Botolphs, in the first chapter of *The Wapshot Chronicle*. First we see the houses one by one, but each house recalls a family and each family suggests a story. That was how Faulkner proceeded too.

Like Faulkner again, Cheever depended at every moment on the force and richness of his imagination. Faulkner was preeminent in that gift, but Cheever had more of it than other writers of his own time, and he too created his "little postage stamp of native soil"; Westchester and St. Botolphs are in some respects his Yoknapatawpha. *Falconer,* the novel he liked best among his own works, was named for an imagined prison in Westchester County, but he usually pronounced the name in an English fashion: "Faulkner." Mightn't that be a form of tribute to the older novelist?

The two men had other points of resemblance, besides their common fondness for hard liquor. One trait of a different sort was their frequent use of symbols from the Bible, as if they were the last two Christians in a godless world. But I wanted to make the more general point about Cheever that he was carrying on a tradition. His age group or cohort has included many gifted novelists: Bellow, Welty, Updike, Malamud, to name only a few. I will never try to assign a rank to each of them like a schoolmaster noting down grades. Cheever may or may not be the best of them, but he is clearly the one who stands closest in spirit to the giants of the preceding era.

Most of the American authors admired in our time did their best work before they were forty-five. Many of them died before reaching that age. Most survived into their sixties, but their truly productive careers had been cut short by emotional exhaustion, alcoholism, or by mere repetition and drudgery. It was Scott Fitzgerald who said, "There are no second acts in American lives." We produced no Thomas Hardys or Thomas Manns (exception being made for Robert Frost) and no one who made a brilliant rebeginning after a crisis in middle life. More recently there have been other exceptions and Cheever is one of them. His career in literature not merely started over but had a last act as brilliant in a different way as the acts that preceded it.

After he published *The Stories of John Cheever,* honors came pouring down on him like an autumn shower. Among them was a doctorate from Harvard (1978), a Pulitzer prize for the stories, which also received the award for fiction of the Book Critics' Circle, both in 1979, the Edward MacDowell Medal in that same year, and finally, in 1982, the National Medal for Literature. He accepted the honors gladly, not with the indifference he had displayed toward the few that had been granted him in earlier years. Once he had acted like Faulkner, as if on the assumption that readers didn't exist; now he was delighted by their response. He gave public readings of his stories, most often of two favorites, "The Swimmer" and "The Death of Justine." His face and his Bay State voice became admiredly familiar on television. He was photographed on horseback, like Faulkner in his last years. Meanwhile he had started a new novel for which he had signed, so we heard, a magnificent contract. To interviewers he said merely that it would be "another bulky book." There wasn't much time to work on it in the midst of distractions. After he had spent so many years in the shadows, even his New England conscience would have absolved him for basking a little in a transcontinental light.

There is often an essential change in writers as they grow older, something beyond a mere ripening of earlier qualities. (I am thinking here mostly of men and not of women, who are likely to follow a different pattern.) The writer, if he has something of his own to say, begins under the sign of the mother, which is also the sign and banner of rebellion—against tradition, against the existing order, against authority as represented by the father. The change comes after a middle-aged crisis, or even before it in many cases. The writer becomes reconciled with his father, indeed with all the Fathers who suffer from having wayward sons. (Here again women are different; they are likely to sign a truce with their mothers.) Cheever said more than once that the Wapshot books were "a posthumous attempt to make peace with my father's ghosts."

Whether men or women, writers find themselves going back in spirit to the regions where they spent their childhoods. For more than forty years Cheever had been a Yorker, not a Yankee; he had been mistakenly called a typical writer for *The New Yorker*. Now he rebecame a New Englander. One can be more specific: he became a Bay Stater, a native son of the Massachusetts seaboard, which has a different voice and different traditions from those of the Connecticut Valley. If Bay Staters are of Puritan descent, they trace their ancestral histories back to the founder of the family. In John's case the founder was Ezekiel Cheever, a minister highly respected by Cotton Mather, who preached his funeral sermon. John quotes Mather as saying, "The welfare of the Commonwealth was always upon the conscience of Ezekiel Cheever . . . and he abominated periwigs." The commonwealth of letters was always on John's conscience and he abominated all sorts of pretension, almost as much as he abominated pollution and superhighways.

While writing *Falconer* he had still smoked furiously; "I need to have *some* vice," he explained. Now, after a struggle, he gave up smoking as well as drinking. In default of vices he practiced virtues, especially those native to the Bay State. That breed of Yankees are distinguished, and tormented as well, by having scruples; they keep asking themselves, "Was that the right thing for me to do?" John must have asked that question often in his prayers. Another Yankee precept is not to speak ill of people even if they are rivals. John, if he had grudges, now managed not to express them (except for a mild grudge against the fiction editor who had rejected "The Jewels of the Cabots"). He had become conservative in the Bay State fashion, that is, in manners though not always in politics, this last being a field that he continued to avoid. There was, however, one Yankee precept, "Be reticent about yourself!" that he now flagrantly violated. I suspect this was because he had come to regard himself as a fictional person, the leading character of a novel that he was composing not in written words, but in terms of remembered joys and tribulations.

The true Bay Stater discharges his obligations, and he sets high store by loyalty to his family, to a few old friends, and to chosen institutions. John became a devoted churchgoer, though he didn't often stay for the sermon. He worked for the institutions that had befriended him, as notably Yaddo and the American Academy, where he served for three years as chairman of the Award Committee for Literature. In that post he had to read some two hundred novels a year; it was another of his unrecompensed services to the commonwealth of letters. He paid off his moral debts to friends; one example was his making a trip to Chicago in order to speak at a dinner held in my honor. He was like a man who puts his affairs in order before setting out on a journey.

The journey started, as always, sooner than was expected. In July 1981 John had an operation for the removal of a cancerous kidney. The operation appeared to be successful, but a few weeks later John was barely able to walk. The cancer had metastasized to the bones of his legs; then it appeared as a burning spot on his rib cage. There was no hope left except in chemotherapy and radiotherapy at Memorial Hospital. Once again John spoke of himself dispassionately, as if he were a character in fiction. He told an interviewer for *The Saturday Review,* "Suddenly to find yourself with thousands and thousands seeking some cure for this deadly thing is an extraordinary thing. It's not depressing, really, or exhilarating. It's quite plainly a critical part of living, or the aspiration to live."

Those were arduous months for John; I think one might call them heroic. Doggedly he prepared a manuscript for his publisher, though it was not the bulky novel he had planned. *Oh, What a Paradise It Seemed* was no more than a novella, but, like all the best of his work, it was accurate, beautifully written, and full of surprises. It appeared in the early spring of 1982. A few weeks later he wrote me, "I fully intend to recover both from the cancer, the treatment and the bills."

I last saw him in Carnegie Hall less than two months before his death. The occasion was the ceremony at which, among the recipients of lesser awards, he was presented with the National Medal for Literature. His face was gaunt after radiotherapy and almost all his hair had fallen out. I said that I admired him for having made the trip from Ossining and he answered, "When they give you fifteen thousand dollars you owe them an appearance." He hobbled out to the rostrum leaning on a cane—or was it two canes? From my folding chair in the wings I couldn't hear his little speech, but I heard the great rumble of applause; John had nothing but friends.

A few minutes later we met and embraced in an empty corridor; I remember feeling that the treatment at Memorial had altered his body. It was more than fifty years since John had first appeared in my office at *The New Republic.* We were two men who had grown old in the service of literature, but our roles had been transposed: John was now older than I and was leading the way.

1983

NEW ENGLAND LIFE

Essays and Reflections

Connecticut Valley

Zebulon Trumbull at sixty-five is like a cider barrel set on two short legs. His girth is tremendous; so is his strength. He can lift the rear axle of a Buick unaided. He can lift a fifty-gallon barrel full of cider, but he won't take a drink of it afterwards, not even to slake his thirst. Years ago his only brother died of drinking cider.

Zebulon Trumbull has no children. The money he inherited year by year, as branch by branch the Trumbull family died out, will eventually go to his wife. If she is no longer alive, it will go to his second cousin in Bridgeport.

On the four-hundred-acre farm that his great-grandfather bought from the Indians, he tried for nearly fifty years to make a fortune. He grew tobacco, good tobacco, too, but fertilizer was expensive and all the help were lazy. He ran a dairy with blooded stock, but half his cows were condemned as tubercular. He raised chickens and sold them off; he raised turkeys and lost them to the foxes. He ran a sawmill for two years; then he became a huckster. He traded horses all over the state, till automobiles drove them off the roads; he still boasts that he never got the worst of a bargain. At present he repairs antique furniture and studies the genealogy of his family, which first settled near Providence in 1652. He pores all evening over his one book, a family history; it cost him $25. His hands are scrubbed, so as not to soil its rag-paper pages, but his nails are black and there is dirt in the deep creases of his fingers, dirt that has stayed there forty years, since the days when he hoed tobacco plants in the August sun.

He is not quite used to the electric lights in his new house, nor to the hum of the electric refrigerator in the kitchen. Last year, for a good price, he sold his four hundred acres and moved to town.

Mr. Denison, who bought the Trumbull place, is generous and hurried. His friends tell you that Jim Denison is a good guy, that he deserves his success: God knows he had to work for it. He works too hard; he drinks too hard when he isn't working. He is the best advertising copywriter in New York City. His hands move nervously; his face is gray, deep lined and flabby. Mr. Denison is a middle-aged man at thirty-five.

It was his wife who convinced him that they should buy a farm. She is a homely woman, low voiced and friendly, who dresses in tweeds and has no trouble keeping servants. She used to own a dog, but she felt so bad when he died that she never would have another. She buys antiques—rarely from Zebulon Trumbull, whose prices, she says, are outrageous. With the help of local labor, and some encouragement from her husband, she has remodeled the Trumbull house, painting it a light cream with Chinese-blue shutters and building a pergola where the outhouse used to stand. Last spring she had the carpenter pull down the barn that closed the long view into the valley.

It is a shame, say the Denisons, that the fields below the house are growing up in sweetfern and sumac. They would like to buy sheep to keep down the weeds—but who would care for the sheep during the winter? It's so hard to find help that you can trust, and there are so few natives here in the valley. But isn't it a comfort to have such nice summer neighbors—artists and writers and all that! Sometimes it seems that all the really intelligent people in New York are moving to the country.

The Denisons are known for their hospitality. Every Saturday night they give a party, to which they invite the writers, the painters, the editors, and the Norwegian musician from North Dakota who bought the Levi Adams place. Their invitations are rarely refused. Mr. Denison can mix an insidious cocktail, and there is a barrel of two-year-old Connecticut applejack in his cellar.

Parties at the Denisons are noisy and good humored. Mr. Denison drinks eight or ten slugs of applejack; he says they rest him after a hard week at the office. He talks about the novel he would write if he weren't held to his desk—if he had plenty of time like you writing chaps. The writers and painters don't laugh at him behind his back; they kid him to his face like the good fellows they are. The Norwegian musician plays jazz, very intelligent jazz to which nobody can dance. The artists and writers play ping pong, or go for a stroll with someone else's wife. There is a good deal of loose talk, a few dirty jokes are told, not in whispers, but there is no real evil. Everybody is tired of Greenwich Village affairs; everybody is over thirty. Sometimes the crowd plays Anagrams, or Murder, or even old-fashioned Hide and Seek, with the lights out and couples darting over the maple-shaded lawn in the moonlight. About one o'clock Mr. Denison, dead drunk, goes to sleep on the couch. There is the sound of motors starting, and the dirt road is swept by headlights.

I usually walk home from the Denisons' parties. After the last car has passed, the road is very quiet. The country loses its ravaged daytime look: the roofless barns seem whole and the fields well tended. The mullein stalks in the moonlight are like tobacco; the goldenrod might be a ripe field of wheat.

The Casey boys lead an easy life. In the summer they work at their trades, and there is always more work than they can do. In the winter they hunt, or chop wood, or sit by the kitchen stove and drink hard cider.

Joe Casey is fifty-four. He was married once, but his wife left him because she couldn't stand his drinking. Tom Casey, the baby of the family, is forty-nine and has never married. The two boys live with their mother, a woman of eighty who remembers her girlhood in Donegal. Their father's sword hangs over the mantelpiece, its scabbard worn away diagonally at the tip from dragging for two years through the Virginia mud.

The Casey boys often speak of their father. An immigrant boy, he enlisted in the Union army; he rose in two years to the rank of second lieutenant. He came to this Connecticut valley with no baggage except his sword. Here the struggle was longer, but at the end of twenty years he had his own house and his own land free from mortgage. In those days there was joy in owning land, with the valley full of rich tobacco farms, stock farms, dairy farms, and among them fields of dark-green potato plants and light-green oats. The Casey boys are proud of their father: maybe that's the reason they cling to his now untilled land when almost all the Yankee farmers around them have moved away.

Yankee names are disappearing from the valley. The Briggses, what are left of them, now live in Waterbury. Theodore Doane, too feeble to keep a herd of cattle, is staying with his one son, Homer, who runs a garage at the forks of the road. Old Zebulon is the last of the Trumbulls. The Penney tribe, once numerous in the countryside, has vanished; even the Penney houses have rotted into black, weed-grown soil. The Whipples, father and son, live by the sale of milk, eggs, chickens, green vegetables and building lots; their women work till long after sunset; they are saving money against the day when they will all settle in California. "It's so hard hereabouts in the wintertime," they say.

But life is easy for the Casey boys. In the spring, as soon as the cider barrels are empty and the frost is out of the ground, Joe Casey sets to work at his trade; his brother Tom goes fishing. Joe is a mason: he builds fireplaces, terraces and old-fashioned well curbs. Tom is a painter and paper hanger, but he never works till after the trout season is ended. All summer they are busy at good wages; then, in the middle of autumn, Joe Casey sets to work at the cider mill, taking his pay in barrels of cider. Tom Casey goes hunting.

In November, the Caseys put on their best clothes and, more or less sober, go to attend town meeting. There used to be as many as two hundred voters in the town hall; now there are never more than sixty; last fall only thirty men and women assembled from a town which covers nearly fifty square miles. They always talk of old times and high taxes and the price of land. They argue the question of whether to hire a teacher for next year, or whether to send the town's twelve children to the neighboring city by motor bus. They choose a man—always the same—to represent them in the state legislature. They elect a board of assessors to reduce their own taxes and to raise the assessment of the farms bought by what they call the summer people. Then, more or less sober, the Casey boys go home to spend the winter hunting and chopping wood and sitting by the fire. The snow seeps down; the roads are closed to automobiles; only the postman passes three times weekly in his sleigh. "The country looks like itself in the wintertime," Tom Casey says. "It's like when Pop was living," Joe answers as he goes to the cellar for another pitcher of cider.

Early in May, when the arbutus buds are opening in the woods and the roads are dry enough for motor traffic, the summer people come trooping back. There is the sound of opened shutters, of carpets beaten in the yard. The first smoke rises from a dozen chimneys, to mingle with the haze that sleeps over Tory Hill. The housewives lay plans for a rock garden here, for a terrace or a second fireplace; they must get Joe Casey if he's sober, and really the new maid is unbearable. . . . Then, pausing to look at the hilltop, where the oak buds are a smoky green, they say, "Isn't all this beautiful! Aren't you glad we live in this lovely valley!"

During July and August, the summer people travel incessantly along the valley roads. They drive to the Whipples' for milk and eggs, to the Denisons' for a highball, to Green Pond for a swim. They have social functions of their own—gin parties, ping-pong parties, barn parties, yes, and musicales—which they attend in force. Over the weekend their houses are crowded with guests from the city, who exclaim between two drinks, "Oh, how I envy you this lovely old farmhouse!"—"Yes, isn't the valley beautiful," the summer people agree. Yet there is something purely formal in their agreement, something beyond mere boredom with their guests and irritation at hearing the same statement repeated too often. The summer people are not of this country; their hands are not black with its soil; they do not depend on its seasons or live by its fruits.

In autumn, when the neglected orchards of the valley are heavy with apples, and grapes turn purple on the vines, and the fields are dotted with gentians almost the color of the autumn haze, the summer people prepare to go. They sprinkle mothballs in the closets, they lock the shutters, they store their bright lawn furniture in the empty barns. Their cars, waiting at the front gate, are piled with suitcases, unfinished manuscripts or paintings, vaseline glass, and the two Hitchcock chairs they bought at such a bargain. For a moment they wait before starting the motor. They look at the hills, where the oaks are changing color, at the fields overgrown with wine-colored sumac; they look down at the blazing maples in the swamp. Somewhere in the woods a hound is baying on a cold scent; the sound of Joe

Casey's axe drifts down from the hill. "Isn't the valley beautiful in October," the summer people repeat without conviction. "Aren't you glad we live here," they say as they drive off.

1931

Town Report

❧ This isn't a piece about Middletown or Anyburg or Sauk Center. The country towns here in New England all bear a family resemblance to one another, but they also have individual characters that can be learned only by living in them. They are more or less united as communities, more or less friendly to newcomers, more or less dominated by cliques that are more or less conservative and sometimes corrupt. But all of them are different from small towns in other parts of the country, and I suspect that all of them have been rapidly changing since the war, in fashions that are not always apparent to their own inhabitants.

I suspect, but I can't be certain. One effect of this war has been to broaden our political interests while narrowing our social horizons. Friends who live within thirty miles of us used to be regarded as neighbors; now we can see them only by saving gasoline for weeks to have a little surplus. Our cousins in Pennsylvania might as well be living in Omaha, or the moon. And so, in setting down the wartime record of one little town, I wonder whether it is at all unusual or whether it is typical of the country as a whole.

Sherman is a town only in the New England sense; in New York it would be an unincorporated village, in Pennsylvania a township, and farther west nothing more than a school district. It consists of about twenty-five square miles of land shaped like a narrow slice of pie—a valley ten miles long with a lake in the south, farmland in the north, and a range of wooded hills on either side. The back roads are full of abandoned farms like those described in Slater Brown's novel, *The Burning Wheel*. North of the village, locally called the Center, there are twenty fairly prosperous dairy farms. Summer cottages are clustered along the shores of the lake and scattered through the hills. The winter population is about 450.

Small as it is, the town has its own probate judge and its own representative in the Connecticut General Assembly. As for local officials, it has so many of them that I have never been able to make an accurate count, although thirty-five are listed by name in the annual report, which doesn't bother to mention three or four constables. Most of these officials are elected for terms of one or two years, but a few are appointed, including the dog warden, who happens to be a Democrat. The first selectman, who acts as a mayor or burgess, more than earns his salary of $500 a year. With a few exceptions, the other officials either serve without pay or else receive fees for the work they actually perform. One of them makes a living by holding three town offices and driving the school bus.

Except for Republican politics, Sherman has no native industries, and there are only three products of any importance: milk, scenery, and good roads. About one-third of the inhabitants are supported by dairy farming, and most of the others either work on the roads, which are maintained or subsidized by the state, or else they supply various goods and services to the summer people who come to enjoy the scenery. At least that is what they used to do before the war.

Sherman today has twenty-nine men and two women in the armed forces—about seven percent of its people and substantially more than the average for the nation. About one-third of them enlisted voluntarily, including an aviation cadet and two army nurses, besides half a dozen men in the navy. I heard that one boy thought seriously of becoming a conscientious objector, but he changed his mind at the last moment, and it now seems that he has become an uncommonly good soldier. Most of the men neither try very hard to get into the army nor take any steps to keep out of it. There is a somewhat passive attitude, as if they said—and in fact I have heard more than one man saying—"When Uncle Sam wants me, he'll come and get me and I'll be ready to go."

Uncle Sam doesn't want the farmers, most of whom are now in their fifties, but they complain of not being able to find help, and this at a time when they are being asked to keep bigger herds. The summer people had to mow their own lawns or let them grow into hay. To keep a maid is a dream that most of the housewives have forgotten. Building has stopped completely, and many of the carpenters and plumbers are finding jobs in airplane factories; at any rate they are moving to Bridgeport and Hartford. Sherman has only two war workers now living here, a grandfather more than seventy years old and one of his younger sons. They work twelve hours on the night shift at Bridgeport, besides driving fifty miles each way.

It is surprising how little talk one hears about the war. Maybe it's because I don't get around as much as I should, or don't catch everything that is said. I note, however, that the radio at the grocery store was turned on for the World's Series but not for news reports of the fighting in the Solomons. Ten years ago when farmers on the back roads talked about "the war," they meant the American Revolution, during which this countryside was infested with marauding Tories. The Civil War and the First World War left no such lasting impressions, for the fighting was far away—and New Guinea is even farther. What is near at hand is food and fuel rationing, high prices, and the shortage of unrationed articles like prunes and alarm clocks and bacon. About all these matters there is grumbling, but rather less than I expected to hear. Sometimes a man will say, "Those people in Washington . . ." as if he blamed them for everything that was going wrong; but the same man will volunteer as an airplane spotter or a fire warden. Nobody thinks that we will lose the war, but there are signs of deep uncertainty about the future. People say, "It's no use making plans any more," and that is a bitter remark for New Englanders, who like to know what they will be doing in twenty years.

So far the most obvious change in Sherman life has been produced by the rationing of gasoline and tires. Eight miles from a railroad station, the town had learned to live on rubber. There is a state highway two hundred yards from my house, and I used to hear the hum of tires as cars shot past at seventy miles an hour. Now the highway is empty half the morning, and then a car passes as slowly and silently as if it were driving behind a hearse. Nobody can take long trips. Hardly anybody thinks of driving to New Milford or Danbury—the nearest large towns—without inviting his neighbors to come too.

At first the church suffered from gasoline rationing, but I understand that with people learning to share rides, attendance is almost back to normal. Sunday school has been resumed, after being abandoned during the summer; the children are now taken there in the school bus. There is absolutely no sign, however, of the religious revival that is supposed to be felt in wartime. Activities that used to be connected with the church are now centered in the town hall.

Indeed, that little white Gothic chickencoop has become more important than any other building in Sherman. It used to stand empty from week to week, being opened only for town meetings and an occasional square dance or chicken supper. The town clerk kept his books and papers at home. Now the hall is open every day, with the clerk at his desk, the selectmen or the assessors meeting, and the rationing board receiving applications (which, incidentally, it handles with great fairness). In the evenings the hall is lighted for meetings connected with war or politics—for lectures on gas masks, fire protection, or first aid; for Republican caucuses and rallies of the fire company. One feels that the community has been drawn together by the new tasks it is called upon to perform.

Some of its former activities have been discontinued; for example, there are not many purely social gatherings. Sherman used to be known as the eatingest town in Connecticut. Two years ago its women compiled and published a *Sherman Cookbook,* with local recipes that are widely followed— and they are good ones, too. It used to be that every event was celebrated and every organization was financed by a covered-dish luncheon, a clambake, a turkey dinner, or a cake and jelly sale. But public meals are difficult to arrange in wartime, and many of the organizations that depended on them for support have become inactive.

Meanwhile the war has created new organizations—too many of them by far, and with functions that in some cases are vague or conflicting. The rationing board, however, has a definite job and is doing it well; it will end by exercising a tremendous power over civilian lives. The observation post has been in continuous operation since the day after Pearl Harbor. It has the services of 150 airplane spotters in summer and 90 in winter, each of them standing guard for three hours a week. A service committee has been forwarding letters and packages to the Sherman boys in the armed forces.

The local defense council is charged with supervising a host of activities, those listed in its report as Air Raid Wardens, Agriculture, Auxiliary Police, Emergency Housing and Evacuation, Finance, Fire Wardens, Courses, Medical, Women's Division, and Salvage—in other words, the whole complicated pattern created in Washington by the Office of Civilian Defense, on the model of what had been done in England. The trouble is that events here aren't following the English model. Serious air raids are becoming more unlikely and it is the countryside instead of the cities that is being evacuated. I should guess that the muddle in civilian defense cost the administration more votes than the loss of the Philippines.

And yet new organizations continue to proliferate. An hour ago I was interrupted by a visitor who urged my wife to become the coordinator of something or other; I didn't catch all of the high-sounding title. The actual work involved was organizing a course in forest-fire prevention to compete with courses already being given in first aid, home nursing, and nutrition, not to mention others. In spite of having a coordinator, the new course would apparently not be coordinated with earlier activities, even those of the local fire warden. The visitor, who was very nice and rather apologetic, had to carry out his instructions from Washington, where the course had been carefully and no doubt soundly planned, but without any notion of what is actually being done in towns like this.

A great deal is being done, and done willingly, in spite of all the confusion. Although some of the defense activities are being performed in a perfunctory fashion, as perhaps they deserve to be, others are taking root in local life. To mention one example, the naming of fire wardens led naturally to the organization of a local fire company, a step that had been hopefully discussed for several years. Until the war we had been forced to depend on the fire company from New Milford, which does excellent work in its own town, but which is so far from Sherman that often a house burned down before it arrived—and even then it charged $50 for making the trip. After the chief fire warden suggested that we could do the work ourselves, the selectmen appropriated $1,500 to buy a second-hand fire truck, and the firemen collected money to buy hose. A firehouse is being built by volunteer labor, with materials furnished by the town. It is an achievement like those we used to admire in travelers' stories from Russia.

When the time came for the national scrap collection, it was the fire company that undertook to do the job. We gathered at nine o'clock one Sunday morning—twenty-five or thirty men and seven or eight trucks, each with a route assigned to it. The driver of the truck on which I rode was the Republican candidate for the General Assembly. I was running against him and we joked about it sometimes during the morning, when we weren't too busy carrying old iron, but nobody was much concerned about our political rivalry, considering that no Democrat has carried the town since Cleveland's second term. At almost every house a pile of scrap was waiting. People said, "I had three old cars, too, but I guess they were shipped to Japan." Or else, "The Japs got in ahead of you, Howard. You'll have to go out to the Solomon Islands if you want to find my tractor." For people here, the scrap iron sold to Japan has come to stand for all the errors in our foreign policy.

From one house we hauled away a weatherbeaten Ford that was rooted in weeds and looked like an enormous vegetable; from another we drove off in a caravan, with a hayrake hitched to the back of the truck and a buggy hitched to the hayrake. The big pile in a corner of the schoolyard had been growing all morning and afternoon; it was now about as large as a brownstone house lying on its side. Digging into it, one could reconstruct almost everything the town had ever been. There were saws and axes, ox chains, farming implements (some used for crops no longer grown in western Connecticut), dozens of heavy milk cans, old trucks and tires, kiddie cars, a box of tennis balls—in all, the record of a town that had passed from lumbering to herding to general farming, and then to a mixed economy of dairying and providing vacations for city people; that had traveled in a century and a quarter from pioneering to weekending—and now was moving in what direction? If it had not been for the war, Sherman might have become an outer suburb, with gentlemen's estates in the midst of desolate fields. So far, the war has preserved its farms and has carried Sherman backward in time through the automobile age toward the period when it was an isolated community furnishing most of its own food and its own amusements. It is in most ways a better and friendlier town in wartime than it was in peace.

That Sunday we collected 25 tons of its relics, or about 110 pounds for each inhabitant. It was more than the state or the national average, but less than we might have collected if we had planned our work more carefully or continued it longer. And that might stand as a general comment on our effort in wartime: it is better than the average, and in spite of some confusion it is probably better organized, like the community itself, but it is not half the effort we are capable of making or will have to make before the end of the war. As for what is being done in towns bigger and smaller than Sherman, I haven't heard and I would like to know.

1942

Along the Housatonic

The Housatonic rises in Mud Pond, near the summit of the Berkshires. It flows northwest to Pittsfield, then south through most of Massachusetts and all of Connecticut to Long Island Sound, having a course of 160 miles as the fish swims, although the distance is about 50 miles shorter by crow's flight. It is not an important river commercially; it is not even navigable above the head of tide at Derby; nor is it remembered for battles that took place at fords or bridges: a massacre of fleeing Indians during King Philip's War and a couple of skirmishes during Shays' Rebellion are its whole military record. It is not a noble river like the Hudson or the St. John in New Brunswick, not an imperial river like the St. Lawrence; but it is a pleasant, even a lovely stream in most of its course; it is full of trout and bass; it never has disastrous floods or shrinks to a trickle in August; and it is regarded with a steadily quiet affection by the people in its valley. Rich men chose to live there after the Civil War and there were decades when Lenox and Stockbridge were dominated by the hundred-roomed and hundred-servanted "cottages" of the robber barons. But writers preceded them into the valley, did their best work, departed; and writers have returned there now that most of the rich are gone. *Moby Dick* and *The House of Seven Gables* were written during the same year, in valley farmhouses only a few miles apart.

The book that Chard Powers Smith has written about the Housatonic is one of the best in the generally disappointing Rivers of America series.* It is one of the best because Smith has put more work into it than most of the other authors have put into their volumes: he has consulted more records, talked and written to more people, traveled more extensively through the valley and lived there long enough to play a part in town politics. He is a little like the man who died on Cape Cod at the age of eighty-six. "Although not a native," said the obituary in the local paper, "Mr. Jones came to Orleans at the age of two." Although not a native, Smith writes like a Housatonic patriot, with an intensity of conviction that holds his rambling story together. On a recent trip through the valley, I was glad to see his book displayed in bookstore windows from New Milford to Pittsfield.

I should like to recommend it to all the valley people; and yet, as a critic

*See Vincent McHugh's comprehensive review of the first twenty-three volumes in the series ("Oh Shannadore," *The New Republic,* May 31, 1943).

and former Pennsylvanian, I can't help pointing out its faults, most of which it shares with the other volumes in the same series. Its emphasis, like theirs, is historical or antiquarian rather than geographical and social. It is full of interesting anecdotes about Abigail Williams and Jonathan Edwards; it has a fine chapter on the Tallyho Age in Lenox; but it fails to tell us anything about the soils of the valley and their influence on agriculture. It tells us comparatively little about the contour of the hills, which are low but continuous to the eastward, whereas the higher mountains on the west are broken by several water-level passes; that explains why the valley has always looked to New York more than to Boston and why the speech of its people is closer to Standard American than it is to the dialect of the eastern seaboard. Smith says nothing about the valley speech and mentions its humor without quoting examples. He gives only a vague notion of how the valley people earn their livings. One would think from his remarks that writing and subsistence farming were the two principal professions; the truth is that writers, however famous, are statistically unimportant in the population, while subsistence farmers began to disappear from the valley more than a hundred years ago. Today the valley lives chiefly on summer residents, repairing their automobiles, selling them gasoline and groceries, building the roads on which they travel and remodeling the houses in which they live. The surviving farmers are industrialists producing milk in sanitary barns that are like small factories, and eggs in electrified three or four-story henhouses. They are so far from subsistence farming that they don't even raise grain to feed their cows and chickens. Their bread, their butter, most of their meat and part of their vegetables, in cans, are bought in the nearest chain store.

Smith tends to idealize the Yankee farmers, forgetting (although he knows) that there are few Yankees left on the land. Most of them have moved into the villages, where they make the best small storekeepers and bankers in the United States. About half the farms in the southern part of the valley are operated by Swedes or Poles; about a quarter of them by the children of other immigrants; less than a quarter by men of New England stock. There are Catholic churches in most of the towns, with sermons in Polish and sometimes Slovak or French as well as English. Most of the Catholics are Democrats, most of the Protestants are Republicans, so that town elections are complicated by religious and racial issues. Smith tells us nothing about these recent conflicts. There is a sense of unreality in his book which I think is connected with the thesis he is trying to prove.

He believes—to put his argument baldly—that the Housatonic Valley has been the scene of a long struggle between the forces of God and the forces of the Devil. The forces of God are the early Puritans, the farmers of all times and the latter-day writers, educators and artists who have settled in the valley. The forces of the Devil are the industrialists and those who work in their factories: what he calls the "urban irresponsibles whose first interest is to indulge themselves." God is symbolized by forests and farmlands and white villages sleeping under their elms; the Devil by slums and smokestacks and summer cottages (unless they are set well back from the river and surrounded by at least an acre of empty land). The Devil has conquered Pittsfield, at the upper end of the valley, and Shelton and Derby and Stratford, where the Housatonic enters the sea; but in all its middle reaches the river flows through a wilderness broken only by God's farms and the houses of God's intellectuals. Smith favors legislation or zoning ordinances that will make this part of the watershed a permanent refuge for artists, farmers, and writers.

As a resident of the valley, I can't say that I support this idea of setting it apart as a sort of Indian reservation for intellectuals. It would hardly be fair to the residents of the industrial cities that surround it, but they are not my immediate concern. I am thinking rather of the intellectuals themselves, and the effects on them of living in a sort of privileged and irresponsible quiet. Is that the good life for which they are seeking? It seems to me a fine sort of life, for a time, but only on condition that it be preceded and followed by a plunge into practical affairs. Writers and artists can't stay in a refuge forever, except at the cost of losing their sense of community with the people outside. Perhaps the worst of all the maladies from which they can suffer is the spiritual dry rot that assails moderately successful people with moderate incomes when they live in a moderately rural area at a moderate distance from the metropolis and try to erect a wall against strangers with immoderate clothes and voices. They will find that although they haven't built a wall against ideas and emotions and sympathies, these too will be kept away by their zoning regulations and their No Trespass signs.

1946

Election Night in Sherman

At eight o'clock on the evening of election day, the moderator locked the front door of the Sherman town hall. The two vote-checkers, Democratic and Republican, made a final count and signed each other's duplicate tally sheets. There were 292 names on them, including those of 19 men and women in the armed services, and 258 persons had cast their ballots, or 88 percent of those eligible; it was the largest vote ever recorded in Sherman.

All day the atmosphere inside the town hall—not half so large as Mrs. Luce's living room—had been that of a big, informal reception. The new minister was there with his pretty wife, greeting members of his flock as they arrived in family groups. Six of the voters were over eighty and one was over ninety; they talked about old times in Sherman. Nobody talked politics, there being a Connecticut law that forbids electioneering within seventy-five feet of a polling booth; and anyway, after talking politics for two months, most of them were glad that the arguments were over. "Hello, Minnie," they said, and "How many times did you vote?" and there was a great deal of laughter. A table was spread in the back of the hall, with pies and a big homemade layer cake; the ladies of the Opportunity Club were serving lunch to the twelve election officials. The kitchen door was open and you could smell a big pot of chowder simmering on the stove. Going down to vote was almost like paying a Sunday afternoon visit to a French village café.

At eight o'clock, the two checkers, the two ballot clerks, the two box-tenders and the two booth-tenders all rose to their feet; their day was ended and they had each earned $5. One woman, the mother of five grown children, did a stiff-legged jig. Like all the others, except the two booth-tenders, she had been sitting on a hard kitchen chair since six o'clock that morning. An old man in the back of the hall was saying over and over, "But I wanted to vote," and someone else was explaining in a loud voice, "It's too late, Pop. You got here one minute too late."

The moderator took charge of the two padlocked ballot boxes. Old, stained and greasy, they had been fitted with hasps and hinges by a carpenter long since dead. One of them used to hold 500 Remington UMC twelve-gauge shotgun shells; now it held the numbered stubs of the ballots. The other, which now held the ballots themselves, had long ago been filled with

Paine's Celery Compound, a Nerve Tonic. "That's what you Democrats are going to need tonight, a bottle of nerve tonic," somebody said, and nudged me. The moderator put one box carefully on top of the other and, walking like a priest bearing the Host, carried them both into the town clerk's office. A little crowd fell in behind him, and I joined it. I had never seen the aftermath of an election, and besides, my wife was one of the Democratic counters.

What I saw in the town clerk's office was a ceremony hedged about with so many laws and restrictions that it might have been handed down by a priesthood from ancient times. Eight persons took seats at a long table: on one side the Republican registrar of voters and two Republican counters; on the other side the Democratic registrar and two counters, while the town clerk sat at the foot of the table and the moderator at the head. "Is everybody ready?" the moderator asked. There was a murmur or grunt of affirmation. Ceremoniously, he unlocked what used to be the case of shotgun shells and emptied the numbered stubs in the middle of the table. The four counters arranged them in piles of ten, then counted the piles and the eight remaining stubs. "Two fifty-eight, right," one of them announced.

The stubs were returned to their packing case. Now the Celery Compound box was unlocked and the ballots themselves were emptied on the table. They were counted like the stubs, while a dozen spectators leaned forward to see that every act was properly performed. A little boy opened the door, stared for a moment with bug eyes, and disappeared into the darkness. "Two fifty-eight, right," said one of the counters. "Now open the ballots," the moderator said.

As the counters unfolded each ballot, they pored over it to see that it was properly marked, then placed it in one of three piles: straight Republican, straight Democratic or split ticket. Doubtful ballots were handed over to the moderator for his decision, but only one of them was finally rejected, with no protests. All the ballots were strictly anonymous sheets of paper; not even a handwriting expert could have told who had voted for which candidate.

Now the two piles of straight-party ballots were counted, the Democratic counters taking the Republican pile, which was by far the larger, and the Republican counters taking the Democratic pile. There was a serious look on all the faces. The two piles were exchanged for a recheck, which did not alter the results: 154 straight Republican and 55 straight Democratic votes. The 48 split ballots came next. They too were sorted into three piles according to the vote for President: Dewey, Roosevelt and other. This time Roosevelt got 31 votes and Dewey 14, the figures being added to their previous straight-party figures. There were two votes for Norman Thomas and one write-in vote for Henry A. Wallace. "Two fifty-eight, right," said the town clerk, after including in his count the ballot voided by the moderator and added up the figures.

The split ballots were sorted into three piles once again, this time according to the vote for Governor. Baldwin led, getting 25 votes as against 17 for Hurley, with 4 votes for the Socialist candidate. And the process of sorting the split ballots continued for each of the 14 national, state, and local offices at issue in Sherman. Standing near the table, I could see how some of the ballots were marked and, whatever the result, they seemed to suggest a good deal of soul-searching. Several Republicans had voted for Roosevelt and Truman, but for nobody else on the Democratic ticket. A very few Democrats had voted for Dewey. Some Republicans had voted against Representative Clare Boothe Luce and Senator Danaher; in fact these two, with Dewey himself, ran a dozen votes behind the rest of the ticket. A few members of both parties had split their tickets in order to vote for (or against) one of their neighbors.

By ten o'clock I could prophesy the results of the state and national elections. This actual count of the ballots was far more revealing than the big returns then being announced over the radio, because here I knew what the votes meant. Roosevelt was going to win; if he could poll more than a third of the votes in Sherman, which had gone Republican by four to one in local contests, he could probably sweep the country. Hurley was going to lose the governorship; he was too far behind the rest of the Democratic ticket. McMahon was running ahead of it and would be our next Senator; there were too many people who disliked Danaher's isolationism. And Clare Luce . . . I guessed wrong about her, after seeing how many Sherman Republicans had voted for her opponent, but then I hadn't allowed for the big vote she was getting from her neighbors in Greenwich.

At ten-thirty the officials finished signing their reports on the result of the contests for each of the fourteen offices. The ballots were put back into the box for Celery Compound; the box was then locked and sealed, like the other for shotgun shells, and both were locked away in a closet. "It was a good job on both sides," one official said. "Nobody can say it wasn't right." The town clerk turned out the lights. Like the moderator and the two registrars, he had been working steadily for almost seventeen hours.

1944

Is There Still Hope for Farming in New England?

Memories first, before we try to summon up the future. Hope is to be found there, I believe, but it depends partly on the world situation (food, fuel) and partly on national, state, and local policies regarding the use of land. We can raise our voices about those policies; indeed, we had better do so without delay. Meanwhile it is a wry pleasure to think about the fairly recent past of what used to be a Connecticut farming town.

When I first came to Sherman more than forty years ago, it was reported by the census as having 330 people and something like 100 farms; I forget the exact number. Most of the farms didn't deserve the name; they were simply fields and a house where an old couple subsisted with the help of a cow, a flock of chickens, and usually a team of superannuated horses. In the valley north of the Center, though, were rich tobacco and dairy farms. The hills were grassy there and dotted with cattle to their rounded tops. On the valley floor were big white houses, red barns, and silos like baronial donjons standing guard over luxuriant fields of corn, alfalfa, and tobacco. Driving past them on a winding dirt road was like exploring Arcadia.

I remember how marginal farms, mostly in the South End, were abandoned as old couples died off or moved to Danbury. I remember when the last field of tobacco was planted during World War II; that year the crop couldn't be sold because the tobacco warehouse had closed. I remember how dairy farmers complained of not being able to earn a decent living and how one after another sold off his herd. More and more houses were built for people who had jobs in Danbury or did free-lance work in New York. The town was becoming residential, and it was also becoming forested as trees crept down from the hillsides and at places crossed the valley. There were no Arcadian vistas any more.

Sherman is still a good town, more determined than most to preserve its rural character, but today it has only three dairy farms. Three other dairymen sold off their herds last spring. Among those herds the best was that of my friend and neighbor Kenneth Edmonds, who, incidentally, had been taking care of my only field. He paid rent for it too: a truckload of manure each fall. I don't know what will happen to the field after Ken stops mowing it, but there was no use pleading with him. Ken was tired; he had been milking cows twice a day, seven days a week, for fifty years. Now he is looking forward to his first vacation.

What is happening in Sherman had already happened in most of the state, and most of New England. Connecticut now has fewer than 4,000 working farms—not half so many as in 1960—and the number includes part-time operations, as well as little factories cranking out eggs or broilers from a production line. Dairying, however, has been the chief agricultural activity, and the state now has only 900 dairy farms, with the total falling by more than ten percent each year. Rhode Island has 700 farms of all types, not many of which send milk to market. The state agricultural college recently sold off its prize bulls, as if to mark the end of an era. In Massachusetts Governor Francis W. Sargent has established an Emergency Commission on Food. He said at a news conference last September, "We must reverse a thirty-year trend which has resulted in the virtual disappearance of food production in this state."

One can hardly blame the farmers for going out of business. They are capable men, for the most part, but they are faced with more problems than a genius should be asked to solve. Manpower is often the most urgent problem. The farmers are growing old—fifty-eight is their average age in Connecticut—and they need help with the chores. Help is almost impossible to find, except at a price the farmer is unable to pay. "The younger generation just doesn't want to be tied up for seven days a week," Ken Edmonds says. "They don't want those hours staring them in the face every day."

Another problem is the high cost of machinery, fuel, feed, fertilizer, baler twine—in fact, of everything the farmer has to buy. Except for roughage, most of which comes out of his own silo, almost all his supplies are shipped in from other parts of the country, at very high freight rates. How much he pays for the supplies depends on the open market (and to some extent on the big midwestern processors, with their notions of what the traffic will bear). The selling price of milk at the farm is something else again: it is fixed by the government and seldom rises as fast as the cost of feed and fertilizer. From 1968 to 1972, gross farm income in Connecticut rose by $6.5 million, while net farm income was falling by $12.2 million. In 1973 net income was further reduced by a fantastic increase in the cost of supplies.

Property taxes are a less serious problem in Connecticut than in some of the other New England states. By the terms of Public Act 490, passed in 1963, a farmer can ask to have his land assessed at its "use value," generally much lower than its value as commercial real estate. The law has reduced tax assessments on farmland by an average of something like sixty-five percent. On the other hand, there has been no reduction in state or federal inheritance taxes. The state tax is high in Connecticut, and it is levied on the same estimate of net worth as the federal tax. When a farmer dies, the Feds move in to value his land at the inflated price that a developer might pay for it. The farmer's heirs might wish to stay on the land, but instead they have to sell it off as the only way to find money for the tax collectors.

Inflated land values are perhaps the greatest present threat to agriculture in New England. The threat is all the greater for a special reason, namely, that the best farmland, fairly level and well drained, is also the best for residential and commercial development. It used to be the marginal farms that were abandoned; now more and more, as population spreads, it is the richest farms that are taken over. How can a young dairyman—granted that there are still a few of these—compete with a real-estate syndicate eager to invest foreign money? How can he afford to pasture cows on land that will cost him from $1,000 to as much as $10,000 an acre?

In the South and Midwest, older men with capital still buy land for the income it will yield from crops or cattle, but the present yield in New England is too low in relation to land values for anything but tax-loss farming (and not much of that). In Connecticut, for example, the last 900 dairymen are working seven days a week for an average return of 3.9 percent on the market value of their land, stock, and equipment. They could sell off everything, pay a capital-gains tax, invest the remaining proceeds in bonds or certificates of deposit, and—to judge by the financial pages—they could earn much more than their present farm incomes by living in idleness.

So once again, what are the prospects for a revival of farming in New England? I still think that the long-term prospects are good, owing to worldwide shortages of food and also to the fact that western and southern farmers are now facing many of the same problems (besides such problems of their own as drought in the High Plains and deteriorating cropland). But the short-term prospects are bleak, and even our distant hopes might be foreclosed. That is, our New England farmland might be lost forever unless steps are promptly taken to help the remaining farmers stay in business and encourage younger men to take their places.

The first step might be a joint resolution presented for adoption by the various state legislatures. It might read something like this: *Resolved that the preservation of open farming and grazing land is to the best interests of the people of* [Connecticut, Vermont, etc.] *and is an effort deserving the aid and encouragement of the state government.*

What good, you might ask, would a resolution do? At the very least it would lead to wider discussion of an urgent problem. If the resolution is adopted after many arguments have been heard, it will provide a reasoned basis for various measures that must be taken if farming in New England is to be maintained at anywhere near its present level, not to speak of its being revived or extended. Some of the measures will interfere with the plans of land speculators, while others will cost the states money. New

Englanders, like Scotsmen, always want to know why public money should be spent.

And why should it be spent in an effort to preserve farmland? Why should we continue trying to compete with western agribusiness? Why shouldn't we resign ourselves to importing all our food from other parts of the country: milk from Wisconsin, potatoes from Idaho, lettuce from Arizona, and apples from the state of Washington? Or again, why should we mourn—as most of us do—when one farmer after another is forced by age and economics to abandon his fields and let them grow up into scrubby woodland? Or when he sells them to a developer with plans for still another residential suburb, a vacation community, an industrial park, or a super-shopping center under acres of asphalt?

Here I won't repeat the ecological answer: that this populated region needs meadows and streams, woods and wetlands, a diversity of open spaces to depollute the air and maintain a supply of drinkable water. "The farmer is the keeper of these lands," says a thoughtful paper recently issued by the Connecticut Conservation Association. "He is the steward of the land. As long as he remains, these resources remain. When he is gone, all too often these irreplaceable natural entities are buried."

Yes, the ecological answer is true and reasonable, every word of it, but my own feeling for New England goes beyond reason into the darker realm of love and aversion. I love the countryside as it was—and as it is today in scattered areas like the Upper Connecticut Valley, the Lamoille Valley, or the Harlem Valley across the state line in New York. I hate to live in the midst of neglected fields, which seem to reproach me; I even hate to drive through miles of scrubland crossed at intervals by stone fences. A deprived and resentful landscape seems to be closing in on me. When the road comes out into open farmland, I feel a sense of relief, as if I were drawing a free breath after years in prison. "Isn't this fine, for a change," I say in mantalk, while my wife uses the forbidden word: "Yes, it's beautiful."

Beauty in itself isn't enough to persuade a state legislator that he should vote for an appropriation, but beauty in New England has an economic value. Almost the whole region has found that tourists are an important source of revenue. The better the region looks, the more tourists will be attracted, not to mention vacationers and permanent residents (for whom there is room enough, if their new communities don't gobble up the farmland). The more farms are preserved, the more pastures are reclaimed, the better (more beautiful) the region will look, and—as most legislators already realize—the more it will comfortably yield in state and local taxes.

That is by no means the only economic argument for a revival of agriculture. Every farmed or grazed or gardened acre produces something that adds to the wealth of the community—and the statement is true even when the farmer is losing money. If he makes it instead, much of the money goes into improving the farm or the neighborhood. Think of the big white hand-some clapboard houses and the brick houses, weathered pink, that dot the New England countryside or cluster in villages. Except in coastal areas, most of those houses grew out of the soil, either directly or indirectly—directly, if they were built with money from corn, tobacco, cattle, Merino sheep, or Morgan horses; indirectly, if they were built by merchants or bankers who prospered from dealing with local farmers. Now that so many of the big houses have to be propped up with New York or Boston money, they seem to me a little less substantial.

"Don't make subjective judgments," I tell myself. "Don't say anything that isn't realistic." Well, here are a few realistic statements.

Every good field abandoned is a loss to the community. Henceforth the field produces nothing, though in thirty years it might yield a meager crop of firewood or pulpwood. If it becomes part of a residential development, this in turn produces nothing (except from a few backyard gardens, rather more of these in 1974 than in 1973). Essentially the new residents are here in their role as consumers, and almost everything they consume is trucked in from a distance. Even their incomes are imported from the larger towns where they work in offices or factories. The new residents are pleasant people and they make a contribution to the community by showing good will and public spirit, but what they contribute in taxes is seldom enough to pay for what they demand in services (new schools, sewers, paved highways kept free from snow, and everything else that a suburb expects). When a farming town in Connecticut goes residential, taxes on old-time property owners are very soon tripled or quadrupled, and they are forced to sell off their acreage.

Once again that isn't the whole story. Those farmed acres in New England once supported—in many areas they still support—a network of local industries and commercial enterprises. Depending on the type of farming, there are (or were) canneries, creameries, cheese factories (now surviving only in Vermont), carding mills (now a few in Maine), feed mills, slaughterhouses, tobacco warehouses, and woodworking plants willing to pay a farmer cash for a few wintercut logs. As farming dwindles in one area after another, those local enterprises vanish and the skills they encouraged are forgotten. The remaining farmers not only lose their local outlets but feel lonelier than ever after the Grange Hall becomes a franchised super-market. There are personal tragedies involved. I think of E. A. Robinson's miller, the one who hanged himself after a last word to his wife:

"There are no millers any more,"
Was all that she had heard him say;
And he had lingered at the door
So long that it seemed yesterday.

"That is Robinson in a sentimental mood," I tell myself; but I remember that the private sentiment is connected with a blow to the public economy of our whole region.

The process has gone too far to be simply reversed. When or if farming is revived in New England, it will have to be a different sort of farming, either more intensive, or on a broader scale. Meanwhile some practical steps can be taken to halt the decay, to put heart into the remaining farmers, and to keep the countryside open by restoring the pastures.

The White Paper on Agriculture in Connecticut puts forward several measures that would help to keep farming alive in the state. Among these it lays most stress on the creation of "agricultural preserves" and on the purchase by the state of "development rights" to open land. Later I shall have something to say about that purchase. As for creating agricultural preserves, it is a practice started by California in 1965. It has been rather more successful in New York, where the enabling act was passed in 1971, and it is now being considered for adoption on a wider scale by New Jersey.

In New York such agricultural preserves, or districts, are initiated by the farmers themselves, who must agree, in each case, that 500 or more contiguous acres should be placed in the district. Their application is reviewed by the county government and discussed at one or more public hearings. If approved by both the county and the state, the district can be officially protected. Protection means briefly "No development," but it has other features as well. Local governments cannot restrict farming practices—such as spreading manure—beyond the requirements of health and safety. Public agencies that want to acquire land in an agricultural district must prove that other acceptable sites are not available. Public-service districts are restricted in their power to tax farmland for services (water, sewage, etc.) that farmers do not require. Also commercial farmers can request annual property-tax assessments based on the agricultural value of their land.

Each agreement runs for eight years, after which it must be reviewed to see whether the land it covers still meets the requirements for an agricultural district. So far, such districts comprise 1.5 million acres, or one-fifth of the best farmland in New York. Apparently the agreements have worked where adopted, and they have led to some glorious battles with public utilities and dam builders, notably in the rich Schoharie Valley. The Connecticut Conservation Association recommends a similar system of preserves for its own state, but with refinements embodied in the still-pending New Jersey plan.

Since the system will reduce the tax basis of local governments, the CCA recommends that the towns be reimbursed for what they lose. The purchase of development rights would also cost money, and—rather than a bond issue to supply it—the CCA believes that it should come from a statewide tax of perhaps four mills on real-estate transfers.

The CCA also suggests other measures that would help to keep Connecticut farms in operation. Briefly they are: (1) subsidies to farmers who permit hunting, fishing, and picnicking on their land; (2) farm markets on state-owned land along highways or even in state parks; (3) college workshops for farmers on management and production techniques (but who would milk the cows while the farmer was attending the workshops?); (4) better training and placement programs for farm labor (and perhaps subsidies to make farm work more competitive with industry); (5) a low-interest revolving loan fund to assist in farm improvements; (6) lower taxes on farm buildings as well as land; (7) negotiating lower insurance costs; and (8) educational loans or grants-in-aid for students planning to be farmers.

Most of those eight measures are directed toward solving the special problems of Connecticut, which is prosperous, thickly peopled, and in immediate danger of losing all its farmland, besides most of its open space. In northern New England the state governments have less money that can be devoted to loans and subsidies. The remaining farms there are different, with fewer plowed fields, except in the Aroostook and the Lake Champlain Valley, and more of the land is in pasture. The immediate problem, the one that demands thought and subsidies, is how to keep the pastures open.

My friend the novelist Wallace Stegner, who lives on the West Coast but owns many northern Vermont acres, has some lively comments. "The horrid fact about New Hampshire," he says, "is that too many city people loved it too much, and hence bought chunks of it, and having no skill or time for farming, pronounced *famine,* they let it grow up to weeds and choke-cherry and spruces and tough little cedars. In Vermont things haven't gone as far as in New Hampshire (I'm totally ignorant of Massachusetts and Connecticut), but they're going.

"We have discussed, in Greensboro, some alternatives: reforesting, which produces a fourth-rate wilderness"—[but not always]; "cooperative mowing and plowing, which is hard to do in the face of Vermont individualism and recalcitrance; and hippy occupation, which takes care of a garden plot and not much more. No city feller can afford, by himself, the machinery it takes to keep a farm's hayfields and pastures open. He has to *be* there to do it with stock, because cattle and sheep won't eat maple seedlings and ash seedlings and so on after they're a year or two old, and neither will they eat ferns and junk and weeds after the first few weeks of the growing season. Result: leave stock out of a pasture or a woodlot for a year or two and there's no recovery—you have to plow or poison, and start over.

"My guess is that an association or cooperative of people determined to keep the pastoral (as opposed to the wilderness or the subdivided) character of New England would get substantial support—clutches of tractors and machinery here and there, clutches of hired hands who would plow up, harrow, disk, etc., and keep open those farms that have ceased to be farmed, and fallen into the hands of professors from Princeton, the Mafia, California speculators, Florida speculators, and local peasants determined to make a pile subdividing. Once the farms are opened, they can be kept open with grazing, as you suggest—either sheep or cattle, if they're managed right, and rotated among the fields properly, will do it."

I like Stegner's idea of landowners' cooperatives; the situation is desperate, and volunteer action would help immensely. But my own guess is that the cooperatives, if they were to thrive, would need state aid and encouragement, perhaps in the form of subsidies for reclaiming pastures. State road crews might be made available for mowing and brush cutting (of course at a fee to the landowner). Controlled burning is another suggestion. It is a very old practice in the Maine blueberry barrens, but elsewhere in New England it has never been widely adopted, I suppose for fear that the fires might spread. Why not have pasture fires that are supervised by the local fire department? Again there is the great question of fencing, which is indispensable on grazing land, but is also expensive. In some areas the old stone fences might be mended once again; they would still make good neighbors. For areas where they were never built, or would cost too much to repair with high-priced labor, might it be possible to invent or adapt some cheap form of portable fencing? I think about those miles of snow fencing that highway departments keep in storage: might they be rented out during the summer?

Then I remember England, where I saw sheep farmers driving from one pasture to another with truckloads of fence panels, which apparently they had made for themselves out of crossed saplings.

Those suggestions are made from the depths of my inexperience, and I hope that the various agricultural colleges will set themselves to finding better answers. Meanwhile I might quote again from Stegner's letter. "I have a friend," he says, "whom perhaps you know—Frol Rainey of the U. of Pennsylvania Archaeological Museum—who has installed forty or fifty sheep on his Greensboro farm, and hired a retired farmer to live in the farmhouse and look after them." I do know Professor Rainey and know his farm as well; it is a fairly level hilltop and, until the milking herd had to be sold off, it was said to be the highest dairy farm in Vermont. Stegner continues, "It's not a paying proposition as yet, but there's substantial federal support, and with more acreage and a bigger flock, he might make it go." I hope he makes it go, and if he needs more acreage, he can probably rent it at a reasonable figure—not buy it—from neighbors eager to have their pastures kept open. With the present high cost of acreage, fairly large-scale farming on leased land has become a possible development in New England.

For the farmer such a practice has two obvious advantages: it enables him to broaden out his operation, and it greatly reduces his capital investment. For the landowner, leasing his land to an active farmer also has advantages (beyond such payments as he might receive, which would not and should not be large). It would maintain the value of his land and the attractiveness of the neighborhood. In states with laws like Connecticut's Public Act 490—New Hampshire has recently adopted a similar measure—it would permit him to apply for a lower tax assessment on his property.

When I gloom about the situation on walks through abandoned fields, it seems to me that the practice of leasing land for agriculture might be vastly extended. Associations of landowners—Wallace Stegner's suggestion—would have more acreage to offer than individuals. And what about the land trusts that are becoming more numerous in southern New England, to meet the threat that a whole town will be built or paved over? One such trust is active in Sherman. So far it has acquired only forest and scrub and swampland, but isn't cultivated farmland even more precious to the community? Some of the trusts have talked about venturing into this new field. Nature Conservancy, which I think is the only trust that operates on a national scale, has been offered about 1,800 acres of Connecticut land in Bridgewater and New Milford. George D. Pratt, Jr., who made the princely offer, is a lifelong conservationist who attached a condition to the gift. There are three farms on the land, and Pratt wants to have them kept in operation. So far Nature Conservancy has had no experience in farm management. Two of the farms are rented and hence present no serious problem, but the third, in New Milford, is the richest and most productive dairy farm in the neighborhood. Fortunately Pratt's experienced farm manager, Peter Petersen, has agreed to go along with the deal and to train a successor before he retires.

Land trusts that will operate or lease out farms are only one of many possibilities. What about the broad tracts of New England that are owned by the states or by the federal government? Most of this land is utterly unsuited to agriculture and should be kept as wilderness or devoted to tree crops or recreation, but there are areas of richer soil whose use might be recommended. I think of interstate highways with their habit of seizing more land—often in fertile valleys—than is conceivably needed by present or future traffic. Some of the surplus land is mowed once a year by the road crews. Couldn't it be grazed or plowed by farmers, at no public expense, so long as nothing was built on it? Also I think of the Saratoga Battlefield across the Hudson, an expanse of 2,432 acres most of which used to be farmland. It is a handsome park only part of which is visited by the public; the rest is woodland or meadows that are mowed—again once a year—by the National Park Service. If they were grazed instead, the magnificent view over the Hudson Valley would be preserved and the land would look more as it did when Johnny Burgoyne surrendered.

Returning to the private sector, what about ski resorts, a subject on which my ignorance is abysmal? I know, however, that trails and slopes have to be kept free of brush, and I presume that much of the work is done with defoliants such as the Army used in Vietnam. Sheep, however, are the ancient and still the best mowing machines for steep slopes. Mightn't sheep growers add to their incomes by contracting to do a sprout-removal job for resort operators? There are problems involved, but I should guess that most of these will be solved after we have lost most of our grazing land and after the rest of it becomes more precious to the region and the hungry world.

In the case of highly productive land in immediate danger of being taken over by jerry builders, some public agency—state, county, or town—might buy the land to keep it from going out of production. That bold step was first considered by Suffolk County, at the eastern end of Long Island. There the situation is deteriorating. Suffolk has been a very rich agricultural county, famous for potatoes, ducklings, and cauliflower, but its farmland is rapidly disappearing under suburban developments; very soon it will have vanished. Apparently Suffolk farmers have not made use of the New York law that permits the creation of agricultural reserves. The law offers many advantages, but not enough of them, in this case, to counterbalance the glittering offers of real-estate speculators.

Two years ago John V. N. Klein, the County Executive, came up with the proposal that Suffolk should float a bond issue big enough to pay for half its remaining agricultural land—that would be 30,000 acres—and then lease back the acres to operating farmers. The proposal was beautifully simple, and it attracted inquiries from twelve states that thought of adopting it. In New England it would be justified only in the case of highly productive acres—truck farms, for example, or the shade-grown tobacco fields of the Hartford Basin, important to the economy of the state, but now being built over. Even in rich Suffolk County, it involved more money than the county legislature thought it could raise; the proposal had to be scaled down. In a later form it undertakes, as a beginning, to preserve 12,000 acres of agricultural land. Some of the acres would be bought outright, as in the original scheme, and leased back to farmers. More of them, however, would not change ownership; the county would simply buy "development rights" to keep them from being built upon or subdivided. Meanwhile the price of Suffolk land has continued to rise. Even development rights would now cost more than Klein's earlier figure of $45 million, a sum that the county legislature was willing to make available. Last spring he had to request an additional $15 million, with the request still pending.

The purchase of development rights by a public agency—if the rights are worth money and the agency can pay for them—is clearly of advantage to farmers who want to stay in business. It gives them fresh capital that can be used for stocking and improving the land. It reduces their tax assessments in states where they haven't the benefit of a law like Connecticut's Public Act 490. When a farmer dies, the Feds can't appraise his land at its development value, which has ceased to be part of his estate. His heirs have a smaller inheritance tax to pay and, if they wish, they can still be farmers.

Those are a few of the measures by which New England farms might be kept in operation, while waiting for an agricultural revival that is likely to come, but might otherwise come too late. Some of the measures had better be adopted promptly, if our region is not to become a wilderness hatched and spangled with housing developments. So far we have been waging a purely defensive struggle against the panzer divisions of invading bulldozers. We win victories here and there, but we are certain to lose the war unless we can assemble other forces, including an agricultural interest strong enough to undertake a counteroffensive against the spoilers.

1974

A Letter on Growing Melons

❧ Dear Jeff, Dear Marissa: So you plan to have a melon patch next year. That presents you with something of a challenge, though truly not a great one, even if New England is not regarded now as melon country. It used to be so regarded all through the nineteenth century, when our local markets were supplied with muskmelons and watermelons in season by local gardeners. On the last day of August 1839, when Henry and John Thoreau set out for a famous week on the Concord and Merrimack rivers, their homemade rowboat carried melons from their home patch as part of its cargo. At Hooksett, not ten miles south of Concord, New Hampshire, they found a commercial grower so proud of his melons that he guarded them at night with a loaded musket. "We had come away up here among the hills," Henry writes, "to learn the impartial and unbribable beneficence of Nature. Strawberries and melons grow as well in one man's garden as another's, and the sun lodges as kindly under his hillside . . ."

Without having seen your Vermont place, I assume that the sun lodges as kindly there as it used to lodge near Hooksett Falls. Full sun all day is the principal requirement of melons. The hotter it is—granted that other things are equal—the sweeter the melons will be. Cold weather is their deadliest adversary. I shouldn't advise planting them where there is likelihood of frost after June 1 or before September 15. They need those 106 mild nights if they are to ripen.

Forgive me for speaking in general terms, as if from behind a grandfatherly beard. Melons will grow anywhere that tomatoes can be picked well before the end of August. They will flourish anywhere that tobacco used to be grown commercially, as, for example, in the Connecticut Valley as far north as Bellows Falls. In New York State the famous Hand melons are harvested from a broad terrace above the Hudson, about twenty miles due west of Arlington, Vermont. Though I haven't talked to local gardeners, I imagine that melons are grown a hundred miles farther north, in the Champlain Valley. I remember a popular cantaloupe called Lake Champlain that has long since disappeared from the seedsmen's catalogues.

At home, in northwestern Connecticut, where we sometimes have a frost June 1 (but never June 2, and I'd like to know the reason), I have been growing a few hills of cantaloupes and watermelons for the last forty years. One year we had a frost September 1, but I saved most of the melons that still hadn't ripened by covering the vines with sheets. I remember losing only one crop; it was the year when I became vainglorious and tried raising those forty-pound southern watermelons, which obstinately refused to ripen. The following year I went back to Early Northern Sweets, not quite half as large, but just as good to eat. When these disappeared from catalogues—I think because they had too many seeds—I became converted to Burpee's Fordhook Hybrid, which ripens just after New Hampshire Midgets and before the earliest cantaloupes.

Choosing the right seeds will be your winter problem, when the catalogues arrive. I recommend Burpee for melons (without prejudice to Joseph Harris, my favorite for other garden seeds). Look first at the new hybrids, most of them early-ripening; they have extended melon country a few miles farther north and back into the hills. Besides the Fordhook Hybrid watermelon, an excellent choice is the Burpee Hybrid cantaloupe, which I have found to be the earliest, the most dependable, and one of the most delicious. Burpee Early Hybrid Crenshaw, ripening about a week later, can be a New England gardener's boast. It is a very large (up to fourteen pounds), thick-fleshed melon that is better-flavored than California-grown casabas. But don't count on more than one big melon per vine.

In addition to seeds, you will need a few garden supplies to start and establish the melon vines. Essentials that I keep in the cellar are a roll of black Pliofilm (sold as "black plastic mulch"), a few dozen Jiffy-7 pellets (with trays to hold them), and a package of Hotkaps. Black Pliofilm is something to which you, Jeff, as an organic gardener, might object; you might prefer a thick layer of some natural mulch, such as wood chips or litter or spoiled hay. Those organic mulches are splendid for cold-resistant vegetables—peas, lettuce, potatoes—but they have a serious disadvantage when used with melons. Besides keeping the soil moist and free of weeds, which is all to the good, they keep it cool, and gardeners tell me that they delay the ripened fruit for a week or more. Black Pliofilm, on the other hand, is wonderful for heating the soil to the proper temperature for melons.

As for the other supplies, Jiffy-7 pellets consist of dried peat moss combined with inorganic plant nutrients. Simply put them in water and they swell into little pots ready to plant your seeds in. (Once again, as organic gardeners, you might object. In that case buy fiber pots instead and fill them with a mixture of compost and sand.) Nobody objects to Hotkaps, though, and they enable you to set out your vines as much as two weeks before the last frost.

Let's imagine now that frost is out of the ground and shadbush is ready to blossom. Before May 1 the melon patch should be plowed and hoed or harrowed. If you insist on using no commercial fertilizer, spread plenty of compost or manure, for melons—in the old-time gardener's phrase—are gross feeders. They like wood ashes, if you have any left in the fireplace. Be sparing of lime, though, in the area where your watermelons are to be planted, for they do best on mildly acid soil.

Stick markers into the spots where your hills will be—five or six feet apart for cantaloupes, seven or eight feet for watermelons. Four hills of cantaloupes and two of watermelons should produce more fruit than you two could eat in season, but you might like to plant more and freeze some of the melons (Crenshaws are said to be especially good for freezing) or give them proudly to neighbors. For each hill, dig a hole twelve inches deep and put two forkfuls of manure in the bottom of it. Cover the manure (or compost) with topsoil and replace the marker in the center of each hill so that it projects three inches above the ground.

Now you are ready to spread the Pliofilm. That is the hardest operation for a home gardener, and it ought to be reserved for a still day because the wind plays hell with plastic mulch. It has to be unrolled, drawn smooth (except for little bumps above the markers), and weighted down with fireplace billets or bricks or shovelfuls of dirt to keep it from blowing away; it's a job on which the two of you might work together.

Everything that follows will be easier, so long as you observe a pretty strict timetable. Here is my own, as worked out over the years.

May 1. Soak the Jiffy-7 pellets in water and watch them swell into little pots. Ten pots fit into a plastic tray. Plant three seeds in each pot, then place each of the trays in a plastic bag and tie the bag shut. The trays should be kept for a week in a warm place, for example, in a cupboard.

May 8. By this time many or most of the seeds should have sprouted. Carefully remove the plastic bags and place the trays near a sunny window. But don't keep them there more than a week or the seedlings will become leggy.

May 15 (if it's not a cold day). Cut holes in the plastic mulch around each of the markers. Every package of Hotkaps contains a round fiberboard setter, and this can be used as a pattern for the holes. Water the hills generously. Carry the trays of plants to the melon patch—by now almost all the seeds will have sprouted—dig shallow holes close to the markers, and set out the pots, usually three to a hill. Handle them carefully, for melon seedlings are fragile. Cover each hill with a Hotkap, following directions printed on the setter. Hotkaps will protect the seedlings not only from frost but also from flea beetles, their first insect enemy.

June 1. Cut a hole in the top of each Hotkap and dust the young vines with a general-purpose garden dust (or with rotenone, if you insist on being organic). Then remove the Hotkaps and thin the vines—if you can manage that without breaking them—leaving five to the hill for cantaloupes and three to the hill for watermelons.

And what else must you do? Nothing, practically speaking, except wait for the melons to ripen. They haven't many enemies in this area. Oh, yes, they are sometimes infested with aphids, and I find it wise to apply before August 1 a garden dust or spray containing Malathion (again rotenone or nicotine dust will do the work, but not quite so effectively). Wild animals haven't been much of a problem for me. Rabbits don't touch the vines, woodchucks neglect them for beans or even ripe tomatoes (which isn't to say that I neglect the woodchucks), and what casual damage I have suffered has been from field mice or voles in a bad season. Raccoons? Thanks be to Satan, their overlord, the raccoons of this neighborhood haven't learned to eat melons, though I have heard disturbing reports from a distance. If they learned about melons here, I wouldn't know what to do short of abandoning my patch. Raccoons are the gardener's wiliest enemies. Once give them instruction in nuclear physics and they would soon take over the country—tomorrow the world.

Back to the melon patch after tearing two leaves from the calendar. Let us imagine that the raccoons have held off for another year, busy as they doubtless are in somebody's big cornfield. It is August 15 and the first melons should be ripe—but how is the gardener to know when to pick them? After a time you learn the signs for each variety. Thus, Burpee Hybrid cantaloupes turn pale gold under the netting and have a translucent look, almost like yellow Chartreuse. Crenshaws brighten from leaf green into squash yellow. Watermelons are more secretive, but the ripe ones have a hollow sound when thumped. Sometimes the sound is doubtful, but then you can cut out a plug with a sharp knife and see whether the flesh is deep red. If it is only pink, the plug can be replaced. There is a simpler test for cantaloupes, namely, to lift the melon gently with both hands. If it comes off the vine, there is nothing left to do but chill and eat it.

I guarantee the taste as infinitely superior to that of melons—even the best—picked green in California or Colorado and jolted across the country. Dear Jeff, dear Marissa, those melons will inflate your pride and restore your faith in the New England soil. Eat on until you reach a state of blissful indigestion.

Yours,
Malcolm Cowley

1975

A Handful of Poems

Boy in Sunlight

The boy having fished alone
down Empfield Run from where it started on stony ground,
in oak and chestnut timber,
then crossed the Nicktown Road into a stand
of bare-trunked beeches ghostly white in the noon twilight—

having reached a place of sunlight
that used to be hemlock woods on the slope of a broad valley,
the woods cut twenty years ago for tanbark
and then burned over, so the great charred trunks
lay crisscross, wreathed in briars, gray in the sunlight,
black in the shadow of saplings grown
scarcely to fishing-pole size: black birch and yellow birch,
black cherry and fire cherry—

having caught four little trout that float, white bellies up,
in a lard bucket half-full of lukewarm water—
having unwrapped a sweat-damp cloth from a slab of pone
to eat with dewberries picked from the heavy vines—
now sprawls above the brook on a high stone,
his bare scratched knees in the sun, his fishing pole beside him,
not sleeping but dozing awake like a snake on the stone.

Waterskaters dance on the pool beneath the stone.
A bullfrog goes silently back to his post among the weeds.
A dragonfly hovers and darts above the water.
The boy does not glance down at them
or up at the hawk now standing still in the pale-blue mountain sky,
and yet he feels them, insect, hawk, and sky,
much as he feels warm sandstone under his back,
or smells the punk-dry hemlock wood,
or hears the secret voice of water trickling under stone.

The land absorbs him into itself,
as he absorbs the land, the ravaged woods, the pale sky,
not to be seen, but as a way of seeing;
not to be judged, but as a way of judgment;
not even to remember, but stamped in the bone.
"Mine," screams the hawk, "Mine," hums the dragonfly,
and "Mine," the boy whispers to the empty land
that folds him in, half-animal, half-grown,
still as the sunlight, still as a hawk in the sky,
still and relaxed and watchful as a trout under the stone.

The Living Water

> In the hot afternoon,
> in the burned meadow,
> the brook is a bloodstain dried
> black on the dry gray stones.
>
> In the hot afternoon,
> in the hillside pasture,
> climb where the water flowed
> last spring, there is life beyond
>
> the broken fence, in the locust grove,
> there is water standing in pools
> and a kingfisher darting over
> the minnows trapped for his feast.
>
> Climb on and find the ravine.
> Crickets are silent there,
> but over a breast-high ledge
> is heard the trickle of water.
>
> The banks are steeper (climbing),
> the shade is deeper (stumbling),
> the pools are deeper (climbing),
> and here they are empty of minnows.
>
> See, in their depths at last
> the arrowlike shadows of trout.

In the hot afternoon, from the hillside pasture,
climb to find water, stumbling into the gorge,
climbing beyond to the vine-entangled swamp,
where catbriars hide the brook that now runs deep
and trout are cool in their sunless kingdom. Climb,
stumble and climb, for the source of it all is here—

> here the final and secret pool,
> with green scum at the edge of it,
> a cloud of midges over it,
> and bubbling from the depths of it,
> stirring the frog's eggs and the fishes' eggs,
> here the source, the limpid and living water rising from white sand.

Natural History

1. Piney Woods

> Teeth on the saw,
> teeth on the rake,
> trout in the brook
> pine in the brake—

The big trees sing to the little trees
  in the pine-crowded brake,
"Here is a twigful of sky," they sing,
"that we will stretch out our limbs and take.
Here is a seep of rain to drink
and rotting leaves to yeast our bread.
Give us the last of your earth," they sing,
  "that our great roots may spread."

> Gorging on mould,
> engrossing the sky,
> the big trees grow.
> The little trees die.

2. The Silvery Fishes

From the vast of it,
from summer fields pegged flat beneath the sky,

enormous sunlight blazing out of them,
   I hid myself away
under the water, under green water,
where silvery fishes nibbled at my thighs,
   and heard them saying:

"We swam upstream for three days and three nights,
for three days drifted southward with the current,
and nowhere found a limit to the world.
   It is shaped like a willow branch.
Heroes came forth, but none could ever swim
   to the tipmost leaf."

A kingfisher cast his shadow on the water.
The fishes hid away beneath a stone.

3. *A Resentment of Rabbits*

At our house not even the rabbits are scared.
   Why, they come out by day
and sit on the doorstep chewing euonymus leaves.
"Rabbit," we say to them, "Rabbit, go away.
   Feast on delicious weeds,
   alfalfa in the fields,
or dewberry blossoms under the night sky."
   Rabbit there on the step
Atwitches a sensitive lip
and fixes us with the dot of a motionless eye.

4. *The Red Branch*

      Sky after sky of windless blue;
      warm days, but with a secret chill.
      The forest wall is green except
      for one red branch on the hill.

      Quiet the leaves, as on a board
      dead butterflies are pinned,
      except for one red branch that stirs
      in premonition of a wind.

      Soon the September gale, too soon
      the bare branch, the leaves blown.

Now, in the mid-September truce,
one leaf drifts down.

5. The Dog Fox

When little daily winds have died away
and turkeys climb to roost in the apple tree,
across the snow night creeps so gradually
no eye can mark the cornerstone of day.

Now tightly draw the blinds against the dark
and see in lamplight how the room awakes.
Listen . . . through the tangible silence breaks,
out of the woodlot, a dog fox's bark.

A creak of rusty hinges in the wind:
his voice was like the rasping of a door,
and when it ceased the darkness instantly

became so hugely silent that behind
a final range of hills we heard the sea
grumbling with all his voices at the shore.

From Where the Forest Stood

We were writers by trade but also countrymen.
Our world was a forest in which the smaller trees
were overshadowed and yet in some measure protected by the giants.
Then came the autumn gales
and the tallest trees were among the first to be uprooted.

From where the forest stood we look out at a different landscape
No broad fields anymore like those where we ran barefoot,
no briary fencerows for quail to shelter in,
no green line on the horizon like that which used to mark
the edge of the big woods.
Everywhere in the flatland, the best farming country,
are chickencoop houses in rows, in squares and circles,
each house with its carport, its TV antenna,
its lady's green cambric handkerchief of lawn.

An immense concrete freeway gouges through the hills
and soars on high embankments over the little streams,
now poisoned, where we fished for trout.
It is lined equidistantly with toy-sized cars,
all drawn by hidden wires to the shopping mall,
where they stand in equidistant rows.
From a hillside we watch their passengers go streaming into
    the supermarket,
not one by one, but cluster by tight cluster.
Do they speak to each other in a strange tongue?
There must be giants among them,
but distance makes them all look smaller than the men and women we knew.

The Urn

Wanderers outside the gates, in hollow
landscapes without memory, we carry
each of us an urn of native soil,
of not impalpable dust a double handful,

why kept, how gathered?—was it garden mould
or wood soil fresh with hemlock needles, pine,
and princess pine, this little earth we bore
in secret, blindly, over the frontier?

—a parcel of the soil not wide enough
or firm enough to build a dwelling on
or deep enough to dig a grave, but cool
and sweet enough to sink the nostrils in
and find the smell of home, or in the ears
rumors of home like oceans in a shell.

The Long Voyage

Not that the pines were darker there,
nor mid-May dogwood brighter there,
nor swifts more swift in summer air;
    it was my own country,

having its thunderclap of spring,
its long midsummer ripening,
its corn hoar-stiff at harvesting,
   almost like any country,

yet being mine; its face, its speech,
its hills bent low within my reach,
its river birch and upland beech
   were mine, of my own country.

Now the dark waters at the bow
fold back, like earth against the plow;
foam brightens like the dogwood now
   at home, in my own country.

A Conversation Between
Father and Son on New England Life
(with Robert Cowley)

✿ At times I have difficulty associating my father, Malcolm Cowley, with his most famous book, *Exile's Return* (1934), his account of American writers in the 1920s. I'm glad to find that it has acquired something of a classic status, but I'm far prouder of the fact that some of his best work—*And I Worked at the Writer's Trade, The View from 80,* and *The Dream of the Golden Mountains*—was written in the last few years. It can't have been easy. He was eighty-five this past summer.

Chalk one up for country living. My father and my mother—she recently turned eighty-one—own seven acres in Sherman, Connecticut, a village some seventy miles north of New York City. We came there in the summer of 1936, when a trip to the metropolis and back was not just an excursion you made each weekend but an adventure. As a child growing up in New England, I found the great divide was still this: are you a native or not? Though I was hardly two, and though I might live in Sherman for the rest of my life, I could never hope to attain that distinction. My family were considered outsiders, doomed to be "city people" forever.

It has been a long time since Sherman was one of those *Ethan Frome* places where old folk lingered at the end of a remote road with a cow, a few chickens, and a presumed burden of memories. Perhaps the town never was like that; certainly it hasn't been in my lifetime. But there was another Sherman that *has* disappeared, something of a self-sufficient arcadia. My father will point out his study window at the long hill that crowds the western horizon and recall that six sawmills were once in operation on it. Today, you can stumble on packs of wild dogs up there. The roadside platforms with their early-morning freight of heavy metal milk cans are gone: about twenty years ago, the big dairies announced that farmers must store milk for pickup in inexpensive glass-lined tanks holding 10,000 gallons. It was a requirement that immediately wiped out all smaller dairy farms in the town.

If Sherman has managed to preserve some of its rural character, my father is partly responsible. I don't think that is too much to say. As chairman of the zoning board for twenty years, he tried to keep Sherman from surrendering to the patternless subdivisions and garish commercial sprawl that have spoiled so much of the American landscape. From an airplane you can see the result: the suburbs actually end and the country begins at the south end of town.

In 1968, when he turned seventy, my father retired from the zoning board. That was the year when his collection of poems, *Blue Juniata,* appeared, and one night he gave a reading for the town. Then came a surprise. He was presented with a silver plate engraved with the words:

> To MALCOLM COWLEY
> In grateful recognition of many
> years of service
> to the town of Sherman

"I was a native now," he told me, "but it had taken a long time." You might say that the process of becoming one is what the following discussion is all about—beginning in Pennsylvania at the turn of the century.

ROBERT COWLEY: I find it somehow fitting that you, of all people, were born in the country. You arrived in the summer of the Spanish–American War, didn't you?

MALCOLM COWLEY: Yes, I was born August 24, 1898, in a farmhouse near Belsano, Pennsylvania. The town was seventy miles from Pittsburgh, where my father was a doctor.

RC: That first experience with the country was almost your last, as I remember.

MC: My mother was alone because my father had been summoned down to Norfolk, Virginia, where his younger brother was supposed to be dying of camp fever. He recovered. So Mother, alone in the big house except for my Aunt Margaret—virgin and slightly crippled—was in labor for two days. Tanny, as we called my aunt, became so terrified that she shut herself in a closet. Finally, my mother's moans attracted somebody passing on the road in a horse and buggy—there was no telephone at the time. He drove to the nearest mining camp and came back with the company doctor, who arrived during a thunderstorm and saved two lives.

RC: There's something I've long meant to ask. What is your earliest memory?

MC: Oh, my earliest memory is being brought in to my grandmother, who was deaf and used an ear trumpet. She was sick in the parlor, which was the room I had been born in. She died when I was four.

But for the rest, the earliest memory would be the first time I wandered off into the woods and found the Vinton Lumber Company had just cut our big timber. The woods were all covered with peeled hemlock logs.

RC: In one of your poems you describe "the woods cut twenty years ago for tanbark / and then burned over, so the great charred trunks / lay crisscross, wreathed in briars. . . ." I take it that the countryside was being ravaged even then.

MC: Even then. And more then. In my earliest childhood there were still great tracts of first-growth hemlock and beech and maple—some of the loveliest woods I've ever seen. The Vinton people got in there with a logging railroad we called "the stump dodger." At the foot of our hill a train with six carloads of logs would go down every afternoon, until finally the whole area was logged clean.

But the coal mines hadn't sulfur-poisoned the streams yet, at least not near us. The streams were still full of fish. I spent all my time barefoot, going fishing. I would go barefoot from the middle of May until the middle of October, when we went back to Pittsburgh. At the end I would have to walk a mile to school in my bare feet over frozen ground. I still remember that.

RC: You seem to have been left alone a good deal of the time.

MC: I was a fortunate child in that I was moderately neglected. It meant that I could run as wild as a weaned colt in an unfenced pasture. I would disappear from the house after breakfast—or sometimes without breakfast—go into the woods, and be gone all day. I came to feel that the countryside belonged to me and that I belonged to the countryside.

RC: For someone growing up in rural America around the turn of the century, how was life different? Was there something special about it?

MC: Well, there *was* something really special. In the first place, poverty. Real poverty in that area. In the second place, people ate what they could produce. Potatoes went into the root cellar. Apples were gathered, pressed into cider, and the cider boiled down into apple butter, which would stand on the shelves in the pantry. They even had flour ground from their own wheat. They'd have a cow and a couple of pigs. In the fall you'd hear the pigs being killed by having their throats cut, their terrible wails going over the whole country. But by the end of the winter people actually didn't have enough to eat. And they would have lots of children. I pity those farm wives. The farm wives didn't wear shoes, except on Sunday. They had bare feet, huge slabs of bare feet like slabs of bacon, and usually wore calico dresses. It was all truly primitive and truly a household economy.

RC: What do you think were the best things about the country when you were growing up?

MC: Absolute freedom was the best thing—I mean, for a boy. There was hardly a No Trespass sign in the whole of Cambria County. You could go anywhere your legs would carry you—or, if you had a horse as I did, you could go anyplace the horse would carry you. You could go into anybody's woods and hunt, you could go into any stream and fish; you could wander over old fields anywhere. The only rule was you had to be home for supper.

So, freedom was the first thing—that sort of scope and possibility. And the second was self-dependence. If you wanted to live well, you had to live well on food you grew yourself.

RC: Do you think we've lost that sense of freedom?

MC: Yes, that is something in the past of this country that has disappeared. I watch children being brought up—including you, you know—and they aren't allowed to do dozens of things that I was allowed to. Your mother wouldn't let you disappear in the woods for the day.

RC: I think it's even more constricting for kids now than it was for me.

MC: It's *much* more. Starting out when they're three years old, in nursery school, they have to learn a form of communal living. We're always rubbing elbows with people now.

RC: How has the end of that limitless freedom you once knew affected American life in general?

MC: That is a thought that is very hard to develop. But the increasing lack of freedom has most certainly produced a mass instinct by which any sort of new fad will spread all over the country and everybody will become affected by it—and then suddenly the fad will disappear. It's the same way with political reactions, when suddenly the country changes its mood and our whole government is actually overturned. The development of the "mass man" is one of the most threatening things that is happening to us. Of course, the most threatening is the destruction of natural resources. The land itself, the air, the water. Minerals. Everything is being used up.

RC: Let's go back to Belsano for one more moment. How has it changed since you were a boy?

MC: One thing is the road. With the road being widened and surfaced, the houses all stand within ten feet of it. There is no more of this business of barefoot boys scuffling in the dust of the road or hanging around the porch of the general store. The creeks have turned yellow with sulfuric acid from the mines—though I hear that some of the streams have been cleaned up. All the big timber is gone. The fields are overgrown; there are hardly any fields left any more.

RC: What happened to the house where you were born?

MC: That was a terrible thing. It was taken over for a roadhouse. The big room where I was born was the barroom. In the summer of 1968 I went in there and had a beer. Then I drove on without looking back.

RC: You started coming to Connecticut in the mid-1920s. What attracted you here to Sherman?

MC: Sherman filled a sort of pattern in my mind. If you take American literary history, the pattern is Concord: somewhere that is a couple of hours from the metropolis and yet out in the midst of fields. Sherman was like

Belsano, only not so poor. You could live here in quite a primitive fashion. Most of my friends were—you might call them Thoreauvians. When the writer Slater Brown was beginning to remodel his farmhouse, old Charlie Jennings, from whom he had bought it, came over to watch the work. "Well, Mr. Brown," he finally said, "I'm glad to see you ain't putting in one of them bathrooms. I always said they was a passing fancy."

RC: What did Sherman look like when you first saw it?

MC: The main road in the valley was not paved. It ran through very prosperous farms, lush tobacco and corn-fields. The hills in back were pastured so that the woods you see now were not woods at all. It was a little vision of Arcadia. Connecticut was almost all farmland in those days. Sherman was all farmland.

RC: Move ahead to 1936. You'd been living in New York City for five years when you decided to settle in Sherman for good. The way you managed it still seems unbelievable.

MC: I was determined to live in the country, so I kept looking for a place up here. Peter [the artist Peter Blume], who had a house for a rent of $10 a month, said that there was an empty barn across the road, and why didn't I buy that? Finances became an obstacle. I had in the bank $300. So here is the how-to recipe that nobody could carry out today.

My secretary offered to lend me $1,000 without making a record of it. So I accepted that loan. I paid $1,300 for the old barn and seven acres, and then I had an equity. On this equity of $1,300 I could at the time borrow $6,500 from the local bank, and with that we could set out to rebuild the barn into this house. But houses always cost more than you think they should: I had to take out a second mortgage of $1,600 from a generous woman in New Milford, Connecticut. Then the house was still unheated, so to buy a furnace and radiators, I made a further loan of $1,300 from another bank. In a little more than six months, I ended up with a house, a cornfield, a briar patch, a trout stream, and an enormous aggregation of debts. Figured out, it came to about $10,800 in all, on my original investment of $300. Credit was so cheap at that time. Just imagine having a 5½-percent mortgage today.

RC: Well, you got your wish, but what about Mother? She'd spent her whole life in the city.

MC: There was one time when the three of us were driving to New York. We came to the state line, and Muriel said, "Rob, never forget that you were born in New York City."

RC: I take it, then, that life in the country was hard on Mother at first.

MC: It was unnecessarily hard. She came to the house one summer and said, "I can't stand it any longer. I was crossing the bridge and I saw a rat as big as a small dog." "How did you know it was a rat?" I asked her. "It had a bare tail." And I said, "That was a possum." But she still didn't like it.

Another time she had to put up the bars at the gateway to keep cows from getting in, and she had laid the bars down by the side in the grass, but the grass was really poison ivy. Well, she knew poison ivy after that.

Slowly she became adjusted to the country. Now she finds trouble readjusting herself to New York. But she never learned to share my idea of subsistence living. I could never tempt her into chickens.

RC: How did a place like Sherman take to newcomers in those days? It was still very much an old New England town, isolated and self-sufficient.

MC: When strangers moved in from the city, they were not greeted warmly, but neither were they greeted with the hostility that they met with in some places. The senior Mrs. Osborn said to Muriel [Mrs. Cowley] at the meat counter of the old village store, "Oh, the city people. I don't mind them as long as they don't try to *help* me." Later, Mrs. Osborn was asked about a newcomer to Sherman. She said with distaste, "She's the *friendly* type."

Oh, those wonderful New England remarks. Old Mrs. Edmonds was talking about her daughter, and Muriel said, "She had a hard time having her baby, didn't she?" Mrs. Edmonds, still ironing, said "*She* thought she did."

RC: I remember, as a boy, how people in this town always seemed to look after one another. Do they still?

MC: They don't because they don't know one another as well. For a long time they did, though. If a barn burned down, there was immediately a benefit held for the farmer who'd lost it. If a farmer was sick at harvest time, the other farmers would pitch in to get his harvest in.

RC: That sounds quite different from Belsano eighty years ago.

MC: Yes, it was. Sherman had much more community spirit. In Belsano, nobody ever went up the back roads to see whether families had enough to eat during the winter, which they didn't. Here the town would take care of destitute people. The first selectman would give them an order for groceries.

RC: How do you account for the difference?

MC: It's something in the whole New England system which settled towns. A town was built around a church, and a church was a community of the faithful. Politics, the town government, and the town meeting pulled everybody together. For people who were thought of as belonging to the community, there was always that helpfulness in New England. I think much more than in Pennsylvania. Tremendously more than in the South.

RC: What are the biggest changes you've witnessed since you moved here permanently in 1936?

MC: Farms going out of business, in the first place. There may have been forty in Sherman that year; at present there are three. Fields that used to be pastures become overgrown, first with brush and then with trees. Not with good trees. Other farms have been subdivided. The whole land has gone into a mixture of subdivision and scrub forest. The great problem besides the decline of farming is just keeping the land open. Once the land grows up into scrub forest, there are no more views. People come to New England for the views, and then they use up the farmland and there are no more views. There are more woods in New England now than there were fifty years ago.

RC: I believe they call the phenomenon "woodland sprawl." Do you ever envision all that scrubland being made into field again?

MC: Yes, I do, but it's one of the dreams I have to shove aside. As the pressure for food grows, I can imagine whole suburban developments being bulldozed down and turned back to farmland.

RC: What about the people who choose country life now—have they changed, too?

MC: They're not so homogeneous as they used to be. These days you get so many executive types who move from one part of the country to another that the sale of a house isn't permanent any longer. It will have to be sold again when the owner is moved to California. Or Texas. But there are also social divisions arising between white collar and blue collar. We have some very serious ruckuses over taxes and zoning. All this results in less social cohesion.

RC: Zoning has always been a touchy subject here.

MC: I feel that zoning is often carried too far. You know, when I was head of the zoning commission in Sherman I had a simple formula for suggesting what the regulations should be. I drove around town and asked what people were doing. Anything they had been doing for years was legal. For example, Edna Barnes had a rooming house up on Barnes Hill. I said, "How many roomers has she?" Somebody said six. So the regulations permitted rooming houses with not more than six roomers. The zoning law passed and didn't meet with a great deal of resistance.

RC: Do you think people go overboard in an attempt to protect the environment?

MC: You can't go overboard in actually protecting the environment. But it ought to be that people can earn their livings in the town. I also find myself on the side of those who want to hunt and fish—especially when it comes to controlling two terrible pests. One is deer, and the other is raccoons. Now, in a farming community deer and raccoons are both kept within reasonable limits. But the suburbanites who don't have any gardens come in and say, "Aren't the deer sweet? People should be forbidden to hunt them"—forgetting that people as well as deer and raccoons have to live in the area. A sort of balance of nature should be maintained, and that's where environmentalists are likely to go too far.

RC: You cited the fights over zoning—and I know you would add stringent protection of the environment—as manifestations of class division in towns like Sherman. Do you feel that the country has become too much the province of the well-to-do?

MC: That is a big question. The people who have enough to live on are really in a way walled off from the people who haven't enough to live on. I don't like that at all. What I would like is a community that is more or less self-contained, a community where the things you need are many of them produced right there. Instead, milk comes from the outside. Most vegetables come from the outside. It seems to me that all the food we eat must taste a little bit of diesel fuel.

RC: Is it still possible for young people without money to live in the country?

MC: It is still possible. It is more difficult. There are no great careers open here—a career, for example, in literature. You have to be in much closer touch with the metropolitan center. And it's the same with people earning their money in any way as free-lances. Even lawyers. For doctors, the country is a sort of paradise.

But there are many ways of making a marginal living. A young couple can come out and live by doing odd jobs, which is impossible in the city. That is, if you don't have silly ideas of pride. I know a man of forty and his wife, who started out mowing lawns and doing painting jobs. He ended up by first buying a house and then having another house willed to him by a widow whose grounds he had been taking care of. So that now he is much better off than the people whose lawns he still mows.

RC: If it's tough being young in the country, what are the problems of aging?

MC: One of the great problems is expense. It costs a lot, especially if you can't drive a car any longer and have to find drivers. Or somebody to help around the house, somebody to take care of the grounds when you can't run machinery any longer. Nevertheless, you have a feeling of support. You're living in a community that knows you. To take one little example, the cars don't run you down as you pick your way across the road with a cane. Or when your wife goes shopping at the local IGA supermarket, she runs into people who know her and help her with her bundles out to the car.

RC: How do you handle the winters?

MC: You have to handle them by getting help. But if you have fuel enough, and your house is snug, then you can live as comfortably in Connecticut as you can in Florida.

RC: Is it your impression that people who live in the country are getting older?

MC: They indeed are, and that is the trouble.

RC: How are places like Sherman trying to cope with that fact?

MC: The little towns of New England are showing enterprise in taking care of their older people. They have "Over-60" centers, for example, or mini-bus service to their shopping centers, so that life does become easier. But we feel here in Sherman—or many people feel—the lack of small and limited housing for older people. One condominium for "Over-60s" would help a great deal. That's one of the points where conflict arises between the suburbanites and the longer-time residents. The suburbanites don't want any condominiums in town.

RC: Talking about all these problems, I wonder if we're beginning to lose sight of the advantages of living in the country. What are they?

MC: Air, water, and trees. And outside of that there is a certain largeness and leisure of life. Leisure, or the choice of what you're going to do on any given day—that doesn't exist in the city.

RC: What are the things that have made you happiest about living in the country?

MC: I don't know. Sometimes going out of the house and looking at the fields or the garden and seeing how it's growing has made me as happy as anything else. And, of course, I was crazy about fishing when I was younger. That combines the joy of walking with the sound of running water and the thrill of catching a fish. You can still find places to fish, although there are too damn many No Trespass signs. But after you become old enough you can disregard the No Trespass signs because you know the people on the land.

RC: Do you think that living in the country has made you a better writer?

MC: In some respects, because it has made me more conscious of things. I like a "thingy" style, not an abstract style. Sometimes when I read writing full of abstractions I stop and say, "Now, what the hell does he mean?" When you read something I write you know damn well what I mean. The language is simple, and the figures of speech have to do with actual objects, persons, and animals.

I used to go wandering off into the woods, and after an hour or so I would begin thinking or dreaming or reconstructing something I wanted to write. The most grievous blow to my writing came when my legs went bad on me and I couldn't "walk" an article any longer.

RC: Do you think Americans sometimes oversentimentalize living in the country?

MC: It doesn't seem so to me. Of course, anybody can oversentimentalize anything. I can't emphasize too much the beauty of growing old in the same place that you were young in, with people you've known for half a century. That is something that Americans often lack.

1983

Publication Data

"Hawthorne in Solitude": Originally published as "Introduction" to *The Portable Hawthorne*. New York: Viking, 1948. Previously collected in *The Portable Malcolm Cowley*, Donald W. Faulkner, editor, New York: Viking, 1990.

"The Hawthornes in Paradise": Originally published under the same title in *American Heritage* 10, December 1958. Previously collected in *The Flower and the Leaf*, Donald W. Faulkner, editor, New York: Viking, 1985.

"The Five Acts of *The Scarlet Letter*": Originally published under the same title in *Twelve Original Essays on Great American Novels*, Charles Shapiro, editor, Detroit: Wayne State University Press, 1958.

"A Case for *Blithedale*": Originally published under the title "Hawthorne as Tragic Artist: A Fine Study." *New York Herald Tribune Book Review*, May 8, 1949.

"Mystery at the Old Manse": Originally published under the same title in *New Republic* 191, December 10, 1984.

"The External Emerson": Originally published under the same title in *New Republic* 120, June 13, 1949.

"Melville Among His Champions": Originally published in two parts under the titles "Mythology and Melville," *New Republic* 123, October 30, 1950, and "An Indispensible Guide to a Fuller Understanding of Herman Melville," *New York Herald Tribune Book Review*, November 11, 1951.

"The Poet and the Mask" (excerpts): Originally published as "Introduction" to *The Complete Poetry and Prose of Walt Whitman*, New York: Pellegrini and Cudahy, 1948. Previously collected in *A Many-Windowed House*, Henry Dan Piper, editor, Carbondale: Southern Illinois University Press, 1970; and *The Portable Malcolm Cowley*, Donald W. Faulkner, editor, New York: Viking, 1990.

"The Buried Masterpiece" (excerpts): Originally published as "Introduction" to *Walt Whitman's Leaves of Grass: The First (1855) Edition*, New York: The Viking Press, 1959. Previously collected in *The Portable Malcolm Cowley*, Donald W. Faulkner, editor, New York: Viking, 1990.

"The Real Horatio Alger Story": Originally published as "The Real Alger Story" in *Horizon* XII, no. 3, Summer 1970, incorporated from material originally published in *Time*, August 13, 1945, and *New Republic* 113, September 10, 1945. Previously collected in *A Many-Windowed House*, Henry Dan Piper, editor, Carbondale: Southern Illinois University Press, 1970.

"The Two Henry Jameses": Originally published in two parts as "The Return of Henry James," *New Republic* 112, January 22, 1945, and "The Two Henry Jameses," *New Republic* 112, February 5, 1945. Previously collected in *A Many-Windowed House*, Henry Dan Piper, editor, Carbondale: Southern Illinois University Press, 1970, and *The Portable Malcolm Cowley*, Donald W. Faulkner, editor, New York: Viking, 1990.

"Robert Frost: A Dissenting Opinion": Originally published in two parts as "Frost: A Dissenting Opinion," *New Republic* 111, September 11, 1944, and "The Case

Against Mr. Frost II," *New Republic* III, September 18, 1944. Previously collected in *A Many-Windowed House,* Henry Dan Piper, editor, Carbondale: Southern Illinois University Press, 1970.

"Edwin Arlington Robinson: Defeat and Triumph": Originally published under the same title in *New Republic* 119, December 6, 1948. Previously collected in *After the Genteel Tradition,* Carbondale: Southern Illinois University Press, 1964.

"Eugene O'Neill in Connecticut": Originally published as "A Weekend with Eugene O'Neill" in *Reporter* 17, September 5, 1957. Previously collected in *A Many-Windowed House,* Henry Dan Piper, editor, Carbondale: Southern Illinois University Press, 1970.

"Hart Crane in Search of a Home: A Memoir": Originally published as chapter 9 of *A Second Flowering,* New York: Viking, 1973.

"Van Wyck Brooks's 'Usable Past'": Originally published as "Introduction" to Van Wyck Brooks, *An Autobiography,* New York: E. P. Dutton, 1965. Previously collected in *A Many-Windowed House,* Henry Dan Piper, editor, Carbondale: Southern Illinois University Press, 1970.

"Two Views of George Santayana": Originally published in two parts as "Santayana at Harvard," *New Republic* 110, January 17, 1944, and "Santayana in Society," *New Republic* 112, April 30, 1945.

"One Man Alone" and "Farewell to the Last Harvard 'Dandy'": Originally published in two parts as chapter 5 of *A Second Flowering,* New York: Viking, 1973 (a shorter version of this appeared in *Yale Review* 42, April 1973), and as "A Farewell to the Last Harvard 'Dandy'" in *New York Herald Tribune Book Review,* September 9, 1962.

"S. Foster Damon: The New England Voice": Originally published as chapter 3 of *—And I Worked at the Writer's Trade,* New York: Viking, 1978; a shorter version of this appeared in *Southern Review* n.s. 4, Winter 1968.

"From Savannah to Emerson": Originally published as chapter 15 of *—And I Worked at the Writer's Trade,* New York: Viking, 1978; a shorter version appeared in *Southern Review* 11, April 1975. Previously collected in *The Portable Malcolm Cowley,* Donald W. Faulkner, editor, New York: Viking, 1990.

"J. P. Marquand, Anthropologist of the Boston Story": Originally published as "The Boston Story," *New Republic* 104, March 3, 1941.

"Time Abolished": Originally published as chapter 6 of *A Second Flowering,* New York: Viking, 1973.

"John Cheever: The Novelist's Life as a Drama": Originally published under the same title in *Sewanee Review* 91, Winter 1983. Previously collected in *The Flower and the Leaf,* Donald W. Faulkner, editor, New York: Viking, 1985, and *The Portable Malcolm Cowley,* Donald W. Faulkner, editor, New York: Viking, 1990.

"Connecticut Valley, 1931": Originally published as "Connecticut Valley," *New Republic* 65, January 28, 1931.

"Town Report, 1942": Originally published under the same title in *New Republic* 107, November 23, 1942. Previously collected in *The Flower and the Leaf,* Donald W. Faulkner, editor, New York: Viking, 1985.

"Along the Housatonic": Originally published as "Whose Housatonic?," *New Republic* 115, August 19, 1946.

"Election Night in Sherman, 1944": Originally published as "Election Night in Sheridan," *New Republic* III, November 20, 1944.

"Is There Still Hope for Farming in New England?" Originally published in *Country Journal* 1, September 1974.

"A Letter on Growing Melons": Originally published as "Melons from Your Own Patch," *Country Journal* 2, January–February 1975.

"Boy in Sunlight," "The Living Water," "Natural History," "From Where the Forest Stood" "The Urn," and "The Long Voyage": Originally collected in *Blue Juniata: A Life,* New York: Viking, 1985.

"A Conversation Between Father and Son on New England Life (with Robert Cowley)": Originally published as "Malcolm Cowley: Countryman," in *Country Journal* 10, October 1983.

Author/Title Index

Note: Reference numbers in boldface type refer to chapters on the author or to works reproduced in full.